W9-BDG-760

THE IRON WAY

The Iron Way

*Railroads, the Civil War,
and the Making of
Modern America*

William G. Thomas

Yale UNIVERSITY PRESS

New Haven & London

Yale University Press books may be purchased in quantity for educational, business, or
promotional use. For information, please e-mail sales.press@yale.edu (U.S. office) or
sales@yaleup.co.uk (U.K. office).

Designed by James J. Johnson and set in Ehrhardt Roman type by Tseng Information Systems, Inc.
Printed in the United States of America.

Library of Congress Cataloging-in-Publication Data
Thomas, William G., 1964–
The iron way : railroads, the Civil War, and the making of modern America / William G. Thomas.
p.   cm.
Includes bibliographical references and index.
ISBN 978-0-300-14107-8 (hbk.: alk. paper)
1. United States—History—Civil War, 1861–1865—Transportation. 2. Railroads—United States—
History—19th century. 3. Railroads—Confederate States of America—History. 4. Confederate States
of America. Army—Transportation. 5. United States. Army—Transportation—History—19th century.
6. United States—Territorial expansion—History—19th century. I. Title.
E491.T53 2011
973.7′1—dc23
2011020608

A catalogue record for this book is available from the British Library.

This paper meets the requirements of ANSI/NISO Z39.48-1992
(Permanence of Paper).

10 9 8 7 6 5 4 3 2 1

To my parents

Come forth from behind your cotton bags! I have no long gun to reach ye. Come, Ahab's compliments to ye; come and see if ye can swerve me. Swerve me? The path to my fixed purpose is laid with iron rails, whereon my soul is grooved to run. Over unsounded gorges, through the rifled hearts of mountains, under torrents' beds, unerringly I rush! Naught's an obstacle, naught's an angle to the iron way!

—Herman Melville, *Moby-Dick*, 1851

Contents

THE IRON WAY

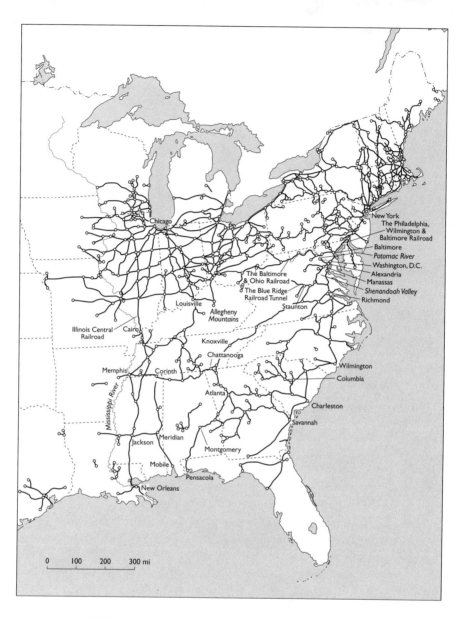

The United States in 1861, showing principal railroads and junctions.

Prologue

Time & space are annihilated by steam [and] we pass through a City a town,
yea a country, like an arrow from Jupiter's Bow.

— Asa Whitney, after his first ride on a train

IN 1844 Asa Whitney took his first railroad trip, and the experience was simultaneously exhilarating and daunting. Seasoned as he was in business and politics, Whitney was not fully prepared for what happened to him that day on the train. A New England merchant and tireless railroad promoter, Whitney had become convinced that the nation needed to build a transcontinental railroad not only for reasons of military security but also as a means to capture, and even redirect, the flow of the world's commerce onto American shores and across the U.S. interior. His first trip on a train through upstate New York seemed to Whitney a moment of great consequence: hurtling across the state, he felt as if someone had suddenly unleashed the power of the gods. Overcome by the experience, he missed a whole town, Schenectady. He searched for metaphors to describe the feeling. The effect of traveling across and slightly above the land, he decided, was like riding an arrow shot "from Jupiter's Bow."

Like many others, Whitney had trouble understanding where all of these changes would lead. He worried about what the powerful new technology would do to the American people. "The whole population seems in motion," he sighed. Crowds crammed into hotels, cars, depots, and waiting rooms. They stuffed food down their throats and "dined on the high pressure plan" in the few minutes before their departure. The accelerating sense of time, he thought, might lead some to think the world was coming to an end. Indeed, after riding the train Whitney concluded that one religious sect's prediction that the apocalypse and end times were rapidly approaching was at least somewhat understandable.[1]

The top speed of Whitney's train reached just twenty-five miles per hour, but the experience was intense and unprecedented. Although Whitney expected to be able to gaze at passing villages through the train windows, the movement of the train made that difficult. He described the effect as disorienting, dizzying even. "This constant locomotion," he recorded in his diary later that day, made distant objects seem "in a whirl." Nothing appeared "permanent" to him, and the "lightning speed" of the train left the trees "waltzing."[2]

"The mind too goes with all this," Whitney wrote; "it speculates, theorizes, & measures all things by locomotive speed, where will it end?" This Whitney could not predict, but he worried about the future with railroads, steam, and telegraphs. "Can it be happy? I fear not," he confessed.[3]

Asa Whitney was not alone. Nearly every writer and politician, and probably most citizens, searched for things to say about the railroad, the remarkable invention that seemed to change so much so quickly. The United States had some 3,000 miles of railroad track in service in 1840, nearly 9,000 miles in 1850, and over 30,000 miles by 1860. And the railroad was not the only technological wonder to consider. The same year Whitney took his first trip on the railroad — 1844 — Samuel F. B. Morse tested his new telegraphic device for the members of Congress. The wires ran along the tracks of the Baltimore & Ohio Railroad, and Morse signaled on May 24 "what hath God wrought" to the joy and amazement of all those gathered around him in the U.S. Supreme Court building to watch the miraculous machine. Morse's telegraph spread quickly. In 1846 there were 146 miles of telegraph line, but two years later, with the urgency of the Mexican War, companies strung the wires from New Orleans to New York City, and by 1850 the nation had put up 10,000 miles of the electric network.

Many Americans saw great potential in the railroads and telegraphs to define progress, promote civilization, and enhance democracy by opening up communication. Newspapers hailed the technology and began devoting ever increasing space to the doings of the railroad business. John L. O'Sullivan, editor of the *Democratic Review* (New York) and the man who first called the nation to fulfill its "Manifest Destiny," considered America a "skeleton framework of railroads" with a "nervous system of magnetic telegraphs."[4] Leading artists, painters, and authors, some of them hired by the newspapers, some by the railroads themselves, took up the locomotive as a subject. They depicted its entry into the American landscape as natural and sublime — in ways that confirmed the widely circulating ideas about American progress.

The railroads emerged as not only the leading industry of the period but also the most visible indicator of modernity. Americans in the 1840s and 1850s saw how railroads transformed business opportunities, social relationships, and the physical landscape around them. They could not know that the railroads would be key players in an American civil war. Ideas about the unity railroads would bring eventually collided with the reality of political schism, social conflict, economic competition, and, ultimately, war.

Harriet Beecher Stowe used railroads in *Uncle Tom's Cabin* as a proxy for everything modern and advanced about the country, even though the South was laying track with slave labor as fast as the North was with free. "Unsophisticated" places in *Uncle Tom's Cabin* were those "where there are no railroads," she wrote. Poet Walt Whitman, in *Leaves of Grass,* extolled the democratic promise of the technology: "Type of the modern — emblem of motion and power — pulse of the continent . . . Law of thyself complete, thine own track firmly holding . . . Launched o'er the prairie wide, across the lakes / To the free skies unpent and glad and strong."[5]

But it was Herman Melville's *Moby-Dick* (1851) that revealed the ways technology, networks of trade, and resource exploitation came together in the modern world. In his 500-page epic of whaling and the human condition, Melville evoked the relentless power of steam machinery and the unavoidable moral dilemma of the industrial nation. When introducing Daggo, the enormous black harpooner, and the racial diversity of the whaler crews, Melville's narrator, Ishmael, likened the workers to "the American army and military and merchant navies, and the engineering forces employed in the construction of the American Canals and Railroads." And Ahab, the impassive, monomaniacal captain of the doomed *Pequod*, was like a locomotive: the "path" to his "fixed purpose is laid with iron rails."[6]

Something of Ahab's confidence and fixed purpose was shared across America in these years because the world seemed all of a sudden to have gotten smaller. According to nineteenth-century Americans, railroads "annihilated space and time." They defied conventional restraints of power and speed, and, above all, they reconfigured the way people thought about their own mobility. Their effect was so profound, so pervasive, that those places without railroads and telegraphs in the nineteenth century measured time and distance by how close they were to the growing network. The chorus of railroad enthusiasm reached full voice in the 1850s, when Americans became more convinced than ever that technology would change their world. The popular literary magazine *New Englander* in 1851 was typically breathless in its assessment of the effects of railroads, telegraphs, and steamships. Better communication, it thought, would make Britain and France friends, not bitter foes. And in America, the *New Englander* predicted technological progress would end slavery and seal the Union forever. "Every rail laid along our mountain ridges, every steamboat wheel which disturbs our mighty streams, is adding a rivet to the union of these States, which the intrigues and bluster of neither Northern nor Southern demagogues can sever."[7]

Henry David Thoreau, however, was skeptical of the new technologies, and his anxieties have resonated across the years. "Men have become the tools of their tools," he mused in *Walden* in 1854. After the sectional political crisis of the early 1850s, Thoreau doubted whether the telegraph would enhance meaningful communication between distant societies. "We are in a great haste to construct a magnetic telegraph from Maine to Texas," he noted, "but Maine and Texas, it may be, have nothing important to communicate." The rapid advance of technology inspired a tangle of emotions: trepidation and awe, consternation and wonder, fear and admiration, anxiety and confidence. In his journal Thoreau wondered "if this enterprise were as noble as it seems." He doubted if the "snort" of the locomotive or its "steam-cloud" were truly "innocent," "disinterested," or "important."[8]

The common thread running through the American experience in these

William H. Bartlett, *Viaduct on the Baltimore and Washington Railroad*, 1836.

Completed in 1835, the viaduct on the Baltimore & Ohio's Washington branch
was an engineering wonder—the first multispan stone bridge built on a curve.
Designed by Benjamin Latrobe, the bridge appeared to defy conventional
limits of speed and gravity. (Courtesy of the author)

years, Thoreau so clearly understood, was a widely felt alteration that railroads,
steamships, and telegraphs made possible in the relationship between space and
time. This profound shift was something anyone experienced when traveling on
the railroad as Asa Whitney did, whether the individual was a company president,
a general, a soldier, an emigrant, or a runaway slave. Tens of thousands of Americans boarded the trains each day. Even in the South, on the Richmond & Petersburg Railroad, hundreds of African Americans rode the rails every month, some
as slaves but others as free blacks.

In the South slavery proceeded to expand in concert with the railroads, and
the relationship has seemed contradictory or paradoxical. Watching slavery from
afar, some Northerners naively assumed that America's technological advances
would be joined by moral and material progress and slavery would be ended as
a result. Slavery, they thought, was incompatible with modernity. And yet, we
know today that slavery in various forms and guises has persisted. Unfortunately,
slavery has proven not at all inconsistent with modern society.[9]

Slave labor built thousands of miles of railroads in the South. This work
went forward with picks and shovels, axes and wheelbarrows, mules and carts.
Even more surprising, if not very well known at the time, southern railroads were
quick to begin purchasing slaves to help operate and maintain their lines. And

because the hard labor of construction was never finished, even on railroads that celebrated their completion there seemed to be no logical stopping point for the use of slaves on the railroads. The modern technologies, it seemed, might extend slavery rather than render it obsolete.[10]

Far from being inconsistent or antimodern, therefore, white Southerners were committed to slavery as the central principle of their society's modern development, and they used railroads to extend this vision. The separation of the South and the North into contending nation-states preceded their outright conflict in the Civil War, and took shape amid larger global changes. The regions developed into "contending territorial empires," becoming more antagonistic as they simultaneously grew more similar and interconnected. We must look for the ways each experienced a process of social adaptation, economic expansion, political organization, and identity formation. Such change was almost imperceptible at times, so slow, gradual, and uneven was the process. Historians have looked for signs of an "irrepressible conflict" and instead have found more similarities than differences between the rival sections. In fact, the North's and South's most striking similarity was their confidence and belief in themselves as modern. Much of this unshakable opinion came from their experience with the railroads. They conducted the war with unprecedented determination and violence, based largely on these beliefs. The conflict between the sections revolved around fundamentally geopolitical issues — slavery, railroads, and expansion — at the same time as and in relationship to their emerging ideological differences. The explosive question of slavery in the western territories gathered momentum, not coincidentally, with the huge burst of railroad growth, staple-crop agriculture, and immigration in the 1850s.[11]

The Civil War and the railroads were twin engines in the development of modern America, operating with independent causes and effects but simultaneously and in relation to one another. Their story — the convulsive working out of war, technology, and the modern nation over three decades — is the subject of this book.[12]

We begin this story in 1838, when Frederick Douglass used a printed timetable to board a train in Baltimore at the precise moment of its departure and rode it to freedom in Philadelphia. This dramatic (and private) escape from slavery on the railroad was something he concealed from white slaveholders for as long as possible. A decade later, around 1848, the United States absorbed vast new territories from its war with Mexico and began to recover from the long recession of the previous decade, inaugurating a new era when the place of slavery and railroads in the nation moved to the center of culture and politics.

Despite the rapid and widespread changes in the South, historians have often dismissed southern railroad development before the Civil War. The lines of argu-

Receipt for sale of slaves to the Mississippi Central Railroad, March 5, 1860.

Railroad companies in the South routinely bought slaves in the 1840s and 1850s, often purchasing thirty to fifty at a time. The "asset" would be carried on the company's annual balance sheet, often listed as "the negro account."

(Courtesy of the Newberry Library)

ment go something like this: railroads were antithetical to the plantation system of the South, because slavery encouraged local production of cheap goods and low consumer demand. Furthermore, the southern railroads were built with different gauges (width) of track, so few of them were connected, and therefore to talk of a railroad "system" in the South is a fiction. One historian has summarized, "Because southern railroads relied so heavily on individual states, a 'South' simply did not cohere before the Civil War."[13]

As we will see, however, quite the opposite occurred. The South's railroads ushered in "the South," unifying and forming the region in powerful ways. The South's investment in railroads and other technologies was consistent with the rest of the nation, its gauges and "system" not materially different. The South's business and railroad leaders spoke in a language of expansion similar to that of the North, and they faced many of the same obstacles to financing, constructing, and running their operations. Railroads and slavery became fused in a relationship that reinforced one another.[14]

Both North and South in the 1850s poured their energy and resources into railroad construction and expansion. Each staked its future on the opportunities and possibilities of steam power. Each created a vast "second nature" system of rail and wire, which obliterated natural barriers and radically changed the geography of its sections. When the war came, Americans, North and South, were full of confidence.[15]

During the Civil War, Americans experienced the railroads in a new, more direct and immediate way. Millions traveled to great embarkation camps and depots along the railroads to enlist in the army. Once in the war, they walked and marched great distances to the battlefields, but they also packed into troop trains and raced forward on the railroads, at times right onto the battlefield. Although horses, mules, and oxen carried and pulled much of what Americans transported, the rails became vital lifelines as armies extended farther and farther into hostile territory.

By the end of the war a strategy to run a massive interstate military railroad system guided the top northern commanders in their aim to destroy or control all of the South's railroad lines and junctions. When Union commanders assembled their forces in ways that took full advantage of the technologies, when they practiced a new form of war making, they demonstrated the nearly unassailable confidence of the modern nation. Rather than taking caution from their experience, Americans took the lesson that anything could be accomplished with enough modern technology, properly focused.[16]

Nineteenth-century Americans, in short, experienced something similar to our circumstances today when the so-called flattening of the globe raises as many questions and problems as it does answers and solutions. They confronted a rapidly developing set of technologies that made their world smaller, faster, and more intricately complicated. They participated in and witnessed the vast expansion of the nation across space and through time. And they found themselves at war on a scale they could not have imagined.

Long after the Civil War, one former slave, Ike Derricotte, recalled that the trains brought the news of the war to Confederates and the enslaved alike. He remembered "how people watched and waited to hear dat old Georgia train come in." The train's arrival was a moment of congregation for the community. Everyone gathered at the depot to divine the events taking place far away but that would have far-reaching effects close at home. "De way dat old train brought 'em de news was lak dis," he explained. "If de southern troops was in de front, den dat old whistle jus' blowed continuously, but if it was bad news, den it was jus' one short, sharp blast. Believe me, evvybody sho' did listen to dat train."[17]

But the railroad meant radically different things to different people. For Derricotte, its whistle might have signaled that freedom was coming—while for the slaveholder it might have indicated a complete reversal of fortune. Railroads, telegraphs, and steam engines offered Americans various, sometimes contradictory and simultaneous, possibilities. They could be used both to facilitate and to retard slavery; they could be arranged both to revolutionize offensive war and to transform defensive strategy; they could act both as an asset and as a vulnerability.

And after the war they could be used to both enable freedom and sustain discrimination and oppression.[18]

This book seeks to lay out a different paradigm for how we understand the Civil War in our history. You will read here about the Civil War as one of the first great modern nation-state struggles, indeed as a global, geopolitical event. Two nations collided, each drawing on the same heritage and political ideologies, each defining its identity in opposition to the other, each expanding rapidly across the continent, and each gaining experience and certainty from the widespread use of railroads and modern technologies. The gigantic battles and huge casualties of the war testified to the seriousness of the Confederate claim to nationhood and to the modern ideas and practices at stake in the conflict.

Before, during, and after the war confidence and immense faith in progress and modernity took root in American society, but how these values influenced the process of national formation and consolidation in the South and the North remains largely unexplained. In this respect the war took place in a much wider context than we have traditionally recognized. Because the South and the North built their respective societies around links to the broader transatlantic world, their contest took on immediate international dimensions. Railroads were the first enterprises to seek foreign capital on such a large scale, far ahead of the federal government. And the bondholders, investment bankers, and traders in London, Paris, and Frankfurt in the 1850s increasingly played a key role in American expansion. The global banking network that took shape around the railroads constituted an important modern development for both Northerners and Southerners—a set of technologies, like the railroads, which could be channeled in very different directions. The relationships that grew up around railroads in the banking sector came into sharp focus during the war itself when the Confederacy attempted to gain international recognition and to take its place in the field of the world's nation-states.[19]

For many years historians focused on a "modernization" thesis in explaining the coming of the Civil War, and this view stressed the divergent pathways of the North's and the South's economic and social development before the war. My argument does not revisit this approach or use the term "modern" in the same way.[20] Here the concept of modernity refers to a series of practices, ideas, and experiences that led Americans to see their world, first and foremost, as exceptional. Similar views came forward in Britain and Europe in this period when the industrial revolution altered everything from how people dressed to what they read. The modern seemed distinct, separate from earlier periods in history. And this historical sensibility, of a break in time, suggested how modern people thought of themselves.

Everywhere they turned, Americans saw change in the fundamental elements of energy (steam and electricity) where for generations there had been nothing but continuity (horsepower and manpower). Most significantly, modern people came to see nature as set apart from human society. George Perkins Marsh in *Man and Nature* (1864), for example, hoped to reveal the need for the management of forests, but he premised his work on the following idea: "The fact that, of all organic beings, man alone is to be regarded as essentially a destructive power, and that he wields energies to resist . . . tends to prove that though living in physical nature, he is not of her, that he is of more exalted parentage."[21]

The explosion of machinery and the mastery of science seemed to indicate, to Marsh and others, that humans could control and direct much more of the creation than anyone ever anticipated. In this period Americans came to trust great networks and systems and, just as importantly, to invest them with meaning.

Still, we cannot take nineteenth-century Americans at their word, and their self-realization as modern does not necessarily mean that they had reached some higher moral stage of civilization. Because white Southerners saw themselves and their slave society as modern, the most obvious contradiction was resolved, at least temporarily, by the North's crushing of the South and ending slavery. The story of how railroads—as the major symbol and enactment of modernity in both northern and southern societies—were built, destroyed, rebuilt, imagined, used, feared, and desired shows just how uncertain the path was out of slavery and into the world of emancipation.

When we consider what was modern about American society in the nineteenth century, we need to set aside older dichotomies of North versus South and instead understand how both regions shared in the defining and constructing of a modern world. Part of the broader Atlantic economy and society, the American regions were neither exceptional nor mutually exclusive. They were hybrids of one another and of the Atlantic as well in shape and outlook. To be modern in the nineteenth century was a way of thinking and acting in the world. Modernity, above all, was a lived experience shaped by its creators in their local surroundings.[22]

Three broad concepts surrounding this experience are woven throughout this book. The first is that the hallmark of modernity in mid-nineteenth-century society was personal mobility. Those who controlled their own bodies, their movements, and their geographic surroundings experienced what they thought was modern. Those who did not or who had their movements curtailed and restricted were placed outside of the modern world. The railroad offered a powerful extension of the body—of personal mobility—for anyone who rode in its cars. And this embodiment of personal mobility was seized and defended by all classes, races, and genders, including African Americans, Native Americans, women, and workers, among others. The fight for personal mobility took many forms. The railroads and the war, more than any other forces, provided the opportunities to reimagine one's personal mobility and the context in which to take action on that imagined extension of the body—to move through space and time. Fugitive slaves,

Irish immigrants, southern planters, northern farmers, and London investors all participated in the great expansion of personal mobility of this period. And their experiences suggested entirely new definitions of citizenship and participation in the modern nation.[23]

Second, the railroad became one of the most obvious, and the most prevalent, forms of symbolic technology in nineteenth-century society. To use today's terminology, the railroad had many and diverse "interfaces" to its system and, like the Internet, performed all sorts of tasks for Americans, slowly altering how people saw themselves, their futures, and their opportunities. In this respect the railroad was one of the first transformative technologies in American history. Because the railroads issued stock with elaborate certificates and interest-bearing coupons, kept payrolls for employees to sign on a dotted line, printed timetables and rate tables, commissioned art and photography, and produced locomotive engines that arrived at depots around the nation, they instantiated a series of actions well beyond those intended by their managers. To look at a timetable, to sign a payroll, to tear off and sell a stock coupon, to consult a network map, to board a passenger car—these actions were performed by humans who actively participated in translating the railroad's manifestations for their own lives, for their own purposes.

The railroad's many interfaces did not ordain any particular action or sequence of events. They were contingent on how people used, understood, and interpreted them. A woman might read a timetable against an array of other knowledge about places and how she traveled through them and at what times she might be willing to arrive or depart. Maps showed depots and stations neatly spaced in increments, but all who studied the increasingly elaborate atlases of that era brought their own dossier of information to the table.

As a result the railroad's time and space extensions could be found in a host of hybridizations—maps that performed a particular set of connections, tables that altered economic relations, and station platforms that provided the stages for not-so-chance encounters. Those who saw themselves as modern manipulated these new interfaces. Indeed, the control of them, and of knowledge about them, was an important and highly contested arena of modernity. Frederick Douglass, one of the clear victors in the battles over modernity, actively shaped and controlled these interfaces through his autobiographies. If we are to understand better the modern transformations nineteenth-century Americans experienced in these middle decades, we need to look closely at the many interfaces that accompanied the railroads and the telegraphs and how Americans put them to use in their daily lives.[24]

And third, as nineteenth-century Americans developed the railroads, and then as they went to war with these new technologies, they rehearsed through their physical performance the modern sensibilities and ideas they increasingly adopted. During the war more people traveled to diverse parts of the nation than they ever had done previously, and as they flew over high bridges and raced through deep tunnels on the trains, they witnessed firsthand the ways nature was controlled, mastered, and stripped of its limitations. The principal and most obvious association they made was that modern peoples and nations could marshal empirical data, and control and build global networks that advanced moral progress. These broad constructions were wrapped up in what nineteenth-century Americans considered their national identity—theirs was a modern "civilization." Their view of history only confirmed these beliefs. The steam age seemed to them to create a new epoch, one of undeniable progress.

A good number of self-delusions developed out of these experiences, and these too persisted throughout the nineteenth and into the twentieth century. Some are with us still. Our own faith in technology and moral progress, and in the control of nature, proceeds unchecked. We might pause, therefore, and look back at how nineteenth-century Americans handled the burst of technology, war, and nation-building in their society.

One final point concerns the way this book relates to the sources assembled during its research and the techniques used in its argument. This is a work of digital history, a hybrid of different interfaces to the past. Nearly every document and piece of evidence, as well as the tools used to examine the sources behind this book, are all publicly available through the Digital History Project (http://digitalhistory.unl.edu) and the "Railroads and the Making of Modern America" digital project (http://railroads.unl.edu). I have hoped to create a book and digital project that are interdependent and complementary. This book, in other words, took the shape it did in large measure because of the digital tools and technologies deployed in the research process and the influences of a growing field of digital scholars. Furthermore, in seeking to uncover the role technologies played in the nineteenth century, this work is also concerned with our current period of technological and social transformation—a time that many are calling the Digital Age.

What is digital history? Certainly, digital histories use the powerful computational, spatial, and analytical tools now available to scholars to raise questions, see patterns, and make associations in the evidence that otherwise might not occur. This book proceeded side by side with the digital project, and each informed the other.

But digital histories also help us think differently about how we know what we know about the past. When we digitize a timetable, or encode a text, or create a database of employees from an original payroll, we work through the partial, the fragmentary, the contingent nature of our history. We are reminded as well that the people in the past whom we study lived complex and meaningful lives not captured entirely by the spotty records that remain: original letters, government reports, photographs, maps, and books. Indeed, many of these records, especially those of the government or the railroad corporations, were created for particular reasons having little to do with the lives, ambitions, and hopes of the people mentioned in them. Digital historians seeking to reconstruct the social world of nineteenth-century America depend on these records, but by importing them into a digital medium these historians attempt to interrelate and shape the information in ways that might make invisible histories much more visible. They create models and visualizations about historical questions, and attempt to uncover patterns and relationships not otherwise apparent.[25]

Readers of this book can participate in the digital history too. In some cases this might mean simply viewing an original document referred to in the pages that follow—for example, the Mississippi Central Railroad Company's bill of sale for the purchase of over twenty enslaved people in 1860. In other cases readers might examine the personal letters of soldiers and railroad engineers, scan the payrolls of construction crews on the U.S. Military Railroads, or review the timetables, lithographs, and rate tables of railroads in the Civil War.

But readers will find more than a document collection online at digitalhistory. unl.edu. A digital history project is by its nature less archival and more exploratory, less about ensuring preservation and more about inviting and enabling inquiry. Because digital history work is concerned with interpreting the past, not just measuring patterns or structures within it, we need to resist the temptation to place all of our faith in the empirical—a legacy, in part, of the railroad era and its modern practices. And given the explosion of statistical and informational visualizations available in the PC and Internet era, such as geographic information systems (GIS), digital historians need to be skeptical of the seductive power of data. Rather than processing information to reach "conclusions" with these new technologies, we are instead creating models of humanistic inquiry for readers to hold up and examine closely. The digital project accompanying this book attempts to reproduce some of the complex interfaces of the railroad system, and to allow readers to get a closer look at their constituent parts and perhaps ask their own questions about these sources.[26]

So, in three major areas of the research, digital technologies opened up key questions at the heart of this book, and they remain open for your investigation online. First, you can use the spatio-temporal models specifically designed for this project mapping the growth of the railroad network between 1840 and 1861 against U.S. county level census data on slaveholding and population. This material is available as a Google map application and can be explored for examining slavery's complex, highly local development along the railroad corridors of the South.

The second model available online is a time line and map of African American movements and events on the railroads during the Civil War that were recorded in *The War of the Rebellion: A Compilation of the Official Records of the Union and Confederate Armies,* the U.S. War Department's 128-volume series of Union and Confederate reports and correspondence. This spatio-temporal index, although limited to military bureaucratic texts, opens up the experience of African American labor and emancipation to further inquiry. A similar time line of guerrilla attacks on railroads was also developed from the *Official Records*.

Finally, we created a set of concordances for "railroad" terminology in the reports and correspondence of military commanders in the 1862 and 1864 *Official Records* volumes. The textual analysis of Sherman's and McClellan's correspondence provoked me to develop the idea behind chapter 7 on "The Railroad Strategy." The full texts of Sherman's and McClellan's official records, reports, and letters, and the computational tools to compare them, are also available.

So, I invite you to read, search, explore, and consider not only the work before you here but also the accompanying digital history available online. There you will find the work of the "sub sub-librarian" of this narrative but you should be warned, as Melville did of his "sub sub's" work, that "however authentic" the sources may be, they offer "a glancing bird's eye view of what has been promiscuously said, thought, fancied, and sung of Leviathan, by many nations and generations, including our own."[27]

PART I

Tools

To accomplish his object, Ahab must use tools; and of all tools used in the shadow
of the moon, men are most apt to get out of order.

—Herman Melville, *Moby-Dick*, 1851

Chapter 1

Slavery, the South, and "Every Bar of Railroad Iron"

THE day was Monday, September 3, 1838. Frederick Douglass arrived quietly at the railroad platform in Baltimore, Maryland. He was resolved to make his escape from slavery. His plan was simple but dangerous: to board a train to Philadelphia. He felt watched, as if he might be identified at any moment, seized, and taken into custody. His fears were not unrealistic—he had worked in trades all over Baltimore for white men who regularly rode the railroad, and he had met dozens of free blacks who might notice him. He could be questioned by the conductor and hauled off the train at any point along the way. To disguise himself, Douglass dressed as a sailor, and he carried false papers that indicated he was a free black. The tactic was bold, but its success depended on Douglass's self-confidence. He had to be convincing, act naturally, and not call attention to himself.

Instead of purchasing his ticket in the Baltimore station, where he might be noticed, Douglass decided to board the train quickly and buy his ticket once on board to avoid any unnecessary waiting. Using the railroad's elaborately printed timetable as his guide, Douglass timed his arrival at the station just as the train was pulling out. He "jumped upon the car . . . when the train was already in motion." Later, Douglass reflected on the precision of his escape and its consequences: "In choosing this plan upon which to act, I considered the jostle of the train, and the natural haste of the conductor, in a train crowded with passengers, and relied upon my skill and address in playing the sailor as described in my protection, to do the rest." When the conductor came into his car to collect the tickets, Douglass later admitted, "This was a critical moment in the drama. My whole future depended upon the decision of this conductor." Douglass felt agitated on the inside but outwardly he was calm and "self-possessed." The conductor asked him for his papers, Douglass obliged, and the conductor moved on.[1]

But another danger lurked. More than anything, Douglass feared that someone might recognize him on the train. "The train was moving at a very high rate of speed for that time of railroad travel," Douglass recalled, "but to my anxious

Samuel J. Miller, *Frederick Douglass*, 1847–52. Cased half-plate daguerreotype (plate: 5½ × 4 in. [14 × 10.6 cm]), Art Institute of Chicago.

Writing an open letter "To My Old Master" in 1848 in his newspaper, Douglass explained his escape this way: "The probabilities, so far as I could by reason determine them, were stoutly against the undertaking [his escape]. . . . It was like going to war without weapons. . . . One in whom I had confided, and who had promised me assistance, appalled by fear at the trial hour, deserted me, thus leaving the responsibility of success or failure solely with myself. You, sir, can never know my feelings."

mind, it was moving far too slowly. Minutes were hours, and hours were days during this part of my flight." He tried to keep to himself, but it seemed that at every stage of his trip someone he knew boarded the train. With each new passenger he recognized, Douglass's heart pounded furiously like the heart of a "fox or deer, with hungry hounds on his trail, in full chase."[2]

First he encountered "a young colored man named Nichols" on the railroad's ferry across the Susquehanna River. Because there were no bridges yet over the river, the railroad company ferried passengers across, a common practice on the nation's rail system. Unfortunately for Douglass, in the transfer of passengers there was even more opportunity for him to be seen and perhaps recognized. Nichols approached Douglass and asked "dangerous questions," and Douglass had to move to another part of the boat to avoid him.[3]

Then, once back on the train going north through Maryland into Delaware, Douglass saw one of his most recent white employers at a depot stop. Although the man was in a southbound train, the two trains pulled into the depot at the same time, and the two men could see one another through the windows "very distinctly." Douglass froze, but in the space of a few seconds the trains parted and he had escaped recognition a second time. Later, still another man, a German blacksmith whom Douglass "knew well," seemed to recognize him even in his sailor disguise. The man stared "very intently" and tried to place Douglass in his mind. Douglass was convinced that the German immigrant "had no heart to betray me" and "saw me escaping slavery and held his peace."[4]

Despite these narrow escapes, Douglass achieved his freedom and arrived in New York City less than twenty-four hours after he had begun his journey. The trip, which covered over 200 miles, would have taken two weeks ten years earlier. Douglass's experience illustrates that all sorts of people could be found on the railroad cars and in the depots. Personal mobility was more possible than ever before and indicated much of what Americans thought was modern about their society. Yet in an address delivered in New York City nearly fifteen years later, in May 1853, Douglass claimed that slavery "has an enemy in every bar of railroad iron, in every electric wire, in every improvement in navigation."[5]

A popular idea in the North was that modern communication and transportation would break down slavery and, conversely, that slavery could not survive amid the new technologies. America in the 1850s, after all, was a nation in motion. Mobility brought social mixing and enhanced the possibilities for equality and opportunity.

Frederick Douglass kept his exact means of escape secret for over forty years largely because he thought the railroad and its possibilities were too important to reveal to slaveholders. In his 1855 autobiography *My Bondage and My Freedom*, Douglass wrote that it was his "intention to withhold a part of the facts connected with my escape from slavery." Seventeen years after his escape, Douglass thought,

MARYLAND.

RAIL-ROADS.

(329) F'M WILMINGTON TO PRINCESS ANN Va.

Via Georgetown.

To New-Castle	5	
St. George's	10	15
Cantwell's Bridge	7	22
Smyrna	14	36
Dover	12	48
Camden	3	51
Canterbury	5	56
Frederica	5	61
Milford	8	69
Milton	12	81
GEORGETOWN	8	89
Concord	11	100
Laurel	6	106
Salisbury	16	122
PRINCESS ANN	15	137

(330) F'M GEORGETOWN TO EASTVILLE, Va.

To Milesboro'	8	
Daysboro'	5	13
St. Martin's, Md.	10	23
Berlin	8	31
Poplar Town	2	33
Newark	6	39
Snow Hill	8	47
Sandy Hill	9	56
Horntown, Va.	7	63
Modest Town	14	77
Drummondton	10	87
Onacock	7	94
Bell Haven	11	105
Frank Town	5	110
EASTVILLE	9	119

CANALS.

(331) F'M DELAWARE CITY TO BLACK CREEK.

Chesapeake and Delaware Canal.

| To Black Creek | 13½ | |

STEAM-BOAT ROUTES.

(332) F'M NEW-CASTLE TO CAPE ISLAND.

To Delaware City	7	
Cape May Light	52	59
Cape Island	4	63

(336) F'M BALTIMORE TO WASHINGTON.

Baltimore and Ohio RR.

To Relay House		8
Washington RR.		
Elkbridge Landing	2	10
Annapolis RR.		
Junction	10	20
Beltsville	4	24
Bladensburg	6	34
WASHINGTON	6	40

(337) F'M BALTIMORE TO PHILADELPHIA.

Via Elkton and Wilmington.

Maryland, Philadelphia and Wilmington RR's.

To Canton	3	
Stemmer's Run	7½	10½
Chase's	5½	16
Harewood's	1½	17½
Gunpowder	2½	20
Perryman's	8½	28½
Hall's ✕ Roads	3½	32
HAVRE-DE-GRACE	5	37
Cecil	1	38
Charleston	5	43
North-East	3	46
Elkton	6	52
Newark	6	58
Stanton	6	64
Newport	2	66
WILMINGTON	4	70
Naaman's Creek	8	78
Marcus Hook	2	80
Chester	3	83
Lazaretto	4	87
Gray's Ferry	7	94
BALTIMORE	3	97

(338) F'M BALTIMORE TO PHILADELPHIA.

Via New-Castle and Frenchtown RR.

By Steam-Boat to		
Fort McHenry	3	
North Point	9	12
Pool's Island	12	24
Turkey Point	24	48
Frenchtown	17	65
Frenchtown RR.		
New-Castle	16	81

By Steam-Boat to		
Marcus Hook	13	94
Chester	4	98
Lazaretto	5	103
Fort Mifflin	5	108
PHILADELPHIA	8	116

(339) F'M BALTIMORE TO WHEELING.

Via Harper's Ferry, Cumberland, Union and Washington, Pa.

Baltimore and Ohio RR.

To Relay House	8	
Ellicott's Mills	7	15
Elysville	6	21
Woodstock	4	25
Marryotsville	4	29
Sykesville	3	32
Hood's Mills	3	35
Mount Airy	9	44
Monrovia	6	50
Ijamsville	4	54
Monocacy	5	59
FREDERICK	3	62
Doup's Switch	4	66
Point of Rocks	4	70
Berlin	6	76
Knoxville	3	79
HARPER'S FERRY, Va.	3	82
Duffield's	5	87
Lee Town Road	4	91
Kerneysville	2	93
Drakesville	4	97
MARTINSBURG	4	101
Tabb's	3	104
Hedgesville Depot.	5	109
Black Creek	4	113
Licking Water Station	5	118
HANCOCK	5	123
St. John's Run	5	128
Rockwell's Run	10	138
Doe Gully Tunnell	2	140
Water Station	9	149
Pawpaw Tunnell	3	152
Little Cacapon	4	156
Paterson Creek	13	169
CUMBERLAND	8	177

National Road.

By Stage to Frostburg	12	189
Little Crossing	13	202
State Line	3	205
UNION, Pa.	32	237
Brownsville	12	249
Hillsboro'	12	261
Washington	14	275
Claysville	10	285
West Alexandria	6	291
WHEELING	14	305

Phelps Traveler's Guide, 1850.

This pocket atlas listed over 700 railroads, steamship lines, and canals in the United States and their routes of service, state by state. Frederick Douglass probably consulted a rudimentary timetable in the Baltimore newspaper or one posted at the depot for the Baltimore to Philadelphia route, described here twelve years after Douglass made his escape from slavery on the Philadelphia, Wilmington, and Baltimore Railroad.

(Courtesy of Archives and Special Collections, University of Nebraska-Lincoln Libraries)

slaveholders would parse his narrative for clues and hints and for "a train of events and circumstances." So he controlled and manipulated the account of his railroad escape, aware that the timetables, depots, and conductors in the nation's railroad system could be turned to enforce slavery. Only later, in his 1881 autobiography, did Douglass reveal how he managed to arrive in New York. "My means of escape," he wrote, "were provided for me by the very men who were making laws to hold and bind me more securely in slavery."[6]

But railroads could extend slavery in the South just as easily as they could enable Douglass to escape. The South in the 1850s, moreover, was alive with the idea that railroads and slavery together could transform the region, possibly affirm the South's place in the advanced societies of the world and secure its political future. Indeed, as leading white Southerners attempted to fold slavery into the modern society they were busy creating, they began to resolve what seemed like a paradox—whether slavery and modernity could coexist. White Southerners, like their counterparts in the North, placed great faith in the railroads, but they turned to slave labor to build, operate, and maintain these enterprises. The railroads purchased and hired thousands of slaves, transformed the slave trade market, and played a significant role in the rapidly increasing price of slaves. By the end of the 1850s slavery and railroads were joined in double harness, propelling the South's economy and society forward.

Although African Americans used the railroads to strike out for freedom, southern railroads became some of the largest slaveholding and slave employing entities in the South. Slavery, it seemed to many white Southerners, was perfectly compatible with the most modern technologies. *De Bow's Review*, the South's journal of industry and business, aggressively promoted railroad development and hailed the new technology because it "destroyed space, lengthened time, and created a new world." All of these changes, *De Bow's* argued, would surely benefit the South and its system of slavery.[7]

The numbers of slaves working on the railroads in the 1850s confirm that this sentiment was widely shared. On the North Carolina Railroad in 1852 there were 1,493 black men and 425 black boys working to lay track and construct the line. They lived in shanties or camps along the road, spread out in smaller divisions or sections. By 1860 the Atlantic & Gulf Railroad had 1,200 slaves cutting its line through the woods of south Georgia. According to one accurate estimate, based on figures drawn from railroad annual reports, over 14,000 slaves worked on the railroads in 1860 across the South. Since no single southern plantation used more than 1,200 slaves, the railroads in the 1850s stood out as some of the largest users of slave labor in the region. Women were not exempt from this work either. They too were forced to toil in the grading camps, wielding picks and shovels and pushing wheelbarrows. Some slaveholders leased women to the railroads as often as they did men, especially in the railroad building boom in the 1830s. Women also worked in the camps, cooking and washing. But by the 1850s the railroads mostly worked large crews of men and boys, some of them exclusively so.[8]

Railroads worked the largest numbers of slaves, moving them into isolated and diverse regions of the South, presenting scenes of the most brutal treatment, yet at the same time initiating a ripple effect of increased mobility, opportunity, and imagined space and time. In *The Emancipator*, for example, a narrative by an anonymous "Runaway Slave" described the dangerous work of railroad construction. This individual was hired out to the contractors for the Hamburg and Charleston Rail Road, which was "cutting and slashing" its way through the pine forest of South Carolina. "Every hour in the day we could hear the whip going," he explained. He found himself working alongside women who were pushing the heavy wheelbarrows up the embankments on high "skids," fifteen or twenty feet off the ground. When the workers fell or slipped, "it was very dangerous business." Boys and girls were forced to go behind and throw all the large chunks of earth up onto the roadbed. "There was hardly a day that some of the slaves did not get crippled or killed."[9]

Furthermore, railroads were a primary reason for the rise in slave prices throughout the region in the two decades before the Civil War. The massive public investment in railroads across the South had recursive effects on slave prices. Railroad construction increased the demand for slave labor because contractors scoured the South to hire and buy slaves wherever a new railroad was built. Competition for labor drove prices up. But thousands of miles of new railroad lines also opened up the interior South to plantation agriculture, dramatically lowering transportation costs to ship cotton to market as well as to ship supplies back into the plantation districts. Railroads extended the opportunities for cotton production and made the crop even more profitable. As new lands were brought under cultivation, planters needed more and more labor. As railroads were built, they increased the demand for slave labor. Slave prices shot up.

The most recent economic analysis of slave prices has shown that the southern states' public subsidies to build railroads totaled hundreds of millions of dollars and created an intensified "boom in railroad construction." Slave prices, therefore, were a product not only of the coldhearted market efficiency of cotton, but also of public policy decisions. The investment in railroads stimulated the South's slave based economy in ways that seemed to confirm for white Southerners the very basis of their society—slavery.[10]

Infused with cash from investors, profits, and state subsidies, railroad companies began buying hundreds of male slaves. The Louisville, Cincinnati & Charleston Railroad, for example, at its first stockholder's meeting in 1841 passed a resolution that the board of directors was "authorized as soon as the means and credit of the Company will permit, to purchase for the service of the rail-road, from fifty to sixty male slaves between the ages of sixteen and thirty." It was adopted unanimously and without argument or discussion.

By the mid 1850s the benefits of slave labor seemed almost too obvious to state. The president of the Mississippi Central Railroad explained to his stockholders in 1855: "I am led to the irresistible conclusion, that in ease of management, in economy of maintenance, in certainty of execution of work—in amount of labor performed—in absence of disturbance of riotous outbreaks, the slave is preferable to free labor, and far better adapted to the construction of railways in the south."[11]

Although hundreds of railroad companies hired slaves from local slaveholders, railroad account books reveal a startling story—the extent and scale of corporate slave ownership. The meticulous entries on the balance sheets show how boards and presidents used their positions to sell, finance, and market slaves. Often when a railroad switched from hiring slaves (see below) to purchasing, the company bought quickly and spent lavishly. In May 1857 the Vicksburg and Mississippi

Edward Beyer, *The High Bridge near Farmville*, from *The Album of Virginia*, 1858.

In the 1850s, using some of the best available engineering talent, southern railroads built some of the longest tunnels and bridges in the United States. They used slave labor almost exclusively.

(Courtesy of the Library of Virginia)

Railroad purchased three slaves for $7,000, then one month later spent another $4,000. A year later the company sold several slaves for $6,000, and then bought fifteen more slaves in 1859 for $20,000. Later, the company president loaned the company some of his slaves, valued at $6,000, and the entry was marked on a separate ledger account. The ledgers included stark entries for "Negroes Sold" and "Negroes Purchased" and presented carefully entered line items such as "negro boy Bill Sailor 1,400." The railroad bought and sold women, children, and men, and the name and amount for each one were recorded for the balance sheet.[12]

By 1860 many southern railroads were deeply invested in slaves and increasingly reliant upon them for operating their trains.[13] The South Carolina Rail Road Company held 90 slaves and was among the top 200 slaveholders in the city of Charleston (out of over 2,800 total slaveholders). In rural Autauwga County, Alabama, the South and North Railroad, with 121 slaves, was the largest slaveholder in the county. In Baldwin County, Alabama, the Northern Railroad held 41 slaves and ranked among the top twenty-five slaveholders in that county. Although many slaveholders in the South held similarly large numbers of slaves, and some planters held many more than these companies, the railroad companies as a group in the 1850s put to work over 10,000 slaves a year in the South and individually amassed holdings in slaves that rivaled the largest planters in the region.[14]

Railroad directors and officers also personally held slaves. They pursued the new technological opportunities of railroading from within their position in the slaveholding elite. In Virginia, among the directors and corporate officers of the state's fifteen railroad companies in 1859, 87 out of 112 directors held slaves. Those who did not were head engineers or superintendents, men who worked directly for the companies, often at the start of their careers. The average number of slaves held by the Virginia corporate directors was twenty. Some held over ninety, and many held over fifty. The list of directors in Virginia, furthermore, included many of the top slaveholding families in the state with extensive, large-scale plantations. Virginia's fifteen railroad presidents, despite the demands of running these new systems, included eight slaveholders, four of whom held over thirty slaves. The lower officers held slaves too. D. S. Walton, the engineer on the Richmond and York River Railroad, held two slaves. Every class of company ownership and senior management, moreover, from engineer to president, secretary, treasurer, superintendent, and director, included slaveholders.[15]

Northerners who traveled south on the railroads saw firsthand how slavery was being adapted to these modern settings. When one northern journalist arrived in Savannah, Georgia, the railroad station there stunned him. "To say that Savannah, Georgia, is likely to have the most complete and elegant railroad station in the country (besides being one of the very largest) may be a matter of some surprise to northern and western railroad men," he reported. The building was 800 feet long and 63 feet wide, designed in a modern style and rivaled only by the railroad stations in Boston and Baltimore. The road was equipped with engines shown at the New York Crystal Palace Exhibition. The yards included six parallel tracks, with over three miles of railroad. It was by any measure a remarkably large and extensive facility. The shops held the best workbenches and lathes in the business, all in all "the best we've seen."[16]

Each of these railroads, outfitted with the most up-to-date equipment, was worked and made possible by slave labor. According to the *Advocate*, southern railroads had achieved through slavery an extraordinary level of quality construction at half the cost of northern and western railroads—all because of slavery. At a cost of $15,000 per mile to construct, the southern railroad tracks prompted "astonishment in more northern communities." Northern and western tracks often cost twice as much to build, averaging by most estimates at the time between $30,000 and $35,000 per mile.[17]

Some Northerners concluded that there was much to admire about these southern efficiencies: no contractors scamming the roads for high profits, no inflated costs and padding of contracts, no secret deals whereby promoters keep the public at arm's length while they engineer a boondoggle. In the North great consternation followed the railroads. George Perkins Marsh, a prominent Vermont railroad commissioner, issued a detailed report meant to expose the "sorcery by which [northern railroad managers] turned corporate misfortune into individual gain." Marsh wrote, "I loathe with all my soul" railroad management. He considered nearly all of them "rogues" and "thieves."[18]

By the late 1850s the South's railroads therefore appeared to be quite a contrast. The "best engineering talent . . . in the world" was in the South building railroads. Led by its public men, the white South seemed to have sidestepped the financial scheming and shenanigans that afflicted some northern lines.[19]

All over the South railroad companies used slave labor to battle the region's many natural barriers. Impassable swamps, dense forests, and high mountains needed to be overcome. This demanding, physical work—grading, bridging, and tunneling—required hundreds of men spread out in camps along any projected railroad line.

In the 1850s southern railroad companies raced to break through one of the principal geographic obstacles in the region—the Blue Ridge mountain chain, which was some 700 miles long. Running from northeast to southwest through the states of Virginia, North Carolina, South Carolina, Tennessee, Georgia, and Alabama, this rough, mountainous backcountry separated the interior south of the Mississippi River from the Atlantic coast south. As early as 1836, South Carolina's U.S. senator John C. Calhoun recognized the role that railroads could play in altering this geography: "Unite these and the future is sufficiently ours to make us industrially independent at least." He had pushed to "bind the Republic together" and "conquer space" with federal support for internal improvements. Calhoun thought that a railroad route from South Carolina through Georgia to the Tennessee River would "do more to unite . . . the slaveholding states than can be effected by anything else." The project, he believed, would "change not only the commercial [affairs] but the politics of the Union." Most of all, he hoped to link the West and the South, because, as his fellow South Carolina railroad promoter James Gadsden argued, "if they [the West] do not come to us we will be overwhelmed by the power that has combined for our ruin."[20]

Many southern leaders, following Calhoun, believed that Nature—the landscape itself—favored the South in the race to Mexico, California, and the West. Weather played a role too, they thought, as heavy snows, bitter cold, and ice blocked more northern than southern routes through the mountains. Ease of construction and grading were also widely discussed advantages. Slavery further enhanced their operations, white Southerners thought. During the congressional debates in 1858 over the location of a proposed transcontinental railroad, Senator Alfred Iverson of Georgia proposed two routes, one northern and one southern, both federally supported, and emphasized the southern route as the cheapest to build and the most reliable to run. But northern congressmen opposed the measure and ignored the arguments for the southern route's low cost and reliability.

"We cease almost to be considered as parties having rights," Iverson lamented, echoing the concerns of John C. Calhoun eight years earlier. "Nature itself declares in our favor but her voice is disregarded."[21]

The idea that Nature favored their region was a persistent theme in the late 1850s among southern expansionists, and it became an important refrain in the years leading up to secession and the Civil War. The political implications of the notion could not be ignored: they hinged on what Nature bestowed and how people—a society, a civilization—reconfigured Nature to their own advantages. The basis for most of these claims came from the experience with railroads. Up and down the mountainous chain separating the seaboard from the interior, projects got under way in the 1850s to break through Nature's barriers and substitute for them a second nature of rails, tunnels, embankments, grades, and structures.[22]

The southern states laid down over 8,300 miles of track in the 1850s, a huge increase over its 1840s network. In fact, 75 percent of the total railroad mileage that the Confederacy would have at the start of the Civil War was newly constructed in the 1850s. Only the northwestern states of Ohio, Illinois, Indiana, Michigan, and Iowa could match this new mileage or boast a similarly rapid growth rate. The two regions, the South and the Northwest, shared equally in the claims of vast progress, constructing almost all of the 22,000 miles built in the United States during the decade. Their beautiful depots, brilliant locomotives, and buoyant enterprises were plain to see (see Appendix, Table 1).[23]

The southern states spent more than $128 million in state aid on railroad building before 1861. Government bonds and stock purchases paid for over 57 percent of the South's total railroad investment. In the North and West, however, public investment was on the wane and accounted for much less, approximately 20 percent of the total. In Virginia the state and local governments spent over $31 million on railroad development, nearly 70 percent of the state's total railroad construction capital.[24]

With a total of more than $252 million invested in its rail network, the South constructed not only one of the most extensive rail networks in the world but also an advanced vision for its economic and social future. The feverish railroad building in the 1850s coincided with the rapid transfer of slaves into the southwestern region, and slave prices skyrocketed with the expansion. Some of the fastest-growing slaveholding regions of the South were also the fastest-growing railroad regions. Missouri spent more than any other state on rail construction in the 1850s, and in the same decade its total slave population rose 30 percent. Even within older slave exporting states, such as Virginia, one-third of its counties experienced rapid slave expansion. Slavery, it appeared, could follow the railroads and might potentially thrive in the western territories.[25]

As both North and South moved west, the different gauges (widths) of railroad track did not materially hinder the process of regional growth, nor did these differences inhibit regional unification and common interest. Rather than a re-

Railroad Access Correlation

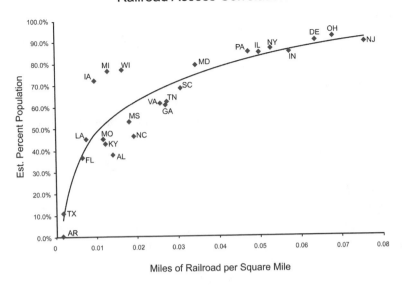

Railroad access trend line by state, 1861.

Using a fifteen-mile buffer around the railroad networks for each state in 1861, and an algorithm to distribute a county's population across the landscape, this estimate of the percentage of county residents who had access to the railroad depots shows the South's advances in the 1850s. The addition of more railroad miles reached a point of diminishing returns in every state.

(Graph and map by C. J. Warwas, Center for Digital Research in the Humanities)

calcitrant, late adopter of the "standard" 4-foot 8.5-inch gauge, the South experimented with different gauges just as other regions did. Pennsylvania alone had railroads with four different gauge systems. Indeed, the closest study of the development of different gauge systems in the United States reveals just how innovative the South was in the decades before 1860, as it followed much of the leading expertise coming out of Great Britain. By 1860 there were nine major subregions with distinct gauge standards across the United States. In this regard the North was no more unified in its gauges than the South. There was no standard gauge in the United States at this time.[26]

Even with a mix of different gauges, in 1861 almost 10,000 miles of railroad track linked up cities and towns across the South. The region boasted hundreds of junctions, depots, and terminal points, so many that despite the South's vast geography (compared to much of the Northeast) the level of railroad access for its free population nearly matched northern states and exceeded them in the number of depots and junctions per capita (see Appendix, Table 2).

At the same time, for every state there was a saturation point, a point of diminishing returns, in the development of railroad mileage and access to the network. Here, too, the pattern of southern development was impressive and consequential. Beyond a certain point each mile of railroad added to a network served an increasingly small percentage of the population. For example, Ohio, one of the leading states in railroad mileage, had 295 percent more miles of railroad track than South Carolina in 1861, but only 22 percent more of its population was serviced by its railroad network. The southern railroad network reached its most densely populated areas and, relative to the North, it brought proportionately more of its residents into contact with the railroads.[27]

In a decade the South had vaulted itself into a comparable position with much of the North in its access to railroads and all that they signified. The states of Georgia, Tennessee, Maryland, Virginia, and South Carolina, despite their difficult mountainous terrain, led the South in the percentage of free residents living within fifteen miles (a day's journey on an oxcart) of a railroad depot. In these five states over 60 percent of residents lived in what we might call the railroad access zone. Although some northern states had higher percentages of residents living along the railroads, the South's overall per capita density of railroad structures, such as depots and junctions, for its free population was higher in many states than in the North. Mississippi and South Carolina, for example, had 3.1 and 4.8 depots, respectively, per 10,000 free residents, while Ohio had 1.7. By this measure, taking into consideration what was built on the ground, whites in the South could claim by 1861 an extraordinary level of railroad penetration, investment, and accessibility (see Appendix, Table 3).

And although the South had relied for decades on its extensive river system for transportation and communication, railroads became the essential means to break the region's geographic barriers. The rail network created a "second nature" system, overlaid on existing rivers and natural features. The vast and complex natural geography of the South only heightened the significance of the newly assembled web of iron rails, ties, and locomotives. Plank roads, turnpikes, macadamized roads, and even canals combined with railroads to create a deep transportation "system." Because steam-powered railroads in the 1850s required a depot every eight to twelve miles for watering and fueling, the technology created a high level of access whether the populations it served were dispersed or concentrated.[28]

In Virginia, which led the South in its efforts to create a comprehensive, modern transportation "system," the state financed a massive tunneling operation to break through the Blue Ridge Mountains. At the time of its completion in 1857 the Blue Ridge Tunnel was the longest in the United States and one of the longest in the world (at 4,273 feet). To dig this tunnel (without the aid of dynamite or nitroglycerin explosives, both of which were yet to be invented), Virginia's state engineer, Claudius Crozet, negotiated with grading contractors to assemble at the foot of the mountains west of Charlottesville a force of 280–315 "hands," of which

The ruins of the Blue Ridge Tunnel, as it appears today.

The Blue Ridge Railroad and Blue Ridge Tunnel were built by the state's Board of Public Works. When the railroad company's chief engineer, Claudius Crozet, requested slave labor, the board had to decide whether the state should purchase slaves for the project. The tunnel has long since been abandoned, but the brick and stonework is the original, much of it slave-built.

(Courtesy of Jean Bauer)

as many as 175 might have been enslaved and the rest being Irish immigrants. He employed fifteen "overseers" and a whole range of specialized laborers, including blacksmiths, drillers, quarrymen, pickers, carpenters, drivers, and foremen. Subcontractors handled the grading of the railroad line using both enslaved laborers and immigrant Irish laborers for the backbreaking work of clearing the forest, removing tree stumps, and digging up the earth to make embankments.

A few of the hired slaves—Robert Mickum, Abraham Ward, and Thomas Burns—were specialized skilled workers, all three of them blacksmiths. After several years of working on the Blue Ridge Railroad, these three enslaved men had become the highest-paid employees on the entire payroll, at $1.50 per day. Not all of this money went to Mickum, Ward, and Burns; some of it instead went to their owners. On some railroads, such as the Richmond, Fredericksburg, & Potomac (R. F. & P.), slaves could earn extra money, above and beyond what the company was obligated to pay the slaveholder. The R. F. & P. paid several slaveholders $100 to hire men for the year, but each of them earned another $60–$70 on top of that. Such earnings depended on skill levels and whether the company was understaffed in a busy time of year.[29]

In 1851 Crozet's force at the Blue Ridge Tunnel had swollen to 471 men, and recruiting workers was getting difficult. He began to turn even more to slave labor. Cholera, strikes, and work stoppages interrupted the work on the east side of the mountain, where the Irish lived in shanties. After his first year Crozet concluded "that it will be advantageous to hire as many negroes as practicable for the Tunnel." The reasons were simple enough, if stereotypical. Crozet had little patience for the Irish workers' concerns, their culture, their families, or their religion.[30]

The decision to use black labor wherever possible on the project came down to a starkly simple truth—black labor could be forced to work, and to work longer. White labor was "occasionally troublesome," according to Crozet. And whenever white labor was scarce, Crozet knew that he could not "dismiss [them] as freely as proper discipline might require." On the other hand, he could not hire slaves regularly "owing to groundless apprehensions in regard to working in the Tunnel." After convincing local slaveholders that the Tunnel work was safer than they imagined, Crozet at first concluded that working with both white (free) and black (enslaved) labor on the site would guarantee progress. There would be "less interruption of the work and we shall have the whites employed under better control."[31]

But as white labor left the project for other jobs, Crozet needed large numbers of laborers quickly. White labor prices—as well as slave labor prices—were going up. Only a large infusion of one or the other workforce would suffice. Crozet finally struck a deal with a slave broker to hire forty to fifty slaves for the tunnel. What Crozet feared more than anything was a slowdown in the work, and only by exploiting slave labor to its fullest extent could he ensure "an economy in the way of progress."[32]

Time and money. Progress and cost. These were the variables Crozet balanced as the Blue Ridge Tunnel project lurched forward through cholera epidemics, strikes, and accidents. Slave labor, unlike that of the Irish workers, could be forced to work wherever and whenever necessary to complete the project on schedule, whether there were accidents or not.[33]

When southern railroads could not buy or lease slaves from planters, they turned to other means. One ready source of labor was state prisons. Virginia's governor and legislature decided to experiment in the hiring of convict labor and authorized the leasing of slave prisoners to companies in 1858 in its "Act Providing for the Employment of Negro Convicts on Public Works." The governor of Virginia, John Letcher, negotiated the contracts and in 1860 sent over one hundred men and sixteen women to work on the Covington & Ohio Railroad. Another symbolic effort to reshape the South, the C & O project had been praised by George Fitzhugh in the dedication of his widely read treatise defending slavery, *Cannibals All! or Slaves Without Masters.* The slaves sent to work there (over 300) found themselves pitched into the largest construction project in the state.[34]

When slaves, whether convicts or not, began working on the railroads, companies saw immediate advantages. For slaveholders, too, the prospect of hiring out their slaves to the railroads was so financially attractive that few passed up the opportunity. Once slaves were sent to the railroad, however, it might be months before they were returned. Paul Smith, an ex-slave from Athens, Georgia, recalled that his father had worked on the first railroad in the state. When the family's slaveholder died, the administrator of the estate "hired out most all" of the slaves to work on the railroad. The slaveholder's wife had little say in the matter, and "it was a long time 'fore she could get 'em back home."[35]

As southern states financed and built thousands of miles of railroads, white Southerners were investing in multiple potential outcomes. Their network could help the South become more independent, even as it sustained broader national growth. Sectional and national purposes therefore resided together comfortably, if tenuously, in the South's expansionist vision. But during the 1850s, when northern railroads began altering trade routes to the growing Great Lakes economy around Chicago, the balance shifted. What once appeared complementary—sectional and national intentions—struck an increasing number of white Southerners as potentially antagonistic.

Southern promoters saw their efforts as embedded in a wider geographic context, defined in large part by competition with the North. They were especially concerned with what the northern trunk line railroads were doing to redirect commerce in the Mississippi Valley and, as they saw it, to erode the South's "natural position." "An extraordinary effort is required," one company's president explained, "on our part to arrest the ebbing tide." He proposed a rail line to stanch the drain of commerce out of the region to run north from Louisiana to Missouri and then on to Iowa, a route "socially and politically, national in character, and eminently calculated to harmonize all sectional prejudices."[36]

Railroad leaders in the South, then, talked out of both sides of their mouths. They spoke of national unification that railroads might bring and sectional rights that railroads would ensure. They exhibited, like their counterparts elsewhere, a remarkable confidence and vision for the ways that the railroads would transform space and restore "natural" alignments in a way that favored the South. The president of the Memphis, El Paso and Pacific Railroad—the name itself indicated the sort of expansionist bravura of the South in the 1850s—explained that his road would develop not only the agricultural potential of Texas, but also the mineral wealth of New Mexico, "and the northern States of the Republic of Mexico, Chihuahua, and Sonora." These opportunities "cannot fail" to indicate to "every one who is at all acquainted with the practical working and advantages of Rail Roads, of the vast amount of business which will be done on this road."[37]

In all of the rhetoric of national unity and railroad growth, there was an intense competition for resources, commercial supremacy, and expansion. Southern railroad presidents in the Southwest spoke of growing cotton in New Mexico, a new market made possible by the railroads, and slavery its logical consequence. Plans for a transcontinental railroad in the 1850s took shape in this political and social context. Nearly every political leader considered the potential transcontinental railroad a "great national thoroughfare uniting the Atlantic with the Pacific, connecting Europe with India."[38]

And railroad promoters everywhere, including in the South, argued that "railroads create the trade they need." The idea was both alluring and threatening. It went beyond confidence or optimism. It was understood as a kind of natural, economic, and technological law whose operations were in effect whether the citizens of a state or city wished it or not. Every state's leading men, none more so than those in South Carolina, were acutely aware of the consequences of their state's potential isolation. For over a century at the center of Atlantic trade, many seaboard states saw clearly the ways railroads were reconfiguring the nation's borders, geography, and commerce. Because the railroads connected places, linked subregions, and crossed natural barriers, their potential prompted a series of questions for those who supported and opposed them: what is our region, who are our allies, and where are we going?[39]

The backbreaking work of grading, digging tunnels, and laying track went forward almost exclusively with enslaved labor in the South. But as railroads were completed across the region, other changes followed. The buying, selling, and hiring of slaves in the 1850s were also transformed by the railroads and telegraphs.

If railroad companies were buying slaves by the hundreds, and leasing them by the thousands, they were also shipping them from one part of the South to another as part of a modernized slave trading system and market. With the growth of railroads and telegraphs in the South, slave trading took on the characteristics of other markets: time-sensitive information, networks of buyers, rapid transit, and national reach. Slaveholders and slave traders increasingly used and adapted these technologies. Slave sales took place at railroad junctions, and slave traders located their operations near the railroad. Up-to-the-minute information, telegraphed from markets all over the South, affected the sales and prospects of traders. Railroads offered different prices for shipping "gangs of negroes, ten or more." The ease with which this technological transformation took place, and the monstrous implications of it for the institution of slavery, should not be dismissed. If cotton was the engine of slavery's growth into the 1850s, then railroads constituted a second phase, equally merciless, exploitative, and disturbing.

Buyers used the telegraphs to deliver instructions for purchasing arrangements, and they used the railroads for orchestrating quick deliveries. "Bring the negroes on immediately" meant load them on the trains as soon as possible. "I can be down tomorrow with five (5) Negroes," one seller from Lynchburg wired a Richmond firm.[40]

E. H. Stokes, a slave trader in Richmond, sent "drummers," or agents, into the South along the railroad network to buy slaves for the trade. One of these agents, a young man named Winbush Young, wrote the Stokes firm daily and telegraphed routinely all of the latest information he could gather. "I sent you by train three (3) negroes, cash eighteen hundred dollars," he telegraphed from North Carolina. Stokes's other agents fanned out along the rail lines, stopping at the rail junctions, renting wagons and moving into the surrounding countryside. They kept in constant contact with the Richmond office by telegraph, seeking authorization for prices they paid and reporting the state of the market from the localities along the line. As they worked their way across their territory, they bought larger and larger numbers of slaves. To make money for the firm, they served as the overseer and hired out their services and the slaves, usually to large businesses such as the railroads.[41]

In 1857 a slave named Jourden H. Banks found himself pulled into this highly modernized slave trading system. He grew up in the Shenandoah Valley of Virginia and watched as his sisters and family members were sold in the 1850s when prices for slaves spiked. His own turn came on June 16, 1857, when he was sent to the smith shop on an errand, only to discover that it was a ruse and that he was to be sold the next day. He was tied up in a wagon and hauled to Staunton, Virginia, where he was shipped on the railroad to the big slave markets in Richmond. He was sold on "the auction-block" for $1,484 to an Alabamian named S. S. M'Kalpin, who had purchased over twenty-eight slaves and planned to lease them to the railroads. M'Kalpin shipped all of the slaves by railroad through North Carolina, South Carolina, and Georgia, to Montgomery, Alabama. From there they were shipped by steamer over 100 miles and then loaded into wagons and taken to the farm. Between the summer and the spring planting of cotton the next year, M'Kalpin sent Banks and the others to work on a railroad under construction nearby.[42]

By his own admission Banks had some misplaced confidence that "the man who would come twelve or fifteen hundred miles to buy me" would provide reasonable treatment, but he found out quickly that the distance he had traveled would offer no such assurances. Upon arrival at the farm Banks was shown his cabin, but it had no beds, no sheets, no pillowcases, nothing but a dirt floor. "I was perfectly confounded at the sight," he remarked. He was put to work on the railroad crew along with the others, and, on September 5, 1857, a confrontation with the overseer became for Banks "the great fight." Another man had been singled out and whipped for failing to keep up the pace, and Banks had refused to help hold him down for the whipping. When the overseer turned on him next, Banks fought back and shoved him down "to get a bite of the dust." Banks made his decision then and there beside the railroad tracks to "strike" for freedom. He wielded his pick as a weapon, and he beat both the overseer and M'Kalpin senseless, to the point that they were "literally crawling about on the ground." Then he dropped the pick and ran.

Banks took off first for the cane brake swamp near the railroad, but once deep in the thickets he circled back to the railroad line. Using it to guide his way through the countryside, Banks "remembered the direction in which I heard the running of the cars" and followed the railroad and the North Star. He came to the end of the Ohio and Mississippi Railroad's unfinished line. From there he followed the barely laid-out road northward, taking advantage of its "straight line." Eventually, he reached the Ohio River and ferried across it. When he reached the Illinois Central Railroad line, Banks followed it to the center of Illinois, where he hired himself out as a farm laborer.[43]

Banks's journey took him thousands of miles from the Shenandoah Valley in Virginia along the railroad into the Deep South, to Alabama, then back again northward along the unfinished railroads to the Ohio River. His long experience on the railroad, first as a slave being transported into the market, then as a slave hired to work on the line, and finally as a fugitive on the railroad, provided an escape from both the status of chattel slavery and from the massive system that slavery in the South had become.

The modern development of slavery with railroads and telegraphs, the deepening of the South's commitment to it, and the extension of railroad technologies proceeded together and in relation to one another. For white southern leaders, slavery became more and more mobile. They came to believe that the railroad ensured slavery's and the South's future.

All sorts of schemes floated to the surface of public discussion in the euphoria of railroad development the 1850s. Some planters even thought that reopening the African slave trade might work in concert with the South's railroad projects. In 1859 the *Semi-Weekly Mississippian* newspaper published a letter suggesting that by reopening the African trade thousands of slaves could be brought to the state for work on the railroads. At the same time, "every white person in the state,

Andrew J. Russell, *Slave Pen*, Alexandria, Virginia, c. 1861–1865.

Railroads transformed the way slaves were sold and transported. The slave market boomed in the 1850s with the expansion of railroad construction across the South, and traders moved along the network using the telegraph to make and finalize deals. This slave trader was positioned strategically one block from the Orange & Alexandria Railroad depot.

(Lot 11486-H, No. 10, Division of Prints and Photographs, Library of Congress)

females and infants inclusive," would have a right of "pre-emption" and the opportunity to buy these slaves over five years, during which time they would be laboring on the railroads. The companies would get free labor, the state would get railroads, and white Mississippians would get slaves.[44]

For many black Southerners, however, despite their hard labor on the railroads and the cruel treatment they experienced, the railroad came to have powerful meanings associated with freedom. Anne Broome, a former slave born in South Carolina, was told as a child that she was brought into life not by a stork but instead by a train. Her mother told her a birth story over and over again that she was brought by the first railroad train "dat come up de railroad track, when they built de line." According to this family fable, Anne's parents saw a baby on the cow catcher of the engine and her mother told her husband to "run out dere and get our baby befo' her falls off and gets hurt under them wheels."[45]

There were good reasons for these associations. Enough black slaves escaped along the railroads, like Jourden Banks, that apocryphal stories of freedom found wide circulation. Frederick Douglass, Henry "Box" Brown, and other ex-slaves wrote about the ways they gained their freedom, often figuratively linking their escape to their loco-mobility—the embodiment of train travel movement.

These stories made their way northward as well. Henry David Thoreau helped Henry Williams escape from slavery by getting him safely aboard a train bound for Canada. While they waited, Thoreau asked Williams how he had made it all the way to Massachusetts. Thinking that slaves guided their flight by the North Star, Thoreau was surprised by Williams's answer: "They frequently followed the telegraph when there was no railroad."[46]

Recent detailed research into the ways slaveholders mortgaged slaves and then used their human property as collateral for extending their operations even further indicates the massive expansion of slavery under way in the immediate years before the Civil War. With slave prices rising steadily in the 1850s, largely because of the boom in railroad construction and operations, slaveholders used their chief asset to gain more capital for expansive economic development on the western frontier. Slaveholders leveraged the value of their slaves to buy not only more slaves but also new technologies—steam engines from Cincinnati, boilers from New York, and sawmill equipment from Baltimore. Between 1855 and 1860, in one small parish in Louisiana over 25 percent of slaves were listed as human collateral on loans to slaveholders. Millions of dollars were raised in this fashion, as capital allowed slavery to build on itself.

The implications of this activity between, say, 1856 and 1861 might be understood in this way: the southern thrust into Kansas was not measurable in how many slaves were on the ground there in 1857 but in the extent to which slaveholders could leverage slaves to extend themselves into these new places, to achieve the possibilities that their enormous assets afforded. In other words, even immediately after the U.S. Supreme Court's Dred Scott decision seemed to open the territories to slavery, slave property might not need to be physically moved in order to extend the reach of slavery. Slave property elsewhere in the South could, and did, provide the collateral for the purchase of slaves, buildings, railroads, structures, equipment, and other assets to be located in these western lands (see Appendix, Table 4).[47]

Put differently, the rise of free labor ideas in the North and the advancement of modern technologies in the United States might not have led inevitably to a "natural," gradual, or nonviolent end to slavery. Instead, railroads appeared to enhance slavery's social and economic potential at the very moment of its impending political eclipse. This persistent juxtaposition, perhaps as much as any singular political event, energized and aggravated the sectional conflict between the North and the South.[48]

Chapter 2

Railroads, the North, and "The Velocity of Progress"

WHEN Asa Whitney put his plans for a transcontinental railroad before the American public and the United States Congress in 1849, he placed a giant map in the front page of his treatise, "A Project for a Railroad to the Pacific." At the center of the page, and of the world, stood the United States, strategically poised to link Asia with Europe. "The entire commerce of the world must be tributary" to the United States, Whitney asserted in his typically grandiose prose. "Nature" aligned the United States as the great middle nation of the world. However, forces were already in motion that might subvert this natural advantage, and so, he suggested, time was of the essence. The United States needed a direct link between its coasts and a plan to network the nation.

The problem, Whitney admitted, was how to initiate the work as a truly "national" project without creating sectional side-effects and regional biases. Whitney knew very well that the only previous precedent for such a similarly large endeavor was the controversial Bank of the United States, which took "the means and earnings from one section of the Union to be squandered in another." The Bank divided a generation, and split the young republic into fractious, feuding, and fiercely competitive political parties.

Although Whitney never really explained how his transcontinental railroad proposal would alleviate, rather than inflame, sectional passions, he tried to persuade Congress to pay attention to "the geographical division formed by nature" that favored the United States. The world's economies flowed, he pointed out, through the mountain barriers, river corridors, and desert spaces on the continent. Nature guided commerce, he argued, and only a massive industrial reconfiguration of these forces could alter natural patterns. By "forcing the commerce" through a shorter route, railroads would redirect the natural flow of goods and capital. Whitney's point was meant to impress his readers: nature determined commercial position, but human progress in the steam age would reconfigure the globe and, indeed, defy nature.

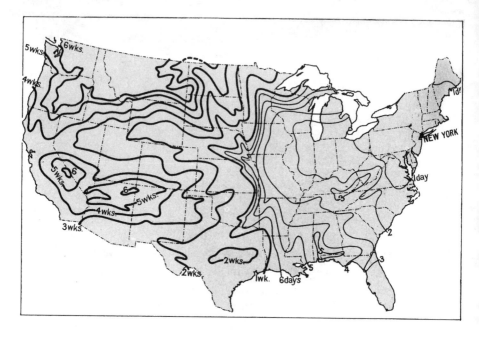

Charles O. Paullin, "Map of the Rates of Travel in 1857 from New York City,"
in *Atlas of the Historical Geography of the United States.*

Paullin's map remains one of the most widely reproduced visualizations of the social changes
brought by the railroad. While New York, as the largest U.S. city, increased in importance
in the 1850s, other regional hubs, such as Baltimore, Maryland, and Charleston, South
Carolina, competed for supremacy and status on the rapidly advancing railroad network.

(Washington, D.C./New York: Carnegie Institution of Washington and
the American Geographical Society of New York, 1932)

But Whitney knew that to convince skeptics he had to go further and so
he explained the value of the transcontinental railroad in terms many northern
supporters could understand: as an instrument to Americanize, employ, and
settle the thousands of immigrants landing at the nation's eastern port cities. He
pointed out that the immigrant workers would become "independent" men who
would "make their own bargain, and work no longer than was for their best interest." These men would eventually settle the less-expensive western lands and
make a start as free laboring yeoman farmers. The Pacific Railroad, therefore,
would liberate, not enslave; it would protect the republic, not endanger it; and it
would offer relief to America's institutions rather than strain or distort their pil-
lars. Whitney's appeal found wide support.[1]

But the process of expansion that Whitney outlined had deeply sectional
effects. As Southerners in the 1850s pushed Congress and Secretary of War Jeffer-

son Davis to give the southern route due consideration, the Pacific Railroad became mired in sectional bickering and eventually it stalled.

Increasingly, railroad development took on partisan meanings. If white southern leaders embraced railroad development, so too of course did Northerners. Just as southern leaders associated the expansion of the railroads with the expansion of slavery, Northerners began to associate their technologies with free labor. As they did so, widespread ideas about labor, land settlement, immigration, abolition, commercial supremacy, and the natural flows of commercial expansion became interwoven with railroad development. The Republican Party took up these ideas and by 1860 led the northern movement for railroad expansion into the West. A whole generation of young men, active in politics, business, and community life, became what we might call "Railroad Republicans." Their faith in the technology, in its possibilities for a particular vision of American expansion, not only matched the white South's growing confidence but also helped Abraham Lincoln win the presidency in 1860.

All eyes, Republican and Democratic, turned in the 1850s to the new lands in the West. The United States' vast territorial acquisition in 1848 after the Mexican War was immense, encompassing the present states of Arizona, Utah, Nevada, Colorado, New Mexico, and California. These lands totaled over 500,000 square miles and were the equivalent in size to about half of the nation in 1850. The settlement of these places and the potential for their development took shape amid a booming confidence in the power, reach, and consequence of railroads and telegraphs.

An important consequence of the rush to build railroads in the South in these years was to enhance southern identity and to fuse slavery with railroad development. For the South, the incomplete network of railroads managed to unite white Southerners who were separated by vast rural spaces and overcome the region's significant natural barriers. By 1860 the most highly populated places of the South were linked in ways unimaginable just a generation earlier. Only western Virginia, a significant exception, stood out as a major population of white Southerners out of reach of the southern-oriented rails. The leading southern business journal, *De Bow's Review*, considered the South in a "race of civilization" with the North, and few indicators of success were more important, or more closely watched, than the railroads.[2]

The intensity of this contest, and of the widespread feelings that accompanied the political battles, did not derive just from the fact that there were new lands to fight over and claim. The railroad offered the North a means to meet slavery's rapid extension, and immigration made it possible to populate these open lands quickly. The process of accelerated northern railroad growth, combined with the opening of new territories, raised for the white South a doubtful future, potentially an eclipse in power, influence, and wealth.

But the North's expansion too brought a measure of self-doubt and concern. Northerners had to reconcile their free labor ideal with the reality of large railroad corporations in their midst, operating by their own rules and managing huge payrolls of wage-earning workers. They did so in part by seeing their society as providentially gifted, as one defined by material and social progress.

As both sections hastened to extend rail lines into the West in the hopes of influencing the new territories, each tried in the language of the period to make the western regions "tributary." William Henry Seward, the influential U.S. senator from New York and a leading voice in the antislavery movement, spoke of a "new equilibrium" in the nation's geography, one not between north and south but instead between the east and "the boundless west." Seward's famous "higher law" speech on the floor of the Senate in 1850 dramatically challenged the idea that slavery was protected by the Constitution—Seward argued that slavery should be seen as "temporary," and freedom as "perpetual." But he also described a United States "empire," a society propelled by "steam locomotion" and "telegraph communications, unknown when the Constitution was adopted." The Union, Seward believed fervently, had taken on a life of its own. The nation's geographic and material progress, its growth across space and through time, was so powerful that "no other government" could exist on the continent. The nation was a "globe, still accumulating upon accumulation, not a dissolving sphere."[3]

Nowhere was this process more evident than in Illinois, Kansas, Indiana, and Iowa. Technology, whether railroads, steamships, or telegraphs, seemed to white Northerners a virtual guarantee of a peaceful future, the means to accentuate modern development and bring along anyone who resisted progress. The single biggest project in this region was the construction of the Illinois Central Railroad, which had acquired a massive (and the first) federal land grant—a whopping 2,595,000 acres. One of the main effects of the Illinois Central during the 1850s, however, was to show Americans in both sections just how fast, and dense, and internationally significant, northern free labor development could be.[4]

Year by year in the 1850s rail lines extended toward Chicago, Illinois, and the city grew in importance. Maps and atlases featured panoramas of the city, showing all of the railroads leading into the great metropolis. When a businessman or emigrant came into Chicago, the city seemed to bristle with energy and accomplishment. Visitors noted both the natural majesty of the prairies around Chicago and the scale of the city that unfolded before them. John Munn, a New York businessman who took his first trip to Chicago in 1850, returned four years later on the newly constructed Michigan Central Railroad, in his judgment "one of the best built & managed Roads of the whole country." He was impressed by its "remarkable degree of precision & promptness." His train made a run of 282 miles in eleven hours "without any deviation from the time table."[5]

Boston & Worcester
Railroad timetable, 1862.

The railroad timetable
was an astonishingly complex innovation. At first,
timetables were printed
on small cards because
local railroads, such as
the Boston & Worcester, made just one or two
runs a day over a short
distance. But the 1850s
marked a major shift as
hundreds of new junctions came on line in the
Midwest and South. Railroads in the 1850s operated primarily as passenger lines, and timetables
for longer lines became
increasingly intricate.

(Library of Congress)

When he arrived at Chicago, though, Munn realized that he was witnessing
an important transformation. He had become "a convert . . . to the idea here that
this is to be *the* City of the West." Indeed, Munn left Chicago in May 1854 convinced that it would be "the terminus of thousands of miles of Rail roads, radiating to all points & [bringing] into its limits the agricultural wealth of the garden
of three States." He was right.[6]

Later, traveling the Chicago and Rock Island route, Munn ruminated on
everything he had seen up to that point. Anyone who took the journey to Chicago,
he thought, would have his or her mind opened by the experience. They would
possess "more extended views of our country." For such travelers, "the 'West'
will no longer be a vague idea, but an embodiment of a rich dream of beauty and
wealth."[7]

Part of the Illinois Central Depot, Chicago (*Harper's Weekly*, September 10, 1859).

"The awakening of the great Northwestern country has commenced at Chicago," *Harper's* reported. (University of Nebraska-Lincoln Libraries)

John Munn's speculations were not unlike those of wealthy white Southerners about their railroads, but Chicago and its environs had made an impression not easily captured in words. The railroads were shaping Illinois and the Northwest in ways that appeared visible to the naked eye, but they also provided the means for thinking in grander terms, for seeing an intoxicatingly bright future.

When the Illinois Central's lands were opened for sale beginning in 1852, northern expansion onto the great prairies of Illinois and Iowa defied most people's expectations. The numbers of settlers, the mobility of immigrants, and the development of the towns along the Illinois Central line all indicated the staggering challenge that Illinois and its great railroad posed to the South. The southern half of the route—the Mobile and Ohio Railroad, which also received a land grant—appeared in the Illinois Central's typical advertisements and guide maps as a great white void, a total blank as if it did not exist, while to the north the eastern trunk lines dominated the routes to Illinois and suggested the pathways for potential settlers. Such intentionally misleading maps were a common tactic among competing investors and companies. But the effect of leaving the South off of many northern company maps was plain—immigrants and settlers were shown where to go and, by implication, where not to: namely, the South.[8]

In 1855 and 1856 the Illinois Central started to sell its lands in earnest and marketed them to all comers. The job fell to a local assistant named Benjamin F. Johnson, whose duty it was to monitor the progress of the road and give tours of the prairie to interested land customers. Johnson noted that the men on his tours began "to open their eyes" and that the key selling points that "struck them" were the price of the land and the increase in population. Johnson, for his part, enthused over the beauty of the prairie as a land of "unbounded fertility" and "agricultural wealth." Cattle could graze their fill in an hour and grow fat beyond belief. Timber stands in the little creek beds were enough to put up fences and strong houses. The soil itself could not be matched anywhere, and it could never be exhausted. And because the prairie was not heavily forested, a farmer did not have to invest in land-clearing to improve the acreage.[9]

Some of the men touring the line, it turned out, were investors in the railroad's bonds, securities that were backed by the value of the land granted to the railroad. These "land bonds" constituted a new financial instrument, and these investors, based in London, personally examined the land to get a sense of what literally underlay the Illinois Central's borrowing. The Europeans had expected the place to be a "swampy inferno" and began their tour with some degree of skepticism. They found instead that the land itself had value and, they concluded, would all but ensure the success of the road.[10]

The land sales on the prairie were followed closely in London banking circles. The rapid growth of American investments in London was part of a larger international network of information, finance, and trade. Foreign investors in 1853 held over $43 million in U.S. railroad bonds, about 25 percent of the value of all U.S. railroad company bonds. Most of these investments were in eastern railroads. Baring Brothers and N. M. Rothschild & Sons banking houses began the trend of British investment in the U.S. market in 1852 when they made big purchases of the Pennsylvania Railroad bonds. But the Illinois Central and its federal land grant changed the character of the British market. According to the most complete history of British investment in the United States, the Illinois Central's new land bonds gave the illusion of total security and as a result "completely captured the British investor's imagination." In addition, the open prairie lands "hinted at a practical Utopia."[11]

More than an investment, the land seemed to provide the basis for all future regional wealth, enriching all parties that might become involved with it. Indeed, Johnson set about proving "the extraordinary proposition that the *subsoil under our richest soils is capable of producing as largely as the soil itself*." Formed over thousands of years of rainfall, salt leaching, and natural processes, the prairie soils possessed a wealth simply waiting to be unearthed. They constituted an agricultural gold mine.[12]

Few documents explain what transpired in the 1850s in Illinois quite as evocatively as the 1860 Illinois Central guide to its lands published by Johnson's office.

One table detailed the growth trajectories of forty-six towns on the line and indicated an average increase in population of 2,760 percent over the 1850s. These towns not only grew rapidly but also filled with migrants from New England and northern states. Just eleven of the forty-six towns were listed as having predominantly southern migrants, these from Kentucky and Tennessee.[13]

The transformation of Illinois, then, was nothing less than explosive in these years. The Illinois Central advertised intensely and attracted settlers from England, Canada, Vermont, Germany, and Ireland. Large numbers came from Pennsylvania, Ohio, New York, and New England. The town of West Urbana in Champaign County provided a useful example: solely a depot in 1854, two years later it had a population of 1,500 and its farm property values had increased 100 percent. The county also grew between 1850 and 1860: its improved acreage jumped from 23,000 to 170,000 acres, and the value of its farm property skyrocketed from $478,000 to $5,178,800. Carbondale, another Illinois Central depot town, stood as a lonely, recently surveyed railroad stop in 1852, but over five years the place attracted over 1,200 residents. Cairo, too, increased its population in the 1850s, by a remarkable factor of ten.[14]

The scale of the Illinois Central building project defied easy calculation and testified to the dramatic reshaping of the lands by the railroad. The first survey parties went out on the prairies from Chicago on May 21, 1851, and the first contracts for grading work were put out nearly a year later, in June 1852. That year 14 miles of track were laid, then another 118 miles in 1853, 300 miles in 1854, and 195 miles in 1855. In three years 627 miles of track were placed on the roadbed, but this achievement represented only one part of the work.

The expansion of the Illinois Central in the 1850s also took place in a particular context of increased mobility. The heightened state of personal and social movement created newly visible opportunities. Capital flowed across the Atlantic Ocean through Canada and New York to Chicago and out onto the prairie. London investors, many of them free trade and free labor liberals, traveled to the region, strode out onto the tall grass prairie of southern Illinois, inspected the soils, and ended up holding over 66 percent of the railroad stock shares. Northern farmers and immigrants were equally mobile, moving onto the Illinois plains with startling rapidity. The railroad itself brought workers to the prairie and, in some counties, put up more buildings and structures than what was already standing, all in a stunningly short period of time.[15]

The explosive growth came to an abrupt halt, however, in 1857 when a massive banking panic hit the United States. The panic changed the pattern of migration across the country and significantly altered the pace of railroad extension. Traffic slowed. The Illinois Central almost went bankrupt. Investors in London, New York, and Boston were called on for capital contributions to keep the railroad from going under. Workers were let go and construction projects halted.

One of the Illinois Central's principal east-to-west migration routes ran over the Terre Haute and Richmond Railroad in Indiana. In April and May of both 1856 and 1857, before the panic, through passengers flooded the Terre Haute's trains on their way to the new lands of the Illinois Central. Over 18,000 emigrants took the railroad in one month in these years, and passenger receipts for the company ballooned, swelling profits and expectations. But in June 1857 the slowdown had already begun and by October 1857 local passengers outnumbered through passengers for the first time in years. For the Terre Haute and Richmond, revenues started to plummet (see Appendix, Table 7).[16]

Despite the economic slowdown, the railroads had produced, in Illinois and across the Northwest, an enormous payoff in the agricultural sector during the 1850s. They channeled the migration of people and capital onto the prairies, so much so that each new mile of railroad, it has been estimated, brought about 32 Germans, 19 Irish, 7 British, and 200 (largely northern) Americans into the Midwest. The railroads increased land values, spurred farm acreage improvement, and concentrated urban growth. They revolutionized the grain trade in the Great Lakes region, redirecting it along the newly opened trunk lines to the eastern ports—the Baltimore & Ohio (B & O), the first of these great linkages, but also the Erie, the Pennsylvania, and the New York Central. They siphoned off trade otherwise bound for the Mississippi River and New Orleans. This shift came "at the expense of the South" and led the South ironically to become self-sufficient in foodstuffs by 1860, a turn of events valuable to the Confederacy in the war. But there were other ways that the railroad shaped a revolution in spatial and temporal relationships, ones which challenged northern society and its ideas about free labor.[17]

In one of the most important developments for northern society and politics, a new class of American workers emerged across the northern states with the rapid expansion of the railroads. While the southern railroads hired and bought slave labor, the northern companies turned to recent Irish immigrants and native-born laboring men from the cities and towns along their lines, and these workers were the vanguard of a modern, systematized, large-scale labor force. At first, the railroad companies employed dozens of workers, but by the 1850s the northern roads had hundreds, and then thousands, on their payrolls. One historian has estimated that the number of railroad workers tripled between 1840 and 1860, with the greatest surge in the 1850s. Most estimates suggest that there were about 15,000 railroad workers in 1850 and 75,000–100,000 by 1860. The B & O alone, for example, employed 6,467 workers in 1857 at its shops, construction sites, and stations. The company was the largest private employer in the city of Baltimore, one of the largest cities in the nation at that time.[18]

By 1860 railroad work was one of the fastest growing industrial sectors in

The railroad depot at Pittsburgh (*Harper's Weekly*, December 4, 1858).

Pittsburgh celebrated 100 years since Fort Duquesne was captured from the French — the railroad depot stood on the site of the old fort, a symbol of the city's modernity. By 1861 Pennsylvania possessed over 500 depots, so many that 85 percent of the state's population lived within fifteen miles of a depot. (University of Nebraska-Lincoln Libraries)

the United States. With numerous regulations, odd hours, and long distances, the work was unlike any other industry, however, and it came to be seen both by the workers and by northern society as peculiarly modern.

It should not be surprising that in these years of rapid growth there were violent conflicts and competing visions over the changing workplaces of northern railroads and what they indicated about northern society. Northerners saw their society as founded on "free labor" principles — the idea that independent working men were neither chattel nor employees beholden to higher powers. Workers, at least according to the middle class, should move upward, not remain permanently in the laboring class. Their mobility would come either through industrious application of their talents and self-discipline or through the expansion of towns and farms across the West. The Republican Party, in particular, embraced an idealized vision of northern free labor society.[19]

But the new railroad workers presented Northerners with a potential contradiction. This labor force worked for highly capitalized companies that employed them by the thousands; large numbers of them were unskilled and permanent wage earners. Many of them were Irish and were dismissed by the middle class as unfit for independent status, and yet they benefitted from various opportunities for advancement in a host of generic trades. Indeed, the largest northern railroads began to act as catalysts for regional employment in ways that supported the general ideals of free labor. Rather than wage slavery, railroad work in the North provided fair opportunities for advancement through skill and experience. A man could move into railroad work through a number of trades—he could move in and out of the work as necessary. While perhaps not fully independent—that is, a landowner—he stood on his own.[20]

Most of all, railroads created a new class of northern employees in counterpoise to the South's newfound uses for enslaved labor on its railroads. Northern farmers could tell themselves that cotton was regionally distinct and peculiarly suited to slavery, that free labor was superior in the cultivation of every other crop, and that free labor outproduced the slave South in wheat and corn. But the North and the South applied their free and slave labor to the same work on the railroads, and as a result created opposing labor systems in the most visible modern industry of the day.

And nearly all railroad workers in the North were white men. In 1860 the U.S. census taker for Philadelphia found not a single black railroad worker in the city. The Chicago, Burlington, and Quincy, as well as the Illinois Central, hired white men only.[21] Of the B & O's nearly 6,500 workers, less than a dozen were black or of mixed race. A handful of black men served as blacksmith helpers and draymen. Thomas Jackson was a porter. Emory Willmore cleaned passenger cars for the B & O. He worked out of Cumberland, Maryland, and had acquired $1,300 in real estate there. But he was a lone exception. As a rule, the B & O hired almost entirely a white labor force—despite the fact that Baltimore was home to the largest number of free blacks in the South—over 38,000.[22]

Railroad work, therefore, took on special significance in the North as white man's work. Some of the most detailed records that we have about northern railroad workers, in fact, come from the Baltimore & Ohio, the oldest railroad in the United States. The B & O became the first major interstate railroad in the nation, and despite its location in a slave state (Maryland), the company became a prominent free labor railroad, setting the example in labor relations, practices, and organization for the Ohio and other northwestern roads to follow.

Some northern companies used a contracting system, essentially outsourcing their train operations to a head man. The Philadelphia, Wilmington, and Baltimore Railroad, as late as 1857, contracted directly with its engineers who ran and operated the road's machinery; they in turn subcontracted a crew to work on the train. The only employees of the company, therefore, were the other company officials and the men at the depots. The engineers, as independent contractors, bore the responsibility for disciplining and organizing their workers.[23]

But the B & O developed a much more bureaucratic organization, and northern railroad companies in the 1850s increasingly followed the B & O's lead. One of the first steps companies took was to write and publish their rules for employees. Rules became ever more complex and hierarchical. "Study well the Instructions on back of this Table," the Illinois Central's Chicago branch warned its employees in its 1856 timetable. The rules were situational and contingent—all employee actions were interpreted and measured against guidelines, but many acts were specifically and unequivocally required. The rules were to be followed, but following them required judgment and case-by-case application. Consequently, there was great variation in the way the rules might be applied and, as a result, great opportunity for failure.

With one of the largest workforces in the nation, the B & O employed over 2,300 laborers, 315 machinists, and 268 carpenters. In fact, the company maintained over 300 different job titles on its huge payrolls. Of the top ten occupational categories for the B & O, just three were operating trains—190 conductors, 194 engine men, and 255 brakemen. The overwhelming bulk of the B & O's employees did not even ride on or operate the trains, but instead supported the sprawling enterprise in general trades, such as carpentry, machine tending, and blacksmithing. Beyond these major job classifications, the B & O hired dozens of more general workers: 101 engine cleaners, 82 machinist apprentices, 51 bricklayers, 53 clerks, 32 iron molders, and 43 firemen. Stablemen, coppersmiths, tinners, cleaners, coopers, mail carriers, stock tenders, quarrymen, and an architect all found employment with the B & O. Seven women, Margaret Englert, Mary Hinsey, Peggy Morris, Ann O'Keefe, Amelia Motter, Bridget Brennan, and Sarah Mally, worked for the B & O cleaning station houses or passenger cars. Other railroads likewise hired women in these positions. A handful of women, often Irish immigrants, worked on the construction crews and tunneling gangs in the East (see Appendix, Table 5).[24]

The diversity of the railroad jobs was remarkable in itself, but the geographic diffusion of them was wholly unprecedented. The B & O employees covered three states and stretched across dozens of counties at over 115 different work locations. Baltimore, not surprisingly, held the most workers—962 men worked the yards at Camden Station. But the top ten largest sites of the company's workforce included Piedmont, Virginia, with 210 employees, and Martinsburg with 259. In remote, mountainous Marshall County, Virginia, a place farther west than westernmost Pennsylvania, the company had 340 workers, mostly carpenters, masons, and laborers, relining the Board Tree Tunnel. Over 200 employees were doing the same to the Welling Tunnel, located in Littleton, Virginia, just a few miles shy of the Pennsylvania state line. These tunnels and the men who were camped there working on them stood over 250 miles west of Baltimore (see Appendix, Table 6).[25]

In the 1850s railroad work became the fastest growing nonfarm occupation in the northern economy, but its work had significant spatial characteristics that set it apart from other industries. "Division" employees, for example, had no fixed

Railroad Workers, 1850s.

Few original images remain of railroad workers in the 1850s, especially of
construction crews, whether free labor or enslaved. Northern railroad companies
employed thousands of men on their payrolls in a dizzying array of occupations.

(Library of Congress)

geographic location. They were what would later be called "the running trades,"
and these workers' place of employment was not precisely fixed. They floated
between major stations along the line. Some lived in Baltimore, others in the
smaller towns to the west; regardless, they did not live in the exact place where
they worked. All of these job classifications were held by white men on the B & O

Surprisingly large numbers of workers could move in and out of shops, tunnel operations, construction crews, and track-laying gangs, even on mature rail-

roads like the B & O. Although rules and regulations appeared to diminish the workers' independence, and as a result to contradict the free labor ideal, much of the railroad work on the B & O intensified growth along its corridors and offered workers the means of advancement within their region.

To be sure, the work was also unpredictable and subject to fluctuation. When downturns in the northern urban economy occurred, these workers were hit hard. And after the Panic of 1857, they were especially receptive to the appeals of the Republican Party—the party of free labor, the party of opportunity in the West. Moreover, these workers experienced a "hidden depression" throughout the 1850s. They represented about a quarter of the North's electorate, and they faced competition from immigrants, depressed wages, and a significant decline in real income. Working men were particularly attracted to the Republican Party, especially by its claim that the expansion of slavery in the western territories limited the opportunities for free white men. In 1860 they made up a key voting bloc in the Republican column, supporting Abraham Lincoln in large numbers across the North.[26]

As a result, between the economic downturn in 1857 and the election in 1860, the character of free labor on the railroads could not have been more important. The B & O's construction projects, continuing well after the company's celebrated completion in July 1857, were in full swing when the Panic hit. In fact, thousands of workers fed on the B & O's reinforcement of its numerous tunnels and were pulled into its central stations and shops. In the 1850s immigrant Irish labor along the B & O did not, as it turned out, flow directly west onto the land rich prairies, but instead settled into distinctly subregional loops of hiring, employment, and opportunity. These patterns showed that a high proportion of railroad work was generic and applicable in a range of close settings—blacksmithing, laboring, cleaning, apprenticing, helping, carpentry, and stonework. Although laborers made up the single largest job category for the B & O, they were just 35 percent of the total workforce. Two-thirds of the employees, in other words, had other quite generic jobs, not exclusively found on railroads, including not only machinists and blacksmiths but also stonecutters, bolt cutters, locksmiths, and weigh masters.

Given the almost unique characteristics of railroad work in the 1840s and 1850s, especially how its spatial unevenness shaped the towns and cities along the lines, railroad workers had particular opportunities to be mobile, but their movements were not exclusively westward, as accounts of the railroad "boomers" have suggested or even as Republican leaders at the time often predicted. Instead, among northern free labor railroaders, both immigrant and native-born, the everyday pathways of their work led them to migrate within any major railroad's region. Out of approximately 400 workers on the 1842 B & O payroll, 95 of them were still with the company fifteen years later. Nearly half (48 percent) of these men stayed in Baltimore during that time, while 27 percent migrated westward from Baltimore and 10 percent moved back east into Baltimore. Indeed, all told, 62 percent of these long-persisting employees stayed in the same exact location between 1842 and 1857. Overall, the B & O workers who can be tracked from 1842 to 1860 maintained a strong connection to the company, despite a series of strikes in the 1850s.[27]

As a result, in the North it appears that railroad work, especially its spatial configuration and diversity, played a key role in shaping the context of free labor ideology. Railroad labor had special significance in the 1850s, as sectional rivalries developed and slaveholders moved slave labor into the western edges of the South. Railroads, such as the B & O, crossed the Alleghenies and connected the eastern seaboard cities to the Midwest farms and urban centers. With the rise of the Great Lakes agriculture and economy, these developments suggested how railroads might transform and realign the regions. Laborers who moved on and off the payroll, who shifted from west to east to find work, who remained within a subregional market, counted on certain opportunities to arise. Free labor promised a form of stability that slavery, at least as it was developing on the southern railroads, unquestionably threatened.

Out in the Northwest, meanwhile, the prospects for free white men in the railroad industry were slowing down in the late 1850s. Railroad workers had found steady opportunities in the mid 1850s but the Panic of 1857 halted many new construction projects, throwing men out of work. Competition was intense for the remaining jobs. Some men returned to their farms. Others drifted along unemployed. By 1860 Samuel B. Reed, one of the leading construction engineers on the Mississippi and Missouri Railroad and a Democratic Party loyalist, could find no work at all in Iowa. He and his partner John Boyle were underbid on contract after contract. One of their competitors for an Iowa job came all the way from Greenfield, Massachusetts, to preempt them. "There is nothing to be made in this western country now as there is too much competition in the way of railroading," Boyle lamented. With Iowa a nest of cutthroat rivals, and with Missouri's governor vetoing state aid bills necessary to complete its railroads, Boyle concluded in 1860 that "railroading seems to be dead."[28]

Reed and Boyle decided to head south into Alabama in October 1860 and look for work on the South's western frontier. With so many northern projects shuttered, Boyle imagined the South as "the country to do work in." With the presidential election in full swing, their trip that fall took them to Memphis, Tennessee, and then on to Vicksburg, Mississippi, along the railroads. Carrying a letter of introduction from the former Democratic governor of Illinois, Reed made little headway and he found that the economic recession had finally caught up with parts of the South and delayed projects around Vicksburg and Montgomery, Alabama. Despite the lack of work, Reed's railroad trip to the South seemed only to confirm his Democratic political views. The slaves, he thought, were "contented and happy," with "no care for the future." They were dressed far better than the laboring classes of the North, according to Reed. Returning to his farm in Illinois, Reed looked forward to supporting Stephen Douglas in the upcoming presidential election in November 1860 and making "the black Republicans quail in their shoes."[29]

It is difficult to say whether railroad contractors, such as Reed and Boyle, were more uniformly Democratic or Republican in their politics in 1860. But they were part of a massive movement into the West of both native-born and immigrant railroad workers. The Irish immigrants on their construction crews identified initially with the Democratic Party, and many remained loyal to the Democrats in 1860. But the native-born men began to take up the Republican cause. They believed in the free labor principle for white men, and their experience with the railroads reinforced these ideas. The slowdown in northern railroading in the three years leading up to the presidential election of 1860, moreover, caused some men to turn to the Republicans even if, like Reed, they disparaged southern blacks and even if they grudgingly admired the wealth produced by southern slavery.

In sum, the American railroad system, although disconnected and disjointed, had sprung up in a remarkably brief period. And because of the speed and vast scope of these developments, investors and businessmen tried to assess what they meant for the American nation. After the Illinois Central land bonds revolutionized the British interest in American investments, and after the Baltimore & Ohio's great success and stability demonstrated that enormous dividends were possible, London bankers and individual investors began buying American state bonds, railroad stocks, and railroad bonds.

In 1859, at the peak of his reputation and career, Richard Cobden, an influential British Member of Parliament and prominent international free trade and antislavery advocate, took an extensive railroad tour of the United States. As a major investor in the Illinois Central's stock, Cobden attended the stockholder's meeting and inspected the company's every operation.

He traveled nearly 4,000 miles by railroad across the United States. He swept down from New England to Philadelphia, Baltimore, Washington, D.C., and out west to Ohio, Indiana, and Illinois, and then south briefly to Holly Springs, Mississippi, and back up through Missouri and Illinois and then east to Washington, D.C. He did all of this in just twenty-four days. Cobden calculated that what took him a week in 1835 to travel he could do in fifteen hours in 1859.[30]

Like most British travelers, he spent very little time in the South, but Cobden did come face to face with slavery, as he toured a tobacco factory in Hickman, Kentucky, and a cotton plantation and cotton gin in Holly Springs, Mississippi. In both places he noticed the ways slavery had been adapted with modern practices. The president of the Cairo and New Orleans Railroad held slaves on his cotton plantations, and as Cobden inquired further into slavery in Mississippi, he found

Richard Cobden, a leading Liberal in Parliament, was also invested in the Illinois Central Railroad.

He took two major trips to the United States, first in 1835 and again in 1859. During his first trip he traveled on railroads for a total of just ninety miles, from Lowell, Mass., to Boston, and then to Providence, R.I. On his second trip, twenty-four years later, he traveled 4,000 miles on American railroads.

(Image from John Bright and James E. Thorold Rogers, eds., *Speeches on Questions of Public Policy*, Vol. I [London: Macmillan and Co., 1870].)

out that nearly all of the railroads were hiring slaves, especially "skilled negro mechanics," who fetched for their slaveholders $400 to $500 a year.[31]

These encounters with slavery along the South's quickly developing western borders did little to dampen Cobden's overall enthusiasm for the expansion and progress of the United States. To a friend Cobden tried to explain what he had seen in the free states: an unbridled optimism, a faith in progress, opportunity, and statistical success, and a calm assurance that nature had favored them. "Nobody can doubt the future" of the free states, he wrote. "Their faith in the destiny of coming generations becomes a part of their estimated power when measuring themselves against the old world. — They are the only people who in their statistical works carry on their progress into the future. — Take a table of the past growth of Chicago, for instance, & you will see, in addition to the exports & imports to the present time, an estimate of their increase for a dozen years to come. — Such a people cannot be beaten or humbled by present misfortunes. They take refuge in the future. — which offers them advantages over the whole world."[32]

The passage is worth quoting at length because Cobden found in the North something so radically different from the "old world" that he could hardly contain his enthusiasm. He was convinced that the "vitality, force, & velocity of progress" in the North was unique. The material and technological advances in American society, moreover, had "moral" repercussions. Societies, whether European or North American, revealed their moral character through civilized material and social progress. Some Americans complained to Cobden that their republic was "going back politically," descending into an abyss of sectional corruption and conflict after the "Bloody Kansas" slaveholder versus free settler conflicts, the financial Panic of 1857, and the Dred Scott decision annulling the Missouri Compromise. Despite the obvious national ambitions of the slaveholders, Cobden could not believe that the future would bring conflict. His breathless trip across the prairies, up and down the line of the Illinois Central, convinced him that civilization and moral progress would follow the railroad. In this belief he was not alone.[33]

Indeed, southern whites drew the same conclusions about their society. We have already seen that the extension of railroads gave white southern slaveholders the means to build new businesses using their property rights in slaves as collateral. The growing rail and telegraphic networks, ruthlessly in the hands of slave traders, enhanced the slave trade, shaping it into a modern, information-oriented and time-sensitive market by the late 1850s. When they stopped to consider the matter at all, white Southerners viewed these developments, however dismal, as part of modern progress. The networks gave slaveholders the ability to project slavery across space and through time into the western borderlands with a scale and speed that had important consequences for the ways they thought about their region and its growth.

The decade before the Civil War has recently been considered a kind of "cold war," when northern and southern economies took shape around competing social and cultural arrangements. Railroad building in the North brought immigrants and dramatically increased its proportion of men of military age relative to the South, so much so that the North's numerical majority of young men jumped from 2.33 to 1 in 1820 to 3.31 to 1 in 1860. Slavery's dynamic trajectory of growth across the landscape, however, could not be discounted. Southern slaveholders possessed an important advantage through their property rights—the uninterrupted capability to move slaves at will wherever they wanted and with full legal protection. They were able, as a consequence, to reach across space and to extend their operations into new territories and settings. In addition, if confronted with an unusually large harvest or a compressed and intense period of work on a railroad, they could force work from women and children, extending their control over time and its restraints. Northern railroads, even with their extensive rule books, could not control time and space in the same way.[34]

With railroads, slavery was now more mobile than ever before. Railroads, as we have seen, participated in slavery's exploitation. As southern railroad developers adapted slavery into the service of the new technologies, the flexibility of slavery could not have been more apparent, nor its reach more extensive, nor its consequences more alarming for many Northerners. Cobden was optimistic about American democracy and the "western region," but he witnessed growing racial animosity in the North. Despite living in "an age of progress," white racial attitudes were hardening and "growing stronger in the Free States."[35]

These changes hardly indicated what was to come—a national civil war—but they were part of the war's coming and the course it took. For the white South the transformation of the landscape, the great engineering feats of the railroad companies, and their extensive use of enslaved labor were all tied to the widespread belief that "nature" favored the region. Indeed, nature needed to be conquered and mastered from the malarial swamps of the Tidewater to the craggy passes of the Allegheny Mountains. The effort to take this step required a massive scale of enterprise, state investment, and adaptive forms of slavery. Every southern state participated in this movement, and in the context of the newly acquired western territories the stakes were increasingly significant. Few realized that the intensely competitive railroad building in both the North and the South was working to consolidate and bring into counterpoise the sections, forge their identities, and give meaning to their claims of superiority. The confidence that came from these activities was easily applied in the Civil War to the defense of the nation and its purpose. For both Confederates and Unionists, therefore, much of what they needed to fight the war could be found in their experiences with the railroads.[36]

PART II

Leviathan

So there is no earthly way of finding out precisely what the whale really looks like. And the only mode in which you can derive even a tolerable idea of his living contour, is by going a whaling yourself; but by so doing, you run no small risk of being eternally stove and sunk by him. Wherefore, it seems to me you had best not be too fastidious in your curiosity touching this Leviathan.

—Herman Melville, *Moby-Dick*, 1851

Chapter 3

Secession and a Modern War

F OR Ephraim C. Dawes, a young student from Ohio studying at the University of Wisconsin in Madison, the fusion between the Republican Party's free soil politics and the railroads' frenetic expansion could not have been more obvious or personal. In 1856, as Bloody Kansas convulsed with violence and fraud, young Dawes followed the congressional campaign of his uncle William P. Cutler, who had served as president of the Marietta and Cincinnati Railroad. Nearly every letter he wrote between 1855 and 1860 included an inquiry into the progress of railroads, their operations, and the fortunes of the Free Soil and Republican Party candidates.[1]

Dawes's heroes were John C. Frémont, the Republican candidate for president; Salmon P. Chase, the abolitionist governor of Ohio; and Cassius Clay, one of the founders of the Republican Party. These men appeared willing to stand up to the South. No issue was more important than the Wilmot Proviso, which aimed to bar slavery from the territories acquired in the Mexican War. Indeed, their stand on the Proviso would inspire other Republican candidates, Dawes thought, who "will neither give or take an insult." And a few months later, when Ephraim's brother Henry decided to go to Kansas as a free soil settler, Ephraim could hardly contain his excitement. "I am [going to Kansas] too," he brashly declared, "I've always wanted to go."[2]

Ephraim Dawes wanted to go to Kansas to take a stand against slavery and to mark the territory for free white men. And in 1856, with railroads linking up New England and the Northwest and forming a dense web, many settlers could consider such moves in these terms. Railroads brought formerly distant regions into unexpectedly close proximity—New England free labor, antislavery, and abolition advocates were so much nearer to Kansas in 1856 than ever before. The Dawes brothers could look at a railroad map and see the lateral lines leading to Kansas. Along the borders, including some of the fastest growing slaveholding counties in the South, slavery was no longer a distant threat to Northerners but instead a visible presence three or four depot stops away. Slavery's strongholds were measurable in minutes on a railroad timetable from places in the free North.[3]

The reverse was also true, of course, and the free labor society of the North was reachable in minutes from the South. The controversy in Kansas, the rise of the Republican Party, and the frenetic pace of railroad building in the Northwest up to 1857 helped bring young men such as Ephraim Dawes into wider networks of reform and politics.[4]

In this highly charged context of sectional rivalry and railroad competition, Dawes was not unusual in his energy or commitment for the Republicans. The young Republican movement brought together men and women with great faith in the technological and material progress that surrounded the railroads. When the war came, Dawes volunteered and joined the 53rd Ohio Infantry as a first lieutenant. Between 1861 and 1864 he fought his way south with Sherman's army, from the Battle of Shiloh to the Battle of Atlanta, where he was wounded severely. His brother, Rufus R. Dawes, joined the Union cause as well and led a company of Wisconsin men in the "Iron Brigade," the tough northwestern regiments in the Army of the Potomac. Writing years after the war, Ephraim Dawes looked back on the spring and summer of 1861 as a time when "the war of words which preceded the battle engrossed all minds."[5]

The "war of words" and the development of a separate southern national identity took place so seamlessly within the material and technological progress of the age that their relationship has sometimes appeared contradictory. Northerners such as Dawes looked at railroads, and the labor and industries that sprung up with them, and concluded that they were so advanced as to preclude slavery. Southerners looked at the same things and drew the opposite conclusions—surely their railroads proved the advanced state of their society and showed no incongruity with slavery and its extension. Both constantly invoked railroads as self-evident markers of their society's modern success, and at the same time spoke in the vaguely unifying language of national progress and purpose. Yet, as we will see, these associations were equally suited to vastly different potentialities: secession, separate development, competition, war, destruction, and conquest could and did flow naturally from these common wellsprings. When they did, the scale and destruction of the war between the northern and southern nations surprised nearly everyone.[6]

In towns and cities across the North, such as Marietta, Ohio, where Ephraim Dawes lived, a new form of civic celebration came with the railroads—highly orchestrated and arranged events to mark a technological moment, the opening of a railroad. The grand celebrations that took place in both large cities and small towns provided occasions for sectional rivalry and self-examination. All sorts of out-of-town celebrities—military officials, editors, artists, politicians, and businessmen—showed up with the railroad officials for these events. And when spe-

Railroad completion celebrations became highly orchestrated events.
They served local, regional, and national purposes simultaneously.
And they often featured an excursion trip over the line with artists,
newspaper editors, political leaders, and railroad officials. Stops along
the way showed off the beautiful, large, and bustling station buildings
and depots in the major urban places on the route.

("Passenger Station of the Little Miami Road," from William Prescott Smith,
The Book of the Great Railway Celebrations of 1857)

cial visitors came, their arrival effectively announced the importance of the town. Railroad company celebrations offered hundreds of communities the opportunity to rehearse their allegiances, their connections, their orientation. On such occasions politics could not be ignored.

One of the biggest moments of technological unification before the Civil War honored the completion of the Baltimore & Ohio (B & O) in 1857 and hailed its engineering feat of crossing the Allegheny Mountains. Because the B & O oriented its entire operation toward free labor, and because the Kansas crisis and the Dred Scott decision made sectional conflict more divisive and pronounced in 1857, the B & O's national celebration revealed an uneasy tension.[7]

At the grand banquet in Baltimore, dignitaries and guests made toasts to the railroad and what it achieved. One marveled that the B & O "had, for all practical purposes of transit, obliterated the Alleghenies from the map of our country." Nineteenth-century Americans used dramatic language to convey this idea—railroads, they said, "annihilated" space and time. At the B & O banquet, everyone marveled at "the simple fact" that the party had traversed over 1,000 miles in a few days. "All that distance has, as it were, vanished from under our feet."[8]

Such sentiments were widespread. The grand vistas, the beautiful tunnels, the elegant viaducts, and the steep embankments indicated a range of new possibilities. But the political implications of these new geographical arrangements were unclear. Toasts were made to the "young west" and to the "future Empire" and the nation's "surpassing agricultural wealth, manufactured production, commercial energy, and political power." They were also made to the South and in defense of its rights (that is, slaves).[9]

One guest hailed the railroad as "a powerful agent . . . to republicanize a people."[10] The toasts caught precisely the contradictory spirit of the age. The development of railroads in the East, West, and South spurred expansion across great space and competition for resources, trade routes, and "natural" advantages. Railroad lines reconfigured the landscape and changed the "location" of cities, towns, and even natural features. Hiring and disciplining thousands of workers, the railroads began a process of networking the nation and led to Americans' first and most significant experience in, and with, a national system. In the heated debates of sectional conflict, slavery, and western expansion, Americans at these moments speculated on how the railroads might affect a future war.

Later, in the presidential election of 1860, over 1,000 votes were cast in Baltimore City for Abraham Lincoln, more than in any other county in Maryland and more than in any other place in the South, where Lincoln was not even on the ballot. Indeed, all along the B & O line in Maryland, especially in Allegheny County, where the company had its shops, large numbers of Lincoln voters went to the polls for the Republicans in 1860. There seemed to be little coincidence in this Lincoln support along the railroad.[11]

The B & O, therefore, appeared to be the exception in the slaveholding South that proved the influence of all railroads, whether built with slave or free labor. Railroads and telegraphs could, and did, appear to sway the political and social orientation of new places. Despite its slave state location, in other words, the B & O seemed to be pulling Maryland and western Virginia closer to Ohio and Pennsylvania, rather than the reverse. The lesson for southern slaveholders seemed clear with regard to expansion in the western territories: free labor railroads could sustain free labor societies, and slave labor railroads could sustain slave labor societies.[12]

At nearly the same time, the Memphis & Charleston Railroad held its celebration of completion, but its event turned into a rehearsal for secession. The mayor of Charleston, South Carolina, William Porcher Miles, explained that the railroad would bind the southern people "together more closely and compactly as a homogeneous people, having common interests, common institutions, and a common destiny." He called the internal bickering between southern states and cities competing for railroads "suicidal madness for us, while our citadel is besieged." Miles sharply pointed out, "The time [for Union] has passed." The South cannot "blink" or cry for peace, because "the war has already actually begun."[13]

These defiant sentiments found ready agreement in Virginia, where the *Richmond Examiner* was already fretting that the South's failure to build railroads

Baltimore & Ohio Railroad artist's excursion, 1858.

Following its 1857 grand banquet, the B & O hosted an artists' excursion in 1858
to show off its dramatic vistas and massive tunnels. The men and women took turns riding
precariously on the cowcatcher, *Harper's Weekly* reported, to get a "better view of the grand
scenes which were opening before and around them . . . such was the confidence felt
in the steadiness and docility of the mighty steed."

(Z24.485 Courtesy of Maryland Historical Society)

would jeopardize its security in a sure-to-come civil war. With its exposed position on the frontier of any future Confederacy, Virginia, the newspaper warned, should not find herself "without the means of concentrating troops with the rapidity indispensable to modern warfare." "Modern warfare" would be governed "by steam," and it had achieved a velocity "not dreamed of thirty years ago." The *Examiner* considered it "obvious" that the Covington & Ohio Railroad was a military necessity because it planned to connect the state's largest white population in western Virginia with the points in the East most vulnerable to attack. The future war would be won and lost, the *Examiner* believed, by how quickly and how many forces could be rushed onto battlefields.[14]

Every time a railroad celebration took place in the South, white Southerners, such as Charleston's Mayor Miles, were increasingly convinced that the Confederate nation was already self-evident. The South's railroads took in capital from abroad through state bond sales and participated in the global web of the cotton trade. They stood at the forefront of commerce and engineering. When southern secession conventions met after Lincoln's election in 1860, the same ideas of civilization and progress—what a nation needed to claim modernity—were strikingly evident. What surprised white Southerners throughout the sectional debates over the extension of slavery in the late 1850s was the North's blatant disregard for the underlying geographic advantages that they thought nature had bestowed upon the South. The recent mastery of geography that their railroad building so clearly demonstrated seemed to count for little in the North, and yet the experience gave the white South unprecedented confidence in its modern civilization and slavery's place in its society. *De Bow's Review*, the leading voice of southern national identity, saw the South as "a first rate power" in the world, with an infrastructure to justify and sustain independence if necessary.

Everywhere white Southerners looked in 1860 and 1861, they could find striking examples of material improvements in their society made possible by the railroads. In Louisiana, the New Orleans, Jackson and Great Northern was opened and advertised tickets to New York City, a trip that took three days and sixteen hours and cost $48. The company was opening a new cutoff to the Mobile & Ohio line near Canton, Mississippi, and had purchased a steam excavator to accelerate the work. It owned 45 locomotives, 37 passenger cars, and 503 freight cars. And in 1860 the Great Northern earned $1,272,683 in gross receipts, and cleared $556,712 in net profits for its stockholders. Outfitted with the best new equipment and making handsome profits, the company appeared to be an enormous success in late 1860. Across the South other major lines showed similar returns and contributed to a wide sense of white southern self-confidence.[15]

The rush to build railroads in the South led its leaders to constantly calibrate their region's position relative to the nation's commercial and economic network. As late as 1860 and 1861 the rush was still on. New southern railroads were coming on line, connecting places never before linked and adding to the dynamic of sectional examination and measurement. Passenger traffic surged, but southern freight traffic proved valuable and substantial. In this respect the 1850s marked a decisive period of change for the white South's identity, as modern ideas, technologies, practices, and institutions were instantiated in repeated sequences across the region. The timetable, the depot platform, the locomotives, the bridges, and the tunnels offered evidence to white Southerners of the mobility and success of their society (see Appendix, Table 7).[16]

But it was the timing of the completion of the Charleston & Savannah Railroad in the fall of 1860 that played a decisive role in shaping the secession movement in South Carolina. The railroad's opening celebration took place on November 2, a few days before the presidential election. Speakers at the banquet talked of a fraternal and mutual sovereignty between Georgia and South Carolina that the railroad confirmed. The river border that for so long separated Georgia and South Carolina had been bridged, Savannah lawyer Francis S. Bartow argued, and the states were united by the railroad. The Savannah banquet was such a success that the Charlestonians asked the Savannah men to come to their city for reciprocal festivities.

Not to be outdone, the Charleston railroad men hosted the Georgians on November 9, three days after Lincoln was elected president. Up to then the reaction to Lincoln's election, even among South Carolina's leading politicians, had been cautious. But the South Carolina legislature was in session in Columbia and considering what measures to take. At the railroad banquet, the dignitaries ate turtle soup, duck with olives, lamb chops, and other regional delicacies. Then, Bartow, a self-proclaimed Union man and southern Whig who a week earlier had urged South Carolina not to secede, suddenly changed his position. Bartow encouraged South Carolina forward toward secession in a dramatic speech at the railroad banquet in Charleston. The Georgians, led by Bartow, gave disunion a credibility it did not otherwise have, and gave the South Carolinians what they needed most to take the step of secession: a clear sign of cooperation and southern unity from a neighboring state. Within the year Bartow was leading Georgians into the Battle of First Manassas, where he was killed, the first Confederate general to die in the Civil War.[17]

The moment surrounding Bartow's speech on November 9 was electric. The *Charleston Mercury* reported that "a wild storm seemed suddenly to sweep over the minds of men." They rushed from the railroad banquet hall to telegraph the legislature and to demand a state convention to "sever our connection with the present Government." They resolved to send advance messengers by train to Columbia, where the legislature was gathered. These emissaries sped ahead, rushing to reach the capital in less than a day. They arrived at the legislature to spread the word—that Georgians stood in support of the South Carolinians, that secession ought to go forward immediately, that delay was no longer an option. On November 10, the South Carolina legislature voted to call an election for a state constitutional convention to consider secession. The speed of secession in the Lower South, especially in South Carolina, took on a life of its own. In some forty days seven states seceded, new governments were created, and state legislatures gathered and assembled. Much of this was possible in large part because of the telegraph and railroad.[18]

Those who opposed immediate secession considered the fast pace of the Lower South part of the problem. In Missouri's state convention, delegates condemned "the impatient people" at the head of the secession movement who "are in the habit of traveling by railroad and talking by telegraph." In Missouri, Georgia, and other states, the railroad companies provided free tickets for all delegates to the secession conventions. And the secessionist delegates offered elaborate resolutions in gratitude for each railroad's "liberality" and "courtesy." The

Lower South states received free passes from the South's railroads to send commissioners to the Upper South's secession conventions, where they encouraged the formation of a Confederate States of America.[19]

In no southern state were the debates over secession more elaborate or the stakes higher than in Virginia, where the convention met in Richmond from February 13 to May 1, 1861. If Virginia seceded, the Confederate nation appeared more viable, more substantial, more coherent. The state would bring its vast and advanced railroad system into the Confederacy, as well as the credit in international banking markets that sustained its rail network and its growing factories and ironworks. The delegates, men drawn from every county in the commonwealth, viewed their roles as historic, and intended their speeches to be written down for the ages. All of them understood in similarly grand terms Virginia's position as the leader of the South. All knew that Virginia's decision would have immense consequences for the Union and for the Confederacy.

The majority of the delegates were elected as "Unionist," but their loyalty to the Union, however sentimental and nostalgic, was also entirely conditional. If the new president attempted to coerce the Lower South states back into the Union, or denied them the right of secession, these "Unionist" Virginians might leave the Union altogether, because they firmly believed that states possessed the constitutional right to secede. Although dismayed at the sudden breakup of the Union, they also saw it as justifiable and understandable. More than this, many of these men sympathized with the Lower South. They too despised the "Black Republicans," they too feared the slow erosion of slavery, they too yearned for an independent South to take its place in the world of nations.

As the convention got under way, Virginia's delegates spoke eloquently of their "civilization." They also spoke in unabashed terms about slavery and its defense. Slavery was "indissoluably [sic] interwoven with the whole framework of society," stated James P. Holcombe, who represented Albemarle, the heavily slaveholding county along the Virginia Central Railroad. The South and the North, Holcombe believed, were "two distinct and unfriendly people," and the "gulf" between these people could not be closed. Holcombe compared their separate development to the nations of Europe. Who would expect England and France to be one people, he asked rhetorically. The answer was self-evident.[20]

Like many secessionists, Holcombe believed that the South, as a separate people and nation, needed to expand, and that railroads and telegraphs had altered the geography of the world and how future wars would be fought. Borders were shrinking as the new technologies advanced, and slavery as a consequence was imperiled. For this reason alone, Holcombe argued, the South needed to secede. Every railroad company director who attended the secession convention seemed to agree—as a group they were uniformly secessionist.

An aggressive war on a large, well-developed country, such as the Confederacy, would prove impossible, some delegates thought, "unless by immense and well-disciplined armies." Railroads and telegraphs might lead these armies right to the border of the new nation, but from that point forward, Holcombe maintained, the technologies favored the Confederate nation. They would transform "defensive warfare." As soon as an army in the North began to mobilize, "the busy lightning" of the telegraph would alert the South "in an instant," from the Ohio River to the remotest frontier of Texas. At that moment, in Holcombe's imagined response, "every railroad facility would be used to concentrate an overwhelming force." The railroad journey would do more than just transport or carry the men to the battlefield; the setting of the railroad cars would inspire and stir something deeper. "Our hearts would kindle with the rapture of patriotic enthusiasm," Holcombe gushed, "when we beheld this most powerful agency of nature and art, pressed into the noble service of liberty, crowding with untiring speed by night and by day." The railroad would deliver "thousands upon thousands" and so create a "wall" of men to oppose the northern armies.[21]

Holcombe took the Virginia Central Railroad home to Albemarle in early March and was serenaded at the depot with a brass band upon his arrival. He told the gathering assembled to greet him that "nearly all the ladies & young men are in favor of secession" in Richmond. The young men and women of Virginia who so clearly favored secession were part of a larger nationalist movement across the Confederacy. These young Confederates welcomed the "rivers of blood" that might come in a fight with the North. They thought that the Federal army would "fly like scud before the Moon." As for the delegates assembled in Richmond, they were wasting hundreds of thousands of dollars dawdling in the session; worse, they were "consummate fools" and "drunkards" who could not see their way clear to secede. The young, especially those in Virginia's colleges and universities, made their national loyalties clear, voting in mock conventions to secede, hoisting Confederate and Virginia flags on the main buildings of their colleges, and hounding professors who expressed anything but vigorous secessionism. They also mobilized quickly into local militias and began drilling. The women at Hollins College formed two female drill units. The men took the railroads to Richmond, where they followed the secession convention minute by minute.[22]

Early in the Virginia convention's deliberations, a surprisingly determined movement developed out of the delegates from western Virginia to delay secession. The mountain and Ohio River border counties of Virginia had long held grievances against the eastern part of the state: they felt that they were underrepresented in the legislature, slave property was taxed too lightly, and no state-financed railroad projects were slated for their part of the state. The final charge was undeniable, and, when the convention was called, many of the western delegates had to travel north into Pennsylvania to get on the Baltimore & Ohio Railroad and thence head east to Washington, then south into Virginia. Their roundabout route to Richmond demonstrated the problem. With war on the horizon, they asked, how would Virginia propose to defend them, their families, their homes? With no railroads and no roads to link them, and with steep mountains separating them, the two halves of Virginia could not go out of the Union together, one half exposed, the other secure. Geography, not slavery, separated them, and the natural barriers had not been broken before the war. The result, western delegates proclaimed, could only be the loss and destruction of their section.[23]

Slavery was not an abstract issue in these debates. When Petersburg's Thomas Branch, one of Virginia's leading railroad directors, offered his constituents' views on secession, he began with the idea that slavery was the cornerstone of their society. He offered a resolution to the convention to affirm that *"negro slaves are property."* Somehow, these white Southerners thought, the North had lost its sense of slavery as a form of property and needed to be reminded of the bare, essential nature of the rights the South was going to defend. For his part, Branch felt compelled to state the will of his constituents: immediate secession.[24]

Finally, on Tuesday, April 16, 1861, a day after Lincoln's call for troops to suppress secession in the Lower South, William Ballard Preston, a western Virginian, a director of the Virginia and Tennessee Railroad Company and a holder of eighteen slaves, introduced the Ordinance of Secession to the Virginia convention. For weeks the floor of the convention had been a cockpit for receiving and sending up-to-the-minute information and for sparring over the right course of action. Preston had earlier opposed secession, but like many Virginians he changed his mind. Asking for "God's mercy," Preston cautioned that he was not reacting to either "the influence of circumstance or telegraphic information." Instead, his dramatic proposal came forward only after receiving a hand-delivered report from Washington, D.C., confirming Lincoln's actions. On April 17, 1861, Virginia's delegates voted 88–55 to secede from the Union.[25]

The majority of these delegates already understood themselves to be part of a southern, modern nation on equal footing with the North, as well as with Britain, France, Russia, and Italy. Indeed, a number of delegates placed the idea of the Confederacy in the context of newly forming nation-states in Europe. They saw themselves at the vanguard of modern state formation. Confident in the Confederacy's cause and in its $300 million in cotton exports, its debt-free railroads, and its diversity of small industry and wealth, Virginia delegates saw the South as "an existing nationality." One Virginia delegate asked whether any nation had ever gone to war with such a "commercial" advantage.[26]

In the "war of words" Virginia's delegates shared decisive common ground in seeing slaves as property. They did not need to discuss this at length. As a result, much of the convention centered on constitutional questions—how to secede, whether it was legal, and what the framers of the U.S. Constitution intended. But white Virginia shared a common, and increasingly important, confidence in the viability of the Confederate nation. They gladly shouldered the responsibility to hold up their modern nation-state on the world stage. "Nations act on their interests," one Virginia delegate argued, "not on their sentiments."[27]

As for the South, and indeed for Virginia, it could not act otherwise if it purported to be a nation, to be sovereign in and of itself, to be a civilization worthy of the world's respect. "It is a fact, Mr. Chairman," one delegate concluded, "that there is a separate national existence at Montgomery." The question was when, not if, Virginia would join it.[28]

In the opening days of the Civil War, after Virginia's secession, any fair calibration of the railroad's use in war making might have favored the Confederacy. The South seemed only to have to defend its borders and its limited but useful railroad network, which could be perfectly suited to shuttling troops and supplies across interior lines. Over the course of the war the railroad would do more than provide this service. Eventually, the railroads obliterated the advantage of interior lines, as the Union could use its rail network to outrun Confederate forces moving from one theater to another. At the beginning of the struggle, however, only a few commanders at the highest levels had any experience at all with railroads.[29]

The war's immediate effect was to throw southern railroad companies into a financial and operational tailspin. Destruction of railroad property escalated quickly in the opening months of the fighting and was caused as much by the Confederate as by the Union army. The corridors of movement and the geographic linkages that the railroads created became the primary pathways for the armies and for all strategic decisions. The geography of the railroads became, almost overnight, the geography of the war.[30]

Despite the losses, Confederate railroad companies immediately offered to support the war effort, charging half-rates for military and government traffic. In June 1861, after the Battle of First Manassas, which took place near the Orange & Alexandria Railroad junction, the company's president dismissed the damages to his trains and tracks. He considered the losses worthwhile in light of the cause. Without the railroad, "the state could not have been defended" at Manassas. The Confederacy could rest assured in its capabilities. He also noted that the company would "employ for another year slave labor."[31]

This was one advantage that seemed clear to southern railroad presidents—and for the most part they felt that mentioning it was unnecessary—slaves could be used to run the Confederacy's railroads, while whites could fight in the war. The companies' annual balance sheets and accounts showed just how important slave labor was becoming in the war years. The Richmond and Petersburg Railroad employed 51 slaves in 1861, 70 in 1862, 99 in 1863, and 118 in 1864. The Richmond and Danville reported 270 slaves on its lines in 1862, and 323 a year later. On the Virginia and Tennessee there were 540 enslaved and 225 white workers in 1862—a year later, 569 enslaved and 269 white. In 1863 the Virginia Central Railroad purchased thirty-five "negro men" for $83,484.60. The Mobile and Ohio bought slaves by the hundreds in the war, but slaves increasingly used the opportunity to escape.[32]

Within months of Virginia's secession in 1861, Confederates witnessed widespread destruction of their expensive and modern railroad network, a consequence of the war that few at first thought possible. In Petersburg, Virginia, a city thrust into the war when Union troops moved to capture the nearby Norfolk navy yard, railroad president William Mahone described for his stockholders the process of destruction along his line. Stunned and annoyed by the turn of events, Mahone explained that the company was carefully dismantling parts of the railroad and especially the "beautiful iron superstructure of the Blackwater bridge" in an effort to save the assets of the road and at the same time effectively deny the enemy their use. But the Confederate military intervened, took over the operation, and immediately destroyed the bridge and several miles of railroad. The self-inflicted wrecking was only the beginning, a foretaste of what would eventually come to characterize the Confederate defensive strategies. But Mahone, who would later become a general in the Confederate army, was "at a loss to understand what exigency rose up . . . for this waste of property." The enemy, Mahone argued, had made "no move in adopting the road to his purposes," yet the Confederates destroyed it anyway and "without any intimation to the officers of the company." Not one to steer clear of a controversy, Mahone considered the Confederate destruction of his railroad high-handed, foolish, and unnecessary. After all, he pointed out, the railroad's track gauge was five feet and "to be found only in the southern states." He thought Union troops, unfamiliar with the gauge, would not have been able to use the railroad anyway.[33]

Confident in the technology itself to hold up Union advances, and in the modern 5-foot gauge of the South's newest railroads, Mahone did not foresee the rapid adaptation Union forces would make even in the first year of the war. They quickly reengineered some of the South's railroads, rebuilt bridges, and brought in tailor-made locomotives to support their invasion. In the summer of 1862 the U.S. Army captured the Norfolk and Petersburg Railroad, and within weeks had changed forty-four miles of its 5-foot gauge to 4 feet 8.5 inches. Former slaves helped them, fleeing slavery at Norfolk and Alexandria and working on the railroads. Nor did Mahone appreciate the pattern of self-destruction in the Confederate army's response to the invasion. Willing to make sacrifices, he and other railroad presidents did not know how to react when their "property" was seized and destroyed.[34]

In fact, the Confederate government began to take railroad iron and machinery from some companies and give it to others in the main military transportation corridors. The Alabama and Florida was chartered in 1856 and in May 1861 had just finished its forty-five-mile route to make a connection between Pensacola and Montgomery. But a year later, in November 1862, Confederate officials removed all of its rails and transferred them to the Mobile and Great Northern Railroad.

Similarly, the Pensacola and Mobile, chartered in February 1861, laid five miles of track but the Confederate government seized its rails and machinery as well. The road, according to its annual report, was "ruined." Eventually, the Confederate government authorized the army to take railroad property whenever and wherever needed. Southern railroad presidents threatened to resign, and managers could no longer "see" their operations. So confused were the army's records that managers did not know where their cars and engines were. Coordination between the railroads and the army, uncertain in the best of circumstances, completely broke down across much of the South.[35]

From the start of the Civil War, therefore, the railroads proved both especially vital and uniquely vulnerable. Both qualities made them central to Union and Confederate strategic planning. Railroads drastically reconfigured the speed of transportation, making the distant dramatically nearer. Despite all of the growth in the railroad system in the United States during the 1850s, however, only four gateways connected the northern and southern railroad networks in 1861: one connection between North and South stood each at Alexandria, Virginia; Cincinnati, Ohio; Louisville, Kentucky; and Cairo, Illinois. All were places with large rivers not yet fully bridged. But within each of the two sections, the new railroad networks came alive, coursing with supplies, men, munitions, and artillery, all rushed to the potential points of conflict.[36]

Along the perimeter of the new Confederate nation, federal commanders tried to discern the implications of the South's communication and transportation system for the upcoming war. One Federal engineer noted in early April 1861 that the capacity of railroads in the South changed the dynamic of time, at least for the military, and changed what a "timely" response meant. "The Confederate States can assemble a large additional military force at Montgomery by railroad, and throw it down also by railroad upon Pensacola," he observed. He emphasized that "the question that next arises is not whether this great nation is able with *time* to supply ample means in soldiers and munitions for such a conflict, but whether, having expended nearly all its ready strength in reconquering the harbor fortifications and navy-yard, it could send timely and adequate re-enforcements."[37]

These commanders recognized the potential of the South to defend itself, and, as they searched for points of vulnerability, they scrambled to consult the latest maps. Often these were produced by atlas companies, newly invigorated by the explosion in railroads and railroad travel. Publishers and printers rushed into the market and tried to convey the full scope of the war—its vastness, its detail, and its geography. Often they wrote about "the seat of the war" or "the cockpit of the war," or they drew maps and symbols for others to see the larger picture.[38]

In New York the highly regarded J. T. Lloyd published his American railroad map in 1861, "showing the whole seat of the war." The map was six feet by five feet and located every depot and junction in the nation. It came with a capitalized header meant as much to entice as to warn: "This is the only map issued in

America that has been deemed contraband by the Secretary of War, and is prohibited from being sent South for their use." Lloyd claimed to have produced the most accurate survey of the whole nation's railroad system, and the implications, he thought, were disturbing and obvious. "The people of the Northern States," Lloyd noted, "can see correctly, at a glance, the preponderance of the Southern Country over the Northern and Western States, and will more fully comprehend the reason of the Southern States uniting, by glancing westward at the rich plains of Mexico."[39]

A glance at Lloyd's map would show that the Confederacy, with its massive geographical extent and its railroads pushing west, seemed to have won the race to modernize and extend its society. In the immediate aftermath of Fort Sumter and the secession of the Upper South states, however, the race became oriented toward strategic and military supremacy. At Fort Pickens, for example, which was off the coast of Pensacola, Florida, Federal commanders gathered as much intelligence as they could about the status of the Alabama and Florida Railroad (Montgomery and Pensacola Railroad). From their position in the fort across the bay they could see that the Confederates were hastily working to complete the railroad. They recognized that the finished railroad would materially affect their ability to hold and possess the Federal fort. They could not know, of course, that the Confederates would tear it up nine months later. Instead, they thought that soon the Confederates would be able to bring up on the railroad as many large guns as they needed and could deliver them right to the coast. They could also assemble a large force from the interior quickly, and begin a bombardment and an assault on Fort Pickens. Indeed, the Montgomery newspapers hailed the completion of the railroad because "a number of large mortars and nineteen Columbiads (some of the latter weighing 9,000 pounds) now lying in the depot here, will be sent to Gen. Bragg to assist in battering down Fort Pickens."[40]

Simon Cameron, the Union secretary of war, was so alarmed at the potential loss of Fort Pickens that he requested naval guns and equipment to be transferred to the Gulf to restore "the equilibrium lost since the late completion of the Montgomery and Pensacola Railroad, which has enabled the rebels to multiply their batteries and arm them with large guns and mortars." The railroad, only finished on May 16, 1861, presented an immediate reconfiguration of the offensive capabilities of the Confederacy and, consequently, immediate recalibration of the Federal defenses. In the case of Fort Pickens, the dynamic situation was critical. The loss of the fort so soon after the surrender of Fort Sumter would damage the Lincoln administration's call for troops and possibly even lead Northerners to reconsider letting the Confederacy secede. Cameron stated that Pickens's "military and political importance just now cannot be exaggerated." Union commanders abandoned the nearby forts around Pickens and consolidated their forces there, and they managed to hold Fort Pickens throughout the war despite repeated attempts of the Confederates to take it.[41]

Neu-York Tribune.

VOL. XXII.....N°. 6,579.   NEW-YORK, TUESDAY, MAY 6, 1862.   PRICE TWO CENTS.

THE SEAT OF WAR IN EASTERN VIRGINIA.

"The Seat of War in Eastern Virginia," *New York Daily Tribune*, May 6, 1862.

Railroad atlas and newspaper publishers in New York and Philadelphia possessed vital information on the South's network of junctions, towns, depots, and rails. Newspapers began printing front-page maps for the first time in the war to help readers understand the complex geography of the Confederacy. (From the collection of James A. Rawley)

As the Confederacy hastened to arm and equip volunteers in the first months of the war, it relied heavily and enthusiastically on its railroads. "Arms at Fayetteville off the railroad!" a local commander wired Confederate Secretary of War L. P. Walker on April 25, 1861. Supplies, percussion caps, rifles, troops—all made their way across the South on the railroads, heading toward South Carolina and converging on Federal installations at Harper's Ferry, Virginia; Charleston, South Carolina; Saint Louis, Missouri; New Orleans, Louisiana; and Fort Pickens in Pensacola. Confederate mobilization was ebullient, filled with joyous hurrahs and with a confidence in their capacity to use the railroads and all manner of other technologies to respond to the war. The Confederacy's rail network seemed to come "alive with troops."[42]

Thomas J. Jackson, a professor at the Virginia Military Institute and soon to be known as "Stonewall," led the Institute's Corps of Cadets to the Virginia Central Railroad on April 21. Enthusiastic and disciplined, the cadets were headed to Richmond to support their new national government however they could. Although their train got stuck in the Blue Ridge Tunnel for a few hours, Jackson was pleased to see that, all along the railroad journey to Richmond, "the War spirit is intense." Confederates understood, however imperfectly, that the modern war they were going to fight demanded these technologies, and in the early days of the conflict Confederates gushed with confidence in the South's railroads, its few but now necessary factories, and its yet untested organizational genius.[43]

All along the borderlands between North and South, citizens and commanders made calculations of time, distance, and reach, assessing the strategic significance of the railroads for the war. In early May 1861, leading railroad promoter, organizing founder of the New York Central Railroad, and New York congressman Erastus Corning wrote Secretary of War Cameron to explain the necessity of holding the Missouri railroads in the Union. Corning pinpointed the secessionist movement in Missouri as "along the line of the Hannibal and St. Joseph Railroad" and considered it "scarcely stronger in any Southern State." He also considered it likely that the first act of secession in Missouri would be the seizure of the railroad. Corning pointed out that the railroad "furnishes the only accessible and speedy route by which the Government can communicate with Kansas, Nebraska, and Utah, or with its military posts along the Western and Northwestern frontier to the foot of the Rocky Mountains." Confederate local commanders also saw the region in exactly these terms: as "the principal battle-ground between the North and the South." As one Confederate officer explained, "St. Joseph with its railroad connections, is the key to Kansas, New Mexico . . . , and Utah."[44]

Corning appealed to the drastic changes in geography suddenly thrust upon Americans by the war. Railroads, cities, and rivers took on different strategic meanings in wartime. The geography of war demanded a fresh assessment of what places and connections mattered. "St. Louis in itself commands nothing—is in reality a key to nothing," Corning concluded. "Speed and easiness of communication" were now the essential qualities for consideration. A city's history, its population, even its armories were less significant than its place on a changing network of terrain, road, and rail. Anything that could be moved would be. Railroads had been built for commercial purposes and their junctions selected through a complex negotiation among competing forces—boosters, politicians, engineers, and financiers. Nature dictated some of the decisions and compromises too, as rivers, mountains, and valleys shaped the networks of rail. If some places of wealth and importance like Saint Louis meant "nothing," others just as suddenly meant everything. Places such as Grafton, Virginia, on the critical Baltimore & Ohio Railroad; Manassas Junction, Virginia, just outside Washington, D.C.; and Corinth, Mississippi, a crossroads for the Lower South, suddenly gained significance and meaning out of all proportion to their size, history, or population.

If the perimeters and the railroads intersecting them became vital places, commanders and officials needed to "see" them either through a map or through the descriptions of geography from lower-level commanders. In both railroad building and war making, lower level officials drafted detailed reports for higher

Columbiad guns of the Confederate water battery at Warrington, Fla.,
near Pensacola, February 1861.

With the railroad to Pensacola under construction and finally completed in May,
the Confederates could move large guns and troops more quickly to the coast.

(National Archives and Records Administration)

officials to make out the landscape. Commanders had to see the interior South to
understand it, and they had to master the railroad network to conquer the region.
To accomplish this required maps, reconnaissance, and detailed information, but
not all commanders were able to translate either the scale of their armies or their
strategy into a form of geographic control and supremacy that would be required
to win the war.[45]

Early in the war Union general William Tecumseh Sherman recognized that
controlling and extending the railroads would be crucial to Union victory in the
South but would require unusual, and sometimes drastic, measures. To those who
served in Sherman's army, his angular countenance, his alert gaze, and his lanky
frame betrayed a restless energy. But the warfare he eventually practiced derived
its authority not so much from his personality as from his keen observations and
his geographic acumen. More than most commanders, he sized the South up. He

learned to be a student of the landscape in the war, to study the available maps, and to reflect on his geographic surroundings.[46]

Sherman's trips into the West to survey the Pacific Railroad lines in the 1850s taught him that these technologies, once planned and extended into the land, could have far-reaching political and military effects. "I look upon the Mississippi [River] as America," Sherman explained to Senator Edward Bates in May 1862. The river "controlled" the United States, and it was vital. Railroads, Sherman concluded, "though very easily obstructed and destroyed, are next to Rivers, the best military Channels and should be extended as far as possible." Sherman emphasized that building a railroad would not ensure its operation. These were fragile technologies, dependent on the surrounding circumstances. As for extending the Pacific Railroad through Missouri, which was Corning's concern as well, Sherman recommended that "every hostile inhabitant within twenty-five miles should be removed and the whole line colonized by men of known loyalty." The railroad, although "valuable" in war, was also a potential weakness "because of its easy destruction."[47]

The war prompted such severe thinking. Railroad corridors could be depopulated perhaps as easily as they were filled up with land seekers in the years before the war. The trains could carry away citizens quickly and efficiently. Commanders started to draw zones and perimeters around the railroads, sometimes five, sometimes fifteen, sometimes twenty-five miles in diameter. Civilians within these arbitrary but sharply defined lines found themselves subject to hard scrutiny; their proximity to the railroad exposed them to the unanticipated violence and destruction in the war zones.

By October 1862 Sherman contemplated a war of destruction that would require the killing of several hundred thousand Confederates. In a letter to his commander, General Ulysses S. Grant, Sherman sketched a broad strategy for the war in the West centered around controlling the Mississippi River and around decisive movements to "break the railroad." Again and again, Sherman would come back to the concept of breaking the railroads. And by 1864 breaking them stood at the center of his operations.[48]

Confederates too tried to assess the value of their railroads but for defensive warfare. In the first few months of the war the Confederate losses in western Virginia prompted concerned reaction in Richmond over whether to build a new railroad across the mountains to defend the region. Confederate general Robert E. Lee failed in the summer and fall of 1861 to prevent the loss of the mountain valleys to Union general George B. McClellan's Ohioans, but Lee recognized and protected the strategic importance of the railroad choke points at Covington and Newbern, the little towns that linked into the Virginia Central Railroad and the Southwestern Railroad. Summing up the defeats in western Virginia and assessing the prospects for recovering the region, the *Richmond Daily Dispatch* concluded: "Where our forces in the field have been sustained by lines of railway reaching to them, they have over-matched the enemy; and where they have had to rely for their transportation on dirt roads, they have been driven back by the well-prepared and outnumbering force of their adversaries."[49]

One of the Union commanders most experienced with railroads, in fact, was George B. McClellan, who had served as vice president and chief engineer of the Illinois Central, and as president of the Mobile and Ohio. Upon his appointment to command the Army of the Potomac in August 1861 after his victories in western Virginia, McClellan wrote Lincoln a long, detailed assessment of his strategy for the war. Railroads, McClellan pointed out, "introduced a new and very important element into war, by the great facilities thus given for concentrating at particular positions large masses of troops from remote locations, and by creating new strategic points and lines of operations." McClellan sketched a comprehensive plan to defeat the Confederacy: "We must seize places on the railways in the rear of the enemy's points of concentration," he argued. Savannah, Charleston, Mobile, Pensacola, Montgomery, New Orleans, and even Tampico, Mexico, constituted the targets he selected, and he hoped their capture, along with that of Richmond, would "crush the rebellion at one blow." McClellan was one of the first Union commanders to recognize the importance of simultaneous attacks on the Confederate railroad junctions.[50]

But McClellan's strategic thinking, however comprehensive and well-informed, would become muddled on the battlefield. Young in the position of major-general, he proved indecisive and uncertain in the face of difficult decisions. And he retreated from the idea that the war would require massive destruction, violence, and loss of life. As vice president of the Illinois Central Railroad during the banking panic of 1857, McClellan recoiled from the idea of firing a single man. "I cannot work in the dark," he cried in frustration as share prices tumbled on Wall Street and traffic fluctuated wildly. Later, in 1862, devising a plan for Richmond that required over 100,000 soldiers, he seemed genuinely troubled by the loss of a single one. In his short but stellar career before the Civil War, McClellan had been everywhere—Mexico City, Sevastopol, Chicago, and London—and yet for all of his precocious genius he could hardly understand the nature of the war he would be asked to prosecute. Mildly offended by slavery on close inspection in Virginia, McClellan resisted any war aimed at liberating slaves and he offered only the condescending promise to "throw my sword into the scale to force an improvement in the condition of those poor blacks" after the war.[51]

But a war on railroads in the South, no matter how much McClellan might wish to limit it, would have to confront slavery, so tied together were they in the Confederacy's history, operations, and national aspirations. Commanders such as Sherman and McClellan, but also Lee and Jackson, had always used geography as a necessary component to devising their strategies, but now railroads figured prominently in their plans too. The railroad created a new geography for war, and each would have to contend with this "second nature." The technology was so new in the 1850s that the generation of West Point graduates before that decade had absolutely no training in the strategic uses of railroads in war making. The decade of the 1850s witnessed such rapid rail development in both the North and South that Americans found themselves negotiating new borders, territories, and boundaries all around them. The leadership of the Civil War on both sides knew that railroads would transform warfare, but they did not know exactly how. They had to learn first where all these rails and junctions were and then develop a very new "railroad generalship" for the war itself, but they were unsure how the technology would affect their operations.[52]

Chapter 4

Fighting the Confederate Landscapes

WRITING from the 53rd Ohio Infantry's regimental training camp in October 1861, Ephraim C. Dawes asked his college friend William Stephenson to take the next train, visit his camp, and bring him all the newspapers he could buy. "We are fixed up so we can accommodate you first rate," Dawes encouraged Stephenson. Dawes greeted the war with great enthusiasm, as if it were an invigorating adventure, an opportunity to put his Republican and his Union convictions to the test. When a new captain came into the regiment, Dawes was the man to give him a tour of the outfit, to introduce him to his fellow officers, and to explain the Christian spirituality of the men in the ranks. Dawes proudly pointed out that among the soldiers in the 53rd there was no card playing, no gambling, and no drinking, and the men had elected Methodist ministers for officers.[1]

Thousands of young northern men like Dawes poured into the railroad stations to volunteer for service and take the trip to their assigned camps. In April 1861 the Central Railroad in New Jersey transported southward 16,119 men from New York, the Camden and Amboy took 10,722, and the New Jersey Railroad hauled 8,849. The movement of men on the northern railroads reached its peak that month, as tens of thousands of soldiers pressed into long cars and hundreds of railroad companies strained to carry the unprecedented load. Nearly all northern soldiers traveled by rail at some point on their journey to reach their outfit. Even when they arrived at the edges of the Confederacy, steam and rail often carried them much of the way forward.[2]

Dawes's unit was typical. On September 17, 1861, the first recruits arrived at Camp Jackson in Ohio, and throughout the fall more and more came into camp. On February 18, 1862, the regiment had orders to move out, and a tearful but patriotic departure from family and friends at the railroad depot followed. The troops rode the trains to Portsmouth, Ohio, then took a steamboat south to Paducah, Kentucky. There, on February 23, they were issued Austrian-made rifles, drilled in their use, and outfitted for battle. A few days later they were loaded back on the steamboats and went down the Tennessee River for twelve days until they reached Fort Henry. After another brief respite and another steamboat journey, on March 19, 1862, they disembarked at a place called Pittsburgh Landing. They had traveled over 500 miles, but between leaving their home base in Ohio and fighting the Confederates on April 6, 1862, in the Battle of Shiloh, Ephraim C. Dawes and the 53rd Ohio had not marched more than a few miles.[3]

Ironically, this would change. Carried into the South by steam and rail at the beginning of the war, several years later Dawes and other soldiers in the western armies would do some of the hardest marching of the war. Dawes never recovered from a bitter cold march through the northern Alabama mountains in December 1863. Later, Dawes recalled the "march to the relief of Knoxville" by the 15th Army Corps as "the severest of the war"—without wagons, blankets, tents, or rations, the ground covered in ice and snow, and the men without shoes, their feet bleeding, cracked, and broken down. Dawes's friend William Stephenson caught such a debilitating cold that his friends forced him to resign. Dawes contracted severe rheumatism from the freezing march and suffered from the condition for the rest of his life. Once on the field of battle, and often on marches from theater to theater, the men in both armies walked as thousands of horses and oxen pulled their long wagon trains. Marching over twenty miles a day, Dawes's 53rd Ohio finally ended up in Chattanooga, "at last in a semi civilized state, i.e. on a R. R. [railroad] one end of which rests in the United States."[4]

Throughout the war, soldiers measured their proximity to the railroad as a benchmark for their contact with what they called "the outside world" or "civilization." Mail, news, food, supplies, and fellow soldiers came down the rail lines. To move away from these corridors was to be out of touch with home and with the army itself, and therefore in a different zone of the war.[5]

Charles Kruse, a young Democratic volunteer from Ohio, had a similar send-off, and like Dawes his trip into the South was marked initially not by violence but by long-distance movements across the landscape. "The depot was crowded with spectators," Kruse wrote to his parents as the 50th Ohio left. Women waved handkerchiefs, fife and drums played, and the crowds offered loud cheers for the soldiers as the trains pulled out of the Little Miami railroad station.[6]

Kruse's regiment went by train from Ohio into Kentucky, where he was amazed at the beauty of the landscape and the lush productivity of the farms. The scenery enchanted him, even as his unit grew increasingly apprehensive about the battles that inevitably would come. As the 50th Ohio plunged deeper into the South, Kruse could not keep his bearings, and he felt he was lost, so he wrote home to request a small map of Kentucky. "We are moving about so much that I hardley know whare I am," he explained. As requested, his parents forwarded him a Kentucky map that had been cut out from an atlas, and Kruse was thoroughly relieved. "I can tell right where we are," he assured his parents.[7]

Many northern soldiers like Dawes and Kruse came into the South along the railroads in the first months of the war, and they participated initially in a form

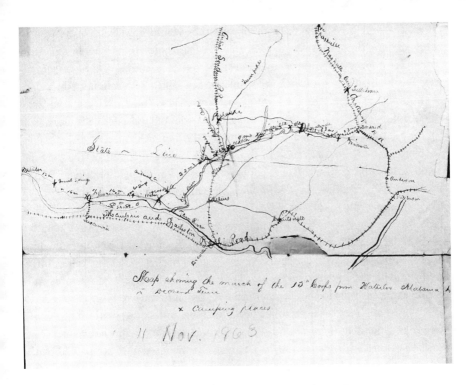

"Ephraim C. Dawes' Sketch Map of His March," November 10, 1863.

An officer in the 53rd Ohio Infantry, Dawes sent this map to his sister after his unit marched twenty-three miles one day and thirteen miles another. Working their way along the railroads in southern Tennessee, the 53rd Ohio had little access to mail and received only "the mildest rumors thro the country." Dawes's map, like countless others, was an artifact of his personal experience, showing the compressed geography of his war and his events.

(Courtesy of The Newberry Library)

of travel and travel writing as they described in letters home the southern landscape and people. Many, like Kruse, wanted maps to track their location and follow along where their units were going, because it was otherwise almost impossible for them to know where they were. The railroad, the landscape, the speed of movement in the war were all disorienting. The South's diverse landscapes were difficult to comprehend. War was not travel, yet the soldiers, and the generals, were sojourning in what amounted to a foreign country.

Confederates also experienced similar movements and dislocations, but their journeys served to inspire their new nation at the start of the war. Some men traveled great distances from one corner of the Confederacy to another. General John Bell Hood's brigade moved from Texas to Richmond, Virginia, in the first month of the war, covering over 1,500 miles on the railroads to get to the Confederate capital. Crossing bridge after bridge and winding their way through tunnel after tunnel, Confederate soldiers saw the nation they would soon defend. As women gathered along these routes at depots, they too participated in the creation of the nation. Ten thousand or more citizens turned out in Richmond to hear Confederate president Jefferson Davis greet the Texans, and one Virginian considered it "an imposing scene." The arrival of so many troops so quickly at the railroad depots, followed by flag ceremonies and the speeches of Confederate leaders, provided a rehearsal for the Confederacy's national loyalties.[8]

Thousands of soldiers took to the railroads, and thousands of civilians migrated across the country. Both Confederate and Union soldiers observed the landscape they encountered and looked for signs of familiarity. Landscape has always played a role in the way soldiers and their families back home have understood the war they were fighting, and the Civil War was no exception. Could a nation as large, modern, and complex as the Confederacy be conquered? Hundreds of miles of railroad crisscrossed the South's border states, as well as interlaced the Atlantic and interior South. With great confidence Confederates were already using the rails to shuttle men and weapons across what military strategists called "interior lines." Throughout much of the Confederate nation, moreover, huge rivers, flooded swamps, and steep mountains created complex natural barriers. All of these features would have to be either negotiated or controlled by the Union army to force the Confederate nation to submit.[9]

The system of rails, depots, and junctions in the South formed a significant part of the landscape of the Civil War, a "second nature." And the natural systems of watershed, elevation, forest, and swamp formed another. The intersection and combination of these first- and second-nature landscapes became especially difficult for nineteenth-century Americans to disentangle.

As Union commanders and soldiers went into the South, they carried preconceived understandings about the best ways to defeat the Confederacy and even about whether the South possessed the landscape of a truly independent nation. Their encounters with the landscape and the people of the Confederacy—both the second nature of rail and infrastructure and the natural systems of river, swamp, and mountain—proved decisively important. Their experience eventually revealed just how vital the railroads were to the Confederate nation and its self-understanding.[10]

The southern places that northern soldiers encountered were recognizably American and modern, but distinct. Many soldiers were sure that the landscape explained the region and its peoples, so they tried to read the buildings, the towns, and the villages for evidence about the society they were fighting. Northern soldiers came into the South as travelers, often gaining their first glimpse of its civilization from the vantage point of a railroad car or a steamship.[11]

Thousands of soldiers from the Midwest came through Kentucky in the first year of the war. Despite hundreds of miles of railroad, Kentucky possessed one of the least developed rail networks among the southern states. Like Louisiana, Florida, Texas, and Arkansas, over 60 percent of its population lived beyond the fifteen-mile zone of the all-important railroad depots. The deep isolation of its population and the beauty of its rugged landscapes produced mixed responses from northern soldiers. With tens of thousands of soldiers marching through Kentucky, the countryside suffered from the foraging parties, stealing, and general destruction of the massive Union armies. George F. Cram, a private in the 105th Illinois, could not believe how much his regiment consumed on the march through Kentucky in the fall of 1862. "You have no idea how much we eat up here," he wrote his mother.[12]

Frankfort, Kentucky, was Cram's first glimpse of the South, and he thought the place "shabby," its state buildings "gone to rack and ruin." The town was on the Lexington & Frankfort Railroad, one of the oldest railroads in the United States. But Cram was unimpressed. The whole state of Kentucky was a "scene of desolation, nearly half the houses unoccupied, large and beautiful orchards, entirely stripped of fruit (scarcely an apple can be bought here at all), corn fields have been ravaged by the hordes of soldiers that have passed through."[13]

As the 105th Illinois moved with General William Rosecrans south through Kentucky to Bowling Green on the Louisville & Nashville Railroad, the pace of the march picked up and many men began falling by the wayside. Cram took account of the country through which he passed: "We marched for miles over high mountains, great huge rocks jutting out over our heads and in some spots trees were growing out as it were from the rocks on the side of the hills." He could barely describe the landscape. When Cram came to Scottsville, Kentucky, a place dozens of miles from the nearest railroad and near the border with Tennessee, he was struck by its isolation. He tried to account for the differences he saw with the North. He looked at the courthouse in the town and considered it so small and insignificant that it looked "very much like a water tank on one of our Northern railroads." The language Southerners spoke was, to his ears, a strange dialect, standard English mixed with black tones and words to make a creole style that he found both amusing and revealingly uncivilized. "Could you be suddenly transported from Wheaton to Scottsville," he explained, "it would be like an electric shock so vast is the difference."[14]

To further document the differences, Cram naturally turned to physical appearance and to the idea that the white Southerners were, in effect, a different race of people. The men were "slim, small and of a pale, sickly color," with long black hair. The women had "an ignorant careless expression." They sit around, he observed, and they loaf, hands in their pockets, "mouths wide open." The people were almost uniformly "secesh" (secessionist), Cram observed, and "beat all for ignorance." Seeing few schools or libraries, Cram concluded that "there is no enterprise nor ambition whatever here." And judging from the landscape, he could not see how such a benighted people could fight or sustain a modern war.[15]

Electioneering in Mississippi: "Rough Riding Down South," *Harper's New Monthly*, June 1862.

Even in the second year of the Civil War, Harper's middle-class magazine was producing travel essays on the South for its northern readers, in this case depicting a trip through the region in the early 1850s. Despite the South's growth in that decade, the piece featured no railroads, instead preferring to depict a rural, backward, isolated, and unkempt region.

Soldiers tried to observe and document what they encountered in the South—an exotic land and an "other" people. Their disdain for both multiplied quickly. Unlike Kentucky, Tennessee possessed nearly 1,200 miles of railroad, and almost 60 percent of its population lived in the zones near railroads. With a more developed rail system than Kentucky by any standard, Tennessee in the first year or two of the war occupied the main western theater of the conflict. Ephraim C. Dawes, who enthusiastically cheered the election of Lincoln in 1860 and enlisted in the 53rd Ohio Infantry in September 1861, compared every place in his march through Tennessee with his home in Marietta, Ohio, but no town could measure up.[16]

After the Battle of Shiloh, Dawes marched with his division into Tennessee in the summer of 1862 under William T. Sherman's command. In June his unit headed to the Memphis & Charleston Railroad to "destroy the road." But the retreating Confederates had already done most of the damage. As he marched deeper into the state, Dawes thought the region a "splendid country" but was shocked to see "all the inhabitants dress in butternut colored clothes and the women chew tobacco, smoke pipes and nip their teeth with snuff."[17]

Soldiers particularly observed the women of the South as alien, but they also drew conclusions about the Confederacy from their encounters with slavery and the enslaved. George Cram saw slaves in Kentucky and thought they "looked well and seem happy." In La Grange, Tennessee, along the Memphis & Charleston Railroad in 1862, Dawes seemed to have found the prototypical South: "Splendid plantations almost illimitable fields of corn and cotton and niggers innumerable," he wrote. It was the most "aristocratic" place he had ever seen: "Ladies very good looking and excessively secesh. Young men all gone to war. Old men all wealthy planters of the Fine old English Gentlemen style. very fat and very lazy." At every town Dawes gave detailed descriptions of the landscape and its people as if he were verifying what he had read in Frederick Law Olmsted's accounts of the South. Olmsted published *A Journey in the Seaboard Slave States: With Remarks*

Hanover Junction, 1863.

Northern soldiers left for the war from railroad stations such as this. Stations also became places to gather for news and information. President Abraham Lincoln passed through Hanover Junction in November 1863 on his way to Gettysburg for the opening of the national cemetery. Crowds gathered to meet the president. (Library of Congress)

Ephraim C. Dawes, 1863.

Dawes fought in the Battle of Shiloh, then protected the railroads in Tennessee with the 53rd Ohio. He was promoted to major of the regiment on January 26, 1863.

(Courtesy of the Ohio State Historical Society)

on Their Economy in 1856, a travel narrative of his railroad trip through Virginia, North Carolina, and South Carolina filled with observations on the South's landscape and people. Like many young Republicans, Dawes read and admired Olmsted's travel narratives.[18]

Dawes's explanations of the South were full of stereotypes, especially about African Americans. "All the niggers in the country would follow us if we would let them," he explained to his sister Kate back in Ohio. "It is kind of hard to turn them off but we cant do anything else with them. Most of the officers supply themselves with servants. . . . A contraband who is tending horse for our Col . . . is a fair specimen of the field hands here. He is stupid as a mule. can hardly talk and implicitly believes everything you tell him. He is I suppose 14 years old. Olmstead's works are true to the life in every respect as regards southern society so far as my experience goes."[19]

Later Dawes colorfully recounted a mission to locate timber for rebuilding railroad bridges. His regiment marched twenty miles with 200 former slaves, led by a "sturdy Ethiopian" guide who used the opportunity to lead the Union soldiers back to his home neighborhood so he could visit friends and secure his belongings. Dawes considered the outing a ridiculous farce with "no other result than escorting a couple of hundred darkies thro the city." Like many Midwestern soldiers, Dawes used these stories to tell his family a lighthearted tale about the South, slavery, race, and the landscapes he encountered. He could not yet see how the former slaves—"contrabands," as they were called—would factor into the army's operations. Nor could he shake off his travelogue-like writing and its references to Olmsted. Other soldiers made similar comments.[20]

When Dawes arrived in La Fayette, Tennessee, he found a "no. 1" railroad station house and was impressed that "the citizens would not allow the depot to be burned" by the retreating Confederate army. But the destruction was everywhere, and increasingly apparent, and the little depot spared in La Fayette was the exception rather than the rule. By August 1862 Dawes, along with the rest of Sherman's army, was occupying Memphis.[21]

The Union army was foraging, confiscating food, and employing black labor wherever necessary. Dawes was amazed at the changes he saw all around him, especially the destruction of the landscape in the wake of Sherman's army. He tried to explain this effect to his sister: "You don't know what war is. You can't appreciate it. Wait till an army overruns the country. Till *all* the male population are in arms till your fences are all burned orchards and barns and chicken roosts robbed, Houses entered and valuables stolen—gardens wantonly destroyed and all manner of excesses committed—not so much by the army as by loose craracters [*sic*] taking advantage of the unsettled condition of affairs."[22]

The war was becoming harder on the civilians and the boundaries between fighting, confiscating, and marauding correspondingly less clear. The full effects of an army in the landscape were not lost on Dawes. He could see that even his unit, with its tight discipline, its evangelical officers, its high morals, and its good men, constituted a veritable machine eating out the land. At Holly Springs, Mississippi, Dawes's regiment "destroyed two big fields of wheat and full 30 acres of green corn besides stealing all the new potatoes in the country and killing all chickens and hogs we could find."[23]

In Virginia between late 1861 and the summer of 1862, a similar sequence of events took place, as tens of thousands of soldiers took railroads into the great Union army encampments outside Washington, D.C., and then found themselves pulled into a massive and destructive conflict. As a newly enlisted volunteer, Bob Taggart discovered, like Ephraim Dawes, Charles Kruse, and George Cram, that his fellow soldiers had few reservations about scouring the local farms for food and anything else easily moved and valuable. They targeted "houses deserted by supposed secessionists" and, Taggart reported, took "many valuable and useful books and articles of furniture." But the officers put a halt to the stealing, at least temporarily, and Taggart was pleased. "It is a real shame," he noted, "the way our soldiers destroy private property whenever they can get a chance. If they happen to come across a deserted dwelling, in which according to rumor a secessionist once lived, there is not a single article left undestroyed or unabused, and sometimes the property of good union men is destroyed." Taggart worried about this obvious lack of discipline and order.[24]

Both armies created vast wastelands of stripped landscapes in the very first year of the fighting. Fences were ripped apart for firewood, trees chopped down for abattoir defenses, and roads reduced to muddy crevasses. In the summer of 1862 the war in the West covered a vast terrain, as the Union army followed the railroads from Corinth, Mississippi, into Tennessee. In the East operations covered hundreds of square miles along Virginia's border. Soldiers came into the war as railroad travelers, noting the wild features of the South's landscapes, reading the region's town layouts and structures for clues to the kind of war they might be fighting. The landscape, by their reading, became part of the war, the first marker of a civilization and, as a result, a legitimate military target or objective.

Perhaps for some soldiers the first casualty of the war was the landscape itself: torn, cleared, and left stripped behind their big armies. Their observations about the Confederate landscape and its people came simultaneously with their witnessing its destruction. Northern soldiers came to understand that to prevail in the war they would need to conquer the diverse landscapes of the South, not just observe their features. It took a series of large-scale confrontations for both the Confederate and the Union armies to begin to look beyond the standard markers of civilization in the landscape and to see the central importance of the South's second nature systems of rail, bridge, depot, and junction, and to understand the role of emancipation and black labor in this enterprise.

In the East, the largest military operation in North American history was getting under way in the spring and early summer of 1862, as Union general George B. McClellan assembled the Army of the Potomac for a massive invasion of Virginia. Despite the density of railroad development in Virginia, especially around Richmond, and despite the Union army's growing strategic experience in the West with rebuilding and controlling long railroad corridors in Tennessee, McClellan's plans for conquering the Confederacy focused squarely on its capital—Richmond. Five major railroads came into Richmond; the city was the Confederacy's biggest node on its rail network.

But there were stark differences between the cleared, settled, and open landscapes of northern Virginia and the heavily forested, remote, and closed landscapes across much of Mississippi, Alabama, Georgia, and parts of Tennessee. And the tidewater rivers of Virginia presented yet another strategic environment altogether. The armies were simultaneously altering the landscape, and there were few reliable maps for commanders to go by. McClellan looked at the wide, open fields of Manassas and thought that the area favored the Confederates—"the roads diverging in every direction, & a strong line of defense" made an attack there especially difficult, he explained to Lincoln. The stripped area around the old battlefield at Manassas was "the most desolate & forbidding spot I ever be-

Cumberland Landing, Federal Encampment on the Pamunkey River, Va., May 1862.

Union soldiers came into the South by steamer and train in the first year of the war. They closely observed the landscape, assessing and comparing it to their northern communities.

(Library of Congress)

held," he wrote his wife, Mary Ellen. So, McClellan planned to circumvent the barren plains and wide rivers of northern Virginia and land his army south of Richmond on the rich peninsula near Yorktown. This dramatic movement would gain "immense results," he thought.[25]

With his extensive background in railroad organization and the military, George B. McClellan became an obvious choice to lead the North's premier army in its most critical theater. McClellan had extensive experience with railroads before the war broke out, first as a surveyor for the Northern Pacific route, then as chief of engineering for the Illinois Central, and in 1860 as president of the Mississippi & Ohio Railroad. In this regard he stood nearly alone among all military officers in the Civil War as the most experienced railroad man to have graduated from West Point and serve in the U.S. Army. Although McClellan had resigned his commission in the 1850s to pursue his career in the new railroad industry, he was quickly called back into service in the secession crisis. In the first year of fighting, McClellan's campaigns in western Virginia secured the line of the crucial Baltimore & Ohio Railroad, and cleared western Virginia of Confederate forces.[26]

Railroads, McClellan recognized, were vital to his strategy of bringing the South to its senses. In his letter to Lincoln outlining the strategic plan for the Peninsular Campaign, McClellan first and foremost thought that coordination of Union forces was necessary to establish control over the South's vital railroads. McClellan explained, "My wish was to gain possession of the Eastern Tennessee Railroads as a preliminary movement—then to follow it up immediately by an attack on Nashville & Richmond as nearly at the same time as possible." After cutting the Upper South from the Lower South, McClellan's plan urged that Union forces be used to "occupy all the avenues of communication" and to "force the slaves to labor for our subsistence instead of that of the rebels." By taking these steps, McClellan reasoned, the threat of "foreign interference" in the war could be put to rest, and the South, he thought, would realize the futility of secession.[27]

The plan was bold and sweeping. His initial orders for General Ambrose Burnside in January 1862 directed Burnside to move from the North Carolina coast inland toward Goldsboro and Raleigh, where there were critical railroad junctions. "The temper of the people, the rebel force at hand, & c, will go far towards determining the question as to how far west the railroad can be safely occupied and held," he cautioned. If Burnside thought he could get to Raleigh, then McClellan ordered him to completely destroy "the main north & south line of Railroad passing through Goldsboro." Render it "impossible for the rebels to use," he emphasized. Furthermore, McClellan hoped for the total destruction of the Wilmington and Weldon Railroad. In February McClellan ordered General Benjamin Butler in Louisiana to "gain possession of all the rolling stock you can, on the different railways."[28]

But at every turn McClellan suggested that his commanders use restraint. He cautioned Burnside against "moving so far into the interior as upon Raleigh." And he imposed limits on what the army should say about these maneuvers and how they might be characterized. "In no case would I go beyond a moderate joint proclamation," he advised, "which should say as little as possible about politics or the negro." McClellan aimed to disable and "isolate" the Confederacy by securing its communication network, but he had no plans to convert the Confederate railroads into avenues of deeper Union invasion or liberation.[29]

Lincoln had other ideas, even early in the war. For his part the president began to outline a strategy aimed specifically at using the Confederacy's railroads for deeper invasion. He preferred that McClellan attack directly south into Virginia and to control both the Orange and Alexandria Railroad and the Richmond, Fredericksburg, & Potomac Railroad (R. F. & P.). He wanted McClellan to use these lines as pincers to press the Confederate army into a vise—in effect to squeeze the Confederacy and shorten the distances to Richmond. Even after McClellan landed the Army of the Potomac on the York River, Lincoln urged him to move his forces on the R. F. & P. to cut off Richmond. At the very least, Lincoln wanted to secure the railroad corridors so as to close the Confederate army's operational territory.[30]

Lincoln's prior experience with railroads may have shaped his views. In Illinois Lincoln the lawyer represented the Illinois Central and other railroads throughout the state. Although he tried cases for and against the railroads, Lincoln went out of his way to solicit the railroad companies and defend them in the big cases. And he routinely pointed out that "locomotion" and "steam power" were transforming the economy and society of the United States. He was, and still is, the only U.S. president to have held a patent—for a device to improve navigation by elevating steamboats over shoals. Few politicians were as prepared as Lincoln to see the advantages railroads presented.[31]

Lincoln's strategy was far from complete, but he was beginning to focus on a central premise: that the Confederacy inhered in no fixed geographic place, and that instead it was sustained through its key institutions and networks. Eventually, Lincoln considered Lee's Army of Northern Virginia to be the most important Confederate institution to destroy. But both Lincoln and McClellan were groping to understand and to articulate the strategic importance of the railroad network in the Confederacy.[32]

Lincoln and McClellan clashed, however, over how to conduct the war and whether military operations should be aimed at bringing the South back into the Union or conquering the Confederate nation. Despite raising the largest army in American history, devising a perceptive and imaginative grand strategy for it, equipping it for massive warfare, and moving it down the Potomac River and up the York River toward Richmond, McClellan placed frustrating limits on the uses of these forces. He was especially proud of his "bloodless victory" at Yorktown and of the positive response to it in Congress. Positioned with his army in front of Richmond, McClellan intended to use the advanced technologies of the day—railroad, telegraph, steamship, and large guns—to convince the enemy that his army was too much for them and that the best course of action would be to stop the secession movement. He was bringing up by railroad the largest number of artillery pieces and shells ever assembled.[33]

But for all of his technical virtuosity, McClellan was unable to grasp just how radically the railroads reconfigured what was strategically vital in the war and how these places might be captured. Nor was he able to understand the depth of Confederate national commitment. McClellan's plan was to cut off the Confederacy's head—in Virginia, in Richmond—from the rest of the South and to undermine the Confederacy through lenient policies toward civilians. If his operational strategy focused somewhat clearly on capturing the railroad corridors around the Confederacy, his campaign to take Richmond treated railroads as a distinctly secondary, even tertiary, concern. In hundreds of letters and telegrams McClellan and his Union staff officers mentioned railroads less frequently than they did "river" or "enemy" or "fort." Slavery and "contrabands" as a topic figured not at all. The Union command's total correspondence can be counted for word frequency to see not only what most occupied their vocabulary but also how word usage changed over time. For McClellan and the Union officers, "Richmond" as a word and military concept became increasingly important. Over the course of the campaign, however, "railroad" terms faded into almost total disuse (see Appendix, Table 8).[34]

McClellan's ideas concerning the war's limits and destructiveness were about to collide with reality in the Seven Days Battles, which were fought between

Keywords appearing in all Union officers' correspondence in the 1862 Peninsular Campaign; the larger the word, the more often it appeared in their writings.

Compiled from U.S. War Department, *The War of the Rebellion: A Compilation of the Official Records of the Union and Confederate Armies* (Lynchburg, Va., and Pasadena, Calif.: Broadfoot, 1985), Vol. 11 (Part III), 1–384.

(Voyeur Tools [copyright 2009] Steffan Sinclair and Geoffrey Rockwell, v. 1.0; graph by Trevor Munoz and the author [September 2009]. This image was generated using Wordle, under a Creative Commons Attribution 3.0 License.)

June 25 and July 1. Before those battles, however, he used every opportunity to deliver Virginia's citizens, and the Confederacy, back into the Union with a policy of conciliation. He wrote Secretary of the Treasury Salmon P. Chase to encourage him to "open trade" on the peninsula in the wake of his army, as a means to "establish our flag." McClellan explained that he was concerned about "destitute" and starving white families in the area, although it seems unlikely that, in the spring of 1862 along the rich banks of the York and James Rivers, the population was experiencing widespread social breakdown.[35]

Throughout McClellan's campaign in 1862, Lincoln inquired about seizing the railroads into Richmond. When McClellan's cavalry captured an engine and six cars on the Virginia Central Railroad northeast of Richmond, McClellan bragged to Secretary of War Edwin M. Stanton that the "railway communications of Richmond are not as safe as they used to be." McClellan's troops destroyed some bridges on the Richmond and Aquia Creek Railroad on May 28, but Lincoln wanted to know precisely where these bridges were and whether the cavalry would hold the railroads. In his response Stanton indicated to McClellan that the administration "rejoiced" at the news "in breaking the railroads and burning the bridges." He thought that "the enemy will feel that blow more heavily than anything since the evacuation of Yorktown."[36]

But Lincoln was not as enthusiastic. In April he pushed McClellan to attack the Confederate army quickly because "they will probably use *time*, as advantageously as you can." On May 17 Lincoln, frustrated by McClellan's slow pace, interfered with McClellan's plans and directly ordered General Irvin McDowell to move from northern Virginia toward Richmond down the R. F. & P. Railroad. Writing on May 28, Lincoln cautioned McClellan that his minor raids against the Confederate railroads around Richmond were not a "total rout" and that he was "puzzled to know why the Richmond and Fredericksburg Railroad was not seized." Repeating that he was "puzzled," Lincoln asked how McClellan could claim to "have all the Railroads but the Richmond and Fredericksburg." Instead, Lincoln pointed out, McClellan had only "the scrap from Richmond to West Point." The piece of the Virginia Central that the cavalry tore up "without more" was "simply nothing," Lincoln concluded.[37]

Instead, McClellan only further concentrated his attention on Richmond, the capital of the Confederacy. In all of McClellan's correspondence with Union commanders during the 1862 campaign, "Richmond" was the third most frequently used word. When General Irvin McDowell wrote McClellan in late May about whether he should use his forces at Fredericksburg to take the R. F. & P. Railroad, McClellan did not bother to reply.[38] Increasingly, McClellan became preoccupied with the size of the enemy force in front of him. He issued general orders for his army to advance "upon the Chickahominy" and urged his men to do so with "perfect coolness and confidence," keeping "well together." McClellan wrote Lincoln to request more troops, because he was already convinced that the Confederates vastly outnumbered him, even as other commanders in the campaign reported rumors from deserters and "contrabands" that the reverse was true.[39]

Despite the Union advantages in manpower, Richmond itself proved unexpectedly difficult to attack. The city's networks of river and rail, as well as its surrounding swamps, created an intricate geography. McClellan had sidestepped hundreds of miles of the relatively open northern Virginia landscape and bypassed several of its major rivers with his water-borne maneuver to the York, but he still confronted a bewilderingly unyielding landscape and a determined Confederate army. He had traded the open fields of Manassas for the thickets of the swampy Chickahominy River and White Oak Swamp.

Richmond's geography was indeed formidable. The city boomed in the 1850s, aided by the James River and Kanawha Canal and the completion of five major railroads and a sixth smaller line. It was one of the most heavily networked cities in the Confederacy, connected to Gordonsville, Petersburg, and Alexandria. No other place possessed more railroads or longer lines of communication. The Richmond, Fredericksburg, & Potomac Railroad connected Richmond to the North, the Virginia Central Railroad to the Northwest, the Richmond and Danville Railroad to the Southwest, the Richmond and York River Railroad to the East, and the Richmond and Petersburg to the South.

With these rail lines extending from its central core, Richmond featured

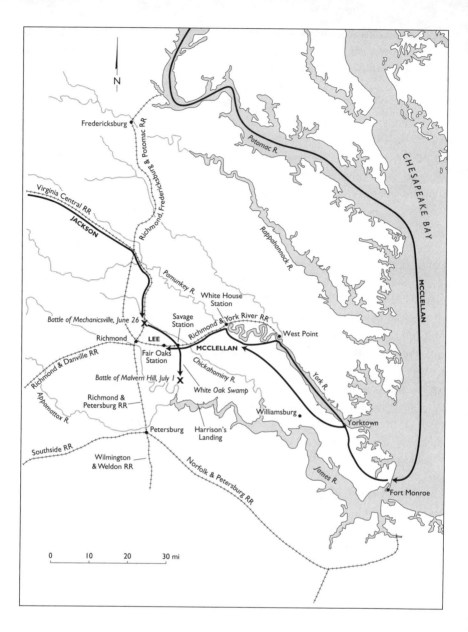

The Peninsular Campaign, March–July 1862.

modern iron foundries at Tredegar Iron Works, the South's largest manufacturing plant in 1860. Moreover, Richmond ranked second only to Baltimore in U.S. flour milling and first in tobacco manufacturing, and these mills established an extensive transatlantic trade network with markets in Brazil and Latin America. Finally, Richmond was the central point in an extremely lucrative and robust slave trade market. By the time of the 1860 census, Henrico County, Virginia (Richmond at its center), contained the highest number of slaves in all of the counties of Virginia, with just over 20,000. Nearly 7,500 slaves were employed in manufacturing. Compared to other southern cities—Baltimore, Charleston, and New Orleans, for example—Richmond led the region in the simultaneous development of manufacturing and slaveholding.[40]

Around the city's eastern perimeter in May and June 1862, McClellan's army loomed on the horizon, like a giant machine in the landscape, kicking up dust clouds, stirring up the waters, and digging up the earth. The Confederate military too began entrenching, impressing the city's slaves to do the hard work of digging and contouring its defenses. Into the city poured thousands of troops from all directions. Richmond, for all of its industry and its commitment to slavery, had an added advantage—to its east stood the swamps of the Chickahominy River, to its north the Rappahannock River, to its south the James River. Nature seemed to have secured the capital, its water and trees forming a perfect wall in the shape of a "7," with Richmond located in the center.

The Chickahominy, moreover, was a broad, slow river; it was so slack that one could be hard-pressed to discern where its banks began and ended, and it was so prone to flooding that it could quickly overspread hundreds of square miles of the flat country that surrounded it. The river bottom was home to dense stands of pine and oak that rooted on patches of soggy ground just above sea level, as if gripping and therefore occupying the only reliable places a man could stand. In between and among these trees was a form of muddied clay so viscous in places it could easily suck down a wagon, a horse, or a man up to the waistline. To the north the Rappahannock River stood forty-five miles above the city, its broad, deep channel offering little cover for an army crossing its reaches. The river ran from northwest to southeast down to the Chesapeake Bay, but above Richmond it was several hundred yards wide—wide enough to require negotiation, bridges, and major planning, wide enough to set up a defensive position on its banks, wide enough to deter cautious commanders from trying to cross it.

Richmond's geographic position, as a result, proved difficult to attack, its natural and second nature systems interlocking in complex ways. McClellan's flanking maneuver by sea avoided the Rappahannock River crossing but brought the Union army face to face with a landscape of interlaced swamps, rivers, and bogs. In all of McClellan's official correspondence and telegraphs with the Union commanders, the most frequently and intensively used words focused on the landscape features surrounding the rivers. Throughout much of the campaign, moreover, the Union command ignored railroads and railroad structures completely, referring to them not once over a span of several weeks.

Soldiers too focused on the unfamiliar Confederate landscape they encountered around Richmond. One Union soldier, Bob Taggart from Pennsylvania, moved up the York River with McClellan's forces in the spring of 1862, and he noted that all at once "everything seemed to change." The shoreline became so low that it could hardly be "distinguished." The vegetation looked "sickly." "Swamps abound," he wrote home, "and no signs of improvement or civilization are visible as far as the eye could reach."[41]

Taggart's regiment landed at White House Station on the railhead. Instead of an outpost of civilization, the little railroad station was, he thought, "a miserable looking place." No fancy platforms, no shining symbols of modern progress, only the army's makeshift offices clustered about the tracks, and around them Taggart observed what he thought were ominous signs of his future: "'Government Hospitals' 'Undertaker's shops,' Embalmers of the dead." Sanitary Commission nurse Harriet Douglas Whetten, on the other hand, was struck by the Chickahominy's sublime nature, comparing its cypresses growing in the water to the "oriental beauty and reminiscences of Arabian nights." Both wrote in the style of travel writers—one to dismiss, the other to romanticize, the southern landscape—but neither was fully prepared for the wreckage about to unfold.[42]

When the army moved along the railroad to Richmond, the stations marked their progress, mile by mile. Eventually, they were four and a half miles outside of the city near a station called Mechanicsville. McClellan positioned his headquarters on the railroad at Savage's Station, and the movement was culminating in a war that, according to Taggart, "looks, feels, and sounds like active service."[43] McClellan's army seemed to have negotiated the complex Chickahominy River, and, using that single railroad, positioned itself on the outskirts of the Confederate capital. The whole campaign appeared a remarkable success. As if picking a lock, McClellan inserted his army into the one slot that nature and second nature systems allowed.

As McClellan prepared to lay siege to Richmond with the Army of the Potomac, he counted on his former Illinois Central Railroad colleague General Nathaniel Banks to prevent a Confederate attack northward to Washington, D.C., through the Shenandoah Valley. Banks and some 20,000 Union troops settled in at Strasburg, Virginia, in the middle of the Valley near the Manassas Gap Railroad extension's end at Mount Jackson. Another Union general, John C. Frémont, threatened to occupy the Valley from western Virginia and headed toward the small Confederate army gathered around Staunton, the critical supply line on the Virginia Central Railroad running east straight into Richmond.

Union commanders, McClellan among them, generally understood the Valley as a possible Confederate avenue of attack on Washington, D.C., and in the first phase of the war they did not appreciate its strategic importance as a corri-

Savage's Station, headquarters of General George B. McClellan, June 27, 1862.

McClellan used the Richmond and York River Railroad to position his massive
Army of the Potomac just a few miles from Richmond. (Library of Congress)

dor for attacking Richmond. So, McClellan ignored the Valley, hoping only that
he would have the time and the troops necessary in his Peninsular Campaign to
capture Richmond. The Union operations under Banks and Frémont in the Valley
were, in this regard, defensive, designed to protect the railroads leading toward
Washington rather than to attack the railroads servicing Richmond.

But these railroads reconfigured the distances and spaces in the war, so much
so that moving up the Valley southwest and away from Richmond actually, because of the railroads, brought the army closer to its objective. This counterintui-
tive result was even more true if the Union army moved on Staunton, Virginia,
and the vital Virginia Central Railroad. Troops from Staunton might pass through
the Blue Ridge Tunnel directly toward Richmond, sixty miles by rail to the east.

The Confederate commander of the Army of the Valley, General Thomas J.
"Stonewall" Jackson, possessed an intimate knowledge of this region, as did his
local mapmaker, Jedediah Hotchkiss. The two men had lived for years in the
lower Valley, Jackson a professor at the Virginia Military Institute and Hotchkiss
a teacher at a local academy near Staunton. Jackson and his brigade gained some

measure of fame at the Battle of First Manassas in July 1861, when his troops took the railroad from near Winchester to Manassas and deployed onto the battlefield just in time to turn back a strong Union assault and ensure a Confederate victory. The rail movement was unprecedented in American warfare. When he received orders, as well as reinforcements, from Robert E. Lee in March 1862 to attack the Union armies in the Valley, Jackson began to conceive of a rapid assault, one in which speed, mobility, local knowledge, and technologies combined to stun and weaken the enemy.[44]

Jackson took on Frémont first, defeating his forces at the Battle of McDowell on May 8, and then he turned northward to confront Banks. To achieve total surprise, Jackson and his troops left the Valley using the Virginia Central Railroad, rode through the Blue Ridge Tunnel, and then disembarked and marched north toward a place called Brown's Gap, where they could slip back into the Valley. Hiding behind the chain of mountains (Massanutten) that divided the Shenandoah into two side-by-side valleys, Jackson marched his army so fast that it seemed propelled as if by railroad. Indeed, his "foot cavalry," as his men came to be called, moved like a train—they went over wide avenues wherever possible, stopping precisely at set intervals, and moving at a consistent, calibrated rate. Jackson managed to bring his army forward at railroad speed even in places where there were no railroads, and the results were stupendous. He arrived in the northern end of the Valley at Front Royal before Banks understood what was happening, and once there created such havoc and confusion that Banks retreated to Winchester. Then, after a battle in front of Winchester, Banks retreated again northward back across the Potomac River to defend the Baltimore & Ohio Railroad line. Following these events by telegraph, Lincoln could draw only a "circle" near Harper's Ferry, within which he thought Jackson's army might be found.[45]

But Jackson's campaign was not over. From Winchester he marched his men south down the macadamized (hard-packed gravel surface) Valley turnpike, again with railroad-like speed, as Federal troops under Frémont and General Irvin McDowell tried to trap him. Rain delayed the Federals more than it did Jackson, and he arrived at the upper end of the Valley before they did. At the little village of Port Republic, Jackson turned and fought the advance column of the Federal army. The long marches, the rain-swollen rivers, and the incompetence of the Federal commanders all contributed to Jackson's advantages. With the Union army spread out across the Valley and having little hope of trapping Jackson again, Lincoln ordered the Federals to regroup. Jackson's army had liberated the Shenandoah Valley from Federal occupation in a matter of weeks.[46]

Having gained a brilliant tactical victory in the Valley, Jackson proceeded to use the railroads in ways no other commander had yet attempted in the war. With near total secrecy on June 17, Jackson, at General Robert E. Lee's request, began to move his entire army out of the Valley and toward Richmond. Lee, who on June 1 took command of the Confederate forces around Richmond, knew that

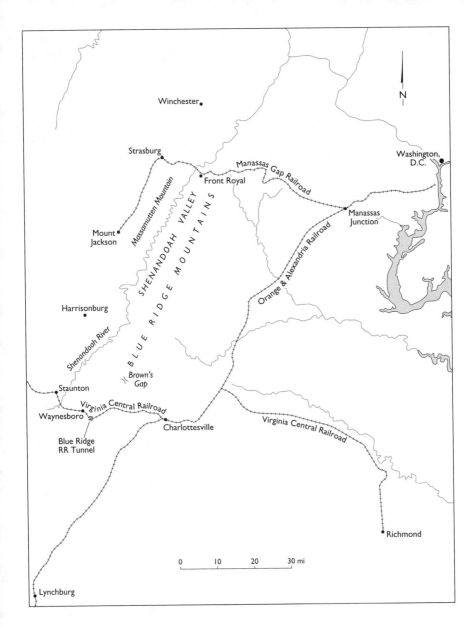

The Shenandoah Valley, Virginia.

speed was essential. He could not let McClellan entrench, bring up his big artillery guns, and slowly strangle the capital.

Jackson marched his 18,500 men to the Virginia Central Railroad station on the eastern side of the mountains, then loaded up equipment and as many soldiers as the cars could carry. The trains shuttled the men forward a full day's march in a few hours. These troops disembarked, assumed a foot march, and the trains backed up the tracks to carry another load forward. This ferrying went on for two days and brought Jackson's army to Gordonsville, fifty-two miles from Richmond. The final leg of the journey to Richmond, however, proved chaotic, as trains slowed down, troops straggled, and rains flooded the roads.[47]

Once Jackson arrived near Mechanicsville, Lee's army launched a series of furious attacks to dislodge McClellan and relieve Richmond. Rain flooded the Chickahominy River and divided McClellan's forces, a major advantage for Lee. Still, the Union forces fought hard, and the Confederates lost thousands, either killed or wounded. The Seven Days Battles became the bloodiest fighting to that point in the war, with over 15,000 Union and 20,000 Confederate total casualties. In the course of the fighting, McClellan made a fateful decision to leave the Richmond and York River Railroad and move his base of supplies to the James River at Harrison's Landing, where the U.S. Navy gunboats might support the Army of the Potomac. No Union army would get this close to Richmond again for two long years.

As McClellan waited on the banks of the James River with the defeated Army of the Potomac, the differences between Lincoln and him over the nature of the war broke into the open. McClellan lectured Lincoln that the war "should be conducted on the highest principles known to Christian Civilization" and that "military power should not be allowed to interfere with the relations of servitude [slavery]." He commandeered the agricultural estate called Shirley plantation as a hospital and went out of his way to thank its owner, Hill Carter, one of the largest slaveholders in the state: "I have not come here to wage war upon the defenseless, upon non-combatants, upon private property, nor upon the domestic institutions of the land [i.e., slavery]." From nearby Berkeley plantation he wrote his wife, Mary Ellen, that he was taking in the "scenery" of the "fine old residences" on the James and that the landscape made him think back to a time before abolitionists and "palm singing Yankees," when the planters probably had "a pretty good time." All they had to think about, he joked, were gambling losses and "the trouble of providing for their wooly headed dependents." When Lincoln signed the Second Confiscation Act, declaring slaves captured in the war "forever free," McClellan flatly objected: "Let the negro take care of himself."[48]

Having pushed McClellan away from Richmond, Lee and Jackson commenced another bold move. Jackson once more took to the railroads, this time heading due north to the Manassas railroad junction, where he defeated the Union army commanded by General John Pope. Pope had issued a series of orders directing his army to confiscate Confederate civilian property, execute suspected guerrillas who attacked the Union railroads, and hold civilians "responsible . . . [if they] commit outrages disgraceful to civilized people and revolting to humanity." Later, Pope clarified his orders when his soldiers engaged in widespread pilfering, saying they had been "misinterpreted" and "grossly abused." Soldiers had "no right to enter houses, molest persons, [and] disturb property." Despite these modifications, during and after the summer of 1862, the war escalated in its destructiveness, violence, and scope.[49]

In northern Virginia the path of ruin in the landscape was extensive: forests were denuded, bridges were wrecked, houses were bombed out, and fortifications were rapidly constructed and abandoned. Sanford Truesdell of the 122nd New York Infantry came into northern Virginia in the late summer of 1862. His unit was assigned to protect the Orange & Alexandria Railroad near the old battlefield of Manassas, where he found the surrounding countryside to be "almost completely deserted" and "ruined." The scale of the destruction baffled him; it seemed to be "guided by one gigantic mind."[50]

Like Ephraim C. Dawes in western Tennessee, Truesdell witnessed little respect for the Virginia farmsteads and landscape on the part of his fellow soldiers. He had seen the older, veteran soldiers go into "fine farm houses" and "ransack every thing," taking what they wanted and "destroying" everything else.[51] Truesdell's regiment marched twenty miles along the railroad as it took up its position. "In the whole distance," he wrote, they "did not see but 2 or 3 houses, all of the buildings near the road being burned." He had not seen "a field of grain of any kind" since he had left Culpepper, Virginia.[52] A few months later, Truesdell's unit moved to defend Brandy Station, Virginia, where "the timber for miles around has all been cut off, most of the barns and out houses took down." The denuding of the trees especially affected him and all he could say of the barren, dreary landscape of war was: "It is lonesome, lonesome, lonesome."[53]

Another soldier compared the war to a tornado. "The work of destruction" that a battle made was something he could hardly explain: "one complete wreck of everything, houses blown to peices [sic] by shells bursting inside of them or burned down, fences torn down and burned up, trees all shattered to peices [sic]." In the little railroad town of La Verge, Tennessee, he found only three houses that were still standing after a battle, and fifty to sixty horses lay dead in the town's streets.[54]

Railroad places were the first to feel the war's effects. Trees were cut not only for firewood to run the trains but also for bridges which were torched, rebuilt, and then burned again by retreating armies. Photographers Mathew Brady, Alexander Gardner, Timothy O'Sullivan, James F. Gibson, and George Barnard captured many of these scenes. They often focused on a landscape entirely transformed by the war—finding treeless, bare land as far as the camera could reach.[55]

The landscape of the Civil War, however motionless in these photographs, changed drastically during the war, and the participants closely observed both its features and its transformations. Northern women, too, went South with the armies as nurses, doctors, and teachers and witnessed and participated in the destruction. Arriving in Beaufort, South Carolina, in October 1862, Esther Hawks saw private libraries "brutally trodden under foot," churches "robbed of all orna-

Ruins at Manassas Junction, March 1862.

Numerous railroad hubs in the Confederacy became sites of repeated fighting, both
large- and small-scale. Here, the ruins were the work of the Confederate army as
it abandoned its forward position in northern Virginia to protect Richmond.

ment," fences "torn away," and even the brick walls for tombs dismantled and
used for soldier's chimneys. Traveling on the railroads into the South and across
the region, soldiers from both North and South found themselves visiting new
territory. Northern soldiers and women travelers wrote letters home filled with
long, descriptive paragraphs on the strange vegetation, crops, fauna, and people
that they encountered in the Confederacy. For northern soldiers, in particular,
the train ride or steamboat journey into the South led them to compare what they
saw with their own homes and towns, and this experience all too often led them
to adopt stereotypes about the South and its peoples. Northerners began to see
that the war would alter the landscape in vast and systematic ways, much as the
railroads themselves had done in the years preceding the conflict.[56]

As they went to war, Americans found that modern warfare created highly
engineered landscapes, ones that wrecked the past and ruined the natural. War

had always entailed destruction, but usually of the enemy forces. The zone of war was limited in earlier conflicts, yet railroad construction had demonstrated that mountains could be bored, swamps filled, and gorges and rivers bridged. Consequently, the zones of the conflict widened in proportion to the railroads. In a modern war between equally powerful nation-states with equally advanced technologies, ideas about limits, natural or human, did not hold for very long. Stonewall Jackson, who shared few qualms about the war's destruction, understood the tactical and strategic value of the railroads for the Confederate nation. Indeed, he formulated an aggressive plan in the aftermath of the Richmond victories. Well aware that the combination of fast marches and, at key points, the use of railroad transportation had confounded the enemy, Jackson proposed to Lee that he divide up his army into "light movable columns." He planned to hit hard and fast any Union army forces in Virginia, to strike north and bring the war to the northern people, and to avoid large, ponderous battles like the Seven Days Battles. Jackson's thinking—ruthless and determined—held that such warfare "best suits the temper of our people." Lee had other plans, however. Jackson's warfare, so clearly successful at the scale of the Shenandoah Valley, would not be applied to the full "cockpit of the war." While Jackson advocated unconventional methods to enable the revolutionary Confederate nation to defeat the larger, more powerful North, Lee and Confederate president Jefferson Davis held to a more conventional strategy—asserting nationhood through massive warfare.[57]

The consequences of these large campaigns were everywhere apparent in the southern landscape. Surveying some of the effects of the recent campaigns, Jackson's mapmaker Jedediah Hotchkiss remarked that "the trees have disappeared" and "houses that never looked at each other" in over a century now "stare each other impudently in the face." He thought that a world, a particular way of life and its landscape, was vanishing before his very eyes. But the destruction would affect the future just as powerfully as it did the present and the past, for "whatever new generation shall live in that land they cannot say they sit under the trees their fathers planted." Referring to the apocalypse, Hotchkiss called this the "'abomination of desolation' that an army produces."[58]

The abomination of the army in the field of battle was something that nineteenth-century Americans witnessed and participated in, and the destruction everywhere raised new questions about the scope of the national war they were fighting. The key question for the Union strategy became whether the war could be fought in a limited way or whether it would demand a wider respect for the national attitudes and experiences of citizens on both sides. In this way the national cause of each helped both Northerners and Southerners convince themselves that the war could and should be extended to the landscape, both the natural and the man-made, however painful the cost. McClellan, Banks, and Burnside resisted such conclusions, limiting their armies and seeking to force a Confederate loss of resolve. In doing so they ignored the recent history of Confederate national purpose and the importance of the vital railroads in creating and sustaining Confederate identity.

Lincoln, meanwhile, studied the railroad maps of Richmond and Virginia intensely. He wrote to McClellan of "the inside track" to meet Lee's army and conceived of the whole geography of the eastern theater as defined "by the different spokes of a wheel extending from the hub towards the rim." Lincoln saw a "chord-line" of turnpikes and railroads that governed the enemy's movements and communication as much as it did McClellan's. Calculating time and distance for every movement, Lincoln wanted McClellan to see what he saw on these maps and to understand the railroad strategy he had in mind, but McClellan did not.[59]

Ironically, Lincoln would never admit that the Confederacy had national aspirations that deserved serious respect, yet he saw most clearly the operational advantages that railroads offered. Commanders on both sides were just beginning to understand how railroads could be used to unmake the places that they had helped create and establish before the war.

And the exploits of Jackson and Lee clearly indicated how Confederates expected to fight with their available resources. At nearly every turn in the summer of 1862 Jackson used the limited railroad system in Virginia to his advantage. He fooled the Federal commanders in the Valley, coming and going by the Blue Ridge Tunnel. He created a shuttle system on the Virginia Central to move his entire force outside Richmond for Lee's offensive against McClellan. And after those victories, he boarded the Virginia Central again, using seventeen freight trains running at ten-minute intervals, day and night, to get his army into northern Virginia to attack the Union army there under General John Pope. Similarly, Confederate general Braxton Bragg moved 30,000 troops from Tupelo, Mississippi, to Chattanooga, Tennessee, traversing over 700 miles by railroad in fourteen days to mount his invasion of Kentucky. With McClellan hunkered down on the James River and Jackson and Lee using the railroads so effectively, the Union's war in the East, however bloody and destructive, would not change until a new strategy could be aimed at seizing and controlling, as Lincoln so wished, the Confederate second nature systems of railroad lines and junctions.[60]

Chapter 5

The Railroad War Zones

INCREASINGLY after 1862, the American Civil War became structured around the railroad network, centered on the boundaries made by junctions and rail lines. Northern generals directed whole campaigns at particular roads and their tributaries. The railroads became an imagined set of guideposts for where the war would be fought and how men and material would be collected and moved onto the battlefield, guiding the way commanders understood the landscape and managed their operations. The railroads were, therefore, the architecture of the war's violence and destruction, a second nature no one could ignore. The setting for this violence, side by side with the most modern infrastructure of the period, bears significance.

In 1862, as northern armies pressed into parts of Tennessee, Kentucky, and Virginia, the general violence of the war escalated. The bloody two-day battle at Shiloh near the Corinth railroad junction in Mississippi gave Americans a new appreciation for the scale of bloodletting possible in the war. Over 23,000 men were killed and wounded in the dense forest fighting there, as both sides used the railroads to assemble and throw forward onto the battlefield the largest armies they could amass. The huge operations McClellan launched to take Richmond indicated to even the most casual observer that the technology of war had reached new levels of sophistication and destructiveness. Land mines, electronically wired command headquarters, balloon aerial surveillance, unprecedented sea-land logistical coordination, and massive artillery formations characterized the Peninsular Campaign, some making their debut in modern warfare. Richmond, like Moscow in the Napoleonic wars, seemed to have survived because the landscape gave the city protective advantages against the size, wealth, and technology of its enemies. But the second nature systems supporting Richmond were equally significant.

Stonewall Jackson's mastery of the landscape in the Valley Campaign and his mysterious movements combined fast marches with rail travel at the key points to confuse and disable the enemy. Jackson's campaign depended on an intense local knowledge of the landscape, on the speed of his army's mobility, and on combining these to achieve deception. The Blue Ridge Tunnel, built by slaves and Irish workers five years earlier, once the longest in the world and since then a statement of Virginia's modern development, provided the critical means for Jackson to outmaneuver his adversaries.

The railroads, therefore, led to a particular geography of the war and its spatial unfolding. Although traditional histories of the Civil War have stressed the battles and campaigns as set pieces and the rivers of the South as especially important barriers, the ebb and flow of the movements and conflicts took shape around the railroad lines. The occupation and conquest of the South unfolded in zones defined by the rails and proceeded across the landscape in patterns along their networks. Occupying the South meant, at least initially, controlling its railroad corridors. In these places near the rail junctions, the Federal army's policies toward the South met their first test.

Because there was no clear and consistent line of Federal occupation, historians have tried to categorize and explain the types of war zones that emerged in the conflict. The zone of Union army occupation, according to historian Stephen V. Ash, created great variation in the Confederacy. First, there were "garrison towns," where the Union forces tried to fortify and hold key places. Second, there was a shifting "no man's land," where neither the Union nor the Confederate armies fully controlled the area. Finally, there was a changing Confederate frontier line, where conflict was especially likely and intense.[1]

In addition, there were huge swaths of interior Confederate territory where no Union army ever penetrated. As late as June 1864, one young woman in the Shenandoah Valley near Lexington, Virginia, had yet to see her "first Yankee" soldier. Her experience was not unusual. Counties across much of Mississippi, Virginia, and even Georgia never saw the Federal army until the waning days of the war, in March or April 1865. Some never witnessed a blue-coat uniform. For these Confederates the war was a distant event, something to travel to rather than something that came to them; of the 833 counties of the Confederate South, less than half (375), according to historian Paul Paskoff, could be identified as "war zones." Only in Virginia, Arkansas, Mississippi, and Tennessee did more than half of the land mass constitute a war zone where battles took place or Federal armies occupied. Over 60 percent of Georgia, for example, never saw a battle or a Federal army.[2]

Both the war zones and Federal occupation policies took shape first around the railroads. The rails funneled the armies into central battle areas and served as corridors for the massive divisions and brigades to move through. The symbols of southern modernity and national independence before the war, the railroads were becoming the means of northern incursion and attack. Paradoxically, the railroads needed to be destroyed by the South in order to save the Confederate nation, and

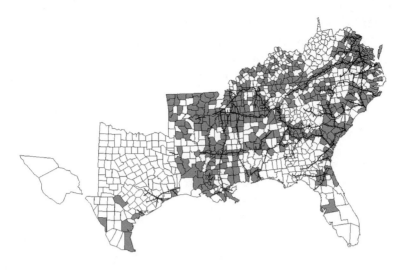

Railroads and war zone counties, 1861–1865.

If the presence of the Union army and/or a battle constituted a war zone, then only in Virginia did the Civil War's destruction touch the majority of counties. Vast sections of the South remained out of the war zone, but over the course of the war destruction tended to follow closely along the pathways of the major lines of communication and transportation. Counties in gray indicate "war zones" (where either a battle or a skirmish occurred, or where the Union army was present). From Paul F. Paskoff, "Measures of War: A Quantitative Examination of the Civil War's Destructiveness in the Confederacy," *Civil War History*, Vol. 54, No. 1 (March 2008).

(Reproduced with permission of Paul F. Paskoff)

they needed to be taken and rebuilt by the North in order to defeat and conquer the Confederate people.[3]

Here, the ingredients of southern resistance and northern planning came to fruition. In late 1862 and early 1863 southern generals relied on a mixture of speed of movement, deception, and local knowledge. Recognizing the importance of the railroad corridors, they launched partisan and guerrilla units to extend these capacities and cripple the northern invasions. The Army of Northern Virginia, under Robert E. Lee, sought more than anything to position the fighting away from the principal Confederate railroad zones. Although Lee's offensives may have been the product of his aggressive temperament, they produced a masterful strategic turnaround between July 1862 and April 1864 in large measure because they disabled, confounded, and blocked any northern attempts at a systematic railroad strategy in the East. Lee changed the location of the fighting away from the Virginia railroad corridors to places in Maryland and Pennsylvania, removed from the southern railroads.[4]

But the Union army's occupation of the South's railroads proceeded first across large parts of the West, especially in western and central Tennessee. Despite the failure of General Don Carlos Buell to take Chattanooga's rail junction in the summer of 1862, and William Rosecrans's painfully slow movement toward that city in the summer of 1863, the Union forces had captured Corinth, Memphis, and Nashville, knocking nearly 20,000 square miles of railroad corridor out of the Confederacy (see Appendix, Table 9). The Confederate retreat out of Kentucky, moreover, brought its rail network under Union control. The Union commanders in 1863, led by Ulysses S. Grant, took over the railroads, freed black slaves along their lines, and ran the railroads themselves.[5]

The zones of war that surrounded the railroads thus became key sites for two important modern developments in the conflict: first, they witnessed new forms of violence in the desperate partisan resistance of the Confederates, and second, they provided the earliest and most consequential movements for black freedom out of slavery. Both of these increasingly visible actions along the railroads inspired northern and southern self-examination about the nature of the conflict and its meaning for their societies. Both also influenced the ways commanders thought about the campaigns. The first two years of the war made clear that defeating the Confederate nation and ending slavery or, conversely, ensuring southern survival and perpetuating slavery, depended to a great degree on who controlled its railroad systems.

When Confederate guerrillas began striking at Union forces and even staged raids across the Union-Confederate border, especially targeting the railroads, they prompted immediate debate about the nature of the war and the strategy that would be necessary to win it. The fifteen-mile zones around railroads had already become the most important avenues into the South and those places where the fighting would become the most severe. Guerrilla and partisan attacks on the Union army's lines of supply and communication exposed their vulnerabilities and exploited their weaknesses. But the violence and vulnerability extended along the network right into northern communities and brought the war home to the North in unexpected ways.

Southern partisans in the border states began organizing units to attack Federal forces as soon as they appeared, and northern commanders and the northern public reacted with concern and even outrage at this form of warfare. Many Southerners, on the other hand, supported the idea of guerrilla warfare as within the bounds of civilized war, indeed as a necessary tool for securing their nation's independence, regardless of the destruction they caused to southern-built, -owned, and -financed railroads.[6]

As guerrillas and partisans entered the field, new forms of violence terrified the northern public and drew on the setting of the railroad itself. To be trapped in a burning railroad car, to be caught by a guerrilla unit, to be robbed and left for dead on the tracks became a different form of violence for Americans, distinct from the violence that led to death on the battlefield. With its peculiar mixture of surprise and chaos, partisan warfare sparked heated debate over boundaries, rules, and conduct in war. The guerrilla attacks also prompted Northerners to consider the available means necessary to end the war. They would need not only to defeat armies and secure the surrender of major cities but also to occupy the South, control it, pacify it, and subdue and secure the region. The battle against the Confederate guerrillas took place most prominently along the railroads and proceeded side by side with the massive effort to defeat the Confederate armies in the field.[7]

Newspaper editors on both sides looked for precedents in history to guide them in their assessment of guerrilla warfare. The *Charleston Courier* cited the guerrilla tactics of the Spanish as an example to follow and warned its readers that they should be ready to adopt extreme measures: "We must enter upon this and every other species of war to exterminate the foul invaders of our soil." The guerrilla war in Spain required Napoleon to station hundreds of thousands of troops there, even though the guerrillas never numbered more than 40,000. Their effect was far out of proportion to their numbers, and Confederates hoped for a similar result. The *Savannah Daily Morning News* likewise supported guerrilla fighting to drive "the hated foe" from the "heart of our country" and "cut off his transportation." In northern newspapers, however, editors deplored the "infamous guerrilla warfare" in the South. They likened the guerrillas to a pestilence, spreading quickly and bent on destruction. The "rebels are organizing these bands daily," one northern editor explained, "and sending them out to plunder and murder loyal citizens."[8]

Northern editors turned to Union general Henry W. Halleck's *International Law*, published in the 1850s and by 1861 widely recognized as the standard treatise defining the rules of modern war. Halleck declared guerrilla fighters to be outlaws. He justified the seizure of any civilian combatant's property as "within the limits justified by civilized warfare" but only by sanctioned army officers in the field. To northern observers Halleck was right to condemn guerrilla warfare as uncivilized, and many northern editors quoted his book's concluding explanation: "Hence, in modern warfare, partisans and guerrilla bands are regarded as outlaws, and, when captured, may be punished the same as freebooters and banditti."[9]

Following Halleck, most Northerners categorically denied these forces any legitimacy and viewed them as outside of the rules of war. In October 1862, as Confederate cavalry raiders tore through parts of Ohio and Pennsylvania, William G. Stevenson began writing a series of newspaper articles about Confederate partisan cavalry officer John Hunt Morgan. Stevenson was a Union man, compelled to serve in the Confederate army until he escaped the Confederates for Union lines in Tennessee. His familiarity bred contempt for the South, as well as concern — that Northerners misunderstood the true "power, unanimity, and the deadly purpose" of the South's leaders and the guerrilla movement. Because the guerrilla bands absolved individuals of any responsibility, Stevenson argued, the guerrillas conducted what amounted to little more than criminal acts. "The essential principle of the system, giving it its power and destructiveness," he wrote, was that the men became "highway robbers in organized and authorized bands." Stevenson went further, criticizing the Confederacy for unleashing "a system which will utterly demoralize all engaged in it; destroy the peace and endanger the safety of non-combatants, and eventually reduce to ruin and anarchy the whole community over which these bands of robbers have their range."[10]

With this logic Northerners tended to treat all partisans, cavalry raiders, and guerrillas as similarly motivated. Yet, there were significant gradations among these forces. The term "guerrilla" was applied by the northern commanders to all activity behind lines whether by regular cavalry units, irregular or partisan forces, or locally formed bands of guerrilla fighters and "bushwhackers." In Missouri, where as many as 27,000 civilians perished in the war and a third of the state's population either left or were killed, guerrilla violence was especially brutal and long-lasting. Indeed, in Missouri, the cycle of bloodshed may have started and been perpetuated by a debt crisis in which the pro-Confederate planters and bankers found that their early financial support for the Confederate cause left them heavily indebted and subject to litigation before largely Unionist courts. Rather than see their property taken in these legal proceedings, Confederate Missourians turned to guerrilla violence. They attacked both civilians and the Union military.[11]

In this respect guerrilla actions both in Missouri and elsewhere were not motivated by premodern sensibilities, nor were they a form of lashing out against central power, the market, or capitalism. Instead, quite the reverse was true. The violence in Missouri and western Virginia in the summer of 1861 escalated when the Union army occupied dozens of counties and defeated the Confederate regular forces. The guerrilla and partisan operators came to the fore in these places, motivated to sustain a modern Confederacy built around railroads, banks, plantation agriculture, and slavery. In Virginia partisan leader John D. Imboden held railroad patents before the war and practiced law; in Kentucky John Hunt Morgan ran a hemp manufacturing and mercantile business; in Tennessee Nathan Bedford Forrest was a cotton planter, slave trader, and city alderman.[12]

By early 1862 the Confederate Congress attempted to regularize the guerrilla forces and passed the Partisan Ranger Act. The measure authorized commissions for units operating in enemy-occupied areas along the border, most prominently John S. Mosby in northern Virginia, but also John H. McNeil and John D. Imboden in western Virginia. As officially enlisted and commissioned soldiers, they could not be executed without trial but were ostensibly subject to standard rules of military justice. Mosby, McNeil, and Imboden orchestrated carefully planned and executed attacks on the Union army's railroads that supplied Washington, D.C., especially the vital Baltimore & Ohio. Confederate general Robert E. Lee ordered Imboden, for example, to attack Federal lines of communication by "destroying bridges, tanks, tunnels, &c., on the railroads" and to "damage in every

Alfred R. Waud, *A Guerrilla*, 1862.

When guerrillas attacked Union forces, the northern public was outraged. Confederate guerrillas and partisan rangers attacked the railroad and telegraph systems, opening up the war to civilians and exposing the remorseless nature of the national conflict. Their activities played a central role in the war. (Library of Congress)

possible way, their lines of communication." Later, Lee told McNeil, "The rupture of the B & O railroad . . . would be worth to us an army."[13]

The first Confederate raider to achieve some degree of notoriety in the North was John Hunt Morgan, who operated in 1862 in Kentucky and Tennessee. A commissioned cavalry officer, Morgan attacked the railroads and supply lines of the Federal army along the Ohio border, prompting the northern public to take the guerrilla threat more seriously.

The Confederate cavalry under Morgan in the summer of 1862 established a new form of warfare aimed specifically at the railroad and steamboat corridors and their vulnerabilities. Morgan developed specialized tactics for his men in these situations, abandoning the saber charge and fighting dismounted like infantry. Using speed and maximum force at the point of attack, Morgan tried to disrupt the Union army's flow of material and men into the South on the railroads. Thus, in August 1862 he attacked the tunnels of the Louisville & Nashville Railroad seven miles north of Gallatin, Tennessee. Because one tunnel was 600 feet long and the other 1,000 feet long, their destruction could potentially cripple the route for years. Morgan occupied Gallatin and captured 375 Kentucky unionists who were guarding the railroad; then he took a train, filled its cars with wood, set it afire, and sent it into the "Big South Tunnel." The tunnel's frame supports burned and the tunnel partially collapsed, putting it out of commission for three months. Tunnels were difficult to collapse without dynamite or explosives (not yet invented), so bridges became the key choke points as they were more easily attacked and destroyed.[14]

Morgan's successes, as well as Mosby's and Nathan Bedford Forrest's, came in part because the Union army had not yet organized itself to defend the railroads, but also because these Confederates thoroughly studied the railroad network and its technologies. In Gallatin, Tennessee, during the 1862 raids on the Louisville & Nashville, Morgan dressed as a federal officer and used the telegraph office to find out the arrival schedule for the trains on the line. He consulted timetables and carefully planned his attacks. He began to carry his own telegraphic box.

Northern newspaper editors, however, characterized the attacks as chaotic and indiscriminate. They stressed the personal and political violence that accompanied partisan warfare.[15] When Morgan's cavalry destroyed a Kentucky state senator's home and burned his store, northern newspaper editors used the incident to whip up resentment. After setting the man's home on fire, Morgan reportedly "said, pointing to the flames, 'You find your loyalty to your abolition Government pretty expensive, don't you?'" Similar stories circulated across the North. No Confederate raid was recounted without its insults and derogatory violence. Nor were these stories presented in the North without justifying a reprisal: "emancipation, annihilation, extermination, and h—— and damnation" for all rebels, one newspaper demanded.[16]

Inevitably, the raids prompted a direct, and harsh, response from Union commanders. General William T. Sherman's occupying army in Memphis faced a growing problem with guerrilla attacks and with sniping on Union supply ships along the Mississippi River. Several Union soldiers were killed. Sherman ordered a reprisal operation against Randolph, Tennessee, where he thought the guerrillas lived. His troops were to destroy the town completely, "leaving one house to mark the place," and to "let the citizens know" the reason for the destruction. But Sherman also tempered his order with the caution not to let things get out of control: "Keep your men within reach of your voice," he suggested. "Take a minute account of every house or piece of property destroyed." But the sniping did not stop, and Sherman began ordering secessionist families expelled from Memphis, and then he oversaw the retaliatory burning of a fifteen-mile zone on the west bank of the Mississippi River. When Memphis citizens protested these harsh methods, Sherman responded that southern civilians "shall experience the full measure of the necessary consequences of such barbarity."[17]

Sensationalized in the northern press, the guerrilla threat was both real and imagined in the North, and it created a series of powerful associations during the war. Guerrilla activity targeting the railroads and telegraphs threatened to expose the weaknesses of these modern systems. Tens of thousands of soldiers might be needed simply to guard the railroads. And the farther the Federal armies went into the South, the more railroad miles there were to protect. Because partisans dressed in civilian clothes or Federal uniforms, lived off the land, used the telegraph to pose as Union officers, and depended on a network of supporters, their very presence cast doubt on the loyalties of anyone in the zone of their operations. Most of all, guerrillas made Northerners question how far they were willing to go with the war and whether the war would ever really end. In this regard the guerrillas' unyielding determination indicated the depth of Confederate nationalism. Conversely, northern reactions to their activities exposed the potential shallowness of northern convictions to save the Union.

Many northern commentators in 1861 and 1862 thought the guerrillas had the potential to become a postwar scourge, and this logic led therefore to a more radical war policy to suppress the Confederate nation and to even greater justifications for violence against the guerrillas and partisans in retaliation for their raids.[18]

Because the guerrillas were targeting the railroad corridors, Northerners came to see the war as a different kind of struggle from earlier conflicts where guerrillas proved a menace. The *New York Times* correspondent in the western theater considered the prospect of a long guerrilla war unlikely. He thought that a protracted conflict was possible only "in a country where there are no railroads and no great rivers." Guerrillas could be "sustained only where there are large interior districts, not easily reached." In his view the South's modern system of transportation and communication was so advanced that guerrillas would have no place to hide. The Confederacy, by this logic, was developed to such an extent that either it would become an independent nation-state or it would be conquered. Unlike Italy or Spain, where guerrillas had hid and fought in earlier wars, he noted, "Guerrillas do not belong to our country and our age. We live in an age of railroads and steamboats." In his view, only eastern Kentucky, southern Missouri, and western Virginia were so unreachable as to sustain active guerrillas.[19]

For the *New York Times* and other Republican proponents of the war, the Confederacy was a region without interior spaces, a country with its subregions so interlaced with an extensive transportation system that guerrillas simply could not persist for generations resisting central authority. Indeed, because guerrilla warfare was impossible in the Confederacy's modern landscape, Republicans thought that the war was a de facto nation-state conflict, a new and modern war, its outcome restricted to total victory or total defeat.[20]

Despite their confidence, Northerners began to fear the reach, determination, and violence of these Confederate raids along the railroads. The system of rails led straight into northern communities, after all, and all of a sudden it seemed that every location on the network could become a possible target. In August 1862 Union soldier Ephraim C. Dawes warned his sister Kate that Confederate guerrillas were capable of striking deep into Ohio. "It would be no difficult thing," he pointed out, "for a few guerrillas to come over and ravage the country and burn M[arietta] for that matter." The desperate fight for Tennessee meant that the Confederates "will [leave] no stone unturned to desolate the border." What bothered Dawes more than anything was the potential for guerrillas to attack his family's home. The railroad made that not only possible but perhaps likely. The guerrillas, he thought, would "not hesitate to invade the sanctity" of his sister's home, steal everything, and "burn the house down." Moreover, the marauders were "quite free in their manners and do not feel themselves bound by any conventional rules of etiquette."[21]

Northern editors played on the fears of the northern public and disparaged the Confederate partisans as a "pestilence," the railroads zones as "infested," and the whole manner of warfare "uncivilized." Yet, the railroads made it possible for Northerners to imagine an attack on their doorsteps. Kate Dawes feared an incursion into Ohio. Morgan demonstrated that these points could be reached, and they were self-evidently worth striking.

Because the railroads carried so much of the mail, news, and freight considered essential to the war effort, and because they served civilians as well as the military, the guerrilla activity along them brought the war home to Northerners in an immediate and important way. In April 1863 Ephraim C. Dawes's 53rd Ohio stood guard over the Memphis & Charleston Railroad and yet guerrilla attacks persisted. Back home in Marietta, Ohio, his sister Kate grew worried for his safety. She wrote him about her fears—that he might be captured, that he might be executed, that the guerrillas could not be stopped, that their surprises might mean he would not see his death coming and have time to prepare, that his death would not be a good death. Dawes assured her that she "need not go crazy" or "trouble" herself at all if he "should be captured by guerrillas." He played down the violence and the uncertainty, explaining that she "need not be at all afraid of our being surprised." When the guerrillas finally did attack a train nearby down the railroad line, Dawes and his regiment rushed to the scene using a freight engine. They covered three miles in seventeen minutes, and Dawes assured his sister that he had enough time to get ready for the worst.[22]

Like many soldiers in the first years of the war, Dawes stuck to the view that violence ought to be limited to the battlefields and, even there, calibrated as carefully as possible toward eventual reunion of the southern states. In western Tennessee, the guerrillas made attack after attack on the northern-controlled railroads, and Dawes's 53rd Ohio was dispatched to hunt down some of the guerrilla fighters. He believed that Tennessee "must be run back into the Union not by burning all the houses and stealing everything in the country but by restoring as far as possible the ancient state of things." For Dawes, whose mission to locate the guerrillas proved fruitless, the solution lay in encouraging civilians along the line of the railroad to turn the guerrillas in. "With proper encouragement," Dawes thought, and with promises from the Union army to restore regular service to the railroads, the citizens might "organize and put down the infernal guerrillas that curse this part of the country."[23]

Not all Union soldiers came to the same conclusion. After John Hunt Morgan's Kentucky raid that tore up seventeen miles of railroad track and cut the supply line to northern soldiers in Tennessee, George F. Cram expected an attack on the South Tunnel, which his unit was protecting. False alarms kept the brigade in a constant state of anxiety and readiness. When Confederates staged a small skirmish, the anxieties of the northern soldiers spilled over into wanton destruction. They located the "mansion" of one of the local Confederate captains "and our enraged soldiers, wheeled out a cannon and level[ed] it." Cram considered the destruction justified. He doubted whether the average Confederate soldier had any will to fight at all and assumed that they were misled by their slaveholding superiors. By this logic, Cram thought, once the South's mansions were destroyed, the fakery at the heart of the rebellion could not but be revealed, and southern soldiers would see their officers in a different light. Cram wondered why the average Southerner "even without clothes" would fight in the war for slavery and slaveholders. He concluded that they were "deluded" by the "big men" into thinking that "Lincoln's robbers were coming down here for no other purpose than to set the Negroes free, incite insurrections, and pillage the country."[24]

Cram did not care for "extremes" and was suspicious of the "too radical" Republicans. But he was also deeply annoyed by the Copperhead Democrats who would give up the war for the Union. As for slavery and emancipation, Cram concluded that he was "perfectly willing to withdraw the [emancipation] proclamation if the rebels would lay down their arms and come back to the Union as it was." Slavery, he thought, "would soon die anyhow."[25]

Like both Dawes and Cram, Charles T. Kruse and the 50th Ohio guarded a series of railroad bridges across deep ravines in Kentucky, near the Tennessee state line. Kruse, who began the war as a Democrat fighting for the Union, was intensely suspicious of Lincoln's Emancipation Proclamation. "I did not come to fight and perrel [sic] my life in the battle field for that cursed raice [sic] of nigers," he wrote his parents in early January 1863. If the war freed blacks, he vowed, "I will kill every one I come acrost."[26]

Within a few days, however, Kruse had come to a somewhat different understanding. The "strength and wealth" of the South was held in slaves and "until their strength is destroyed we can not expect to conqur [sic] them." The destruction of the railroad tunnels and bridges by Morgan's guerrillas seemed only to confirm Kruse's convictions, as he stood watch, fought off boredom, and awaited another attack. Kruse hoped that Charleston, Richmond, and Vicksburg would fall before summer. "Burn them all," he urged, "destroy as we take and they will have nothing to come back after. Not withhold destruction because it is in our country but let us conquer them and we can soon build again." Kruse followed

George N. Barnard, *Fortified Railroad Bridge Across Cumberland River,*
Nashville, Tennessee, 1864.

Confederate guerrilla forces, often operating as regular cavalry units, attacked Union-
controlled railroad lines. They shot into trains, destroyed tracks, took prisoners, killed
Union soldiers, and burned bridges. Union commanders responded by developing block
houses and fortified bridges to protect the vulnerable lines, equipping trains with special
armor, recruiting loyal local citizens to ferret out guerrillas, and dispatching special
counterinsurgency cavalry units to track down the Confederate guerrillas.

(LC-B811-2642, Lot 4177, Division of Prints and Photographs, Library of Congress)

Morgan's exploits in the newspapers and listened to the constant rumors that circulated up and down the railroad. In letter after letter he sent home to his parents, Kruse referred to the elusive Morgan. He had good reason to be concerned. Confederates attacked trains throughout Tennessee in early 1863. In a typical attack on April 13, 1863, 200–300 guerrillas derailed a Union troop train, opened fire, captured the mail, and set fire to the cars. Eighteen Union soldiers were killed and nine Confederate guerrillas died.[27]

Indeed, the Union strategy to defeat Confederate partisans and guerrillas increasingly depended on a systematic effort to control the railroads, run them for the army, defend them with blockhouses and fortifications, and repair them whenever damaged. At turns, the Union army destroyed railroad facilities to cut off or cripple the South's armies, then rebuilt them to serve as networks solely for extending the Union army ever deeper into the South. Tennessee, especially the nexus of rails in western Tennessee between Memphis and Nashville, served as the earliest training ground for Union generals in the importance and reach of the railroads and how to defeat guerrillas and partisans.

In response to the increased Federal security of the railroads, Morgan decided to follow the lines north and stage an attack across the border. Northern railroad companies in Ohio volunteered their employees to guard all of the intersections and road crossings for ten miles on either side of the railroads. But Federal troops captured Morgan in July 1863 in Ohio after he had ridden through Indiana and penetrated farther north than any other Confederate commander would in the course of the entire war. Dozens of his men were killed in the fighting and hundreds captured, but the raid terrorized the border North. That it did not ignite Confederate sympathizers in the region drew some comment but mattered little. Morgan's path of destruction suggested the ease with which rivers and borders might be crossed and the weaknesses in the systems of rail and wire in the North. He was held for a short time in the Ohio Penitentiary near Scioto. But in early 1864 Morgan escaped, jumped on a southbound train near the prison, and made his way back across the Ohio River into the Confederacy.[28]

To some northern observers Morgan's exploits constituted only the most dramatic of what was an increasingly large-scale problem. Guerrillas, partisans, and Confederate cavalry raiders combined in 1862 and 1863 to execute hundreds of attacks. It seemed a deluge. Dozens of Union soldiers were killed, captured, and wounded in these small engagements. The toll was mounting and there seemed no end in sight. And the difficulties in defending against these incursions increased in turn. After a particularly large attack near Humboldt, Tennessee, the Chicago *Times* noted that General U. S. Grant's army depended on a single strand of telegraph wire for 240 miles—which "costs thousands to guard its entire length." Indeed, the *Times* fretted that "history seldom records so large an army hanging . . . by so long and slender a thread."[29]

Guerrilla and partisan forces in the South did more than annoy the Union army along the rail lines. They killed thousands of soldiers and captured large quantities of materiel and arms. Some estimates suggest that more than 30,000 Confederate guerrillas operated in the war along the railroad war zones.[30]

By 1863, with tens of thousands of Confederate guerrillas operating in the field, Union trainmen worried about security more than anything else. One wrote the U.S. Military Railroads commander, Herman Haupt, and complained about the uncertain security of the Alexandria to Manassas route. There were trains rolling down the line with expensive stores "in transit," and there were paymasters loaded with cash "traveling" in the passenger cars. These were easy and attractive targets for guerrillas. And along the line, the railroad had a woodpile where "60 contraband choppers sleep in the woods." The black men every night put "their own pickets out" and were "with difficulty kept at work." They too feared for their lives. Meanwhile, Confederate partisan John S. Mosby and his men prowled along the rail line, hiding in the pine thickets, ready to attack. So, the Union army began clear-cutting and removing all timber within one mile of the Orange & Alexandria Railroad "to break up the lurking places of guerrillas."[31]

When guerrillas attacked a train en route, the situation prompted a host of questions: should the engineer let off steam and put on the brakes, should passengers jump, should the conductor refuse to answer questions? In August 1862, when fifty guerrillas fired into a passenger train on the Winchester Railroad in northern Virginia, the *New York Times* upbraided the conductor for "foolishly" stopping the train. Everyone searched for guidance—how to behave in these alarming situations—but they had little to go on and were often second-guessed.[32]

The back-and-forth cavalry, partisan, and guerrilla raids along the borders of the two warring nations created a widely experienced, or at least imagined, variant of the army's large-scale battles. As Confederates fired into trains, derailed cars, and stopped passengers, as they burned bridges, captured workers, and killed guards, a microwar took place that involved citizens in the North and South in ways the largest battles did not. The ebb and flow of the railroads and telegraphs helped sustain these operations because they were regular, daily, and predictable. And the associations of the railroads and telegraphs with connection, modernity, and "the outside world" only increased the importance of this zone of the war. Until 1864, when Union general William T. Sherman asserted total control over the railroads in his operations, the guerrillas and their exploits suggested that the North might never fully conquer the southern nation.

What often began as incursions to cut the railroads by one side or the other sometimes quickly devolved into all manner of destruction. To "tear up" the railroad escalated into more widespread violence, whether perpetrated by guerrillas or by regular forces. A young Confederate in Virginia, for example, reported to his mother in May 1863 that his unit met the Union cavalry as it tried to wreck the Virginia Central Railroad near Louisa Court House. "They have burned all the bridges over the canal," he noted, "and all the barns and stables and every thing like food on the other side of the River from here." The Union forces tried to destroy the aqueduct over the Rivanna River and they "shot a young man . . . yesterday 3 times and then cut his head off and roled [*sic*] him in the canal right before his mother and Father's eyes."[33]

In another corner of the Confederacy, the *New York Times* correspondent went on patrol in Louisiana with the 177th New York and the 14th Maine to hunt down the "Gonzales" guerrilla band operating along the New Orleans, Jackson and Great Northern Railroad. The Union forces burned railroad bridges, captured twenty Choctaw Indians, torched the railroad town at Ponchatoula, seized a Confederate shoe factory, and sent out teams of "scouting parties" to find Gonzales. One Union soldier got lost, however, and stumbled into the guerrilla camp by mistake. The guerrillas "did not keep him a prisoner but instead blew his brains out with a shotgun." In retaliation the Union forces burned the railroad station at Tangipahoa, Louisiana, took all the sugar they could find in Confederate warehouses, and distributed it "to the poor."[34]

Both sides grew concerned about the lack of discipline that followed such destruction and violence. The Union army, which had created buffers around railroads and telegraphs, meted out severe punishments for cutting the wires or interfering with trains, and began hunting down and killing guerrillas from Virginia to Mississippi. The army also began to consider other ways to deal with the guerrilla menace. The internal violence of eastern Tennessee as well as of parts of Arkansas, Missouri, and western Virginia, were bypassed and contained. Because so much of the guerrilla action centered on the railroads and telegraphs, William T. Sherman came to the conclusion that only total dominance over the rail network would ensure the ongoing operations of his army and render the guerrilla attacks an annoyance rather than a matter of real consequence. Thousands of soldiers in 1864 and a highly organized U.S. Military Railroads repair force were deployed to protect the railroad war zone. Union officers dispatched special units to find the partisans, hunt them down, and prevent civilians from supporting their operations.

In Louisiana the Union army raised a regiment of black troops and dispatched them to defend the New Orleans, Opelousas and Great Western Railroad against Confederate guerrillas. The First Louisiana, also called the "Native Guard," secured the railroad up to Thibodeaux, Louisiana, and along the way helped repair the bridges and culverts that the Confederates had wrecked in their retreat. Black soldiers, writing letters back to New Orleans, commented on every aspect of their service—the "progress" in civilization that the war represented, the insults they tolerated from rebels in New Orleans, the segregation that streetcar conductors tried to impose on them, and the pride they took in rebuilding the railroads "as quickly as they were destroyed."[35]

Blacks in other parts of the South, especially in Virginia, Tennessee, and Kentucky, had already begun to work for the Federal armies to rebuild and main-

*Pickets of the 1st Louisiana "Native Guard" Guarding the New Orleans,
Opelousas and Great Western Railroad.*

United States Colored Troops (U.S.C.T.) recruiters in 1863 fanned out
along the railroads, especially in Tennessee, stopping at depots along the
route to sign up soldiers. Over 180,000 black men volunteered and enlisted
for service in the U.S.C.T. Both white regiments and U.S.C.T. units found
themselves guarding railroads and watching for guerrillas.

(*Frank Leslie's Illustrated*, March 7, 1863, University of Nebraska-Lincoln Libraries)

tain the railroads in the war effort. Report after report indicated black participation in Union railroad crews and enlistment in United States Colored Troops
regiments. Charles T. Kruse wrote from Glasgow, Kentucky, that his regiment
included fifteen blacks "digging up the stumps about the camp and round the
fort" and helping to protect the vital railroad. Blacks were working on the railroads too, often on the "wood train" as choppers and sawyers, but also as firemen,
brakemen, and general laborers. When working on the railroads in remote areas,
however, they were exposed and vulnerable to guerrilla forces, which subjected
those they captured to various fates: reenslavement, beatings, death, and robbery.
Their work for the Union war effort, however, constituted an important contrast

to the guerrilla activity in the railroad zone. Blacks across the South seized emancipation and used their labor and skill to help secure the railroads for the Union army.[36]

This second, and equally important, consequence of the war zones around the railroads emerged in the first year of the war—they were corridors of freedom for thousands of former slaves. The junctions and depots became some of the earliest sites of black free labor work, as northern commanders hired, and sometimes impressed, "contraband" labor along the railroads. Eventually, hundreds were employed by the U.S. Military Railroads machine shops in Nashville. Hundreds more worked for the U.S. Military Railroads in what became known as the Construction Corps, rebuilding bridges and rail lines all over the sprawling Department of the Mississippi. By the end of the war the U.S. Military Railroads was running the longest, and possibly the largest, most comprehensive experiment in black free labor employment in the occupied South.[37]

The earliest evidence of black work on the Union military railroads came from Alexandria, Virginia, in 1861 and early 1862. There, and around Norfolk, Virginia, the Union army established its first control over Confederate territory at important rail heads. In both places the War Department began running the sections of railroads that the Union army captured. Because the Norfolk and Petersburg Railroad employed dozens of slaves, and because the Richmond, Fredericksburg & Potomac (R. F. & P.), which terminated at Alexandria, ran its operation with hundreds of slaves, the War Department found itself nominally in charge of some of these men in 1861. Most worked on maintenance, doing the heavy labor of repair and track laying, but some were brakemen and firemen working on the trains. Others were wood choppers, cutting lumber for ties and fuel.

Evidence remains sketchy about how freedmen moved into this work in the first year of the war, but former slaves marshaled whatever resources they could and offered their labor and skills to the Union cause as soon as practical. Thousands of freedmen were impressed by the Union army in Tennessee to rebuild the railroads around Nashville and haul the army's supplies from the depots to the warehouses. The army provided minimal shelter, and hundreds of black refugees died of disease and exposure in the "contraband camps." But public outrage over the terrible conditions led to improved sanitation and security in the camps. Moreover, work in these places led to freedom, as former slaves demonstrated their value to the cause. In March 1862 northern newspapers reported that ninety-seven former slaves had been transported to freedom in Philadelphia. They took a train north out of Washington, D.C., or perhaps Alexandria, Virginia, and then in Baltimore they switched to the Philadelphia, Wilmington, and Baltimore Railroad. "Most of these contrabands," the *New York Herald* reported, "have been engaged with Banks's division, repairing railroads on the Upper Potomac." Indeed, on April 18, the *Richmond Daily Dispatch* reported that thirty-six

Contrabands at Cumberland Landing, Virginia, May 1862.

In the Peninsular Campaign, Federal forces encountered thousands of former slaves who sought freedom and work in the Union army camps. Even if slaves fled slavery, their status was unclear in the first year of the war. In July 1862 Congress declared such refugees from slavery "forever and henceforth free." (Library of Congress)

slaves had run away from the R. F. & P., almost certainly to the Union army. One of them, a slave named "John Henry," was "owned by Mrs. B. B. Wright," and he was twenty-six years old and described as "5 feet 10 inches high, black, [and] slow spoken." Whether he became the John Henry of railroad legend on the C & O cannot be known, but the R. F. & P. was still looking for these former slaves three months later. None had returned or been recaptured.[38]

In May 1862, when McClellan's campaign for Richmond went into full swing, the presence of the Union army widened and more former slaves fled to the railroad corridors to escape bondage and, wherever possible, to demonstrate their support for the war and help fight it. As Union general Irvin McDowell's forces slowly moved down the R. F. & P. Railroad that month, he gave specific orders that all "colored fugitives" who came into the lines "will be enrolled and registered as heretofore prescribed." McDowell explained further that the ex-slaves would "relieve, as far as possible, the troops from labor at depots and on railroads. These fugitives will wear a uniform badge . . . , to designate them in gangs of tens and hundreds."[39]

Because the Confederate army had pulled up the rails of the R. F. & P. during its retreat out of northern Virginia, as well as burned the big bridges at Accokeek, Potomac Creek, and the Rappahannock River, McDowell used every available resource to rebuild them. The work went forward, he remarked, with "the troops, aided by such colored fugitives as could be had, and, when possible, the work was pushed night and day." The bridge over the Rappahannock was 600 feet long and 65 feet high, and the one over the Potomac Creek 400 feet long and 80 feet high. Rebuilt by the Union troops and ex-slaves working together, these new bridges elicited wonder from foreign officers touring with the Union army in 1862. Each bridge, according to McDowell, "ignores all the rules and procedures of military science as laid down in books." The hastily built bridges were "constructed chiefly of round sticks cut from the woods, and not even divested of bark . . . [were] four stories, three of trestles and one of crib work . . . [and] carries daily from ten to twenty heavy railway trains in both directions." The big Rappahannock bridge was rebuilt in nine working days and contained more than two million feet of lumber. The original structure took nine months to complete, but McDowell's force of former slaves and Union soldiers threw up the new bridges and repaired the railroad in a few weeks. Along the R. F. & P. corridor, McDowell ordered all property necessary to be seized for the Union army. Former slaves were brought into his operations and were paid for their work. "Lumber was taken wherever it could be found," he reported, "nearly all the timber suitable for bridging was exhausted in the vicinity of Potomac Creek." The army commandeered "a large machine shop and foundry, with all the machinery and tools." Former slaves, or "colored fugitives," as McDowell called them, "were employed and to the extent of all that could possibly be procured."[40]

After Lee drove McClellan away from Richmond and took the Confederate army on the offensive in August 1862, the war zones shifted again throughout northern Virginia. Lee's army advanced north, recapturing large sections of the state, and retaking the vital railroads. The Union forces pulled away from their advanced positions along the R. F. & P. Railroad and retreated back up its line toward Washington, prompting the Confederate railroad operators to move back in on the R. F. & P. The superintendent immediately took out advertisements in the *Richmond Daily Dispatch* for the thirty-six slaves who had run away in April and put up an additional five-dollar reward for their recapture. Meanwhile, the Union troops burned their magnificent new bridges over the Rappahannock River, Potomac Creek, and Accoceek Creek, and they loaded the locomotives onto barges and floated them north to Alexandria. As the Union army withdrew up the railroad from Fredericksburg, black families went with the Union forces. Colonel W. W. Wright, the engineer and superintendent of the U.S. Military Railroads, witnessed the evacuation: "The contrabands fairly swarmed about the Fredericksburg and Falmouth stations, and there was a continuous black line of men, women, and children moving north along the [rail] road, carrying all their worldly goods on their heads. Every train running to Aquia was crowded with them." According to Wright, well over ten thousand contrabands walked or rode on the tracks north toward freedom. A similarly large number came to the Union

Andrew J. Russell, *African American Laborers on the U.S. Military Railroad in Northern Virginia*, c. 1862/1863.

From the beginning of the Civil War, African Americans worked on the railroads, transferring their labor to the Union cause.

(Lot 9209, No. 49a, Division of Prints and Photographs, Library of Congress)

army in New Bern, North Carolina, in 1862 and began working to rebuild railroad bridges, load trains, and cut timber.[41]

While such military reports gave accurate estimates of the numbers of contrabands following the railroads north, the total number of former slaves working on the military railroads remained less clear in 1861 and 1862. Yet, the determination of freed people to support the Union war effort and to work for a wage impressed military commanders, and black work on the railroads became so important that it could not be taken for granted. In October 1862 in Norfolk the U.S. Military Railroads employed dozens of black men on the Norfolk and Petersburg line, probably the railroad's former slaves. According to the commander running the operations out of Norfolk, Colonel E. L. Wentz, the "negro force" was "in Government employ." That is, when the army took over the railroad, it began paying the contrabands immediately. But the men were working almost entirely without shoes. And because there were "no shoes in Norfolk" that they could purchase, Wentz worried that even giving the men an advance or paying them their due wages would not solve the problem. With winter weather approaching, Wentz felt "obliged to dispense with their services altogether" unless the government could procure and supply shoes for the men.[42]

Working without shoes, a little over a year into the war, these former slaves along the railroad were nonetheless now free men, working for a wage. On the R. F. & P. line, where hundreds of slaves were bonded to work before the war, in March 1863 black men filled all sorts of positions for the U.S. Military Railroads. In a report detailing the payroll at Aquia Creek, the superintendent listed fifteen "engine wipers (contrabands)" out of sixty-four total employees there. In the Maintenance of Way department, he reported seventeen contrabands as wood sawyers, twenty-six more as wood sawyers at Aquia Creek, and nine as laborers. The men were living in a place he called "Contrabandville."[43]

Despite the work they did and the deprivations they endured, the black laborers on the railroads found themselves treated differently than whites. When Wentz testified before the American Freedmen's Inquiry Commission in 1863, he admitted as much. Over the previous year Wentz said he had "several thousand contrabands" working for him on the railroad. He admired their hard work and told the commission that "on the average" he could get "in this climate 33 pr. cent more work out of them than out of white laborers." But he also let it be known that he paid them half of what he paid white laborers for the same work, fifteen dollars rather than thirty. "I can effect with contraband labor things which I would not undertake with white labor," Wentz explained. Black laborers could take a stack of hard lumber eighteen inches square and sixty feet long and "lift it by main force breast high into the cars." Irish labor, he pointed out, could do no such thing.[44]

Wentz also explained just how many contraband wished to work. Wentz let it be known around Norfolk that he paid fifteen dollars a month and rations. "At any time," he said, he could get "within twelve hours 300 good hands" and 500 willing black men in forty-eight hours. After each job, whether cutting timber, laying track, grading, or moving earth, Wentz simply dismissed the whole force, knowing he could easily hire more. Still, Wentz looked out for these men in a general way, condemning the common malfeasance in the Quartermaster's office, where contrabands were "played" and in general treated poorly, often not getting "near what they are entitled to."[45]

The early use of black labor on the railroads in Virginia grew substantially as the northern forces moved into Tennessee in 1862 and 1863. By 1863 Colonel Herman Haupt, the Union army's brilliant railroad engineer in charge of the U.S. Military Railroads, had created a "construction corps" in Tennessee, with 200 bridge carpenters and 300 contrabands on his payroll.[46] Hundreds were employed in the railroad mechanic's shops in Nashville. This operation was the beginning of a wartime force eventually organized as the U.S. Military Railroads Construction

African American wood choppers' hut on the Orange & Alexandria Railroad.

Black men, many of them formerly enslaved on the South's railroads,
chopped timber for railroad ties, bridges, and fuel for the U.S. Military Railroads.
Stationed at remote camps, such as this, they also faced the constant danger of
Confederate partisan and guerrilla raids. (National Archives and Records Administration)

Corps, which by 1864 employed over 9,000 men to rebuild bridges and repair railroads. Thousands of these men were Northerners, recruited by agents sent to the northern cities. But as many as 1,000 or more may have been freedmen and freedwomen. Thousands of other black workers may have worked on railroads outside of these districts as well.

Because wartime wages were high in the North and because many northern white railroad workers chose to remain with their companies, the military railroad officials in Huntsville, Alabama, employed "quite a number of contrabands." The U.S. Military Railroads was able to use black labor admittedly "at low wages." But these men, like their shoeless counterparts in Norfolk at the beginning of the war, could not afford "clothing for the winter season" because the camp sutlers charged the highest prices they could fetch. So, the railroad officials at the Huntsville station asked the army Quartermaster's Department to sell standard-issue government clothing to the black workers—"such things as they may need"—at the cheaper government rate. Up the chain of command, they argued that the black workers needed provisions and that they would "pay on delivery of the articles" with their wages and that "all that is wanted is authority to sell to them." Finally, the Quartermaster's office agreed and ordered its local officers to sell clothing to the freedmen "when paid for."[47]

Such victories were small but meaningful. As the war went on in 1864 and Sherman's army pushed south from Tennessee into Georgia, the value of the black workers became increasingly apparent on the railroads, and the corridor of their work expanded. Railroad officials became ever more responsive to these men, probably because the former slaves made repeated requests for better clothing and conditions. One military railroad official in Nashville explained to his superiors that there were "four or five Negro men at work for me who have families and they are bothered a great deal to find houses for them." He asked directly: "Can anything be done to build these boys some small houses?" A few days later the reply came down the chain of command: "The houses will be built and on any location [the captain] may select."[48]

In Tennessee black men were working as mechanics in the shops and as blacksmiths. Some worked for government contractors on construction and grading crews. Other freedmen and women worked directly for the U.S. Military Railroads as brakemen, yard employees, cooks, and laborers. Thomas Greggs, Frank Banks, Mitchell Tally, James Coffee, Walter Gilbert, Albert Staples, and Dick Jackson were paid sixty-two dollars a month, the same as the white men on the line. George Jackson, a freedman laborer in the Construction Corps, earned one dollar and twenty-five cents a day, the same as the white laborers. Dan Black, a freedman track layer in an otherwise all-Irish gang, also earned the same as the white men. They rode the trains with government-issued passes all over Tennessee, traveling to wherever their work was most needed.[49]

United States Colored Troops recruiters showed up at the military railroad sites where thousands of black men were working and opened up enlistment offices. Union general Grenville Dodge, charged with rebuilding a railroad in western Virginia, tried to ban recruiters from accessing his workers. He was concerned they would all leave to fight in the war. In Tennessee, near the border with Mississippi, Alabama, and Georgia, the army's senior officers promoted black enlistment up and down the railroad line. General Lorenzo Thomas stopped at the depot in Moscow, Tennessee, on his way to the junction at Corinth, Mississippi. The 53rd Ohio, Ephraim C. Dawes's unit, was ordered to give a "salute at the depot" and to hear Thomas give a speech. Dawes reported that "the recruits for the negro regt. here turned out and were hugely tickled." As for the white soldiers, the reaction was less positive. The speech had "a rather bad effect," Dawes noted that night in his diary. "The men were already converted and did not like to be argued into a thing they had already made up their minds was right," he explained. At another stop on Thomas's tour, the 90th Illinois, an Irish regiment, "hissed" Thomas on the idea of raising black troops at all.[50]

But blacks stepped forward to offer the most detailed knowledge about the

South's railroads and to aid northern commanders in finding and understanding the network, and they volunteered to fight. They possessed critical local knowledge about the railroads, their facilities, their timetables, their schedules, their engineers, and their geographic locations. In December 1861 near Hilton Head, South Carolina, as the Union navy went ashore, several black volunteers contacted Union army officers and offered to go on a special mission to burn the principal railroad bridges between Charleston and Savannah. The commanding engineer of the Union expeditionary force there recommended following up on the offer: "From a military point of view its destruction would be of great value to us."[51]

In other instances black guides located key sites on the rail network and coordinated Union attacks with the schedules of trains. In October 1862 a combined army-navy operation attempted to take out the Charleston & Savannah Railroad near the Coosawhatchie River. Their contraband guide led them to the railroad, where they intercepted a Confederate troop train steaming down the tracks. The Union force "directed a heavy and rapid fire upon it" and destroyed the train. "We left a number of the enemy dead and wounded on the track," the commanding officer dryly summarized.[52]

The war zones around the railroads opened up all sorts of opportunities for black freedom. Black railroad workers at depots and junctions across the Confederacy used the railroads to leave slavery and join the Union cause. As acts of personal mobility, these examples of black emancipation had extended repercussions, well beyond the South. Contrabands migrated in the war to Iowa, Minnesota, and other states in the upper Midwest, where they were both welcomed and feared, given employment and discriminated against. Northern soldiers sometimes sent ex-slaves north on the trains, with letters of explanation for the soldiers' family to employ them on the farm. When several hundred contrabands arrived in Saint Paul, Minnesota, however, rumors spread quickly among whites that more were coming and that they would take advantage of the situation to get jobs vacated by white men gone to fight the war. Iowa, which had barred black settlement in 1851, had about 1,000 black residents in 1860. By 1865 there were 3,600, largely because of the war and the movement out of slavery.[53]

Near the "Long Bridge" over the Potomac River in Alexandria, Virginia, thousands of refugees from Petersburg and Richmond gathered at the end of the war. The Union army built shelters, and a small city sprang up on the banks of the Potomac. In the South, wherever the Union army went, black free labor on the railroads followed. In Louisville, Kentucky, another railroad gateway, approximately 7,000 migrating blacks traveled through the city and across the border to Ohio, Indiana, and Illinois in just one month—January 1864. The war was full of movement for people. Nothing, it appeared, was stationary.[54]

The war zones around the railroads offered immediate opportunities for black freedom and black free labor, as well as a striking contrast to the prewar slaveholding railroad companies of the South. While Confederate officials organized the impressment of black enslaved labor and haggled with white slaveholders over these terms, the Union army offered wages and promised freedom. Black workers showed their knowledge and capability to Union soldiers, and black soldiers were recruited and drawn into military service along the railroads. In the depots, stations, and trains, blacks gained visibility and status; their presence, expertise, and sheer physical labor were undeniably valuable. Before the railroads became visible as the core strategy of the northern command in 1864, they had already become the principal zones for new forms of violence and freedom.

Chapter 6

The Confederate Nation "Cut Off from the World"

WHEN the United States of America split into two competing nations in the winter of 1860–1861, many people in Britain, France, and Europe were surprised at the news. Months and weeks went by in 1860 without much comment on American affairs before the election of Abraham Lincoln. Then, when South Carolina and the cotton states began to secede, many Europeans were caught off guard. Few predicted the breakup of the Union over a presidential election, and almost nobody expected a bloody, long, and destructive war in America. The British businessman and statesman Richard Cobden, who had traveled through the United States just eighteen months earlier, was "astonished" at the news. The prominent London banker Lionel de Rothschild kept as closely informed as anyone about U.S. political and financial affairs through his firm's American agent, August Belmont, who was based in New York City. From December 1860 to April 1861, Belmont wrote mournfully about the looming division of the states, and what he saw as the manipulative behavior of politicians on both sides. He was also clearly pained by the searing experience of a national schism.[1]

From the London office, however, the Rothschild firm replied to Belmont's private letters with worldly realism. "If separation be really unavoidable," they wrote at the height of the crisis, "we hope it may be done peaceably, and the question now with us should be to see how we can turn the altered state of affairs to our advantage." As early as March 1861, other London financiers were already making loans to banking firms in the new Confederacy.[2]

An immediate set of decisions was presented to the London bankers—should they do business with the new Confederate nation? Despite the Rothschilds' consistent antislavery position, and despite the firm's forceful role in the British abolition of slavery, they were pragmatic businessmen and, like many others, had a complicit relationship with slavery. They kept many southern clients, traded in vast quantities of southern tobacco and cotton, and invested in southern state bonds, which financed the huge railroad boom in the South built almost entirely

Lionel Nathan de Rothschild was one of a handful of powerful
transatlantic bankers who emerged with the marketing of U.S. and state
bonds, railroad securities, and agricultural commodities in Europe.
Rothschild held antislavery convictions but expected the Confederacy
to become independent. The firm's southern businesses collapsed in
the Civil War, and the transatlantic bankers' pragmatism and
neutrality effectively isolated the Confederacy.

(Reproduced with the permission of the Rothschild Archive)

with slave labor. And because southern clients sometimes listed slaves as collateral or as assets on balance sheets, the prominent London bankers, whether Rothschild, Peabody, or Baring Brothers, found themselves one step removed from the slavery economy of the U.S. South and, after 1861, the American Civil War.[3]

And, like many observers in Europe, the Rothschild firm could see only one result from the American crisis: two nations, two confederacies, two peoples, North and South, irreconcilably split. It seemed unlikely that the North could force a region as large, wealthy, and modern as the South to remain in the Union against its will.[4]

Clearly, the Confederacy's idea of itself as a modern nation was tied to its standing in the world. To be viable, a nation needed to be globally engaged, to announce its autonomy, and to have that respected and reciprocated by others in the world. These expectations could take various forms—not only diplomatic but also social, not only public but also private. Confederates, especially the planters and businessmen at the center of the nation's institutions, had long been on the edge of shifting borders, and their cultural and economic vitality rested in large measure on their society's openness. Before the war they were connected to plantations in the West Indies, the Bahamas, Mexico, and Cuba, and to banking houses in London, Paris, and Frankfurt. Their cosmopolitanism has gone largely unrecognized until quite recently. Southern slaveholders as a whole constituted a highly mobile, restless, and internationally minded class. They were used to negotiating various networks of association and information—from the transatlantic to the regional, and from the regional to the local. And they saw themselves modernizing their society with railroads and telegraphs in a world that was rapidly taking shape around aggressive nation-states whose borders were becoming ever more sharply defined.[5]

One of the first tests of the Confederacy in its capacity as a nation was the way it would be received in the private transatlantic financial markets. At the beginning of the war the Confederacy had some real advantages in this arena. Lionel de Rothschild and other leading European citizens thought that the question in front of the Americans, and indeed the world, was simply whether there would be peace or war before what appeared to be an inevitable separation.

Cotton occupied only one aspect of the U.S. trade relationship with Britain. Probably as significant, if often overlooked, were the Anglo-American banking houses that had grown up around the industrial expansion between 1820 and 1860. Firms such as Baring Brothers, George Peabody, and N. M. Rothschild & Sons were the most prominent and influential of these bankers. Around 1852 each began investing in U.S. railroads. All told, British capital investment in the United States has been estimated at £60 million in 1854, but the exact size and distribution of this investment remain unclear. At the time, the *Economist*, a leading financial journal, estimated British investment in the United States to be much higher, at £100 million in 1860. Out of the 244 railroads surveyed by the U.S. secretary of the treasury in 1853, 76 reported that they had direct foreign investment in the form of stocks or bonds.[6]

Less visible than equity stock ownership but equally important were bond investments that British and European investors made in the 1850s in railroad company, state, and city bonds. Of the 244 U.S. railroads that reported foreign investment, four-fifths of the total value was held in company bonds. So, in general, while U.S. citizens held stock in American railroads, Europeans purchased bonds.

As an example, foreign investors held $2.5 million of the $3 million in Pennsylvania Railroad bonds, and $7 million of the $19.2 million in New York and Erie bonds. European investors held all of the bonds of the Alabama and Tennessee Railroad. Because the southern states used state bonds to finance railroad construction, British and European bankers invested heavily in these instruments as well, helping to underwrite the decade's massive railroad expansion. Over 70 percent of all foreign investment in the United States in the 1850s was placed in public debt—mostly state bonds. As a result, while cotton occupied significant attention in all quarters, the flow of commercial and financial investment had gone both to the northern and the southern nations, much of it in the form of heavily traded bonds that came with the railroads.[7]

Everywhere European investors looked, the age was one of national formation, war, and technological eruption. The United States and the Confederate States appeared as nations among nations, and part of the wider pattern of the era. In Britain, where radical leaders had widened the franchise, ended the slave trade, and brought down trade barriers, opinion makers applauded the progress of national self-determination. In 1859, as the small region of Piedmont struggled to break free from the Austrian empire and join Italy in a newly formed nation-state based on common heritage and ideas of personal freedom, Britons cheered. When the southern Confederacy broke from the Union a year later, its struggle for national independence seemed similarly motivated and no less worthy. That most of the leading Confederate states' railroads were financed through state bonds with British capital was not widely known, but the connections would play an important role in any potential movement to extend the Confederacy diplomatic recognition.[8]

In 1861, therefore, the American South's claim to national status struck many in Europe as entirely natural and legitimate, if grossly marred by slavery. This paradox of the South as a recognizable nation with an unrecognizable claim to civilization gave Europeans pause. The long history of cotton and its importance in Britain was complicated by the more recent developments surrounding railroads and transatlantic banking. Within a year the American war took shape as something different, and new, and terrible, but with important ideas at stake.

Over the course of the war, the idea of the Confederacy as a modern nation competed with the reality of an ever-tightening blockade. The blockade worked not only to damage the southern economy but also to endanger the Confederate claim to nationhood and jeopardize its modern systems of information, trade, and reciprocal relationships in the world. The combined naval–land assaults on the Confederate ports and the railroad networks that extended from them eventually clamped the South's communications arteries, captured key points on its vaunted railroad network, and did what the naval blockade alone could not effectively accomplish. Together, these actions rendered the South a nation cut off from the world and led white Southerners to reconsider their nation's viability. One measure of the Confederacy's failure was the gradual removal of its citizens from correspondence with the world's modern nations. The northern blockade and later its one-by-one capture of the Confederate ports and railroads became an especially effective instrument in the South's suffocation. The blockade did more than eliminate supplies or restrict the exports of cotton. The blockade affected the way white Southerners experienced time and understood their place in the world.

The blockade went into effect on April 19, 1861, when Lincoln issued a Proclamation of Blockade sealing the commercial ports across the South. Lincoln's order spoke of an "insurrection" and a "combination of persons" who were preventing the regular collection of revenue in United States ports in the South. At the same time, he used formal language indicating he would "set on foot a blockade of the ports" to enforce the laws of the United States and "the law of Nations."

The effectiveness of the blockade has been a matter of some debate. Historians have concluded that approximately 1,800 ships ran the blockade in the war and that as many as 18,000 shipments may have crossed the lines overland, as Confederates exported 500,000 bales of cotton to Britain and France and another 900,000 bales to the North. Over 400,000 rifles and 1 million lead bullets came into the Confederacy through the blockade. By this measure the blockade was a sieve, but by other, less tangible ones the blockade did severe damage. The creeping sense of self-doubt, the growing feelings of isolation, and the frustrated restriction of trade and travel all indicated for Confederate civilians that their modern world was collapsing around them. The Union's increasingly well-organized blockade board began setting and targeting more systematic priorities, focusing mainly on Confederate ports with railroad links.[9]

Once the blockade went into effect, and once postal, rail, and telegraph communications were strained, the South's relative isolation from the world jeopardized its claim to national status and recognition. The most active proponents in Britain for recognizing the South had almost no direct contact with Confederate citizens during the war. Instead, they communicated with William L. Yancey, James M. Mason, John Slidell, and other Confederate diplomats and envoys who made it to Europe. There were no Confederate counterparts to the extensive transatlantic networks and correspondence of Harriet Martineau, the prolific London *Daily Mail* political economist on American affairs, or Richard Cobden, whose U.S. travels gave him wide contacts in government, railroad companies, business, and elite society. Instead, a region—the South—that boasted few international men and women of letters seemed to have staked a tenuous national claim on the basis of slavery, railroads, cotton, and state's rights, a set of principles that could be neither adequately communicated or defended.[10]

As the effect of the blockade took hold in the daily lives of Confederate citizens, the scope of their world began to shrink, and the feeling of being disconnected from the world grew in turn. Confederate civilians put on a brave face and took pride in homespun clothing and making do, but the social effects of their isolation were disturbing. Most immediately, prices skyrocketed and goods once easily available became scarce. Sarah L. Jones, a British traveler in the South during the secession crisis, found herself "blockaded" and stranded in the region. What began as a picturesque adventure into Virginia society suddenly took on a new urgency. In her 1863 reminiscence, *Life in the South: From the Commencement of the War by a Blockaded British Subject*, Jones explained to her readers the shock of war as it appeared in everyday life, concluding that "war is hard to realize." She meant principally that the passing of time slowed down in war in ways that those on the outside of a besieged nation could not fully comprehend. As the regular, twenty-four-hour cycle of mail and correspondence was interrupted, altered, and redirected, she felt that time itself was distorted or warped. While she waited for news, the rest of the world moved at the old pace, making the difference in experiences even more distressing.[11]

The railroads, which so reliably brought mail, news, and passengers from the "outside world" to hundreds of communities, no longer operated in the same way nor, in the case of the Confederacy, with the same extensiveness. They were crowded with troops and supplies, being rushed to the edges of the new nation. And these roads abruptly ended where they had once continued, cut off at the lines of the war zone or captured territory. Jones realized that to get home from Virginia would require a five-day trip by horse through the mountains of western Virginia to a point beyond Harper's Ferry on the Baltimore & Ohio Railroad, and from there a railroad journey west to Pittsburgh and back east to a northern port. With time and geography so radically broken at the beginning of the war, the Confederacy experienced an abrupt moment of truth. Could a nation claim its place in the world if its citizens could not send and receive mail or travel without interruption?[12]

A month after the announcement of the northern blockade, a more mundane but no less momentous event cast white Southerners into unfamiliar territory. The interruption of mail services with the North took effect May 31, 1861. At midnight on that day letters addressed to points in states that seceded were no longer delivered or carried on the U.S. mails. In this early test of its resilience, the Confederate government responded with extraordinary effectiveness. Confederate postmaster general John Reagan raided the U.S. Postal Service, recruited most of the Southerners in the bureaucracy, and reproduced the forms, system, and organization of the U.S. postal system in the South. The mails continued with seamless interruption, at least inside the Confederacy.[13]

Southern banking houses, credit and financial firms, and cotton and tobacco brokers that communicated with their northern and British counterparts, however, had their businesses suspended immediately. The Rothschild firm, for example, kept steady correspondence with agents in New Orleans, Richmond, and Baltimore for years. In early May 1861 Chieves and Osborn, the Rothschilds'

Wreck of blockade runner, Sullivan's Island, S.C.

Blockade runners became increasingly sophisticated, taking advantage of the
latest technological innovations to achieve maximum speed. For Confederates,
the blockade—combined with shortsighted Confederate policies of self-reliance—
slowed time and cut off communication with the world of nations, damaging
Confederate transatlantic ties and claims of modern progress.

(Division of Prints and Photographs, Library of Congress)

tobacco suppliers in Petersburg, Virginia, pleaded for British intervention and
recognition of the Confederacy. "We cannot ship goods to England," they pointed
out, and "we have a large quantity of tobacco for your House now ready, but cannot ship it and do not know when it can be shipped." In the unstable situation
they did not know exactly what to suggest to Rothschild; perhaps, they wondered,
the bankers could charter a small ship and send a consignment of goods through
the British Consul. "Our country is in a sad condition," they explained, but "if
recognized by England this Civil War now existing would be stopped and thousands of Southern business men would be spared for the benefit of mankind."

They denounced the "paper blockade" that Lincoln had proclaimed a few weeks earlier, and they declared what they considered obvious about the coming war: "the South can never be subjugated."[14]

In July the Petersburg firm managed to get a letter to N. M. Rothschild & Sons confirming that they had received Rothschild's replies in June. In late November 1861 Rothschild replied to Chieves and Osborn. For six months, the firm noted, they had not been able to conduct business because of the "stoppage of the communication" with Virginia. Chieves and Osborn were not heard from again until March 1862, and they had not received any letters from Rothschild since June 1861. Using a route from New Orleans to Tampico, Mexico, the Petersburg tobacco merchants hoped to hear back from their bankers as soon as practical. In July Rothschild replied, but the letter never arrived. All four of the banking firm's previous letters had been returned from America undelivered. As of October 1863, Chieves and Osborne had not received a single letter from Rothschild for two and a half years.[15]

For August Belmont, the New York representative of N. M. Rothschild & Sons, the American Civil War threatened to interrupt business, cut off southern clients, and jeopardize the value of all of his American securities. Like other transatlantic bankers, both Belmont and Rothschild were deeply connected to the South's economy and development. Belmont was a Democratic Party leader and when the war broke out had to walk a careful line of support for the Union and the war. Rothschild was concerned with the greater humanitarian tragedy in the nation-state struggle on the American continent. Their weekly correspondence, and that of other similar banking houses, concerned the financial stakes at risk in the war, as well as the complex questions surrounding the possibility of European mediation and intervention. The consistency, range, and detail of their communications about these matters had no counterpart in the Confederacy and played a major role in shaping the outcome of the war.

At Belmont's direction before the war, the London Rothschilds, headed by Lionel de Rothschild, had bought U.S. bonds, state bonds, and railway and canal stocks and bonds. Beginning in 1852, with bond investments in the New York, the Erie, and the Pennsylvania railroads, Rothschild acquired in the next few years large positions in the Pennsylvania Central Railroad, the Illinois Central Railroad, the Mobile and Great Northern Railroad, the Indiana Canal, and the Parkersburg Railway. The London branch of the Rothschilds was circumspect about some railroad investments and about some state bonds, especially in the Deep South, where several states had repudiated bonds in the 1840s. Despite these reservations, the firm became ever more deeply invested in some American securities, taking by their own admission a "great stake" in several. In total their direct American railroad investments amounted to over $500,000. But in addition, Lionel de Rothschild's London firm invested widely in the bonds of Virginia, Missouri, Tennessee, and Kentucky, leading railroad-building states in the

1850s, indirectly helping to finance their slavery-built railroads. In this they were no different than Baring Brothers' and the other leading transatlantic banks. At Belmont's urging, the Rothschilds invested in these southern state bonds, doing so, as he put it, "notwithstanding that they are slaveholding states."[16]

So, the "stake" that the bankers held in both sections was quite significant. Belmont filled his reports to Rothschild in 1861 with warnings that British policy toward the American war should be conservative and restrained. Let the naval blockade of the southern ports do its work, he cautioned, and bring the South to its senses with minimal bloodshed. Develop "energetic efforts to obtain cotton from India, Central America, Australia, + Algeria," he advised, so that both Britain and the United States might break free from "a monopoly" that allowed an "overbearing slave oligarchy . . . to defy civilization."[17]

Belmont had already concluded that the time for rationality had passed and indeed that the Americans were on the brink of a new form of modern warfare with drastic possibilities for destruction. In many European circles, however, widespread misunderstanding of American democracy and of the nature of the conflict abounded. Few understood the federal structure of the American government; fewer still grasped the determination on both sides to fight the war at whatever the cost. One reason for these misjudgments was the time lag in communication across the Atlantic. Although the Atlantic Telegraph was tried in 1860, it failed, and so telegraphic connections extended from the United States only as far as Halifax, Nova Scotia, where steamers carried dispatches to Britain. The steamers took ten days to make the voyage, and the delay meant that the reactions of the British observers were a step behind the unfolding events. But another reason for the difference was sensibility. Schooled in the great power politics of Europe in the age of empire, without a strong conception of a national "people" or purpose, many in Britain did not grasp the significance of the modern nation-state war developing in America.[18]

Indeed, Belmont's 1861 correspondence with Rothschild was full of apocalyptic warnings. Belmont thought it "incredible" that Britain, so long against slavery, would give any status to the Confederacy, a rebellion that had "no other purpose than that of fastening slavery not only upon our Country but also upon Mexico + Central America." British neutrality might only prolong the war, and if the conflict went another year, he thought that the "humane proceedings of a blockade" will be replaced by "a war of extermination by the North [and] West against the homes + plantations of the South." Trying to explain the feeling that had gripped the United States, Belmont suggested, "The people are far in advance of the government."[19]

However, Belmont's weekly correspondence with Lionel de Rothschild and his London associates had a powerful effect over the course of the war. His explanations of the Union's resolve began to educate the British bankers about the nature of the conflict. And the Confederacy's gradual isolation only further contributed to the sense that Belmont's views were correct. All communication from their southern contacts appeared to have been cut off or stopped. "We have nothing," Belmont reported to the London firm, "altho' the mail and the telegraph are in good working order."[20]

The long-standing business relationships and trading routines that Belmont and Rothschild had cultivated across the South began to wither and atrophy. In June 1861 Belmont realized that Richmond's tobacco market was "shut down." He would have to make other arrangements in states he could reach by telegraph, rail, and post. He turned to Kentucky, Maryland, and even Ohio for tobacco. Belmont could see that the conflict was completely reshaping the market. With Baltimore "cut off" from supplies of Kentucky tobacco by the fighting along the Baltimore & Ohio, and New Orleans "closed," New York became the only viable shipping point.[21]

Rothschild was not the only London banker with extensive ties to the South suddenly arrested by the blockade. Baring Brothers bank in London and Liverpool was even more deeply involved in the New Orleans cotton market, indeed in the wider southern commodity markets, despite the firm's northern and anti-slavery sympathies. Baring Brothers' agents in the United States were divided as well—Joshua Bates, a New Englander, supported the North, but Russell Sturgis, also from the North, favored Confederate independence. Like Rothschild, the firm also experienced an immediate interruption in communication with the South. In 1859 Baring's Liverpool offices sold thousands of bales of cotton on consignment, making it one of the largest middlemen in the industry in Britain.[22]

Baring Brothers began rerouting letters to southern clients. On June 1, they predicted that once the "system of carrying on the war" was clear they would formulate a plan "by which the foreign correspondence of the South can be carried on." In the meantime, Baring sent letters via its agent in Havana, Cuba.[23]

Increasingly, Baring found itself in an anomalous position. The firm shipped arms to the United States in large quantities in clear violation of British neutrality, and at the same time it managed accounts for Confederate clients, selling large consignments of their cotton and holding the proceeds on account. Baring's account holders included the most prominent individuals and institutions in the North, mostly New Yorkers and Bostonians, such as Charles Francis Adams and the American Missionary Society, as well as leading manufacturers and businessmen. Yet, Baring also managed accounts for scores of Confederates from Georgia, Louisiana, Virginia, North Carolina, Tennessee, and Alabama. Baring even had an open account for Belle Boyd, the well-known Confederate spy, during 1864 when she arrived in England. The bank kept detailed balance sheets and instructions on how to reach its clients, and for the Confederates a brief notation served the purpose during the war: "under cover to W. S. Waller, Nassau," or "via Wilmington under cover of J. R. Lafitte, Nassau."[24]

Even as the Confederacy's ports were seized by the Federal forces, Baring clients in the South contrived numerous avenues of communication to reach their bankers in Britain. Letters were smuggled across the lines into Nashville, Tennessee, when that city fell to Union forces. Letters were carried by rail to Wilmington and run through the blockade to Nassau and on to Britain until late in the war. Letters were dispatched through Charleston from points nearby in Georgia until the closing of that port. In 1862 the firm still received "reliable accounts" from the South about the extent of the cotton crop, but the network of agents that both Baring Brothers and Rothschild had in the southern cities of Baltimore, New Orleans, Petersburg, and Richmond could hardly maintain the level of sophisticated market communication that they had before the war, even though their networks were strained, not broken. For most Southerners and for the Confederacy as a whole, however, their lines of communication were not nearly as robust as those of the powerful Rothschild and Baring Brothers banks with their agents.

But after the news of Antietam and the Preliminary Emancipation Proclamation reached Britain in early October 1862, the powerful banking houses in Europe, regardless of their prewar investments in railroad and state bonds in the South, would have little to do with the Confederacy. Transforming what British cabinet member William Gladstone a few weeks earlier had said was a "purposeless" war into one clearly for humanity and civilization, the Emancipation Proclamation proved decisive for British banking firms, and had the effect of isolating the Confederacy even further. Each understood that the American war had entered a new and important phase. The losses at Antietam shocked and dismayed the British. On September 17, 1862, in one day of severe fighting on that battlefield, over 3,500 American soldiers died and over 16,000 were wounded or missing. Most estimates put the number of Antietam casualties at nearly 30,000, with both sides sharing equally in the bloodshed. The British, who were traumatized by the deaths of 19,584 men in the Crimean War, could hardly comprehend the scale of the American conflict.[25]

For Lionel de Rothschild, who in 1862 quietly floated the idea of British and French intervention, the news of the Battle of Antietam and the announcement of the Preliminary Emancipation Proclamation indicated only that the war would take much longer. The Confederates, he noted, had "retired in good order," Richmond still had not fallen, and in many respects the North was no closer to ending the conflict than it was six months earlier. He had hoped for a "decisive" result. The "loss of life" was "deplorable" and, Rothschild urged, "something should be done in a conciliatory way to stop it." Although the Emancipation Proclamation might eventually prove a positive development, Rothschild was skeptical of it as a war measure. His British business associates and partners initially characterized the proclamation as "too precipitate for sound policy and . . . likely to cause still greater alienation."[26]

After a few weeks, however, Rothschild concluded that the Americans were so opposed to mediation that there was "nothing more to be said about it" and they could sort out their disagreements for themselves. Keeping his hand in the market, Rothschild bought up $50,000 more in Virginia state bonds when the price fell in late 1862. But when the Confederacy tried to float a loan in early 1863 through Erlanger & Co., a German banking firm, neither Rothschild nor the other banking houses in London participated. Rothschild thought the loan would only attract "the wild speculators," and neither he nor any other "respectable people" would have "anything to do with it."[27]

The fact that British firms rejected the Confederate loans during the war, however, should not obscure their considerable investment in the South before and after secession. The markets in London for American securities and railroad stocks and bonds continued throughout the war. Southern state securities rose and fell with the daily news reports from the American battlefields. So did the prices for U.S. bonds. In late May 1863, Rothschild seemed to track the price of U.S. bonds and Virginia 6 percent state bonds as proxies for the fortunes of the rival nations at war—the United States and the Confederacy. In late May 1863 he reported to his associates in New York that both the Illinois Central and the Erie Railroad shares rose markedly on the London exchange with the dramatic news of General "Stonewall" Jackson's death at Chancellorsville. Railroad bonds and stocks became a kind of daily opinion poll for British financiers and the public. All knew that the decisive events would be resolved on the battlefields—to which the markets responded, if imperfectly. Rothschild and others looked for some kind of sign, both in the market for securities and in the news of American battles, that the conflict would end and that the American war, which had been "such seesaw" and so "sanguinary," would not drag on "indefinitely."[28]

The war dragged on, and as it did so the Confederacy's standing as a modern nation became ever more precarious. Despite its modern railroad systems and telegraphs, the Confederate nation found itself unable to maintain an open channel to the outside world of nations. The Confederacy could rely on only a handful of representatives and contacts in Europe. The prewar southern states had marketed their state bonds abroad, but unlike the northern railroad companies, their state-financed and slavery-built railroads were led by directors with little experience in Europe.[29]

During the war some leading Confederate citizens ran the blockade and conducted business in London, but the risks were considerable. Rose O'Neal Greenhow, a Confederate spy whose fame preceded her everywhere she went, tried to present the Confederate cause to European leaders and society, but she found her nation isolated from international affairs and unable to communicate with the outside world.

Greenhow was a spectacular presence, a woman spy whose daring exploits in the first year of the war landed her in a federal prison in Washington, D.C. Her protests against the Lincoln administration and her fearless defense of the

Confederacy helped her become an international celebrity. She was exiled to the South in May 1862, transported by steamer to Fortress Monroe, and sent across the lines to the Confederates. In Richmond she was greeted as a hero and received at the Confederate White House by Jefferson Davis.

A year later Greenhow waited in Charleston to run the blockade. She planned to take the South's claim of nationhood to England, publish a memoir of her imprisonment, and return to aid the Confederate cause. In late July 1863 she found it "impossible to get out" of the port, so she put off her trip for another month. The Confederate losses at Gettysburg and Vicksburg depressed her, and in her waiting she grew increasingly doubtful. As she looked out over the harbor at Charleston, she began to recognize that because the Confederacy "cannot make big guns" Charleston itself "must fall." Rather than stay in Charleston for what seemed an inevitable defeat, Greenhow decided to go to Wilmington, where she still hoped to make her run through the blockade.[30]

In mid-August Greenhow's blockade runner dodged the Federal cruisers, and after "a close chase all the way" arrived in Bermuda. A month later she was in London, well settled on Regent Street and meeting with Confederate sympathizers. Despite her success and daring, Greenhow realized that the blockade affected every aspect of her cause. She wrote her good friend Alexander Boteler, a member of the Confederate Congress, several dispatches but none of them ever arrived. She received in reply only "unbroken silence." Nevertheless, in December 1863 Greenhow sent another letter to Boteler urging him to send "correct information" to their friends in England, and impressing upon him the need "to counteract the Yankee accounts." The news of Confederate general Braxton Bragg's defeat at Lookout Mountain, she pointed out, was so one-sided and so definitive that the value of the Confederate bonds was cut in half overnight on the market. In her quest to do everything possible to promote Confederate recognition, Greenhow followed every aspect of the London financial markets, including interest rates, the bond market, and share prices.

Greenhow confessed that her "heart grows sick when the mail comes without letters." She wanted the latest news so that she might "have the means of placing it in proper quarters." But months went by and Boteler never replied. In fact, by February 1864, although Greenhow had traveled to Paris and met personally with the emperor, she had heard back from none of her Confederate friends.[31]

Her experience was just as common for the Confederate nation's high officials. Historians have noted the devastating lag time in Confederate diplomatic correspondence at critical moments in the war. Confederate secretary of state Judah P. Benjamin could hardly reach his key diplomats in Europe, James M. Mason and John Slidell. Mason languished for up to seven months without any direct communication from the Confederate foreign office. Benjamin's critical dispatch to Slidell in April 1862 detailing a reciprocal offer for French recognition, perhaps the most important diplomatic dispatch of the war for the Confederates, arrived nearly three months later in France and Benjamin did not receive a reply until October. The Confederate diplomats simply could not count on consistent communication of any kind.[32]

While Confederate blockade runners enjoyed considerable success during the first year of the war, the Union navy began to put more ships on station and the blockade slowly tightened. Then, in 1862, as port cities such as New Orleans fell to Federal forces, the blockade only got stronger. The combination of these events isolated the Confederacy even further. One blockade runner estimated that four out of six ships slipped through the blockade in 1861 and 1862. He made only twelve voyages, however, and when he arrived in the Confederate ports he found a nation whose borders were almost daily changing.

Yet, even under the strain of the blockade, Confederate communications proved resilient and surprisingly adaptable wherever there was an open port with railroad access. Rails and telegraph wire connections could be broken in one place, only to reconfigure the network and how traffic flowed across it. Of course, there was a limited set of configurations for the South's network, but as long as parts of it functioned together the Confederacy remained surprisingly viable.

Some Confederates managed to maintain steady contact with Britain, Europe, and the world. In Petersburg, Virginia, tobacco merchants Chieves and Osborn wrote fourteen letters in 1864 that arrived in London at Rothschild's bank. Rothschild's replies began slowly making their way back to Virginia through the blockade. The communication line ran through Wilmington, North Carolina, and went to Nassau, Bahamas, where a Confederate-leaning British subject, George Chambers, served as go-between, forwarding letters into the Confederacy on blockade-running steamships.[33]

Indeed, despite the war and the blockade, business resumed in late 1863 and early 1864 for Rothschild and for his Virginia tobacco manufacturers. Chieves and Osborne began shipping tobacco from Petersburg to London for Rothschild to sell on consignment, and they began calling in their prewar credit at other firms in Australia, California, Germany, and New York for consolidation at Rothschild's. Another tobacco manufacturer in Petersburg, Reuben Ragland, also worked through Rothschild. Both producers found that Old Twist brand of tobacco from Virginia, especially those boxes manufactured by expert and skilled enslaved laborers before the war began, came into great demand because the quality of tobacco manufacturing had suffered so much. In 1864 these merchants shipped hundreds of hogsheads of tobacco out of the Confederacy through Nassau to N. M. Rothschild & Sons.

The market, however, had changed. Ever since the blockade cut off most southern suppliers, the interruption spawned tobacco production elsewhere. Ohio, Kentucky, and even Canadian tobacco producers stepped up their operations. Their tobacco was inferior to Virginia's but it was also less expensive. Rothschild found that the firm could not sell the Virginia tobacco in 1864 at high enough prices, despite the superior quality of its Old Twist manufacture.[34]

In retrospect, the resilience of Rothschild's connections to the South's principal markets in tobacco appear surprising. Despite the almost complete lack of communication between June 1861 and March 1862, overall between June 1861 and December 1864 Rothschild sent over sixteen letters to Chieves and Osborne, and only two were not received, those in November 1861 and July 1862. Chieves and Osborne, meanwhile, managed to get eighteen letters to London in this same period.[35]

But Rothschild received no more letters from Chieves and Osborne after November 3, 1864, despite steadily sending letters to Petersburg through Nassau in December, January, February, and March 1865. When Wilmington finally fell to Union attack in January 1865, the last open channel to Europe was closed. Observing from New York, August Belmont concluded that the combined land-sea operation in North Carolina "shuts the Confederacy almost entirely out from all intercourse with the outer world." With the fall of Wilmington the South had become entirely an interior country, without any access points at all to conduct business, diplomacy, or exchange (see Appendix, Table 10).[36]

For Confederate civilians their nation's growing distress became most evident in the clogged railways and the failure of transportation and communication systems that had given the society so much confidence. Sarah Jones, the blockaded British woman so sympathetic to the Confederacy, saw nothing but crowded railcars on her torturous journey to northern Virginia as she attempted to get out of the Confederacy. Sick and wounded soldiers lay sprawled in every conceivable position. To her amazement she was the only woman on the train, one of the clearest signs to her of how the war was effacing the former markers of a civilized society in the South. When she arrived in Warrenton at the depot, "The business of war, the miseries of the blockade, and the difficulties of transportation were more than ever apparent." The scene was total confusion: no porters, no office, no platform. Eventually she managed to get to the right train only by allowing herself to be carried along by the crowd.[37]

By contrast, northern women were using the railroads and telegraphs to reach far into the heartland and organize aid societies for the Union cause. At the outbreak of the war, there was little organized coordination for the transportation of sick and wounded soldiers. But northern women spontaneously formed local aid societies and eventually regional and national boards. Mary Livermore, a Chicago aid worker for the United States Sanitary Commission, oversaw 4,000 local chapters in the northwest region, which altogether delivered over 70,000 boxes of hospital supplies to the Federal forces. Indeed, the scale of this coordination was matched by its reach. Livermore took the railroad deep into Wisconsin and Michigan's rural areas and then canvassed the prairies by coach, going eighteen miles from the nearest station to find women to support the cause. "As we dashed along the railway," she recalled, "it took us through what seemed a continuous wheat-field . . . women were in the field everywhere, driving the reapers, binding and shocking, and loading grain, until then an unusual sight."[38]

Livermore saw firsthand what the war was doing out in the country, hundreds of miles from the nearest battlefield and dozens from the nearest railroad station. Women "skillfully" drove the reapers and shocked the wheat. Women loaded grain and worked the machinery. Their brown, tanned skin from fieldwork impressed Livermore, and the hoopless skirts they wore in the fields surprised, even shocked, her. However tempted Livermore was to stereotype these women as uncivilized, unrefined immigrant peasants, she could not. They defied every easy categorization and, instead, were plainly part of the modern war itself.

Livermore not only used the rail network to enlist women at the outer reaches of the North into the central aid effort but also found wherever she went on the rails an unexpectedly patriotic sentiment and a means to fulfill the nation's commitment to freedom. One of the first expressions of solidarity between the home front and the battlefield for Northerners, according to Livermore, occurred when "prompted by generous impulse, men and women boarded the trains as they halted at the stations in cities, and served to the [sick and wounded] men hot coffee." Wherever northern women like Livermore went, the trains were crowded with the men and material of war. These scenes sparked intense patriotism for passengers. All along the routes she traveled, sick and wounded soldiers boarded the trains, and "all were provided for long before they reached" their destination, "for the people on the train became infected with generosity and patriotism."[39]

For Confederate civilians, on the other hand, one of the first signs of their impending defeat became visible in the almost complete breakdown of train service. As blockade runner John Wilkinson made his way from Wilmington to Richmond in December 1864, his train trip revealed a crippled nation. Wilkinson made twenty-one voyages through the blockade and claimed to have carried nearly 7,000 bales of cotton worth $2 million in gold. Yet, the Confederacy's weaknesses were painfully plain. "The progress of demoralization was too evident at every step of my journey," he recalled, "and nowhere were the poverty, and the straits to which the country was reduced, more palpably visible, than in the rickety, windowless, filthy cars, traveling six or eight miles an hour."[40]

The jarring experience of witnessing loss and disconnection especially affected elite Confederate women, whose travel and contacts diminished rapidly beginning in the late fall of 1864. From her home in South Carolina Mary Boykin Chesnut had traveled during the first years of the conflict to Richmond, Montgomery, Charleston, and Wilmington. Much of her travel went uninterrupted. The telegraphs and railroads confirmed the sense of wholeness and unity in the Confederate nation. She could move freely from one part of the Confederacy to another with familiar grace and speed. When Sherman captured Atlanta and

George Barnard, *Boxcars with Refugees at Railroad,* Atlanta, Ga., 1864.

With the capture of Atlanta, General William T. Sherman's army seized an important rail hub for the Confederacy. This image of refugees and African Americans, sitting on rail cars with their possessions, indicates the massive displacement that came with the war.

(Library of Congress)

sliced through southern communications, however, Chesnut feared that the Confederates "will be wiped from the face of the earth." When Sherman marched to the sea, she took refuge in Lincolnton, North Carolina, "a thoroughly out-of-all-routes place." Eventually making her way back to Camden, South Carolina, Chesnut found that everything went wrong on the trains as she waited for hours and hours by the tracks. By late March 1865, her sources of information were reduced to the view from her second-story window. No more newspapers, telegrams, letters, or train travel. When an optimistic Confederate colonel tried to persuade her that hope was not lost for their nation, Chesnut could not believe him. "I pass my days and nights partly at this window," she explained. "I am sure our army is silently dispersing. Men are moving the wrong way, all the time. They slip by with no songs and no shouts now. They have given the thing up. See for yourself. Look there."[41]

Late in the war Chesnut was still at her little window, looking out on the changed world below. A world of emancipation, a world of Confederate defeat, a world of collapse and transformation. "We are shut in here, turned with our faces to a dead wall," she wrote in her diary. "No mails. A letter is sometimes brought by a man on horseback, travelling through the wilderness made by Sherman. All railroads have been destroyed and the bridges are gone. We are cut off from the world, here to eat out our hearts."[42]

Chesnut, like many other men and women, recorded the strange flow of information and knowledge in the last year of the Confederacy and speculated how these changes twisted the new nation's sense of purpose. Citizens in the Confederacy tried to piece together reports from various sources. They gathered at the railroad depots for the arrival of trains, where they received the wounded, the captured, and the soldiers moving from and to the battles. There, they also caught wind of the official dispatches from army officers, and they talked to strangers, swapping rumors and gossip. They stood in the hotel lobbies and outside the telegraph offices and post offices waiting for words about distant events. They even turned to the enslaved, listening to them as never before, catching their whispered comments or asking them outright what they had heard in their cabins and along the paths they traveled. Rumor, or what one historian has called "the grape vine telegraph," became one of the most widely experienced aspects of the war's dislocation in the Confederacy.[43]

A sense of the strain that these developments brought to Confederate civilians can be glimpsed in the diary of Joseph Waddell, a Whig newspaper editor in Staunton, Virginia, and a Confederate clerk, whose support for secession and Confederate independence had been unwavering, though never strongly attached to slavery. Waddell considered the "Yankees" a separate race of people, one that could neither understand nor tolerate southern slaveholders and their worldview. Though he never fought in a battle, nor ever left Staunton, Waddell's war covered a vast geography of information. He gathered snippets of stories from the Gulf of Mexico and the Trans-Mississippi; he followed events along the railroads in Missouri and Texas; he tracked the progress of armies across distant theaters; he combed the few northern newspapers he could get his hands on for information about diplomatic affairs in London, Paris, and Mexico City. He tried, most of all, to sift through all of these partial reports for some certainty, some empirical data to document the progress of the war. By the summer of 1864 he found his task more difficult than ever. Here, for example, is Waddell's long entry for Tuesday morning, July 26, 1864:

> Official dispatches from Atlanta confirm the recent good news from that quarter—if it only holds out! Rumors yesterday of successes on the Potomac, but discredited, . . . The report now is that the Central Bank suffered very little by the burning of the car on the Danville Railroad, but the Valley Bank was almost destroyed—Strange that we can get no definite intelligence.[44]

Joseph Waddell's diary entries became only more surreal, as banks collapsed, Confederate bonds sank, and railroad service became irregular or halted altogether. His modern society ran on "intelligence," but Waddell found that he could not verify much of anything. Official army reports made their way along the broken networks of rail and post office, but even these were suspect, subject to alteration and embellishment. With his Staunton location—the nexus of rail and telegraph, and one of the last fully operational nodes on the Confederacy's network—Waddell and his community experienced widespread gloom, apprehension, and "public anxiety."[45]

All of the modern structures, technologies, and ideas present in the Confederacy's founding depended on intercommunication with the world of nations. Banking structures, and in particular the means of credit and commercial exchange, required the consistent flow of information and knowledge. The railroads in the South had been the first and most visible instances of these modern developments, along with the state bonds that financed them. Virginia's 6 percent bonds, an index of how the Confederacy's modern status might be seen, began a steady decline on the European markets beginning in June 1863. By the summer of 1864 the Virginia bonds were trading around 30 percent of their face value.[46]

As long as these modern systems stood, even if weakened, the Confederacy continued. Indeed, in 1864 the Union's standing was not much better than the Confederacy's. The Union war effort was costing $2.5 million a day. The Federal government total spending before the war had been $63 million a year, but now it was spending that amount about every twenty days. And the government could hardly sell its new bond issues. Gold speculation soared with the lack of confidence and U.S. bonds collapsed in the summer, trading on August 20 at 39 percent of their face value.

The war seemed to have resolved little and weakened both parties to the point of exhaustion. Yet, the northern commanders, led by Grant, Sherman, and Sheridan, came to understand the vulnerabilities of the Confederacy's modern systems as well as their importance to the Confederate nation's identity. They crafted a new form of generalship around dominating the railroads that in its scale, coordination, and thoroughness proved impossible for the Confederates to ignore or resist. Nothing like it had been seen in American warfare before, and nothing better demonstrated the national purposes of the North.[47]

Chapter 7

The Railroad Strategy

FOR the top northern commanders in 1864 the Civil War became a far-reaching attempt to reshape the social and physical environment of the Confederacy—and to demonstrate the reach of the American nation-state. To defeat the South it was necessary to master its nature, to dominate, control, and comprehend its landscapes, its systems, its networks, and its people. No one did this more effectively or thoroughly than General William T. Sherman. His campaign for Atlanta, and then his subsequent march through Georgia and up the coast to Savannah, were the culmination of a northern railroad strategy to win the war. The systematic running of previously independent railroads, under the U.S. Military Railroads, demonstrated what could be achieved with them if properly focused. The ideas behind this strategy had been in development for some time, ever since the first year of the war when Lincoln laid out the importance of railroads to George McClellan and McClellan drafted his comprehensive strategy for Lincoln. But Sherman's vision of the railroads was tied to his larger moral purpose: to end the anarchy of secession.

In this way Sherman, along with Generals U. S. Grant and Philip Sheridan, hitched the railroad strategy to a powerful ideal for the northern public. Their actions showed how dominating the South's railroad network would synchronize the moral imperative of the Union with the idea of progress and civilization. In large measure they also denied the Confederacy its claims to progress, civilization, and modernity. Dominating the Confederacy's railroad systems, indeed turning them against the Confederacy, was not only a military objective, it was also a social and political one, because it erased the history of modern slave society built around these technologies. Although many northern commanders were convinced that railroads were a key military objective, they only gradually came to comprehend their wider strategic significance and tie them to the moral ideas behind the war.

In the midst of the Vicksburg Campaign in 1863, Sherman took his first step toward a more comprehensive strategy along these lines. He surprised himself with the realization that he had mastered the southern landscape. In the complex of swamps, rivers, marshes, bluffs, and cane thickets in Mississippi, Sherman boasted "how perfectly" he "comprehended the whole topography of the place with such limited means of knowledge." To make it easier for his family to follow his movements through the campaign, he sent a map home, explaining to them that "devastation and ruin lay behind us." The landscape around Vicksburg was extraordinary with its "hills and valleys . . . fallen trees, stranding trunks and Canebrake." Sherman had had to concentrate as never before on understanding the natural and man-made systems that encased, protected, and underlay the city. He had to take "all possible advantage of the shape of the ground." By his own admission he was "out here studying a most complex geography."[1]

Sherman's convictions about the larger strategy for the war were shaped in these encounters with the terrain. The contrast with George B. McClellan could not be more stark—McClellan spent little time and energy studying the landscape of tidewater Virginia during the Peninsular Campaign. It appears that Sherman had come to three broad conclusions by the end of 1863. The first was that the "entire South, man woman and child" was against the North and was determined to fight the war out to the finish. Sherman estimated that defeating the South would require over one million men in military service and several years of bloody warfare. Second, he thought that the Mississippi River was the "great base of operations" from which to control and penetrate the South's networks. On July 4, 1863, when Vicksburg fell to the Union forces, Sherman congratulated Grant on freeing "the river of our greatness." Having conquered one of the most important natural systems in the South, he was ready to move on from the river into the interior and to master the rest of the South's second nature networks. "I want maps," he bluntly told Grant.[2]

Third, Sherman was convinced that the North's war would outrun most attempts to contain its excesses and that the hard hand of war would eventually have to affect the civilian population in the South directly. To the white Southerners in Memphis, Tennessee, who had protested his occupation of the city in 1862, Sherman was candid in his harsh expectations. While they could show "courage and bravery," they could not "stay the hand of destruction" that was "setting adrift their slaves, . . . consuming and wasting their fields and improvements, destroying their roads, bridges and the labor and fruits of near a century of undisturbed property." In the Vicksburg Campaign a year later, Sherman estimated that he threw 20,000 artillery shells into the city. "We consumed the fruits of the Country," he explained to his brother, U.S. senator John Sherman, "broke up the important Rail Road communications, whipped the enemy wherever encountered, and secured the Yazoo [River] as a base."[3]

More than ever before, northern commanders followed the "second nature" system of railroads and their intersection with the landscape of mountain, valley, river, and forest. Led by Sherman, Grant, and Sheridan, a form of what we might

General William T. Sherman at Fort No. 7, Atlanta, Ga.,
overlooking Chattanooga Railroad lines, 1864.

Sherman recognized the importance and vulnerability of railroad corridors.
In September 1862 Sherman ordered an expedition to "destroy" the town of
Randolph, Tennessee, because guerrillas had fired on Union steamships from
the banks of the Mississippi River. In 1864 he adopted similarly hard measures
to protect the railroads during his Atlanta Campaign. (Library of Congress)

call "railroad generalship" emerged in 1864. For the Confederates no comparable
successor to Stonewall Jackson came forward to initiate a counterstrategy to the
Union generals. Expecting to fight large decisive battles, Confederate leaders,
such as General Joseph Johnston, who was defending Atlanta, seemed willing to
give up their railroads when necessary. Although southern partisans and cavalry
conducted small raids on northern-controlled rail lines in 1864, Confederate commanders, especially in the Atlanta Campaign, made no serious attempt to seize,

control, and defend large sections of the network that would cut off or cripple the northern invasion. Nor were they successful in moving the theater of combat into Kentucky or outside of the vital nexus of southern railroads in Tennessee.

In the 1864 campaigns, moreover, the Union commanders began to harness their armies to a scale of operations many Americans could hardly comprehend. They relied on the rail systems to coordinate these efforts and to make the logistics for these huge armies possible. On one front Sheridan was seeking to raze hundreds of square miles in the Shenandoah Valley and capture its railroads, on another Grant established a new city outside of the trenches at Petersburg, fed and armed by his specially fitted railroads. Grant's objectives included cutting Lee's army off from the rest of the South, and featured massive maneuvers to seize the rail lines coming into Petersburg and Richmond. On yet another front, Sherman fought his way toward Atlanta along the thin line of rail through Allatoona Pass, Georgia, and then carried out and explained his "March to the Sea" as the most dramatic attempt in the war to reconfigure the environmental and social geography in front of him.

Early in 1864 Sherman took his army on an expedition from Vicksburg to Jackson, Mississippi, and then on to Meridian. The movement was a trial run at the sort of interior marches Sherman was planning for Georgia. It was also an example of how the dismantling of the railroad networks might affect larger strategic aspects of the war. Sherman's army literally took apart the railroad junction and facilities in Jackson. They moved down the Southern Railroad Company line through the depot at Brandon, tearing up the tracks, and finally arrived at Meridian, an important junction with the Mobile and Ohio Railroad. Over 100 miles of track were pulled up, twenty locomotives were blown up, and sixty bridges were destroyed. Sherman reported to Grant on February 27: "We staid [*sic*] at Meridian for a week and made the most complete destruction of the railroads ever beheld." And a week later Sherman reported: Meridian "no longer exists."[4]

This became Sherman's chief goal—to wipe a place from the map, to render it dead or worthless, to irrevocably alter the geographic connections that sustained the Confederacy and its claims to progress. After his expedition to disassemble Meridian, Mississippi, in February, Sherman exhibited few doubts about his core strategy. Uninterested in a large battle with the Confederate forces amassed at Dalton under Johnston, Sherman expected to maneuver his army south from Chattanooga toward Atlanta along the Western and Atlantic Railroad, repairing the line as necessary as he went. To keep the army fed and equipped, he relied on the U.S. Military Railroads, Division of the Mississippi, under Colonel Daniel C. McCallum. The Construction Corps, under Lieutenant Colonel William W. Wright, was to keep the roads open and the Transportation Division, under Lieutenant Colonel Adna Anderson, was to run them efficiently.

The rail lines were not only vital to supply his army but also symbolic of the control Sherman expected to assert in the South. Protecting and controlling them, keeping the supplies to his army flowing, these were the highest immediate priorities, and Sherman took them seriously. When guerrillas and southern partisans attacked the vital railroad line below Chattanooga in July 1864, Sherman gave clear orders to "take no prisoners."[5] As he maneuvered to capture more of the Western and Atlantic Railroad north of Atlanta, Sherman issued general orders to the commanding officer of the troops guarding the railroad at Marietta: "Show no mercy to guerrillas or persons threatening our road or telegraph. . . . no matter how hard their friends may plead." Then, on the same day, Sherman reiterated the point to General John Smith, who was defending the vulnerable railroad tunnel near Allatoona: "If guerrillas trouble the road or wires between Kingston and Acworth, they should be shot without mercy." Although the Union army did not carry out these orders quite so literally, Sherman clearly saw the railroad corridors as special zones where more stringent rules of engagement might apply.[6]

Having given hard orders to defend his rail supply link and having tasked thousands of soldiers with protecting the line, Sherman began his move through the mountains of north Georgia to the south and east along the railroad toward Atlanta. In several calculated thrusts to begin the campaign, he sent part of his army under General James McPherson south and west of the Confederate lines at Dalton. Each move, Sherman contemplated, should "feel" for the railroad below the Confederate position and, if possible, destroy the line and cut off Johnston's army from Atlanta. His first such maneuver, launched on May 8, placed Union general Grenville Dodge's corps two hundred yards from the railroad at Resaca, Georgia, deep behind the main Confederate force up the line at Dalton. After a brief fight at Resaca, Johnston retreated down the Western and Atlantic south over the Oostanoula River, abandoning but not destroying the railroad as he went.

The pattern was set until mid-July. Using McPherson's Army of the Tennessee like a ball on a chain, Sherman swung it to the west and south again and again. The geography of river and railroad cooperated. Every time the Confederates fortified a position, they were up against a river or they found themselves open to Union forces getting behind them to the south.[7]

On May 21 at Kingston, Georgia, Major Ephraim C. Dawes and the 53rd Ohio regiment prepared for another of Sherman's swinging ball and chain blows to begin. Dawes wrote at the time, "Our order says take twenty days rations, ie. part rations, foraging the rest, and start with the expectation of not relying upon the R. R. for anything for that length of time." The movements to that point had inspired Dawes with confidence. "We have the best army," he wrote. "The R. R. cars from Chattanooga ran into Kingston almost as soon as our advance reached there. There is more energy displayed here than I ever saw before."[8]

Indeed, Sherman asked his commanders and soldiers for "superhuman energy" to protect the railroad lines and to free his large army to break apart the Confederate forces. To Secretary of War Edwin Stanton and to the governors

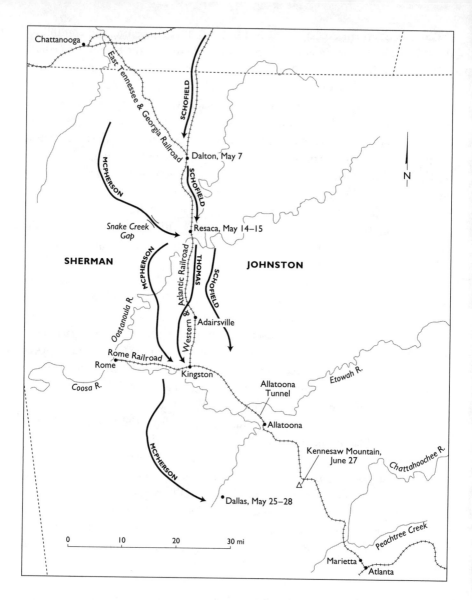

The Atlanta Campaign, May–July 1864.

Keywords appearing in General William T. Sherman's correspondence in the Atlanta Campaign of 1864; the larger the word, the more often it appeared in his writings.

Compiled from U.S. War Department, *The War of the Rebellion: A Compilation of the Official Records of the Union and Confederate Armies* (Lynchburg, Va., and Pasadena, Calif.: Broadfoot, 1985), Vol. 38 (Parts IV and V), including all of Sherman's letters in these volumes.

(Voyeur Tools [copyright 2009] Steffan Sinclair and Geoffrey Rockwell, v. 1.0; graph by Trevor Munoz and the author [September 2009]. This image was generated using Wordle, under a Creative Commons Attribution 3.0 License.)

of western states, Sherman requested militia units to defend the rail centers at Memphis, Nashville, Cairo, Paducah, and the "exposed" rail lines between these points so that the regular army could be marched to "the interior." Sherman impressed upon the governors that the Confederates were "united and inspired with a demoniac zeal."[9] Only by breaking their armies into fragments might they be defeated.

His goal became to dominate the Confederate system, by taking it over and controlling its key junctions. Sherman used the term "railroad" 377 times in his official correspondence during the Atlanta Campaign. For Sherman the railroad was the object—75 percent of the time he used the word, he did so as the object of a verb. The major elements of Sherman's language regarding the railroads suggest that he sought to first break or destroy, then occupy and control.

Indeed, even though the first part of the campaign concentrated on pushing through the natural barriers of mountains and rivers, Sherman used "railroad" language more frequently throughout the entire campaign than he did any other set of terms in his official correspondence. While the Atlanta Campaign, in other words, posed major geographical barriers in the form of "mountains," "hills,"

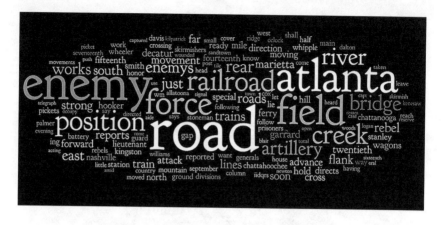

Keywords appearing in all Union commanders' correspondence in the Atlanta Campaign of 1864; the larger the word, the more often it appeared in their writings.

Compiled from U.S. War Department, *The War of the Rebellion: A Compilation of the Official Records of the Union and Confederate Armies* (Lynchburg, Va., and Pasadena, Calif.: Broadfoot, 1985), Vol. 38 (Parts IV and V), including all Union command correspondence.

(Voyeur Tools [copyright 2009] Steffan Sinclair and Geoffrey Rockwell, v. 1.0; graph by Trevor Munoz and the author [September 2009]. This image was generated using Wordle, under a Creative Commons Attribution 3.0 License.)

"rivers," "gaps," and "passes," Sherman more frequently focused on the second nature systems of rail and telegraph. By the last week of August and the first week of September, when his forces closed on Atlanta, the intensity of Sherman's focus on the railroad networks spiked. His correspondence from August 30 to September 4 hammered away at controlling, reaching, and occupying the railroads.

Union commanders of different levels in Sherman's army, from captains to generals, adopted similar understandings of the imperative to dominate the railroads. And the railroad figured prominently in their overall correspondence. "Enemy," Road" (often meaning railroad), and "Railroad" were among the most frequently invoked terms by the Union officers between May and September 1864 (see Appendix, Table 8).

Later, Colonel Wells S. Jones of the 53rd Ohio described the intense fighting to control the railroad and, like many other commanders, the way that the railroads became a geographical landmark. His unit conducted almost all of its fighting in and around a "railroad cut"—a line positioning and guiding their daily operations. Colonel Jacob E. Taylor of the 40th Ohio made similar moves—his unit "struck out for," "proceeded down," "destroyed," and "marched to" the railroad line for days at a time, never losing touch with it. Nearly every regiment, brigade, division, and corps in Sherman's army found itself moving along, parallel with, toward, or across the railroads.

When Sherman's army finally captured Atlanta and its vital rail depots on September 4, 1864, the event had immense political consequences, bolstering Lincoln's reelection campaign (against Democrat George B. McClellan) and raising questions in the Confederacy about Jefferson Davis's capacity to lead the nation to independence. The destruction was staggering, and as in Meridian, Mississippi, at the beginning of the campaign, the dismantling of the rail systems seemed especially significant. Upon entering the city and seeing the ruins of the train depot, one of Sherman's soldiers thought it was a "*perfect smash.*" The big railroad bridge on stone piers over the Chattahoochee was destroyed too. The sight of its wreck inspired drama and emotion. Soldiers paid special attention to the destruction of Atlanta's railroad depots and bridges. These were the largest structures in the southern landscape and symbolic of the South's claim to modernity, wealth, and power. Their wreckage was equally symbolic of the South's loss and incapacity.[10]

One of Sherman's soldiers went back into Atlanta in late October to review the devastation. He found nearly every house "riddled and torn by our shells, here a tall chimney knocked down and there a portico carried away." A poignant example of the Confederate desperation touched him: "Along each side of the railroad were holes in the bank where families had crawled in to escape our iron showers." Fine shade trees were "hacked to pieces." Atlanta was, he concluded, "dead."[11]

Sherman's campaign for Atlanta constituted one of the largest land-based army movements of the war and was enabled in large part by his detailed geographic knowledge and vision. The maneuvers were carefully planned reconfigurations of the southern landscape, aimed at crippling railroad networks and severing southern communities from one another. The principal target became the railroads as much as the cities they served. In the intensity and single-mindedness of his focus, Sherman stood out among northern commanders. By late August he seemed for the most part uninterested in offering the Confederates a battle. Instead, he sought only to knock out the junctions and dominate the railroads in Georgia. By his own measure he had succeeded: he had reduced the Confederacy to "one stem" of railroad "connecting the channels of trade and travel" between Georgia, Alabama, and Mississippi. These slender lines now occupied Sherman's attention. They were all that held the Confederacy together and, if cut or captured, Sherman could control if and how goods and people moved from one city to another. When General John Bell Hood evacuated Atlanta and blew up trains of railroad cars rather than see them captured, Sherman ordered that all "destruction on the railroad will cease" and he concluded that "the object of my movement against the railroad was therefore already reached" and that "it was idle to pursue our enemy in that wooded country." Rather than chase Hood's Confederate forces around, Sherman set about repairing the railroads "about as fast as he [Hood] broke them." Almost overnight, Sherman turned his army from dis-

No. 1. Steam engines "Telegraph" and "O. A. Bull" remained in position
amid the ruins of a Confederate roundhouse in Atlanta in 1864.

The South possessed some of the most beautiful depots and railroad facilities in the
nation in 1861. Sherman's campaigns sought to dismantle the Confederate railroad
system and in so doing deny any claim to modernity and progress. African
American workers stand atop the old Georgia Railroad flatcar.

(George N. Barnard, LC-DIG-ppmsca-18960, Division of Prints and Photographs, Library of Congress)

mantling the Confederate systems to operating them. Later, with the trains and
telegraphs running "with regularity and speed," Sherman concluded that he now
owned, occupied, and held the network.[12]

Much has been written about the destruction that Sherman's army wrought
once it left Atlanta on the March to the Sea, and historians have debated whether
the March was as vicious or as brutal as the rhetoric about it. But the March was
another, even more elaborate maneuver to control the Confederacy's network of
railroads. Sherman gathered information about the railroads from every source
available and used them as guideposts for his operations. Before setting out from
Atlanta, he questioned R. R. Cuyler, president of the Georgia Central Railroad
and a prisoner of war. Based on Cuyler's information, Sherman relied on the rail-

road mile markers to give him exact measurements to the enemy lines in front of him.[13]

Before the March to the Sea one of Sherman's soldiers predicted, "In all probability every enterable [*sic*] house we find will be burned." Nothing this arbitrary took place. Instead, Sherman's operation systematically moved east toward the last remaining cluster of railroad junctions in the Confederacy. Afterward, this soldier explained the March in more careful terms: "We have made a great raid, leaving Atlanta in four columns, marching on four different roads, taking up in a general sweep about an average of forty miles wide through our whole route." They tore up "miles and miles" of the Georgia railroad, then quickly, and deceptively, moved south and entered Milledgeville, "without firing a gun." There they "made the most terrible havoc among the citizens."[14]

Certainly, Sherman's extensive campaigns across the landscape of Georgia took on the qualities of a natural event, something like a huge storm or hurricane. No one in the South really knew its direction or could predict its effects, yet all could recognize its pure, almost natural, power. Sherman himself saw his campaign in starkly different terms. He was convinced that what he was doing was a scientifically based, hard-nosed military maneuver that would be proven in time. The dramatic act of cutting loose from standard communication and transportation inspired some of these understandings, for the March to the Sea seemed to signify a force outside of, no longer tethered to, the boundaries of the technologies of rail and wire. Newspapers did not know where Sherman's army had gone. Speculation about his huge force's operations became widespread and intense. Many of these reports ignored the March's mechanical qualities. The campaign's objectives, route, and duration were specifically tied to the rail systems of the Confederacy. Sherman had studied his maps, pored over the latest census data, and interviewed dozens of locals about the buildings and property on the route.[15]

At the end of his March to the Sea and back in contact with his higher command and the world, Sherman worried about how his army would be supplied but he also breathed the salty air of confidence. "I never saw a more confident army," he wrote his wife, Ellen, in December. "We have lived Sumptuously," he reported. Writing from the field outside of Savannah, Sherman was preparing both to force the surrender of the city and to embark on another march north toward Grant's army. Once he stopped before Savannah, however, Sherman found that feeding and supplying his army when it was stationary was considerably more difficult than when it was under the rhythm it acquired on the move out in the countryside. He considered his options for another movement. His plans, as he explained them to Grant, were vast and well founded. "I feel confident," he told Grant, "that I can break up the whole R.R. system of South Carolina and N. Carolina. . . . And if you feel confident that you can whip Lee outside of his entrenchments, I feel equally confident that I can handle him in the open country." He told Grant of the numerous reviews that he held for the army. He wanted his army to see itself and the fine state it was in. He reiterated to Grant, "This army has a confidence in itself that makes it almost irresistible."[16]

More than any battle, Sherman's Atlanta Campaign and the subsequent March to the Sea demonstrated to the South that its driving economic vision of the Confederacy, based as it was on railroads, slavery, and agricultural wealth, was obliterated. He started on the March with 5,000 head of cattle and wound up in Savannah with over 10,000. He had shot all of the old, broken-down mules and replaced them with fresh horseflesh from the plantations along his route. Former slaves followed every regiment. Sherman characterized his campaigns as "remodeling the enemy's interior lines to suit our future plans and purposes."[17]

Remodeling, as Sherman put it, changed the location or importance of cities as the Confederacy's boundaries shifted and as its "second nature" infrastructure fractured, especially when Sherman moved into what he called the "interior." Charleston, South Carolina—the center point of secession and the symbol of Confederate nationalism—Sherman decided, was worthless. The city was "dead and unimportant" as a military objective, because its rail lines could be cut from Columbia. His army was eating out the countryside around Savannah "for 50 miles." The army's size and destruction were something to behold. "All recognize in my army," he told Grant, "a different body of men than they have ever seen before." In late January 1865, poised to move north from Savannah, Sherman explained to Grant his plans: "I will be sure that every Rail is twisted, rapidly move to Columbia and fill up the triangle formed by the Congaree and Wateree, tributaries of the Santee, breaking up that great center of the Carolina [Rail] Roads."[18]

Sherman decided that the calculus of his railroad strategy had been correct. Moving from Savannah along the rails, destroying them as he went, Sherman found a region where the "rice fields," the "river forest," and the trees looked "familiar" but where "the People are all gone." Blacks and whites fled in different directions, the former to the Union army, the latter deeper into the remaining "interior" South. "Desolation is supreme," Sherman observed in late January 1865.[19]

"We are not fighting Davis alone, but all the elements of Anarchy which have organized resistance to an attempted civilized and compact Government," Sherman explained to his father-in-law. Sherman did not oppose the system of slavery in the South, which he found unobjectionable, but instead found his cause in the "mobs" and "vigilance committees" that had led the secessionist movement. His accidental role as a liberator of the enslaved perplexed him. Instead, he came to his railroad strategy as a way to end the war and crush the men who had started it. Sherman wanted to use his command of these technologies and his geographic knowledge to make the enemy see "how the Power of the United States can reach him in his inner recesses."[20]

In this effort he was undeniably successful. Between February 1864 and February 1865, Sherman had occupied and controlled over 30,000 square miles of railroad territory across three states. By capturing Savannah, with its long lines of communication, he disconnected over 11,000 square miles of railroad-serviced territory (see Appendix, Table 9). Confederate civilians far removed from the path of his army felt cut off, their world shrinking. Sherman's form of warfare was not "total war" in the sense that it brought civilians directly into the conflict or remorselessly set out to target them. Instead, it was network war or railroad war. In this respect the strategy he practiced was distinctively modern. By denying Confederate civilians their mobility, by recognizing the way railroads had become agents of civilization and extensions of politics and society, Sherman not only blazed a path of destruction but also mastered and reconfigured the Confederacy's systems, and in so doing rendered the Confederacy "dead" and "worthless."[21]

A similar process of destruction and geographic domination unfolded in the Shenandoah Valley during the summer and fall of 1864. After years of Union frustration and limited success in the Shenandoah Valley, and with guerrilla forces inflicting serious damage to the Union on the railroads in northern Virginia, generals Ulysses S. Grant and Philip H. Sheridan took a new approach. It also proved pivotal in the attempt by Union commanders to visualize, calculate, and dominate the geography of the South and to master the scale of the war. Sheridan, like his counterpart Sherman, undertook an empirical effort in the campaign—to quantify the systematic control he tried to impose on the Confederate landscape. Although his results were uneven, his methods were unprecedented in their scale and reach.

The Shenandoah Valley, in particular, had been the ground of Confederate victories throughout the war. Federal armies appeared confused and beaten there, as if the land itself confounded them. General Stonewall Jackson used the Valley's geography to his great advantage in 1862, so much so that in 1864 Jackson's ghost still seemed to loom large in the minds of Federal commanders. Certainly it did for the Confederate soldiers whose officers led them on special visits that summer to Jackson's grave in Lexington, Virginia, at the Virginia Military Institute (V.M.I.).

Whether inspired by the memorials to Jackson or not, the Confederates in the Valley began to fight harder and as if they had somehow inherited and resurrected Jackson's blend of speed and forcefulness. The result was that several Federal commanders failed to take control of the Valley in the early summer despite ambitious plans for a coordinated Union attack on the Confederacy. First, in May 1864 Union general Franz Seigel suffered defeat at the Battle of New Market, where the V.M.I. Corps of Cadets went into action for the Confederate forces.

Then, in June, General David Hunter saw initial success when he brought his army into Staunton, Virginia, captured the town, and moved south to occupy Lexington, where he burned several buildings at V.M.I. But Confederate forces caught up with Hunter at Lynchburg, a key Confederate rail junction, and drove him ignominiously out of the Valley into western Virginia. In mid-July General Ulysses S. Grant hoped that Hunter's movements in the Valley would take place simultaneously with those of Sherman outside Atlanta. Grant informed General Henry W. Halleck that "Sherman will, once in Atlanta, devote himself to collecting the resources of the country. He will take everything the people have." Hunter's task was to seize the Virginia Central Railroad at Charlottesville, or, if unsuccessful, then "he should make all the valley south of the Baltimore and Ohio [rail] road a desert as high up as possible." Grant clarified the plan in this way: "I do not mean that houses should be burned, but all privisions [*sic*] and stock should be removed and the people notified to move out."[22]

When Hunter failed at this, Grant turned to General Philip H. Sheridan to "wipe out the stain the Valley of the Shenandoah has been to us heretofore." As with Hunter, Grant expected Sheridan to cut off the railroad junctions in Staunton and Charlottesville and, if at all possible, to move eastward along the railroad to threaten Confederate general Robert E. Lee's entrenched army near Petersburg and Richmond. He hoped to cut the rebels off from their principal food supplies in the upper Valley and southwest parts of Virginia. But Grant's orders implied the removal of people from a vast zone around the railroads and a sweeping seizure of Confederate resources. He suggested that Sherman in Atlanta might, after taking everything, redistribute food "to rich and poor alike" and that, because Sherman will take all cattle and horses, "they will have no use for grain further than is necessary for bread."[23]

For Confederates, especially those from western Virginia, the Valley's landscape conjured up all that was good and blessed about their society. Its mysterious resistance to Federal penetration up to late 1864 could be interpreted as a signal indicating the rightness of their cause. Natural geography, when combined with second nature's infrastructure, might enable the Confederates to ward off the intrusion of the Union army again and again. To a young Confederate soldier in 1862 the beauty of the Valley appeared redemptive—the "romantic scenes" of tearful women cheering on the Confederates in the streets of Winchester and Strasburg inspired him. The Valley was "the most romantic place" he had ever seen, with its luxuriant fields, its turnpike road, its railroad that "crosses a deep chasm on trussel [*sic*] work 130 feet high." The mixture of technological wonder and pastoral scenery created a sublime feeling that stirred his heart.[24]

Such sentiments were not uncommon among Confederates. Stephen Dodson Ramseur, a North Carolina general in Jubal A. Early's Army of the Valley, also described the beauty he saw there in 1864: "pure water, a few vegetables and plenty of fresh meat. Altogether we consider ourselves very fortunate thus far." Ramseur wished that his wife could "see this magnificent Valley—at this beautiful season of the year." He observed: "Although plantations are ruined—and the blackened remains of once splendid mansions are to be seen on all sides, yet nature is tri-

Alfred R. Waud, *Ruins of the Bridge over the Shenandoah River, Loudon Heights Beyond*, 1864.

The partisan war in Loudon County, Virginia, turned especially violent in the fall of 1864. Confederate forces under John S. Mosby captured and killed Union soldiers in retaliation for the burning of civilian homes, and Union general George A. Custer responded by hanging seven of Mosby's men. Then, on November 6, 1864, Mosby executed several more Union soldiers in response. The fighting took place along the Manassas Gap Railroad line and its bridges. (Library of Congress)

umphant—magnificent meadows, beautiful forests & broad undulating fields rich in grass & clover!" If nature had proven resilient, bearing its fruits in the face of adversity and in effect siding with the South, Ramseur concluded, "Truly it does seem sacreligious [*sic*] to despoil such an Eden! by the ravages of War."[25]

In September 1864, as Sheridan's troops brushed aside Jubal A. Early's Confederate army in the Valley and began systematically burning the region's resources, only the partisans under John S. Mosby frustrated their efforts. Mosby's unit stepped up the intensity of its attacks on the Manassas Gap Railroad, which was supplying Sheridan's men. Because part of Grant's plans had called for the depopulation of entire counties along the vital railroads, Sheridan felt justified in taking extreme measures against the guerrillas. In retaliation for raiding the trains, Union forces began burning civilians' homes near the railroad.

A war of reprisal quickly followed. In his report to Lee, Mosby frankly admitted that his command had coldly executed several captured Union prisoners of war caught burning civilian homes. "Such was the indignation of our men," he explained, "at witnessing some of the finest residences in that portion of the State enveloped in flames that no quarter was shown and about 25 of them were shot to death for their villainy." Lee forwarded the report to Secretary of War James A. Seddon without comment on the reprisal killings but noted approvingly, "Attention is invited to the activity and skill of Colonel Mosby." Lee went on to summarize the report's key data: over 1,200 enemy killed, wounded, or captured; over 1,600 horses and mules, 230 beef cattle, and 85 wagons taken from the enemy.[26]

In the Valley Campaign both sides escalated the violence. For Confederate civilian Sue Richardson, Sheridan's campaign brought the terror of the war into her front fields and parlor. She summarized in clipped language the shock of seeing the Union army burning barns and shooting livestock: "reg.[iment] in mountain field, pickets on hill. squads passing, plundering." Richardson paced the house "in breathless despair." Union soldiers came by every day and picked over the place. Then, on October 12, the Richardsons' enslaved "servants" left the farm to head for Union forces and freedom. She heard that the Union army intended to stay all winter and was "building" a railroad to keep supplies flowing.[27]

By October 1864, however, the guerrilla warfare and the counterinsurgency efforts of the Union army had taken an unexpected turn. Union forces were using local Confederate civilians as human shields on the trains in northern Virginia to prevent John S. Mosby's men from attacking the railroad. Then Secretary of War Edwin Stanton ordered every house within five miles of the Manassas Gap Railroad burned and all civilians in that zone to be considered bushwhackers. But the tactics did little to deter the violence. Mosby expanded his field of operations, executing a daring raid on the Baltimore & Ohio Railroad. His men killed several Union soldiers, took thousands of dollars in greenbacks, and wrecked the train.[28]

In Richmond the Confederacy's leading newspaper editors were confident that Mosby would attack the railroads, even if he "knew that all who were dear to him were on a train." They believed Mosby would not hesitate for a second "provided he were assured that the good of his country demanded the sacrifice." Indeed, when some citizens petitioned Mosby to stop his attacks because the Union army threatened to retaliate by burning houses, Mosby had "unhesitatingly refuse[d] to comply." To do so would be a "degrading compromise." Mosby considered his attacks "sanctioned both by the customs of war and the practice of the enemy." Mosby, however, refrained from attacking Union trains carrying Confederate civilians as shields, even as he assured Lee that he would "not allow the conduct of the enemy toward citizens to deter me from the use of any legitimate weapon against them." The Confederate secretary of war went further. He endorsed not only retaliation for the Union's use of civilians on the trains but also "signal vengeance" on "all conductors and officers."[29]

Mosby was not the only menace to Early's forces. Sheridan claimed that "every train, every small party, and every straggler, has been bushw[h]acked by the people." When Lieutenant John Rodgers Meigs, son of the Union quartermaster general and a favorite of Sheridan's, was killed on October 3 by Confederate cavalrymen, Sheridan ordered the complete burning of all property within a three-mile radius of the site. Sheridan's officers began systematically shooting captured Confederate "bushw[h]ackers."[30]

Grant's orders to Sheridan by this time included an apocalyptic provision: "Eat out Virginia clear and clean as far as they [Early's army] go, so that crows flying over it for the balance of the season will have to carry their provender with them."[31] Sheridan took these orders quite seriously and by October reported to Grant from Woodstock that "in moving back to this point the whole country from the Blue Ridge to the North Mountains has been made untenable for a rebel army." Later, Sheridan quantified what "this destruction embraces." In his report to Grant, Sheridan listed what he had captured or destroyed between August 10 and November 16:

23,000 artillery rounds
19,230 small arms
1,061,000 small arms rounds
3,772 horses
1,200 barns
7 furnaces
3 saltpeter works
435,802 bushels wheat
20,000 bushels oats
77,165 bushels corn
20,397 tons hay
10,918 beef cattle
12,000 sheep
15,000 swine
12,000 lbs. ham
1 railroad depot
1 locomotive
3 box cars
947 miles of rail[32]

Sheridan sent dispatches to Grant nearly every day in September and October, keeping him informed about the strength of the Confederate forces in the Valley and the overall operations he was conducting there. Grant's orders included as the principal objective of the operation the railroad line of the Virginia Central near Staunton. Sheridan, he hoped, would establish total control not only over the large Valley but also over the railroad that fed and supplied Lee's army from the south and west. In other words, Sheridan was to attempt what Sherman had done in Georgia: wreck the Confederate army in front of him and, as important, wreck the region's capacity to sustain the army. Further, and perhaps most significant, he was to cut off and control the transportation network behind Lee. Sheridan accomplished the first two objectives with enthusiastic determination but only half-heartedly attempted the third.

Despite his claim to have captured 947 miles of "rail," there was little evidence that Sheridan disabled or wrecked the key Confederate lines. The lone locomotive, single depot, and three box cars on his long list of destruction suggested his oversight. Sheridan, for his part, focused his energies almost entirely on crippling the Valley's productive capacities, burning barns, driving off live-stock—so much so that he practically ignored Grant's orders to take control of the Virginia Central Railroad. "When this is completed," Sheridan affirmed, "the Valley from Winchester up to Staunton, ninety-two miles, will have but little in it for man or beast." In his dispatches to Grant, Sheridan kept trying to quantify the destruction. Adopting a refrain common to the Federal commanders on this subject, Sheridan wrote to Grant, "I have given you but a faint idea of the cleaning out of stock, forage, wheat, provisions, + c."[33]

For Confederate civilians in the Valley the destruction there did not need to be imagined, and to them it signaled a complete loss of "civilization." Stephen Dodson Ramseur wrote that the Federal forces and, by extension, the northern people "have put themselves beyond the pale of civilization by the course they pursued in this campaign." For Ramseur the indictment was closely linked to his understanding of the fertility and beauty of the Valley, both of which had been "totally destroyed." Ramseur lamented to his wife, "The Valley is one great desert," using the same noun that Grant had used three months earlier in his directions for the campaign. Within a few weeks Ramseur died defending the Valley, but Sheridan's campaign drew to a close having only partially fulfilled Grant's directives.[34]

Indeed, after Sheridan's troops withdrew back to Winchester, Virginia's governor requested a detailed report from the Shenandoah counties on the extent of the destruction and of what he called the "wrongs and injuries, contrary to the rules of war" perpetrated by the Union forces. Responding quickly to the governor's request and half-expecting some form of Confederate reimbursement, Rockingham County sent commissioners out into the field to quantify the losses in late October and then published their report in early November in the local newspaper. They found that Sheridan's troops burned 450 barns, 3 mills, and 1 furnace, and took about 1,700 head of cattle. Heavily targeted by Sheridan, the county contained not one railroad junction, depot, or mile of track. Despite the burning in Rockingham County, the Confederate railroads supplying Lee's army at Petersburg continued to operate untouched.[35]

Although Sheridan did not control the Valley's networks as Sherman did Georgia's, he did wreck the Confederate army under General Jubal A. Early. Having decided that Rockingham County was the "termination" of his campaign, in late October Sheridan left the Valley on the Manassas Gap Railroad and headed for Washington, D.C. But shortly after Sheridan departed, the Confederates attacked the Union army in a surprise move against the Union bases on Cedar Creek. At first the powerful shock of the Confederate forces pouring fire into the unsuspecting Union camps worked. Telegrams reached Sheridan, who, once in the capital, switched to a special train and rushed straight back to the battlefield.

After their initial success at Cedar Creek, Early's Confederates suffered a humiliating defeat. Their battlefield discipline gave way as soldiers rifled through Union knapsacks and tents, plundering food and equipment. When Sheridan's Union veterans regrouped and counterattacked, Early's soldiers, out of formation and their guard down, fled in near-hysterical panic. Early reacted poorly as well and publicly upbraided his army for its failure, making their loss all the more painful.

For all of the Union army's success in the Valley, December found Sheridan at his base near Winchester, and Grant's orders to take the Virginia Central Railroad remained unfulfilled. Sheridan claimed that, after the Battle of Cedar Creek, "practically, all territory north of the James River now belonged to me." Yet, he controlled neither the railroads nor their principal towns—Staunton and Lynchburg. In his report to Grant filed several months after the war ended, Sheridan justified his failure in this way: "On entering the Valley it was not my object by flank movements to make the enemy change his base, nor to move as far up as the James River, and thus give him the opportunity of making me change my base, thereby converting it into a race-course as heretofore, but to destroy, to the best of my ability, that which was truly the Confederacy—its armies."[36]

In the ice and cold of December, he finally sent his cavalry "to strike the Virginia Central Railroad at Charlottesville or Gordonsville." But the mission failed, as did General George A. Custer's cavalry movement up the Valley to Harrisonburg in the same month. In February 1865 Grant explicitly ordered Sheridan to take the rail nexus at Lynchburg, Virginia, on the Virginia Central as soon as the weather made a strike possible. He informed Sheridan that other Union cavalry raids were to be coordinated so that the railroad network in key parts of the Confederacy might be attacked simultaneously and shut down entirely. After taking Lynchburg, Sheridan was to head south toward Sherman's force on the coast, "eating out the vitals of South Carolina." All of these movements together, Grant maintained, would "leave nothing for the rebellion to stand upon."[37]

Sheridan made his way eventually in early March 1865 south through the Shenandoah Valley and across the Blue Ridge Mountains along the line of the Virginia Central Railroad. He decided not to proceed to Lynchburg after all, nor to venture south toward Sherman's army, but instead to move east toward Richmond. Again writing an explanation months after the end of the war, Sheridan filed his official report of what he called the "Expedition to Petersburg." He included detailed reports by his brigade commanders on what precisely was destroyed and captured. Sheridan's orders from Grant were clear: to destroy the Virginia Central Railroad and the James River Canal, and to take Lynchburg if possible. Sheridan claimed to have effected a "thorough and systematic destruction" of the railroad.[38]

In his postwar memoirs Sheridan recalled that although he avoided Lynchburg he "decided to destroy still more thoroughly" the railroad. At this point, looking back on his campaign twenty years later, he could no longer quantify the destruction. Instead, he could note only that he had "destroyed the enemy's means of subsistence in quantities beyond computation." But in July 1865 his brigade commanders reported official totals of every item destroyed—altogether 49 miles of railroad, 27 miles of telegraph, 7 depots, and 43 bridges. Leaving over 140 miles of the Virginia Central Railroad untouched, Sheridan skirted Richmond to the northwest and arrived from his "expedition" at White House, Virginia, on the old Richmond and York River Railroad line that McClellan had once occupied and that still served in 1864 as a Union supply base. "I was master of the whole country," Sheridan claimed in his memoirs.[39]

Sheridan's Valley Campaign and Sherman's Atlanta Campaign were complementary, even if Sheridan did not control the railroads in the way that Sherman and Grant had expected. Each revealed the systematic nature of the domination its commanders and armies executed. Each produced scenes of terrifying violence for civilians. Each attempted to quantify and measure the war—its losses, its course through the landscape, and its effects beyond the battlefield. Finally, each signaled a modern form of warfare that recognized the importance of networks—fighting aimed at routes, bases of supply, communication, and transportation, and, therefore, unflinching in its severity toward civilians. Because of this, each also prompted severe criticism from Democratic editors and politicians in the fall of 1864. Sheridan's burning of the Valley, in particular, indicated the fierce logic of the modern war.[40]

Sheridan so thoroughly destroyed the Confederate army operating in the Valley that its general, Jubal A. Early, reported back to Robert E. Lee alone, without a single soldier. On March 2, 1865, Sheridan's troopers shattered Early's remnant army at the Battle of Waynesboro, captured the Virginia Central Railroad, and secured its Blue Ridge Tunnel for the Union army.

Sherman applauded Sheridan's work in the Valley as "hard, bull-dog fighting." Sherman had no sympathy for the leadership of the Confederacy. And he considered them to blame for the war and wanted others to see "the awful fact that the . . . men who rule the South must be killed outright." The conquest of territory, Sherman told Sheridan, did not necessarily address this awful fact, and it mattered little to Sherman whether the killing was done "close to the borders" or "farther in the interior." Men such as Ramseur, Early, and Lee were part of "Anarchy," and their actions left the "civilized and compact Government" afflicted. Conquering the southern nation, Sherman decided, required total mastery of the country's rail systems and at the same time the deaths of those Confederates whose national identities could not be extinguished in any other way.[41]

Once in control of key junctions and railroads across the interior of the Confederacy, Sherman's army ran the trains for themselves. For the Union soldiers who rode the railroads into the South and then fought over, around, and on them, the railroad carried them out of the war zone and back into the North. Wounded soldiers were transported off the battlefields by wagons and ambulances, sometimes traveling for miles to arrive at the nearest rail head. Once at a train depot, they often found rest in a United States Sanitary Commission (U.S.S.C.) camp or a hospital. Trains would then transport many of the wounded from the battle zones to larger hospitals in the big cities. These journeys from wagon to rail were not easy. The uncomfortable wagons traveling over rough roads inflicted additional pain, especially for the severely wounded. And because soldiers were being transported from one world, the arena of violence and combat, to another, the arena of civilization and public life, the transition from wagon to rail was full of awkwardness.

Few soldiers' wounds were as grotesque as those of Ephraim C. Dawes, and few journeys were as painful or uncomfortable. A major in the 53rd Ohio, Dawes was with his unit through most of the Atlanta Campaign. In May 1864 he had marched dozens of miles a day with the 15th Corps in the Army of the Tennessee, skirmishing and fighting its way through Snake Creek Gap to Resaca and Kingston. He had already taken his wounded friend William B. Stephenson to the rail depot at Kingston and sent him home, an event that left him "feeling blue." And on May 27, at a little crossroads near Dallas, Georgia, he had privately celebrated his birthday.

The next day he was horribly wounded: he wrote in his diary on May 28, "Had my lower jaw shot off." The minnie ball took out all of his lower teeth, lip, tongue, and chin, leaving a bloody mass hanging and his throat open and bleeding profusely. "The sensation," Dawes wrote a few weeks later, "was as if a red hot iron had been thrust through my face with the speed of lightning." He went down immediately from the impact, and after a few moments of stunned incomprehension he crawled on his hands and knees toward the rear of the battle lines. The litter ambulance took him further to the rear near the field hospital, and when he saw a surgeon Dawes sarcastically wrote in the dust, "Good for thirty days [leave]." He felt, by his own account, "pretty good," but had to sit up in order to keep breathing. When the doctors held up a mirror to show him the wound, Dawes explained to his family that he wanted to cry but instead tried "to smile (with my eyes)." At Kingston he spent the night in the U.S.S.C. hospital, run by a well-known nurse, Mrs. Bickerdycke, but the women there were horrified by his wound. Even a few of the experienced surgeons refused to change his dressings. The next day, June 1, Dawes and thirty or so wounded men boarded the train for

Ephraim C. Dawes and his wife, Francis, 1883.

While a member of the 53rd Ohio Volunteers during the Civil War, Dawes was wounded in the face at the Battle of Dallas in May 1864 during the Atlanta Campaign and was grossly disfigured as a result. A prolific writer of regimental and war histories after the conflict, Dawes was fitted with a prosthetic jaw with lower teeth and adopted a full beard to cover his wounds. Lithographers and publishers used his 1863 likeness for his publications.

(Courtesy of the Ohio State Historical Society)

Chattanooga. The soldiers were the only passengers, and their private car kept them from embarrassment or explanation. Arriving at Chattanooga, however, his face sloughing off and bleeding steadily, Dawes found "no one there to tell us where to go."[42]

The following day, June 3, Dawes took one of the most difficult railroad trips of his life, from Chattanooga to Nashville. Clogged with war supplies and traffic, the trains slowed to a crawl and the journey stretched to twenty-six hours. In his diary he managed to scribble: "a trip that I shall always look on with horror." Dawes sat in the backseat of the passenger car, "partly to keep from being looked at and partly to get a sight of the country." But he could not avoid the attention. "People looking at me annoyed me almost beyond explanation," he later fumed. Dawes had to enlist his traveling companion, a fellow soldier, to shoo away those who gawked. When his old pal, Will Stephenson, met him at the depot in Louisville, Kentucky, Dawes confessed, "Perhaps, I wasn't glad to see him."[43]

On the railroad trip home Dawes wrote his parents and his siblings to explain what he had experienced and to try to assure them that he was still the same man, if grossly disfigured. His determination and stoicism in this regard could have been nothing other than astonishing to his family. Dawes wrote from the train that his wound was "sloughing freely, very painful and offensive" and that he was "nervous and weak." The staring of the other passengers, however, bothered him more than the pain.

While Dawes made his way home, Sherman's huge army captured Atlanta, and while Dawes tried to adjust to a new life at home, his old regiment set out with Sherman on the March to the Sea across Georgia.

After a few months recuperating in a soldier's hospital, Dawes went to live with his uncle and aunt, William P. and Julia Cutler, in Marietta, Ohio, where the former congressman and railroad president helped Dawes get a job with the Marietta and Cincinnati Railroad as a clerk. Later Dawes struck out on his own in a new venture: buying and selling oil leases in western Pennsylvania, West Virginia, and Ohio. Once back in Ohio, Dawes underwent an innovative medical procedure and his case was studied for years afterward in *The Medical and Surgical History of the War of the Rebellion*. In September 1864 Professor George C. Blackman performed an operation designed to restore his lower lip, using "hare-lip and interrupted sutures, with transverse adhesive straps, . . . [and] water dressings." Eventually, in 1867, Dawes was using his barely attached lower jaw with a special set of "artificial teeth" to eat food.

A renowned surgeon, Blackman was also a "moody," despairing "genius." Addicted to opium and reckless with his personal finances, the doctor was bold and dashing with the scalpel. He cut Dawes's cheeks open and stretched the skin to hold an artificial "under jaw and teeth" and to form an "under lip." Dawes took this treatment without chloroform, flat on his back, holding the hands of his brother, Rufus R. Dawes, the commander of the 6th Wisconsin Infantry. But the operation was too much, and Dawes nearly choked to death on his own blood. Unable to breathe, he ripped the prosthetic jaw and teeth out and threw them aside in a panic. A few months later Dawes underwent a second operation with Blackman, and the jaw was fitted properly. In the following months he grew a full beard to cover the "shocking deformity."[44]

Dawes had lost much in the war, including his speech, but his convictions about the promise of railroad technologies and the American free labor economy remained, it appears, intact. Equipped with prosthetics, Dawes wrote histories of the war, keeping the heroism of his regiment, and the stakes in the war, alive for the next generation. His postwar account of the life of his uncle, Republican congressman William P. Cutler, placed slavery and railroads at the heart of the Civil War. The South, Dawes wrote, "had been long preparing" for the conflict by building railroads, and "the people of the North could not be made to believe [it] was impending."[45]

Cutler's experiences in these years exemplified for Ephraim Dawes the wild gyrations of the nation's economy and its convulsive birth of modernity. In 1854

Cutler was a railroad president with 6,000 men working feverishly to lay tracks, but the Crimean War hit and securities collapsed, and he had to discharge the entire workforce. A few years later he had obtained financing in London from an exiled Polish count, and after another round of construction Cutler opened his railroad on April 9, 1857. The banking panic that year brought "disaster and ruin." He had opened his railroad just in time "to receive with fatal effect that blow which staggered commerce." And even though Cutler's Marietta and Cincinnati Railroad held a "commanding position" in 1864 as the shortest route from Cincinnati to the Atlantic seaboard, his efforts to get traffic were hamstrung by his eastern connection to the unfriendly Baltimore & Ohio, which was slowly suffocating the smaller company and waiting to take it over.

While Cutler fought in 1865 to keep his businesses afloat and Dawes battled to recuperate from his wounds, the American Civil War ground to a conclusion. Sheridan, Grant, and Sherman had captured the major railroads in the Confederacy and had driven both General Joseph Johnston (returned to command after General John Bell Hood lost Atlanta) and Lee away from the major cities and into the diminished interior.

Lee's retreat away from Petersburg in April 1865 grew desperate. His army groped its way southwest along the remaining railroad. At Appomattox Station, when Union forces caught up with him, Lee's path forward along the railroad was blocked. Federal forces also took control of the High Bridge behind him, and, as a result, Lee was trapped on the rail line, unable to resupply himself or to reach a useful junction on the now nonexistent network. He surrendered the Army of Northern Virginia and its 28,231 soldiers on April 9. Meanwhile, Sherman continued to pursue Johnston in North Carolina and on April 17 cut him off at the Durham railroad station, separating and isolating the last major Confederate army, and taking its surrender the following day.

After the surrenders, tens of thousands of northern men traveled home from the war out of the South on the railroads. Some were wounded, like Dawes, others simply decommissioned and came out of the war much in the same way they went into it, packed in railroad cars with other soldiers, slowly separating at junctions as they returned to their respective cities and towns. The Pennsylvania Central carried over 24,000 men from Harrisburg to Pittsburgh as they made their way toward their final destinations in northern Illinois, Iowa, Michigan, northern Ohio, Wisconsin, and western Pennsylvania. The Camden and Amboy transported 36,390 soldiers from Philadelphia to New York as they headed for New Jersey, New York, and New England. The Northern Central hauled 50,300 soldiers from New York as they made their way west toward their destinations in northern Illinois, Iowa, Michigan, northern Ohio, and Wisconsin. Over the old coastal Philadelphia, Wilmington, and Baltimore line went 54,910 soldiers, while 15,400 traveled home on the Baltimore & Ohio in the summer of 1865. Soldiers clogged the stations and depots along these lines.[46]

With the war over and the Confederacy defeated, a world of questions remained unanswered. For the Union soldiers returning home, what would they do? For the freedmen and -women in the South, where would they go and what would their freedom mean for them? For the Confederate soldiers and civilians, would they be reconciled to their defeat, and how would they accept the loss of their national quest? Few expected the reconstruction of the South to be straightforward. Military officials were occupying a huge area of the South and operating nearly its entire communication and transportation system. The railroad strategy that won the war left the War Department in possession of forty-seven of the South's railroads. Somehow they would need to be relinquished and returned, but how and with what labor remained unclear. When the railroads began running again, moreover, black freed people could buy tickets or get jobs working on them, and the restoration of the South's modern system could, and would, become the setting for competing visions of citizenship, freedom, and progress in the New South.

PART III

Vortex

I was then, but slowly, drawn toward the closing vortex. When I reached it,
it had subsided to a creamy pool. Round and round, then, and ever contracting
towards the button-like black bubble at the axis of that slowly wheeling circle, like
another Ixion I did revolve. Till gaining that vital centre, the black bubble upward
burst; and now, liberated by reason of its cunning spring, and owing to its great
buoyancy, rising with great force, the coffin life-buoy shot lengthwise
from the sea, fell over, and floated by my side.

—Herman Melville, *Moby-Dick,* 1851

Chapter 8

After Emancipation

MANY years after the Civil War ended, ex-slaves testified that the railroad delivered the Union army into the South. Often, they recalled seeing their first "Yankees" on the railroad. One day late in the war Dilly Yelladay's mother and aunt were taking the cows to pasture on a North Carolina plantation. When they looked down the railroad tracks, "everything was blue." At first, they stumbled in disbelief and fear because "the Yankees were ridin' up de railroad just as thick as flies." They quickly discovered, however, that the train was ringing the bell and blowing the whistle that signaled their freedom. When the Union army came down the railroad tracks, she recalled, her father and all of his uncles "run away an' went to the Yankees" to serve in the United States Colored Troops (U.S.C.T.).[1]

These intense, emotion-filled images and stories of the railroad and the momentous coming of freedom were not just a product of the war years—these associations extended back to Frederick Douglass's escape from slavery and have remained a part of African American legend and history ever since.[2]

Just as powerful were former slaves' widely shared visions of Abraham Lincoln himself coming into the South. One ex-slave, Charity Austin, was born in 1852 and was bought by a planter from Danville, Virginia, who promptly shipped her off to one of his plantations in Georgia. There she saw "husbands sold from their wives, and wives sold from their husbands." But Austin claimed to have seen Abraham Lincoln as well. "None of us knew who he wus," she explained years later. "He was just the raggedest man you ever saw. The white children and me saw him out at the railroad. We were settin' and waitin' to see him. He said he was huntin' his people; and dat he had lost all he had. Dey give him somethin' to eat and tobacco to chew, and he went on. Soon we heard he wus in de White House, then we knew who it wus come through." The railroad brought Abraham Lincoln, the railroad brought the Union army, the railroad brought freedom.[3]

In the immediate aftermath of the war, however, what the railroad would bring remained uncertain. Former slaves knew full well that the southern railroad

Andrew J. Russell, *Military Railroad Bridge over Potomac Creek*, 1864.

This bridge was destroyed and rebuilt several times. In May 1862 General Irvin McDowell employed hundreds of contraband laborers, who replaced the bridge in nine days. Here, in May 1864, the U.S. Military Railroads, again with large numbers of black freedmen, constructed the bridge in forty hours. Photographs such as this one indicated the complexity, cost, and scale of the bridges across many of the South's rivers and also conveyed the precarious, and sublime, ways the railroad was thought to defy nature.

(Lot 4336, No. 37, Division of Prints and Photographs, Library of Congress)

companies bought and sold slaves, worked thousands of them, some of them to death, and seemed to have little regard for their welfare or even their lives. The men who owned the railroads and the companies themselves stood at the center of what had been the Confederate States of America. In the heady days of emancipation, with so much on the line, African Americans also knew that their greatest asset was their skill and their labor, much of it gained from experience working on the railroads and in the fields and factories of the South.

But as southern railroads began to reconcile their accounts after the war, their losses required some kind of statement for their annual reports to stockholders. The Mississippi Central Railroad's annual report contained just one line item alluding to emancipation: "Account of C. S. [Confederate States] Bonds and cost of Negroes now free: $585,237." The Nashville and Chattanooga Railroad president was more direct in his 1867 recapitulation of the losses from the war: "We find from the books that there has been invested in negroes, in Georgia, the sum of $154,348 and negroes sold amounting to $32,805.25 leaving negro investment

$121,542.71." This amount, he rather drily noted, "is now, manifestly, a total loss." With hundreds of thousands of dollars wiped off their balance sheets through emancipation, southern railroads, like the planters who served on their boards, could no longer leverage their human collateral for credit, their preferred method of expansion throughout the 1850s boom.[4]

Surveying the losses from the Civil War, the president of the Atlanta and West Point Railroad struck a hopeful tone in his 1865 annual report. Noting that the "emancipation of the negroes of the company" and the "collapse of Confederate credit" made up over $500,000 in losses for the company, he looked ahead to what emancipation might mean. "Will not the emancipation of four millions of bondsmen," he asked, "with the future control of their own earnings, and their own movements, add greatly to the local travel of the States where they are domiciled?"[5]

He raised an important question. Freedmen would presumably control their own movements, and four million people would have immediate access to the nation's railroad systems. Earning wages, controlling their own time and resources, the freedmen would surely travel. Freedom of movement was one of the most important acts of emancipation. Riding the railroads, going where and when one pleased, was a demonstration, a rehearsal, of what it meant to be free. Access to the railroads was already a mark of first-class citizenship. But African Americans' movements, and their visions of emancipation, would be contested in the years following the war.[6]

As Americans tried to reconstruct not only the South but also the nation out of the destruction and transformation of war, the railroads figured prominently in these plans, and they became symbols of national unity. The success of the Union commanders and their "railroad strategy" in the war suggested to northern financiers what could be possible through more centralized control and management. Ironically, the literal reconstruction of the South's railroads served to unite whites north and south. Yet, for African Americans the railroads also became a crucial battleground for their civil rights. Segregation and discrimination on the railroads were obvious points of conflict, and they flared up right away. Less clear to many people at the time were the ways railroads might align powerful interests competing over visions of the New South. When northern capitalists began stitching together interstate systems, initiating their own form of railroad generalship, they needed willing southern businessmen to cooperate with them. Bringing the South back into the nation, these businessmen thought, might mean sacrificing some of the ideals of the war if necessary.

The modern society the white South had constructed for itself before the Civil War—around railroads and slavery—was half-dead at the end of the war. Although slavery was outlawed by the Thirteenth Amendment, the hierarchy of race and the power of railroads remained for white Southerners to rebuild and reorganize. The Civil War, one historian has pointed out, "had destroyed much of what made slavery so profitable—most notably its railroads, and its bonded labor." Afterward, just when the South needed modern capital and technology the most, the region seemed least able to close "the growing technological gap." But as we will see, the South's railroad companies were far from crippled. Many of their systems were rebuilt by the U.S. Army and simply handed over to their former Confederate owners in 1865, a story long forgotten in the history of Reconstruction.[7]

Given the transformations of rail travel and telegraphic information—the ways that the boundaries of place and time were obliterated and redrawn in the war—the South's reunification into the nation largely would turn on who controlled the rail systems and what they intended to do with them. The future of the South also depended in large measure on what exactly emancipation meant to black and white Southerners alike. Everyone looked for signs that might indicate how, and on what terms, the South might move forward, in the wake of a Confederate nation driven by railroads and slavery.

In the summer of 1865 northern reporters noticed tens of thousands of freed people gathered near the railroad lines, depots, and stations. The *New York Times* correspondent in Atlanta described "crowds of contrabands . . . at every station along the line, the most of them with no fixed employment, and with no definite purpose."[8] Many northern reporters, including those from the *New York Times*, disparaged the freedmen as idle and shiftless, and these stories contributed immediately after the war to a widespread suspicion among whites about black emancipation. When the *New York Times* correspondent went through Florida he described the scene in terms sure to raise alarms for white readers: "At every station we noticed large numbers of black, healthy, good-looking negroes, the larger portion females, decked in their gayest attire, and in a style that would throw the most ridiculous caricatures in the shade."[9] From every corner of the South came similarly dismissive northern newspaper reports that blacks have "simple ideas of freedom" and want nothing other than to get to a Union army camp and live in "idleness."[10]

Although many thousands of freed people congregated along the railroads in the summer and fall of 1865, they had good reasons for doing so, reasons the northern reporters failed to mention. Families hoped to become reunited so they came to the railroads and telegraph lines. The War Department's Bureau of Refugees, Freedmen, and Abandoned Lands, known as the Freedmen's Bureau, attempted to manage the transition from war to peace, from slavery to freedom. The Freedmen's Bureau operated out of offices across the South, most of them located on the old railroad network at depots and junctions the Union army captured.

Freedmen's Bureau officers organized free transportation passes on the U.S. Military Railroads for freedmen to the towns of their loved ones long separated by slavery or to places where they were contracted to work. Many freedmen, whether working for the U.S. Military Railroads, enlisted in the U.S.C.T., or hiring their labor to the Union army, had accumulated enough greenbacks to ride the trains when and where they wanted.[11]

The military railroads offered some of the best jobs in 1865, because freedmen could work away from their former masters on the plantations, gain skills, and have access to travel and independence. In Alexandria, Virginia, thirty-six men were working for the U.S. Military Railroads in August 1865. Many of them were brothers, such as Bob Turner, George Turner, and Lewis Turner, and James and William Roberson. Hundreds of Alexandria's African Americans secured contracts through the Freedmen's Bureau to work on farms across the South—many going on the railroads all the way to Louisiana, Mississippi, Arkansas, and parts of Virginia. Similar negotiations took place at every major southern city, and black laborers made long journeys on the railroads to these locations.

But among the thousands of labor contracts negotiated across the South by the Freedmen's Bureau after the war, few of them were for railroad work. In many places freedmen were already working for the railroads, and the railroad companies did not negotiate contracts through the Freedmen's Bureau. Unlike the year-long contracts on the big plantations, railroad work was more independent work, and it was for an industry that seemed to have boundless opportunities. Over the next two decades railroad workers would constitute one of the fastest growing labor sectors in the nation. Almost as important, freedmen could work *when* they wanted for the railroad—they could pull together some resources and move on to find family, or to look for other work. Although northern reformers and Freedmen's Bureau agents pushed freedmen to sign yearlong contracts, many preferred a much more flexible arrangement in 1865 and 1866. One pattern was especially clear: as families reunited, the men withheld the labor of their women and children. The forced work of women and children under slavery was no longer negotiable, and freedmen expected to work for their families as the head of their household.[12]

Contract work for day labor on the railroad suited their needs and kept their options open. "Large numbers of negroes" paid by the U.S. Army Construction Corps were working on the railroads outside of Atlanta in June 1865. Over the summer black laborers across the South migrated to the towns and cities, many of them working on the government's railroad repair crews. Far from "idle," the freedmen came to the depots and stations of the South with their eyes on the opportunities emancipation offered.[13]

In these places conflict and competition for work happened right away. In Virginia, along the old Richmond, Fredericksburg, & Potomac Railroad at Aquia Creek, the volatile mix of black and white workers and former Confederate and Union soldiers combined in August 1865 to produce one of the first postwar race riots. A simple altercation between a freedman and a white worker who was a former Confederate escalated quickly. Organized mobs of whites and blacks threatened one another with shovels and clubs. The 5th Maryland, a Unionist but nonetheless southern regiment, was called in to break up the conflict. Led by an overaggressive lieutenant, the Union soldiers arrived well after the initial altercation and turned first on the black railroad workers. According to newspaper accounts, the soldiers began to "break in the doors and windows, and drag the negroes from their beds" in the camp. In the chaos a white mob of workers formed, armed with shotguns. One black man was killed in the riot.[14]

Later, after other army units intervened, forty white workers—all of them discharged Confederate soldiers—were arrested, tried, and sentenced to a chain gang for sixty days. "The negroes have been sent back to their work," the Radical Republican *Chicago Tribune* assured its readers, "confident of protection in their rights, and encouragement in their industry." But the Aquia Creek Riot was a sign of a less secure future. Even the *Tribune* a few days later repeated an overblown rumor about the Aquia Creek incident: that the freedmen were plotting to "assassinate all the white laborers employed on the railroad" and that they had gathered up "scythes" and "knives" to carry out a massacre. In the fall of 1865 rumors among whites flew around the South regarding concerns that blacks were preparing for a major uprising in the new year. When Christmas 1865 came and went without an insurrection, nervous whites found other false alarms.[15]

The railroad work at Aquia Creek was part of a much larger U.S. Army project in 1865 to maintain and rebuild some of the South's major railroads. The Union army spent millions of dollars repairing the South's railroads before turning them over to their old companies in September 1865. Far from leaving a desolate and destroyed South, with a prostrate railroad network and no prospect for recovery, the army left thousands of miles of new rail in the South. For some railroad companies in the South, the only losses they sustained were those associated with their "negro funds."[16]

The extent and purpose of this vast rebuilding and reconstruction effort has often been obscured because so much attention has been focused for so long on Sherman's neckties and on the destruction of the rail depots in Atlanta and Columbia. What has been forgotten ever since was just how much of these same railroads were repaired by the U.S. Army before being returned to the companies free of charge. Some historians have deemed the losses to the railroads "incalculable," but in the most thorough accounting of the war's destruction, historian Paul Paskoff has shown that the Confederate railroad system "escaped the war with little or no damage."[17]

As it turned out, the end of the fighting gave some railroad companies a brand new, fully operational system. And the U.S. government did in fact calculate the costs of the destruction. The total expense of the rebuilding effort across seventeen railroads in Tennessee, Alabama, Georgia, Mississippi, and North Carolina came to $12 million in labor and material.[18]

Reconstruction of the South in this respect was literally *re*-construction, a

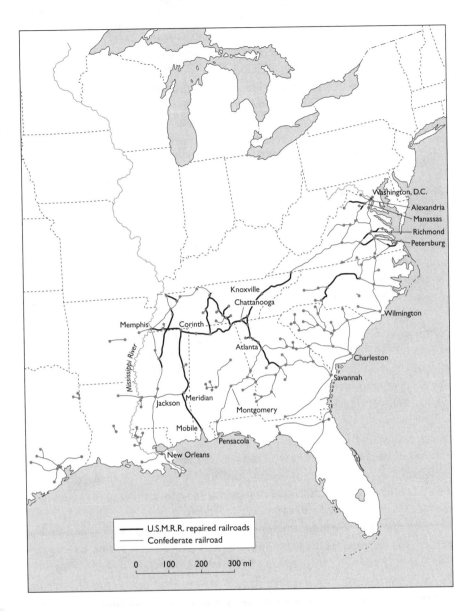

Railroads across the South repaired by the U.S. Military Railroads in 1865.

fact long obscured in the era's twisted history, which the white South remembered only as punishment and subordination, conveniently forgetting the generous terms of their restoration. Colonel William W. Wright, the Union officer
in charge of the U.S. Military Railroads Construction Corps, described in detail these reconstruction operations in his April 1866 report to the War Department. He tabulated every penny spent, every foot of lumber used, every iron spike
driven in to get the South's railroads up and running. The Nashville and Chatta-

nooga, whose president had lamented the "total loss" of $121,000 in emancipated slaves, benefited from the extensive repairs of the U.S. Army, including improvements totaling over $4 million. Wright's Construction Corps paid 4,293 men to maintain and keep that railroad running in 1864 and 1865. The 151-mile-long railroad supplied the Army of the Cumberland in the Atlanta Campaign, but "the superstructure was old," he reported, and "much worn." It had "never been of first class character" because, according to Wright, "the rail used was light." So, his Corps relaid the entire road with new T-rail on good ties. In addition, they laid over 100,000 feet of new side track at the major depots to supply the Union army, and they rebuilt 43 bridges, totaling 21,727 feet (over 4 miles) of new bridging. When the Corps turned the railroad over to the company, the Nashville and Chattanooga was better than it was when it had been seized.[19]

Similar work was done on the other lines, so much so that an entirely redeveloped railroad network in major areas of the South stood ready in the summer of 1865 for civilian use. The Nashville and Decatur line was rebuilt largely by Union soldiers in 1864 to make it basically operational, but then Wright's Construction Corps, with black and Irish laborers, came in and added 14,000 feet of side tracks, rebuilt 41 bridges and 15 water tanks, and spent $1.6 million in payroll and materials on the road. In summary, the U.S. Military Railroads repaired over 1,100 miles of southern tracks, rebuilt over 18 miles of bridging (most of it twice), and laid down 433 miles of new track and cross-ties. More mileage was repaired later. On the Memphis & Charleston's 271-mile route, the Corps rebuilt 13 water tanks and 10 bridges, which cost $88,000, and spent over $75,000 on new iron rails, spikes, chairs, and cross-ties.[20]

No railroad suffered more than the Western and Atlantic (what Wright called the Chattanooga and Atlanta) because of both Union army maneuvers across it and Confederate cavalry raids against it during the Atlanta Campaign in the summer of 1864. The Confederates tore up twenty-five miles of the railroad in a massive raid aimed at disabling the Union's key supply route. And in an effort to cut off Atlanta from external communication, Sherman, just before his November March to the Sea, "very effectually destroyed the road" and gave orders for Wright's Corps to remove sixteen miles of track between Resaca and Dalton. Yet, after Sherman's March was completed, Wright's Corps went back into Atlanta and rebuilt nearly all of the Western and Atlantic, laying down 140 miles of new track and cross-ties, raising 16 bridges, and erecting 20 new water tanks. Close to $1 million in construction labor and $1,377,145 in new material were expended on the Western and Atlantic before turning it over to the state of Georgia and its original corporate officers in September 1865.[21]

To supply this rebuilding effort, the Construction Corps operated five sawmills in Tennessee and Georgia, and these together cut a total of over 5,500,000 board feet of lumber for the railroad bridges, houses, water tanks, and wharves.

Repairing Railroad, Etc.

The U.S. Military Railroads rebuilt the South's railroads in the closing months of the war. African American railroad workers cut timber, broke rock, and hauled gravel for the grading. Their experience on the railroads as trackmen and laborers, as well as firemen and brakemen, continued after the war. In 1880 over 50 percent of all railroad workers in Virginia were black; in Pennsylvania, by contrast, railroad workers were almost uniformly white.

(From *Report of Services Rendered by the Freed People to the United States Army, in North Carolina in the Spring of 1862 After the Battle of New Bern;* Courtesy Texas A & M University Libraries)

Black freedmen worked in the sawmills as well, cutting timber, hauling lumber, and operating steam-driven machinery.

Late in the war, the Construction Corps rebuilt thirty miles of the North Carolina railroads for Sherman's army as it marched north from South Carolina. Repairing railroads from Wilmington to Raleigh, in June 1865 the Corps controlled and operated 293 miles of railroad in the Tar Heel state, and spent over $900,000 on labor to bring these roads up to full service.[22]

The Union rebuilding effort, however, extended only to those lines under the U.S. Military Railroads' control at the end of the war. Over 3,100 miles of southern railroad were seized, captured, and operated by the Union army during the fighting. This represented about one-third of all the railroad mileage in the Confederacy. Ironically, the railroads that remained in Confederate hands the longest suffered the most from the war, as they were run-down, stripped of equipment, and without working capital. Still, some of the biggest slave owning railroads— the Mississippi Central, the Mobile and Ohio, the Atlanta and Macon, the Western and Atlantic, the Raleigh and Gaston, and the North Carolina—were either entirely or partially in Union hands at the end of the fighting, and these were fully restored to operational condition.[23]

In Virginia, too, the U.S. Military Railroads and the army ran and rebuilt railroads in Alexandria, Norfolk, Petersburg, and Richmond. By April 30, when the Union army suspended all repairs on Virginia railroads, over $3.5 million had been spent on labor and materials in the state. In April alone, 4,542 railroad employees operated over 400 miles of track for the army. In the last year of the war, the U.S. Military Railroads' Virginia operations transported over 1.2 million passengers, mostly across the City Point Railroad in the siege of Petersburg. Newly built sections of railroad in Virginia cost the army $1.5 million in materials, much of it spent in April, May, and June 1865. Storehouses, buildings, offices, shops, water tanks, depots, and wharves were also newly constructed, putting the total estimated value of the army's construction and repairs to the railroads in Virginia at $3.3 million. Most of these structures were given to the Virginia railroad companies in early July 1865.[24]

As the Union army pulled out of the South and returned the railroads to their former owners, no item seemed too small to record in the transfer. One Union captain reported on the exact number of jacks, cranes, irons, spikes, screws, saws, augurs, and rope returned in precise detail. His inventory included water coolers, paper cutters, and clocks.[25]

In addition, as the U.S. Military Railroads liquidated its $30 million operations in late 1865, the War Department decided to offer the locomotives, rolling stock, and other equipment to the southern railroad companies on generous terms. Hundreds of railroad cars were simply returned to the companies, while thousands were sold on credit at reasonable rates. Locomotives were put up for sale too, and the War Department agreed to allow companies to use the revenue of future military transportation of U.S. equipment and troops, as well as freedmen using Freedmen's Bureau vouchers, as credit to purchase the available rolling stock at auction. Over 280 U.S. Military Railroads engines and over 3,000 cars were sold directly or on credit to the South's railroads. All of the repairs to these roads were essentially written off and given to the companies when they took possession of the tracks. To qualify for these terms, Confederate railroad companies were simply required to elect "loyal" officers and directors. In other words, the former Confederate directors of these companies had to take the oath of future loyalty, regardless of the history of their secessionist past or their companies' active support for the Confederacy.[26]

Despite this brisk reconstruction effort, many people in the North were under the impression that southern railroads were utterly destroyed, and nearly everyone believed that without proper railroads the region would be consigned to poverty. This view of a wrecked South came largely from northern correspondents who traveled thousands of miles on the southern railroads in the immediate aftermath of the war. From Atlanta, Charleston, and Chattanooga, they filed stories with headlines such as "The South as It Is," and they emphasized the poor state of the South's railroads. Because the South's trains crawled along at twelve miles per hour, while northern trains sped over the tracks at thirty, reporters thought that the South's railroads were at the "embryo state of progress." Convinced that the bridges and roads were probably unsafe and weakened from the war, some reporters suggested that the South's railroads could not pay for their own maintenance. One journalist traveled on a southern railroad that was willing to accept either U.S. greenback dollars or fresh garden produce as payment for a ticket. The story circulated across the North and became emblematic of the dilapidated condition of southern railroads, as well as of their lack of resources.[27]

Yet, less than a year after the war ended, reporters regularly noted that rail service in the South was largely restored. The *Glasgow Herald* in far-away Scotland reported that the Savannah and Gulf Railroad had been in operation for several months and was "thoroughly repaired and in excellent running order." The New Orleans, Jackson and Great Northern reported in October 1865 that trains were running over its entire 206-mile track, and announced in December 1866 that it had purchased from the U.S. government 20 locomotives, 23 passenger cars, and 133 box cars from "current receipts." The road was back in business without having gone into further debt.[28]

Northern journalists reported that quite a few white Southerners had not ridden in a railroad car or ventured more than three or four miles from their homes since the start of the war in 1861. This was an exaggeration, but the idea that people went so long without the modern systems of rail communication—the daily traffic of mail, news, travel, and services—seemed almost incomprehensible to Northerners. Presumably, these former Confederates would need time to reacquaint themselves with "intercommunication with the civilized world" after their "long imprisonment." In this respect some Northerners came to believe that restoring the railroad service as quickly as possible would be the instrument of "comity" between the sections. The condition of the railroads—their service and safety, therefore—served as a barometer for the need to help the white South get back on its feet and reenter the nation. But when the trains began running regularly again, their operations generated as much conflict as they did harmony.[29]

In 1868 many of the South's state-supported railroads underwent a further wholesale change: nearly all of them were privatized and sold off in state after state. South Carolina's governor secretly sold the state's share of the Blue Ridge Railroad for just 1 percent of its face value. Radical Republicans always viewed the state-owned railroad companies with suspicion, because state governors could appoint some of the seats on the boards of directors. Long associated with the planter elite and the extension of slaveholding, the railroad boards gave the governors extraordinary opportunity for patronage appointments and political favoritism. Once separated from the state's ownership, Republicans believed, the railroads might attract northern capital and investment, lead the region's economic diversification, and open up new opportunities for black and white laborers in the sure-to-follow factories, mines, and businesses.[30]

In Virginia, which led the way, as the huge state investment in railroads was transferred to private investors in a series of acts, the state was left with the mountain of debt incurred when the railroads were built before the war—approximately $45 million—but it now had no ownership stake in their businesses. Railroad financier Collis P. Huntington acquired the Virginia Central Railroad and the Covington & Ohio and renamed them the Chesapeake & Ohio Railroad. The state had spent millions of dollars on these lines before and during the Civil War, but Huntington obtained the state's ownership share for nothing but the promise to complete the line to the Ohio River in six years.

By a similar process former Confederate general William Mahone gained ownership over three railroads in southern Virginia, and Pennsylvania and Baltimore parties took control over major lines in northern Virginia. To secure the legislation, the railroad men deposited thousands of dollars into legislators' pockets, threw huge parties, and distributed lavish gifts. All sides charged the others with bribery and corruption. Yet after the flurry of special legislation divesting the state's ownership in one railroad after another, only the old Richmond, Fredericksburg & Potomac remained as a partially state-owned company. Estimates varied, but many observers calculated that the state of Virginia had lost over $26 million in the giveaway.[31]

Huntington's race to the Ohio River in six years would lead to a further exploitation: he asked for permission to use convict labor from the state penitentiary. The origins of the practice extended back to slavery and, in Virginia, to the work specifically on the Covington & Ohio. After the war *De Bow's Review* was already pointing the way toward what would become a growing trend in the South—state after state began renting convicts to the railroads as a way to boost development. In the late 1860s some 200–300 men were incarcerated in each southern state prison, and each institution experimented haphazardly with leasing some or all of their prisoners to railroad companies. Huntington was not the only railroad baron to turn to convict labor, nor was he the only one attempting to reshape the South's economic geography in these years, but by the early 1870s Huntington was leasing 380 black convicts and 53 whites to work on the C & O's tunnels. In 1872, 26 blacks and 3 white men died working on the C & O—11 men, fortunately enough, had escaped.[32]

The politics of railroads across the South became thoroughly wrapped in the politics of Reconstruction. Republicans pushed for the railroads in the hopes that businesses that would follow would bring prosperity and lead the way toward a free labor society. Democrats too supported the projects, often with an eye toward their own political and economic benefit and an end to Reconstruction on their terms, even if it meant colluding with northern businessmen. In some places, such as piedmont South Carolina and upcountry Georgia, local white conservatives joined the Ku Klux Klan to fight the Republicans and their northern railroad allies. Klan violence, much like the guerrilla violence in the war, spread along the railroads and often reached its greatest vehemence in places where black railroad workers were the most numerous, vocal, or active in politics. In Alamance County, North Carolina, where the North Carolina Railroad workshops were located, black and white workers joined the Republican Party. Blacks occupied hundreds of skilled positions on the shop floor and acted with a significant degree of independence. The Klan systematically targeted these men and the railroad that supported them. And further south, hundreds of black workers were attacked in South Carolina, as they worked to grade the railroads owned by northern financier Tom Scott. Black mobility, independence, and political activism, enabled as it was by the northern-financed railroads, prompted swift retaliation by the Klan. In many respects the Klan picked the tactics perfected by partisan and guerrilla units during the Civil War.[33]

Throughout the conquered South, the railroads were the nexus for much of the conflict over black citizenship, emancipation, labor, and mobility. One of the immediate battlegrounds developed around whether railroads should be segregated by race. Before the Civil War northern railroads segregated their cars, a practice that British travelers such as Richard Cobden found remarkable and offensive. Both Frederick Douglass and Harriet Jacobs protested against northern segregation, before and during the war, and some states forced railroads to offer equal accommodations.[34]

But in the South after the Civil War, as in much of the North earlier, the railroads ran their operations based on custom. Typically, companies issued regulations and rules about who might travel in which cars, often simply in the form of oral directions from the conductor. Because transportation companies, whether steamships or railroads, were private enterprises, they had the authority to organize passengers in ways conducive to public safety. They also had a duty as common carriers not to deny service to any particular group. So, many railroads created "ladies" cars, where women of refinement might travel apart from single men. These cars were toward the back of the train, where the smoke from the engine was less overbearing. Because the companies separated women from men, as a reasonable and necessary protection for "ladies," the railroads had no trouble accepting the idea of separating whites from blacks on the same terms and for similar reasons.[35]

Women of color in the South, no matter how refined or well educated, however, were often simply directed to the forward smoking cars. Unwritten rules barred them from sitting in the "ladies" cars, and black men were consigned without question to the smoker as well. No federal laws or state statutes required segregation or governed these company decisions—instead, the practices evolved

Andrew J. Russell, *Bird's Eye View of Machine Shops, with East Yard of Orange and Alexandria Railroad,* Alexandria, Va., 1861–1865.

In the immediate aftermath of the Civil War, African Americans seized the opportunity to work and to travel. Visible just to the left of the railroad shop smokestack and roundhouse stood the old Price and Birch "Slave Pen" at 1315 Duke Street.

(Lot 11486-C, No. 2, Division of Prints and Photographs, Library of Congress)

with the extension of the railroads and seemed to whites the "natural" result of nineteenth-century social life. By this logic segregation was affirmed in state after state as legally permissible under common law.

During the war Congress acted immediately where it could have the most effect—in the District of Columbia. In April 1862, when the Alexandria & Washington Railroad sought congressional approval to revise its charter and allow a uniform link with the Baltimore & Ohio, Congress inserted a provision into its charter that "no person shall be excluded from the cars on account of color." Similar measures followed in 1864 regarding Washington, D.C., streetcars and railroads, as Senator Charles Sumner led the Radical Republicans in efforts to prevent discrimination against black passengers.[36]

Then, on February 8, 1868, African American Catharine (Kate) Brown rode without incident in the ladies' car from Washington, D.C., to Alexandria, Virginia, over the Potomac River. On her return trip back to the District, Brown again took a seat in the ladies' car. But a policeman hired by the railroad to keep hoodlums off the platform spotted her and insisted that she leave the ladies' car, which implicitly was for white women only. Brown refused, saying, "This car will do." She pointed to her ticket and said that she would return in the same car she rode in the opposite direction just an hour earlier—the so-called white people's car. At this the policeman replied loud enough for other passengers to hear, "No damned nigger was allowed to ride in that car anyhow; never was and never would be." He wrenched her wrist, hit her above the eye, and kicked her. Brown held on to the railings in the car, later stating that she was determined to fight to "death," if necessary. But the policeman was joined by a conductor, and the two men dragged her from the car and down the pavement platform, pushing her to the ground. With the help of a bystander, Brown went to the smoking car and rode back across the river, injured and shaken.[37]

A few days later Brown filed a lawsuit, arguing that limiting the ladies' car to only whites violated the railroad's 1863 congressional charter, which explicitly stated that no person could be excluded from the cars on the basis of color. In retrospect, it might seen surprising that Brown managed to bring this suit and then contest the appeal all the way to the U.S. Supreme Court in one of its first rulings on segregation. But the story of Kate Brown's early fight for civil rights grew out of the particular mix of black mobility, railroad consolidation, Reconstruction, and free labor ideas at work in the aftermath of the Civil War.

Brown lived in the District of Columbia and in 1868 was working at the U.S. Capitol as "washwoman" for the ladies' room. Her connections to powerful Republican leaders in the Senate were extensive, so much so that she could recognize by name various clerks for Senate committees, and these ties proved important in her case. Upon hearing about her treatment on the Washington, Alexandria and Georgetown Railroad, Senator Charles Sumner immediately requested that the Senate's standing Committee on the District of Columbia begin an investigation into the affair. Senators Waitman Willey from West Virginia and Sumner from Massachusetts questioned witness after witness about the exact provisions of the company charter and the precise events surrounding Brown's ejection from the ladies' car.[38]

The violence and segregation Brown experienced, by all accounts, was part of a pattern, increasingly a common feature of the South's railroads. By June 1868 Sumner's Senate committee called eight witnesses and considered whether to repeal the company's charter as a punishment for the "outrage" against Brown. The committee found that other instances of segregation had taken place. One of them involved a black man named Seaton from Alexandria, most likely George L. Seaton, a member of the Virginia General Assembly and a prominent builder who owned $15,000 in real estate and $1,200 in personal property.[39]

Brown was twenty-eight years old at the time of her lawsuit. Born in Virginia,

Andrew J. Russell, *"Long Bridge" over the Potomac River*, 1864.

The original footbridge across the Potomac was replaced with this railroad bridge in 1864 by the U.S. Military Railroads, connecting Washington, D.C., with the army's growing camps, hospitals, and defenses near Alexandria, Virginia.

(Lot 11486-E, No. 9, Division of Prints and Photographs, Library of Congress)

she may have been enslaved in that state and come into Washington, D.C., before the war, or she may have been free, living in the District for years before the Civil War. But in 1860 she was free and a domestic servant, living in the household of Edmund French, a prominent New York railroad and civil engineer. However, French, who was in Washington to design the extension to the Treasury Building, died July 7, 1860, at age fifty-three. Perhaps through French, Brown had established connections to the Treasury Department, the U.S. Senate, and the railroad business. Indeed, her brother-in-law may have worked for the Washington, Alexandria and Georgetown Railroad company. By 1870 she was thirty-one years old and working as a "waiter," sharing a house with Lewis Simpson, a Treasury Department worker, and her sister Margaret Simpson, both of whom testified on behalf of Brown in her lawsuit.[40]

At some point after her encounter with the policeman in Alexandria, Brown went to see Alexander T. Augusta, a highly regarded black physician who lived on 14th Street, a few blocks from her home. Augusta, forty-two years old, had been born in Virginia and had accumulated some $10,000 in real estate. A veteran of the Civil War, serving as a Union army medical surgeon with the rank of lieutenant colonel, Augusta had had a similarly demeaning experience on D.C. streetcars in 1864. He too had been ejected from a train after refusing to sit in the segregated section. His case also prompted a Senate investigation led by Charles Sumner. And earlier in 1863 Augusta penned a widely read article in the *Christian Recorder* about an incident in Baltimore in which white thugs attacked him on the train and tore the shoulder straps off his uniform. Turning around the phrase used by Chief Justice Roger Taney in the Dred Scott decision, Augusta claimed that even in Baltimore "colored men have rights that white men are bound to respect."[41]

Augusta treated Kate Brown daily for several months. Because she was spitting blood, he considered her internal injuries "severe." He kept her under close supervision to monitor her "hemorrhage" and prescribed "powders, pills, and liniments" for her injuries. By all accounts from witnesses, Brown was severely injured on the railroad platform. One of the witnesses, Seth Beedy, who was traveling from Maine, was asked by the Senate committee to assess "the degree of violence" that was used. Beedy replied that he could not "define the exact degree of violence" but "it was by violence, and that alone."[42]

Brown's lawyers, Samuel Bond and George Burgess, both well-placed Republicans, claimed $20,000 in damages for the injuries she sustained. Without any personal or real property Brown, they argued, was "compelled to employ" a doctor and she could not work.[43]

Her case arrived at Burgess and Bond's law office and went to trial during a special moment in the course of Reconstruction and in the organization of civil rights in the District of Columbia. In January 1869 the National Convention of the Colored Men of America met in Washington and elected Frederick Douglass as its first president. Douglass and the convention delegates pushed hard for an end to all-white juries in the District. Then, only two months later, on March 18, 1869, Congress passed an act that retroactively invalidated any use of the word "white" in laws relating to the District of Columbia. This blanket revocation applied to any and all race limitations on electors, officeholders, and jurors. Black men were qualified and eligible for jury duty in the District after March 1869, and their names were to be gathered and placed in the box for potential service.[44]

Because of several motions and delays during 1868 and 1869, Catharine Brown's case went to trial in March 1870, nearly two years after she filed suit. The circuit court in Washington, D.C., impaneled a jury of twelve men, who together represented a portrait of the Republican triumph in the war. Ten whose race can be determined were white men, and likely all of them were. These were citizens of property and means for the most part, with large families and some wealth.[45]

The trial lasted three days, and many of the witnesses from the Senate investigation were called again to the stand to testify in the civil case. Brown showed that she had been physically injured, and her physician, Alexander Augusta, testified at the trial. Her lawyers introduced evidence that the Baltimore & Ohio, which owned the Alexandria and Washington, itself owned by the Washington,

Alexandria and Georgetown Railroad, made no distinction on the basis of color for passengers buying tickets on its various lines. They brought in testimony of African Americans who traveled the railroad regularly in Maryland and Ohio and said that they had ridden the B & O's ladies' cars "without molestation." B & O officials testified that the company did not segregate passengers.[46]

The railroad company's attorneys, meanwhile, claimed that segregation was simply the custom of the day on southern railroads, the same argument made eighty years later in the landmark school desegregation case *Brown v. Board of Education.* "In the entire section of the country in which road is located," they pointed out, "it is a custom among all railroads to have such a regulation." They argued that if they did not segregate the cars passenger traffic would drop off to nothing—segregation was necessary, therefore, to have any traffic at all. The jury, however, decided the case in Brown's favor and awarded her damages of $1,500 plus the costs of the trial and lawyers' fees.[47]

After Brown won in the lower court, the railroad company appealed the case to the U.S. Supreme Court. The railroad's lawyers argued that the company had never totally excluded persons of color from being carried in its cars and therefore had in fact complied with the letter of the law—colored persons were carried, just in different cars. Moreover, the railroad's attorneys claimed that the Congressional Act of 1863, regarding the railroad's operation and the required nondiscrimination on the basis of color, had no validity in Virginia, where the segregation took place. Segregation, according to their brief, was reasonable and legal.[48]

But the Court vindicated Brown, holding that the "temper of Congress" in 1863 was that "discrimination was unjust" and "this discrimination must cease." Congress never thought that a railroad would refuse to carry colored passengers at all, since "self-interest" would compel railroads to carry whoever might pay for a ticket. Instead, the Court found, "it was the discrimination in the use of the cars on account of color where slavery obtained" that Congress sought to address. The railroad's argument was "an ingenious attempt to evade" compliance with its charter provisions. According to the Supreme Court, Catharine Brown "was not required to look beyond the ticket, which conveyed the information that this road was run as railroads generally are."[49]

Despite the victory, the implications of the case were severely limited. The Court's legal reasoning would later be ignored in *Plessy v. Ferguson,* the 1896 decision upholding segregation laws, because few railroads were so chartered by Congress. Even in 1873, the *New York Times* pointed out, the "right of railroad companies to make regulations separating the races in their cars" remained in place for those that did not have any restrictions in their charter.[50]

Brown's experience in February 1868 when she boarded the train in Alexandria, Virginia, indicated just how quickly, persistently, and quietly the white South turned to segregation in the aftermath of the Civil War. A month after she was ejected from the ladies' car, *De Bow's Review* told its readers that the South

Long Bridge, 2010.

When Kate Brown crossed the Potomac River on this bridge in 1868 and was forcibly removed from the ladies' car in Virginia, the Washington Monument was only half-completed. Brown's employment at the U.S. Capitol placed her in contact with powerful Republican Party lawyers and politicians. Her lawsuit against the company went to the U.S. Supreme Court five years later. (Courtesy of Margaret T. Konkel)

faced a "negro problem" and that the removal of white oversight after the war would lead to vice, degradation, and failure for blacks. "Without the authority and control of the white man," *De Bow*'s argued, blacks "cannot progress." Such editorials were increasingly common. Democrats charged Republicans with purposeful racial mixing. Pro-slavery defender George Fitzhugh, once a great advocate of the Covington & Ohio Railroad as essential to the South's future, now blasted the project as controlled by Northerners and therefore likely to turn Virginians into subservient shopkeepers. In the pages of *De Bow's Review*, Fitzhugh disparaged the Freedmen's Bureau as a "zoo" and as an experiment in science to see if blacks could be elevated. Ever since the advent of black voting and military Reconstruction, *De Bow*'s maintained, whites had been "robbed and plundered" in a "nefarious design" sure to bring "utter ruin and degradation." The "only thing whites can do," according to *De Bow's*, "will be to SEGREGATE."[51]

Little did Brown know, perhaps, but the Washington, Alexandria and Georgetown was part of a key link in the struggle of various northern railroad interests to gain access to the South. Positioned at the Washington, D.C.–Alexandria gateway, the railroad possessed the only railroad bridge over the Potomac River during and immediately after the Civil War: "Long Bridge."

Two giant companies—John W. Garrett's B & O and Tom Scott's Pennsylvania Railroad—battled for the Washington-Alexandria gateway and the routes that might connect with this bottleneck. In Virginia, where Conservatives were restored to power quickly and where Radical Reconstruction was short-circuited, the state legislature never passed an equal accommodation law prohibiting discrimination by race on the railroads. So, the railroads were free to regulate their cars as they saw fit. Northern financiers made little objection to these social practices, as long as they could continue striking backroom deals with southern Conservatives to bridge the gaps in their systems, acquire convicts from the state penitentiary, and secure local aid to finance construction. Tom Scott, Collis P. Huntington, and others acquired Virginia's railroads at a fraction of their cost, but they were little interested in the fortunes of freed black people like Catharine Brown working or riding on their trains.[52]

In Texas, Mississippi, and Florida, in all of which laws had been passed requiring segregation on railroads in 1865 and 1866 ("Black Codes"), the Reconstruction legislatures reversed course and passed new laws that required equal service.[53]

But these state measures proved limited in effect and vulnerable in court. Many were repealed once Conservatives recaptured state offices across the South after 1870. Others went unenforced. Catharine Brown's experience indicated just how arbitrary the rules were. After the Civil War, as railroad systems were interconnected and reached across multiple state lines, equal accommodation laws were ineffective because they could not apply to interstate companies—the very same companies whose capital and expansion the Republican governments so eagerly sought in these years. Companies therefore made pragmatic decisions. They segregated passengers whether there were laws requiring so or not. Brown was successful before the U.S. Supreme Court only because Congress had acted on a particular railroad company's charter. The arguments the railroad made against her indicated much of what would come to pass across the South in the years to come—segregation was defended as modern, efficient, necessary, systematic, and legal.

Years later, in the 1880s, states across the South, in fact, began to pass a new round of segregation laws that applied specifically to travel within their states. This second wave of segregation was crafted amid signs of rising black expectations and self-assertion in the South, urban racial mixing, deepening white supremacy, and political jockeying within the Democratic Party. Yet, it came after an earlier first wave of segregation embedded in the Black Codes and practiced by the railroads themselves after the Civil War.

Following Catharine Brown's example (although without the advantages of her particular case), black women across the South, such as Ida B. Wells, a Memphis newspaper editor and an early champion for civil rights, began to win lawsuits in the 1880s, allowing them access to the whites-only ladies' cars. Beginning with Tennessee, southern states responded with segregation laws forcing railroads to run separate cars for each race and, by doing so, foreclosed all sorts of scenarios made possible with interstate travel.[54]

Northerners saw railroads as a generic and significant criterion of progress for the South. White Southerners saw them as the means to end Reconstruction and paradoxically to restrict black mobility. But the idea of the sheer necessity of railroad growth after the war meant different things to different Southerners, and the changes that railroads were bringing to the South before the war only continued to accelerate after the shooting stopped. Cotton agriculture spread into the upcountry and piedmont South, just as interior towns swelled, and older port cities languished. Both blacks and whites wanted to turn the force of these patterns to their advantage. Black Mississippians spoke of railroad building as a way to "make this Whole South flourish," and thousands of blacks petitioned to get railroad work in a single Mississippi county. White conservatives also viewed railroads as a catalyst for prosperity but displayed little appreciation for ideas about black free labor. In their view railroads might open up the interior South, as well as encourage immigration and diversification, but only if black labor stayed on the plantations. White prosperity and black freedom of movement could not easily coexist. Railroads could enable the former by foreclosing the latter.[55]

Yet, railroads remained the principal feature in the social landscape of the reunited nation—the means of personal mobility, the carriers of progress and modernity, and the most prominent instruments for wealth, power, and geographic dominance.

We do not know precisely why Catharine Brown traveled to Alexandria on February 8, 1868. Most likely, her trip was to visit family. She seems to have traveled to Alexandria with some regularity. Ironically, we know much more about the railroad rivalries competing to acquire this gateway than about the passengers, such as Brown, who used it. We do know, however, that her ticket—the key evidence in the case—was printed exactly the same as those issued to white passengers. Brown took this fact to mean that she could enter the ladies' car.

Perhaps we can infer something about the clarity of her intentions that day. The railroad argued repeatedly in court that the routine practice on the Washington, Alexandria and Georgetown in 1868 was to run south to Alexandria with three cars in tow behind the locomotive—the smoker, a middle car, and the ladies' car in the rear. Once in Alexandria the engine switched places and the cars were therefore reversed. The ladies' car on the way south became the smoker on the way back north, and the smoker on the way south became the ladies' car on return north. The railroad claimed that Catharine Brown was probably confused by this switching and that she did not know her place or the routine practice along this stretch of the railway. But Brown, in taking the case to court, in testifying, and in every brief her attorneys filed, denied this charge.

The long history of the railroad and its modernity was not over, of course, and the victory that Brown won in court did not prevent segregation. Northern railroads continued to employ almost exclusively white labor, virtually shutting out black railroad workers (see Appendix, Table 11). The Supreme Court's 1896 decision in *Plessy v. Ferguson* upheld railroad segregation laws, and even cited Brown's case, only to dismiss its larger meaning. The Court bent over backwards to separate political from social equality before the law, and concluded that segregation, or social inequality, in and of itself did not constitute unlawful discrimination. From the Plessy case, the doctrine of "separate but equal" sprang forth in American law. Streetcars, railroads, ferries, and eventually highway motels and rest stops were ultimately segregated across the South, a practice that continued until the Civil Rights movement and the passage of the Civil Rights Act in 1964.[56]

But Brown's case shows that in the immediate aftermath of emancipation, black Americans moved across and within the South, their mobility a visible sign of their claim to citizenship, social and political. Like Frederick Douglass before her, Catharine Brown challenged segregation not only through her moral certitude but also through the way her social actions shaped the modern world. Unlike Douglass, whose escape depended on his passing unrecognized, Brown's case depended on the recognition she could gain, and on the network of those who witnessed her treatment. Brown clearly wanted to establish the meaning of emancipation both for a specific time and place—the short railroad trip across the Potomac River that she regularly took—and by implication for post–Civil War America writ large. She won her case in court, but it would take years for the modern world around her to accept and recognize the broader meaning of that decision.

Epilogue

The Road to Promontory Summit

I T is one of the great ironies of American history that the Credit Mobilier Company would become the instrument of corruption in the building of the nation's first transcontinental railroad—the Union Pacific. The Credit Mobilier ultimately became the construction company that handled the contracts to build the Union Pacific Railroad. Over several years it charged the Union Pacific enormous markups on labor and services for construction, and tens of millions of dollars were siphoned out of government grants into the pockets of Credit Mobilier's stockholders. As the Union Pacific rushed to complete the railroad in 1868, its contractors ran up hugely inflated bills on every item—labor, wooden ties, horseflesh, hammers, picks, and shovels.[1]

Credit Mobilier, however, was founded before the Civil War with an entirely different purpose—to finance the South's railroads, free the region from the grip of British capital, and initiate a southern transcontinental route through northern Mexico. Credit Mobilier and its twisted history give us a clear indication of how much the Civil War altered the course of American national development and how in its aftermath a new round of financiers and builders stepped forward out of the war to make the nation and the railroads work to their advantage.

The transcontinental project, so long delayed before the war, had been from the start a colonial effort contested between the North and the South. Both sections competed for the authority to extend their empires into the West. The war interrupted the South's expansion, contained and eliminated slavery as an economic system, and secured for the North its vision for railroad and homestead colonization of the Great Plains. The railroad's land grant, its engineering, its marketing, and its settlement plan were the clearest indicators of the emergence of modern America to come out of the Civil War—a society organized around geographic mobility, technological expansion, and the conquest of nature.

Asa Whitney's 1849 plan for a railroad to the Pacific assumed that the world's commercial flows could, and indeed would, be altered by the railroads. The opening of Cornelius Vanderbilt's railroad across Nicaragua in the 1850s, and his fast steamship lines to and from that crossing point, suggested how quickly global patterns of trade were changing. Natural geographic barriers fell all through the 1850s as tunnels, bridges, and railroads revolutionized spatial and temporal ideas.

Although the Union Pacific was built across the Nebraska prairie, there were other routes and plans competing for U.S. government and foreign investment in the 1850s and 1860s. For years all sorts of powerful interests campaigned for selection and funding as the first transcontinental railroad. A southern-rights newspaper editor and Democratic political operative named Duff Green set up the original Credit Mobilier Company—called the Pennsylvania Fiscal Agency. Green had been prominent on the political scene during President Andrew Jackson's administration, helping start the rise of the Democratic Party, but, like John C. Calhoun, he broke with the Northerners in his party. By the 1850s he was deeply involved in railroad projects he hoped would lead to southern independence. He chartered dozens of companies across the South, and he threw together a construction company to build the railroads. In a flurry of financing and speculative promotion, Green expected the railroads to knit together the South and provide an essential framework of regional unity and identity. He also took the lead in developing a Pacific railroad across Mexico through the South, one that he hoped would connect to the New Orleans, Opelousas and Great Western Railroad. Green secured a charter in Texas with a generous land grant from the state, and then proceeded to ask Mexican president Mariano Arista for a charter to build the railroad to Mexico City and Mazatlan. Mexico gave a charter to the Rio Grande, Mexican and Pacific Railroad Company, as well as generous land grants for it. Green had orchestrated three companies into a southern transcontinental plan linking New Orleans to Texas to Mexico.[2]

Having acquired the charters for this international enterprise, Green found that he needed vast sums of money to build and complete the railroad. The question for Green became where the initial money for construction would come from for such a risky project—where would he acquire ready cash to commence grading and track laying? Hoping to attract some New York and Philadelphia capital for his southern transcontinental route, Green, a resident of Georgia, organized a holding company in Pennsylvania—the Pennsylvania Fiscal Agency. American railroad promoters, like Green, were strapped for cash, and they had to pay contractors (and the workers) in part with "hypothecated" securities below their par value. Green wanted to get cash for construction on much more favorable terms, and so proposed that his holding company would pool and manage stocks and bonds, recognizing that "the use of credit" had become an "indispensable part of the improved machinery" of commerce.[3]

The plan was ambitious indeed, and it was very much a product of its time and place—the U.S. South in the 1850s: the faith in railroads to redirect trade and immigration toward the South; the eagerness to break across Mexico and into the West; the search for capital in England, France, and even Mexico on more favorable terms; and the hypothesis that the South's railroads could be inter-woven through a new round of building. In 1859, when Green's Pennsylvania Fiscal Agency opened its doors, the prospects seemed bright. Dozens of railroad contractors applied to go down to Texas and start construction.[4]

But secession and Civil War intervened, and Green, who at first opposed secession but nevertheless became a Confederate, left the Pennsylvania Fiscal Agency in Pennsylvania and went South for the war. During the war the company was sold out from under Green by the remaining stockholders—to the Union Pacific's quirky but ruthless financier, Thomas C. Durant, who renamed the venture Credit Mobilier in 1864. Green had failed to build a southern transcontinental railroad, but he had succeeded in creating a peculiarly modern instrument that Durant could use. Green had come as close as anyone to solving a problem that vexed every huge private-public internal improvement—where to obtain ready cash for construction at rates reasonable for success. His fiscal agency created one of the first shell companies in American history. It employed no one. Its entire purpose was to obtain credit and extend contracts with limited liability for its shareholders.

All sorts of changes flowed from the Civil War, transforming the modern nation. Green's ouster and the rebirth of the Pennsylvania Fiscal Agency as the Credit Mobilier were perhaps the least visible to the public. But other changes that came out of the war were more plainly obvious. On the Pennsylvania Rail-road the heavy logistical demands of the war led to the "near total eclipse" of the board of directors and to the emergence of powerful manager-directors, such as Thomas Scott and J. Edgar Thomson. The decisions facing the company in the war were technical and immediate and could not be resolved by board commit-tees. Instead, the presidents and vice presidents increasingly made the decisions. Well aware of what the U.S. Military Railroads had accomplished in the war, the Pennsylvania Railroad began assembling a 3,000-mile network in the aftermath of the conflict, taking over other railroads one after another. These maneuvers took place without any stockholder consultation. A new era of business organization had dawned, and other railroad executives followed in the path of the Pennsylva-nia. They bought up rival companies, leased others, and bypassed towns if they did not like the leaders or receive enough support. Uninterested in the larger ide-ologies coming out of the war, such as emancipation and freedom, these profes-sional managers made specific business decisions focused on geographic control. Indeed, the persistence of racism after the war, for example, led some railroads to avoid locating their lines in black-settled towns in the North, cutting off places such as New Philadelphia, Illinois, from the expanding network of rails.[5]

The war brought other lessons, especially the need for a Pacific Railroad. When the war began, congressmen saw that the railroads altered ideas about time and distance. And these changes indicated to them the great military benefits of a transcontinental railroad. One congressman in the 1862 debates on the Pacific

Railroad bill recognized that the army had been able "by means of steamboats and railroads to concentrate more decisive action on any given point in three months, than otherwise could have been done within one year." The debates over the 1862 Pacific Railroad bill showed that congressmen, whether Republican or Democratic, viewed the railroad as a means of advancing the political, symbolic, economic, and military goals of the nation. Because southern congressmen had gone to the Confederacy, there was little opposition to these ideas. Those who registered opposition were almost to a person concerned with the potential for corruption. Led by the Republican vision for the nation, Congress embraced a new set of imperatives in the war—first, that other nations were building similarly vast projects with public support and, second, that the general public of the nation desired the project. Between 1850, when Congress approved the first federal land grants in history (for the Illinois Central), and 1862, when it passed the Union Pacific land grants, arguments about the constitutionality of such ventures virtually disappeared.[6]

A further important change had taken place, one which white Americans also viewed as entirely modern. Backed by the federal government and encouraged by the railroads, white settlers moved onto the Great Plains and forcibly pushed Indian nations out of the way. The colonial project to link up the modern nation, extend its empire, and settle the lands took shape first in Kansas, where the growing railroads in the 1850s were jeopardizing every treaty the U.S. government had struck with Indian nations. The roads were expanding so quickly that white settlement on Indian lands could not be held back.[7]

Tens of thousands of Euro-Americans took the Overland Trail west in the 1850s, settled on the Iowa, Kansas, Nebraska, and Minnesota prairies, and crossed into formerly Native American lands. Between 1853 and 1856, the U.S. government initiated and signed over fifty-two treaties with Native groups, and each of these legal documents duly recorded vast cessions of lands. Indian agents and the Bureau of Indian Affairs inaugurated a series of policies aimed at bringing Native Americans onto reservations and clearing corridors for white settlement and travel. The agency's reports were couched in the guise of "civilization" and the language of progress. But their efforts were aimed at restricting the mobility of nearly all of the Indian tribes, by fixing them on reservations, out of the way for railroad development on the prairies.[8]

In Kansas this process was under way in the 1850s and was characterized by gross fraud. When Lincoln eventually signed new treaties with the Delaware, Kickapoo, and Shoshone tribes during the Civil War, it was the railroad companies that ultimately obtained title to the Indian lands in Kansas.

Events taking place on the Great Plains indicated much about the modern America taking shape. In Kansas a young man named William F. Cody went to work for the U.S. Army Quartermaster Department during the Civil War. After the war Cody went to work for the Kansas Pacific (at that time it also called

Andrew J. Russell, *Engineers Camp, Weber Canyon, the Union Pacific Railroad*, 1868.

This photograph captured part of Samuel B. Reed's team of surveyors for the Union Pacific. Involved in every stage of the construction, Reed was pressed in the summer and fall of 1868 by financier Thomas C. Durant to cut corners on the engineering in Weber Canyon in northern Utah. In early 1869 Reed wrote his wife, Jennie, that the Union Pacific had "squandered uselessly" "immense amounts of money." One month before the Union Pacific's completion, the *New York Times* called its construction "one of the most monstrous frauds that was ever perpetrated upon any Government." (Courtesy of Special Collections Department, University of Iowa Libraries) itself the Union Pacific or Union Pacific Eastern Division). He was a meat pro-vider, hunting bison on the Kansas plains to feed the thousands of workers laying tracks. Cody started out killing twelve buffalo a day and was paid $500 a month. He earned the nickname "Buffalo Bill" and later claimed that he personally killed 4,280 bison in less than twelve months. But in May 1868, after building over 400 miles of railroad, the Kansas venture ran out of money for construction and Cody's contract was suspended. The bison were quickly becoming nearly extinct, in the process reshaping Native American and U.S. government relations.[9]

Simultaneously, to the north the Union Pacific Railroad was also feverishly grading its line and laying tracks. To show off what the Union Pacific accom-plished, Thomas C. Durant organized a major celebration when the railroad's construction reached the 100th meridian. He invited hundreds of dignitaries to the end of the line in October 1866: congressmen, newspaper editors, politicians, and generals. The invitation list looked like a roll call from the Civil War, includ-ing all of the prominent generals and admirals: Sheridan, Thomas, Meigs, Meade, Cullum, Farragut, and Hancock. August Belmont was on the list, along with other New York bankers. Special trains were assembled at Omaha and ferried the guests to the end of the tracks. There they were treated to a special performance: a "wild west" show with 100 Pawnee Indians who danced, rode, and acted for the assembled visitors, even staging a mock attack on the tents at dawn. Durant fretted for months over every detail and pestered the construction engineers and Union Pacific employees relentlessly. He retained a professional "landscape pho-tographer," J. Carbutt of Chicago, to take large prints and "views." And for $1,735 he hired George Pullman to provide his company's new luxury "palace cars" on the excursion trains from Albany, New York, to Chicago and from Chicago to North Platte, Nebraska. The "One Hundredth Meridian Excursion" by all ac-counts boosted the Union Pacific's public image and was considered by Durant and the investors to be a resounding success.[10]

To any casual observer the Union Pacific's scale of operations appeared remi-niscent of the Civil War. In June 1867 the *Cincinnati Gazette*'s special correspon-dent reported that 1,500 "tie getters" were chopping down trees all along the route, wherever timber could be found. One hundred thousand ties were ready for the tracks, 2,000 men were grading the road, and "immense construction trains" stood in support "like the grand reserve of an army." The spike drivers sounded like a "hotly contested skirmish" and the cacophony like "the rumble, and grumble, and roar of the wonderful advance." Everything about the project signaled the exuberance of the age of progress, the confidence in such large-scale projects, and the retreat of nature before them. The *Gazette* could hardly restrain its enthusiasm:

> Civilization rolls here like a freshly risen flood; bears up the former life of the
> wilderness like drift wood, and forces it on before. The track of the buffalo is

marked still, but their herds have gone westward; their haunts centuries old are deserted. All wild animals are following them. The prairie dogs have moved their cities. The ruins are frequent; they attest to the march of Empire.[11]

The "march of Empire" was marked by the conquest of nature, and this narrative for the American nation began to replace the old divisions of the Civil War period. The imperial ideas that surrounded the Union Pacific only became more powerful in the decades that followed its construction. William F. Cody picked up the themes of the Union Pacific's One Hundredth Meridian Excursion and in the 1870s began his own version of the "wild west" performance. In his lifetime Cody had witnessed and participated in the great iterations of transportation technologies—from the Pony Express to the transcontinental railroad—and he believed in a national narrative of American technology and moral progress. His "wild west" celebrated the way Americans battled against nature and the frontier. This conflict, he suggested, was the nation's defining struggle. His shows focused on how white Americans became Americans: defeating the Indians, clearing the plains, building railroads, establishing farms and settlements, and defending them with the U.S. Army.[12]

Neither Cody nor his performances confronted the recent bloody Civil War, the sectional conflicts, or the Confederacy's bid for independence. Instead, Cody's shows emphasized the transformation of the nation through conquest in the West, not the South—over nature and Native Americans, not over railroad networks and fellow white Americans.

Only a few outliers had doubts about this story of American progress and its elevation of technology, conquest, and modernity. Thoreau had been an early dissenter, questioning the moral capacity of the new technologies. Melville too was a prescient moralist. Later, looking back and summing up his experience in these middle decades of the nineteenth century, the historian, philosopher, and writer Henry Adams observed that his generation "was already mortgaged to the railways, and no one knew it better than the generation itself." Adams thought that the railroads were "but one active interest, to which all others were subservient, and which absorbed the energies of some sixty million people to the exclusion of every other force, real or imaginary." Indeed, the railroads contributed to "a steady remodelling of social and political habits."[13]

Adams was not alone in feeling beholden to the railroads. But he was rare in his willingness to think about the broader implications, including the price Americans seemed to be willing to pay for their modern society. Like Thoreau, he had misgivings about the railroad's effect on his generation, and he worried that the age of machines had the potential to become a peculiarly dehumanizing moral force in history. Adams also knew that the great rush to build railroads that resumed after the war's fighting ended, and the finances, engineering, and labor they required, surpassed anything accomplished before the war. As these colossal enterprises went forward, the opportunities for malfeasance, graft, fraud, labor exploitation, and self-delusion multiplied. In the American South railroad promoters turned to convict labor, and hundreds of African Americans died in the tunnels of Appalachia. In the American West dozens of Indian treaties were abrogated and trampled upon, bison herds were hunted to extinction, Chinese laborers were imperiled in the high Sierras, and fraudulent kickbacks were handed out to congressional supporters.[14]

There were good reasons for Henry Adams to be concerned about the machine age. Nevertheless, the largest national project to come out of the Civil War, the first transcontinental railroad, indicated much of what Americans thought was modern about their reunited nation. Its power to advance progress seemed undeniable, its majesty as a feat of engineering unequaled. Few enterprises symbolized the mobility of the nation, and its mastery over nature, more eloquently. At the moment of transcontinental unification in 1869, as Americans rejoiced in the wholeness of their nation, they also recognized something that Cody and others helped us to forget—that the railroads came with the Civil War.

On May 10, 1869, the nation's telegraphs hummed with the exhilarating news that the Golden Spike had been driven at Promontory Point, Utah. As the *New York Times* announced the next day, Americans were "henceforth emphatically one people." When the last three hammer blows fell on the spike, the *Times* explained, "the lightning came flashing eastward, vibrating over 2,400 miles between the junction of the two roads and Washington, and the blows of the hammer upon the spike were measured instantly in telegraphic accounts." At 2:47 p.m. Washington time, 3:10 p.m. New York time, 2:30 p.m. "precisely Philadelphia time," and at 11:47 a.m. San Francisco time, the signal from Promontory Summit came that finally the national project was "Done." With the word received across the nation at the same moment, although recorded at different times, "The Continent was spanned with iron."[15]

Across the nation, in towns and cities, in the East, West, and South, Americans paused to hear these signals and contemplate what they might mean. After the ping of the final spike came across the wires, great celebrations erupted, marked by joy at the national accomplishment and anticipation for its great future. In Chicago one hundred thousand people joined in celebration and marched in the streets in a parade eight miles long. In San Francisco three days of festivities kicked off on May 8, when the completion was initially supposed to take place, and continued until the work was done. In New York bells pealed and churches held hushed services to the glory of the national endeavor. There was a sense of great expectation, and nearly every speaker and news editor talked and wrote of it as an event that literally linked Americans in a synchronized moment of national experience and destiny. The great space of the American continent, it was widely thought, had been conquered by the railroad, and time had been universally if imperfectly bridged by the telegraph.

The country's premier news journal, *Harper's Weekly*, noted about the Pacific railroad's completion that the "remarkable event" was celebrated in Chicago with great enthusiasm while in New York it was received calmly and in a frame of mind "as on the occasion of the capture of Richmond." Americans, perhaps especially in the East, could not help but think at such a moment of the recent Civil War. New Yorkers seemed to slip into the same solemnity that gripped them four years earlier. They sang anthems. They gathered for prayer and contemplation of their changed world and the new achievement's consequences.[16]

Most speakers, whether politicians, clergymen, or railroad officials, took the opportunity to reflect on the whole era from the 1850s up to that day and moment on May 10, 1869. At New York City's old Trinity Church, for example, its rector, Rev. Dr. Francis Vinton, stood that morning at noon to preach a sermon at a special service commemorating the railroad. Vinton was August Belmont's brother-in-law and a widely respected theologian. He had served at Grace Episcopal in Brooklyn Heights before being called to the bigger city church in Manhattan. Looking back, he reminded his congregation that the railroad "was begun when the nation was agitated by war and is finished now when we enjoy a reign of peace." The scale of what the railroad meant, like the war, however, was hardly comprehensible to him, and he searched for ways to express what it had taken to complete the project. "When we contemplate this achievement, we can hardly realize its magnitude," he explained, "three thousand two hundred and eighty-five miles of continuous railway within four degrees of latitude and fifty degrees of longitude."[17]

Vinton, like other speakers that day, also turned to the railroad's larger meaning. He tied the completion of the railroad to the future peace of the nation and thought it would inaugurate an end to sectionalism. "It will preserve the Union of these States," he assured his listeners. The railroad "prevented a separation" and would forever bind "the States of the Atlantic and Pacific into one nation." Vinton was speaking in terms that his listeners no doubt found appealing and understandable. To see the transcontinental railroad in these terms, as somehow naturally unifying, comforted Americans, but it set aside the role of the railroad in the coming and fighting of the nation's bloodiest war and its extraordinary expansion into the West.[18]

The railroad appeared to be the achievement of the war generation, the final field for the great Civil War generals—Sherman, Sheridan, and Grant, all of whom spent some time in the West. "The closing of the war of the rebellion, and the opening of this great road, constitute a new epoch in our history," one speaker explained. American "nationality," "progress," and "power" were altered with the completion of the first transcontinental. The railroad was like the spine and

Completion of the Pacific Railroad, in *Harper's Weekly*, May 29, 1869.

This image was a metaphor for where the nation was going, although it said little about where the nation had been. Created by Alfred R. Waud, one of the most prolific Civil War sketch artists and lithographers, the image suggested a national tapestry of progress. Far from binding the nation, railroads and the culture that developed around them had been one of the root causes of discord and division. (University of Nebraska–Lincoln Libraries) skeleton for the nation with "ribs of iron in every direction." The nation had "telegraphic nerves." Beyond any doubts, moreover, the nation had "proven that it has bones and sinews and blood, on the battlefields" of the Civil War.[19]

At the moment of technological unification, nearly every speaker explicitly acknowledged the Civil War. For the previous twenty years, Americans of every rank, gender, race, and section felt the effects of the great compression of space and time that the railroads and the telegraphs inaugurated. The railroad network, however fixed on the ground with spikes and rails, was so new that its meaning, purpose, use, and consequence were open to the imagination in the period between 1838 and 1869.

An underlying sense of relief, tinged with anxiety, was palpable on May 10, 1869, in the midst of all the fireworks, parades, speech making, and prayer. The day reminded many Americans of the nation's long passage through war and conquest, and the day raised their hopes that the promise of the technology might avert future such struggles.

Those searching for meaning and direction in the events at Promontory Summit tried to imagine a way that the destructiveness and violence that accompanied the nation's technological progress might be turned into a more productive, even utopian, future. Americans in the era of the Civil War placed great faith and confidence in the power of technology to advance moral and social progress. That faith was shared by those who stood in the least powerful ranks of society—Frederick Douglass, Catharine Brown, and countless others who used the railroad to win freedom and claim equality. But Douglass and others knew also that the modernizing world of rail, steam, and telegraph supported numerous competing futures.

The iron way of the railroads, of technology broadly, could lead in any number of directions. In fact, moral progress so often tied to the railroads was equally open to interpretation. The path of the United States out of slavery, through war, and into emancipation proved especially uncertain and awkward. Americans took up the railroads and created competing visions of modernity. In doing so, they revealed that greater access to information, communication, and mobility did not necessarily produce a fairer or richer democratic republic. But what Americans did with the technology, *how* they used it, and especially *who* used it, produced revolutionary changes in society.

Between 1838, when Douglass made his escape from slavery, and 1869, when Catharine Brown's segregation case went to trial in Washington, D.C., Americans built railroads and strung telegraph wires at a furious pace. The lessons learned from their first brushes with the systematizing technologies of the railroad, telegraph, and steamship included a widespread understanding that the landscape and nature could be bent to human will. And the war seemed only to confirm these sentiments, pushing aside the anxieties of an earlier era.

Americans wanted desperately to be modern. During this great period of expansion and national formation, Americans had just begun to assemble an idea of what the railroad was but not what it might mean for their lives and their nation. In this context the railroads became especially important because they changed the way Americans understood the possibilities and challenges of their world. The building of railroads, the wars in the American South and on the Great Plains, and the consolidation of the expansive empire that was the United States were all part of the same process and time period. The Civil War became the first and the greatest unanticipated field for the shaping of the new technologies.

Acknowledgments

MY research for this book would not have been possible without the generosity of John and Catherine Angle, who have supported the University of Nebraska-Lincoln Department of History for many years. John Angle died in 2008, and I will miss him dearly. His enthusiasm, good humor, and positive spirit remain an inspiration. The Angles' support made possible much of the digital research at the heart of this book's analysis and interpretation.

I am indebted as well to the American Council for Learned Societies for the Digital Innovation Fellowship, which I received in 2008, to the Newberry Library for a Short-Term Research Fellowship in 2007–2008, and to the British Association of American Studies for a Visiting Professorship at the Eccles Centre for American Studies at the British Library. Parts of the research were conducted with Richard Healey, University of Portsmouth, and in collaboration with him on an Economic and Social Research Council (ESRC) grant. I presented parts of this work to faculty in the History Department at the Episcopal High School in Alexandria, Virginia, where I was the Ben Geer Keys Scholar-in-Residence in 2008. I gained valuable insights from their close reading and suggestions. I also presented several chapters to the Nineteenth-Century Studies Workshop at the University of Nebraska, where I received valuable feedback from a great group of students and colleagues.

My colleagues and friends have offered cogent criticism as well as plain encouragement at nearly every stage of this project. I feel fortunate at the University of Nebraska to have such generous colleagues — Margaret Jacobs and Andrew Graybill read the entire manuscript and helped me immensely at a critical stage. Edward L. Ayers generously read an early draft of the manuscript and offered his always cogent, thoroughly encouraging, and perceptive analysis. Aaron Sheehan-Dean reviewed the manuscript with a sharp eye for both the details and the larger picture. Whatever faults are in the manuscript are mine. All of the following people have either read chapters or given me suggestions along the way: Anne Bretagnolle, Pete Daniel, Alice Fahs, Gary Gallagher, Andrew Graybill, Richard Healey,

Jeannette Jones, Wendy Katz, James Le Sueur, Tim Mahoney, Peter Maslowski, Jane Moody, Peter Onuf, Ken Price, Stephen Ramsay, James A. Rawley, Anne S. Rubin, Calvin Schermerhorn, Robert Schwartz, Douglas Seefeldt, Adam I. P. Smith, Amy Murrell Taylor, Alex Vazansky, Bobby Watts, Barbara Welke, Victoria Weoste, Laura White, Richard White, Tyler White, Kenneth Winkle, and John Wunder. Students at the University of Nebraska have also given me thoughtful comments and helped research parts of this work and I wish to thank them for their spirited discussions and hard work: Kim Banion, Catherine Biba, Sean Kammer, Kurt Kinbacher, Miles Krumbach, Diane Miller, Kaci Nash, Nathan Sanderson, Vanessa Steinroetter, Nic Swiercek, Michelle Tiedje, Robert Voss, and Leslie Working. Geitner Simmons, editor of the *Omaha World-Herald*, a southern-history expert and modern-day Renaissance "man of letters," generously offered to read the entire manuscript and gave me valuable advice. J. W. Kaempfer graciously helped me get settled in London for research on parts of this book, as did Father Andrew Cain, Christine Cargill, Andrew Ceresa, and Ian and Alison Thomas.

It would be difficult to overstate how much I have benefited from the support and dedication of the Center for Digital Research in the Humanities at the University of Nebraska. This work began as an experiment in digital analysis, and the Center has shepherded for many years "the Railroads project," as we call it. I set out to use the digital project to help me organize, arrange, make sense of, and analyze the materials of this period. Dan Becker, Karin Callahan, Nathan Freitas, and C. J. Warwas worked on the geographic information system we developed for the U.S. railroad network from 1840 to 1861, helping me not only with technical matters but also with ways to conceptualize the project. Ian Cottingham collaborated on efforts to model spatio-temporal visualization and integrate diverse data into maps. I am in their debt. Zach Bajabar, Karin Dalziel, Keith Nickum, Brian Pytlik-Zillig, and Laura Weakly each contributed their expert knowledge to the development of the Web database and archive. Trevor Munoz came on as an intern at the Center in 2009 after completing his Master's degree in Digital Humanities at Kings College, London, and his textual analysis and concordances of *The War of the Rebellion: A Compilation of the Official Records of the Union and Confederate Armies*, Vol. 38, opened my eyes to new ways of thinking about these texts and about Sherman's railroad strategy and the Atlanta Campaign. Part of any digital project entails some pure experimentation, and I am thankful that Stephen Ramsay enthusiastically collaborated on creating directed graphs of the Union commanders' "geographic vision" based on the language in their official reports. Katherine Walter and Ken Price, the co-Directors of the Center, have given me consistent encouragement and supported this research at every turn, for which I am very grateful.

Numerous archivists and librarians have also aided me in this work and generously given their time and expertise. Peterson Brink and Mary Ellen Ducey at the University of Nebraska have tirelessly worked with the remarkable Charles Kennedy railroad collection. Librarians helped me immensely in identifying new source material deep in the railroad records and in other collections, including: Martha Briggs, James Grossman, John Powell, and the staff of the Newberry Library; George Briscoe at National Archives; Greg Prickman at the University of Iowa; Sara Bearss, Gregg Kimball, Brent Tartar, Sandra Treadway, and Minor Weisiger at the Library of Virginia; Edward Gaynor, Heather Riser, and Regina Rush at the University of Virginia Albert and Shirley Small Special Collections Library; Melanie Aspey and Tracy Wilkerson at the Rothschild Archive; Clara Anderson and Moira Lovegrove at the Baring Archive; and Philip Davies and the staff of the British Library. Jean Bauer braved the backwoods of Crozet, Virginia, to locate and photograph the ruins of the Blue Ridge Tunnel for this book. I am grateful for her help.

Wendy Strothman of the Strothman Literary Agency believed in this project at its earliest stages and gave me careful suggestions throughout. My editor at Yale University Press, Christopher Rogers, deserves a thousand thanks, as does Jeffrey Schier for his thoroughly professional help in editing and production. Laura Davulis and Christina Tucker at Yale patiently advised me as I collected and arranged the images for this book. I appreciate greatly Bill Nelson's work on the maps and his almost unbelievable efficiency in producing them.

My family is at the center of my life and this book would not have been possible without their unfailing support. Heather, Sarah, Guy, Janie, Mom and Dad, Jane, cousins, and siblings have all encouraged and supported me and I am so thankful for their enthusiasm and patience.

Appendix: Tables

Table 1. Total railroad mileage (by decade) in the North and South

	1840	1850	Change (%)	1860	Change (%)
North (MA, NY, NJ, PA, OH, IN, IL)	1,576	4,617	290	15,012	325
South (VA, NC, GA, SC, AL, MS, LA)	1,099	1,787	160	7,001	392

Source: Jenny Bourne Wahl, "Stay East, Young Man? Market Repercussions of the Dred Scott Decision," *Chicago-Kent Law Review*, Vol. 82, No. 1 (2007): 368.

Table 2. Access to railroad depots and junctions, 1861
(per capita for free population, per 10,000 persons)

Region	Points (junctions and depots)		Est. population within 15 miles
	Total	No. per 10,000	
South	1,518	1.856	54.7 %
North*	1,636	1.796	62.4 %

*Selected northern states here include Pennsylvania, Illinois, Michigan, Ohio, Wisconsin, and Iowa.

Source: Historical Geographic Information System (GIS), 1861 Railroad Network, Center for Digital Research in the Humanities, University of Nebraska-Lincoln.

Table 3. Access to railroad depots and junctions by state, 1861
(per capita for free population, per 10,000 persons)

State	Total number of junctions/depots	Junctions/Depots per 10,000 persons	Population within fifteen miles (%)
Alabama	117	2.211	38.2
Arkansas	7	0.216	0.4
Florida	30	3.813	36.8
Georgia	152	2.554	61
Kentucky	123	1.322	43.2
Louisiana	49	1.302	45.4
Maryland	83	1.384	79.5
Mississippi	110	3.101	53.4
Missouri	125	1.171	46.6
N. Carolina	133	2.010	46.6
S. Carolina	147	4.879	68.8
Tennessee	152	1.822	62.6
Texas	39	0.925	11
Virginia	251	2.271	61.8
Selected North			
Illinois	426	2.488	85.1
Iowa	73	1.082	72.4
Michigan	97	1.295	76.8
Ohio	413	1.765	92.6
Pennsylvania	504	1.734	85.5
Wisconsin	123	1.585	77.4

Source: Historical Geographic Information System (GIS), 1861 Railroad Network, Center for Digital Research in the Humanities, University of Nebraska-Lincoln.

Table 4. Total number of slaves by subregion

Subregion*	1840	1850	Change (%)	1860	Change (%)
Old South	1,328,603	1,567,052	18	1,748,273	12
Cotton South	617,195	897,531	45	1,203,437	34
Northern Border	457,695	543,098	19	590,189	9
Western Border	78,175	192,683	146	408,612	112

*Old South is defined as Virginia, North Carolina, South Carolina, Georgia, and Florida; Cotton South includes Alabama, Louisiana, and Mississippi; Northern Border encompasses Delaware, Kentucky, and Tennessee; and Western Border comprises Arkansas, Missouri, and Texas. From Jenny Bourne Wahl, "Stay East, Young Man? Market Repercussions of the Dred Scott Decision," *Chicago-Kent Law Review*, Vol. 82, No. 1 (2007): 368.

Source: U.S. Historical Census Browser, Geostat, University of Virginia, http://fisher.lib.virginia.edu/collections/stats/histcensus/.

Table 5. Largest ten occupational categories for the Baltimore & Ohio Railroad, 1857

Occupation	Number employed	Occupation	Number employed
Laborer	2,305	Foreman	230
Machinist	315	Tonnage engine man	194
Carpenter	268	Tonnage conductor	190
Tonnage brakeman	255	Blacksmith	139
Watchman	252	Machinist helper	132

Source: Baltimore & Ohio Railroad Company, printed payroll lists, 1842, 1852, 1855, 1857, Maryland Historical Society. Richard Healey, Katie Dooley, and William G. Thomas, "The Geography of Free Labor: The Baltimore and Ohio Railroad and Worker Mobility in Mid-Nineteenth Century American Society," unpublished manuscript, 2010.

Table 6. Largest ten employment locations for the Baltimore & Ohio Railroad, 1857

Location	Number employed	Location	Number employed
Baltimore, Md.	962	Welling Tunnel	218
Northwestern Virginia R.R.	563	Laying second track	211
Board Tree Tunnel	340	Piedmont, Va.	210
1st Division	259	2nd Division	185
Martinsburg, Va.	259	3rd and 4th Divisions	184

Source: Baltimore & Ohio Railroad Company, printed payroll lists, 1842, 1852, 1855, 1857, Maryland Historical Society. Richard Healey, Katie Dooley, and William G. Thomas, "The Geography of Free Labor: The Baltimore and Ohio Railroad and Worker Mobility in Mid-Nineteenth Century American Society," unpublished manuscript, 2010.

Table 7. Numbers of passengers and total receipts on selected northern and southern railroads in the mid-nineteenth century

| Year | Total no. through passengers | Total receipts | | Ratio |
		Passenger	Freight	
Terre Haute and Richmond Railroad				
1856	134,595	$319,075	$194,612	1.64
1857	97,217	$280,176	$185,380	1.51
1858	64,900	$189,097	$174,104	1.09
1859	52,697	$173,008	$164,492	1.05
Mississippi and Tennessee Railroad				
1856–1857	41,531	$46,151	$67,651	0.68
1858–1859	59,437	$65,394	$105,430	0.62
Richmond & Petersburg Railroad				
1856–1857	89,379	$84,872	$62,654	1.35
1857–1858	72,250.5	$76,188	$61,530	1.23
1858–1859	74,327.5*	$86,650	$63,755	1.35
Virginia Central Railroad				
1855–1856	100,836	$220,285	$255,046	0.86
1856–1857	98,638	$242,680	$268,812	0.90
1857–1858	108,314	$266,109	$291,144	0.91
1858–1859	134,883	$306,312	$319,021	0.96
Virginia and Tennessee Railroad Company				
1853–1854	58,435	$63,580	$96,759	0.66
Pennsylvania Railroad				
1853	1,134,908	$1,069,740	$1,446,261	0.73
1857	884,024	$1,244,858	$3,374,040	0.36
1866	2,483,443	$4,174,192	$11.1 m**	0.37

*Southern railroads counted tickets for slaves and children as .5
**Exact figure is $11,193,565.00

Source: Annual Reports, Charles Kennedy Collection, Special Collections, University of Nebraska-Lincoln Libraries; Illinois Central Railroad Collection, IC 6M4.2, annual reports, Newberry Library, Chicago, Ill.

Table 8. Frequency of railroad terms appearing in Union officers' correspondence, 1862 and 1864

| | 1862 | | 1864 | |
Word	Count	Frequency (per 10,000 words)	Count	Frequency (per 10,000 words)
enemy	486	27.36	495	36.62
river	377	21.23	139	6.81
fort	358	20.16		
Richmond	284	15.99		
Yorktown	260	14.64		
James (River)	203	11.43		
York (River)	190	10.70		
road	169	9.52	623	45.62
roads	155	8.73	124	12.26
bridge	148	8.33	242	17.66
city	146	8.22	25	1.86
railroad	98	5.52	348	26.03
Chickahominy	70	4.90		
telegraph	66	3.72		
trains	49	2.76	66	6.49
depot	43	2.42	30	1.86

Source: U.S. War Department, *The War of the Rebellion: A Compilation of the Official Records of the Union and Confederate Armies* (Lynchburg, Va., and Pasadena, Calif.: Broadfoot, 1985), Vol. 11 (Part III), 1–384, and Vol. 38 (Parts IV and V), from Cornell University, *Making of America;* Voyeur Tools (copyright 2009) Steffan Sinclair and Geoffrey Rockwell, v. 1.0; Trevor Munoz and William G. Thomas, *Railroads and the Making of Modern America* (September 2009), http://railroads.unl.edu.

Table 9. Key railroad points in the Confederacy with affected railroads and territory (using fifteen-mile catchment zone buffer)

Junction	Date of capture	No. of railroads	Zone affected (sq. mi.)
Nashville, Tenn.	February 25, 1862	4	6,292
Memphis, Tenn.	June 6, 1862	4	7,687
Corinth, Miss.	October 3, 1862	3	7,872
Jackson, Miss.	May 14, 1863	4	13,357
Manassas, Va.	October 14, 1863	3	4,006
Chattanooga, Tenn.	November 25, 1863	3	3,143
Meridian, Miss.	February 14, 1864	3	9,503
Atlanta, Ga.	September, 1864	3	4,576
Savannah, Ga.	December 21, 1864	3	11,342
Columbia, S.C.	February 17, 1865	3	3,453
Charlottesville, Va.	March 5, 1865	3	5,548
Gordonsville, Va.	March 12, 1865	3	4,057
Florence, S.C.	March 16, 1865	4	9,562
Goldsborough, N.C.	March 21, 1865	4	8,465
Petersburg, Va.	April 2, 1865	5	6,002
Richmond, Va.	April 2, 1865	5	4,173
Burkeville, Va.	April 6, 1865	4	7,395
Montgomery, Ala.	April 12, 1865	2	7,262
Raleigh, N.C.	April 13, 1865	3	7,049
Lynchburg, Va.	(not captured)	3	16,025

Source: Historical Geographic Information System (GIS), 1861 Railroad Network, Center for Digital Research in the Humanities, University of Nebraska-Lincoln.

Table 10. Captured ports in the Confederacy with affected railroads and territory (using fifteen-mile catchment zone buffer)

Port city	Date of capture	No. of railroads	Zone affected (sq. mi.)
Alexandria, Va.	May 24, 1861	3	2,334
Hatteras Inlet, N.C.	August 19, 1861	—	—
Roanoke Island, N.C.	February 8, 1862	—	—
St. Augustine, Fla.	March 11, 1862	—	—
Jacksonville, Fla.	March 12, 1862	1	1,237
New Berne, N.C.	March 14, 1862	—	—
New Orleans, La.	April 25, 1862	2	**
Beaufort, N.C.	April 1862	—	—
Pensacola, Fla.	May 9, 1862	1	1,940
Norfolk, Va.	May 10, 1862	1	3,156
St. John's River, Fla.	October 3, 1862	—	—
Galveston, Tex.*	October 4, 1862	1	2,008
Port Royal, S.C.	November 7, 1862	—	—
Albemarle Sound, N.C.	May 5, 1864	—	—
Savannah, Ga.	December 21, 1864	3	11,342
Wilmington, N.C.	January 15, 1865	3	7,449
Charleston, S.C.	February 18, 1865	3	8,021
Mobile, Ala.	April 12, 1865	1	4,530

*Recaptured by Confederacy January 1, 1863
**Mileage not available

Source: Historical Geographic Information System (GIS), 1861 Railroad Network, Center for Digital Research in the Humanities, University of Nebraska-Lincoln.

Table 11. Railroad workers by race, 1880

	White	%	African American*	%	Total no.
Maryland	3,440	95	193	5	3,633
Ohio	17,949	99.5	107	.5	18,056
Pennsylvania	25,612	99.5	114	.5	25,726
Virginia	2,670	49	2,807	51	5,477
West Virginia	2,507	85	437	15	2,944

*Includes "Black" and "Mulatto" persons listed in U.S. Population Census

Source: North Atlantic Population Project and Minnesota Population Center, *NAPP: Complete Count Microdata*, NAPP Version 2.0 [computer files]. Minneapolis, Minn.: Minnesota Population Center [distributor], 2008, http://www.nappdata.org. Richard Healey and William G. Thomas, "Mobility After Emancipation: African Americans, Railroads, and the Meaning of Freedom in Ohio and Virginia, 1865–1880," unpublished manuscript, 2010. The above data counts are based on the eighteen NAPP occupation codes that are unquestionably railroad workers; the percentages indicate relative proportions by race. Because one-third of railroad workers did not self-identify as railroad workers, the absolute numbers could change should future work produce revised estimates.

A Note on Sources

Many of the sources used in this book have been digitized and are available in the "Railroads and the Making of Modern America" project. Libraries and archives continue to preserve, maintain, and make available to scholars the most important sources for understanding this period—the original documents. I have also used many of the newly available digital source collections to find materials, including Google Books, ProQuest, American Periodicals Series, and Ancestry.com. Thousands of online articles and documents have been consulted in the research for this book. These research tools have proven invaluable for sifting across collections to discover keywords, individuals, and particular events. I have also consulted secondary sources and dissertations on the Civil War era and on railroads, a large and rapidly growing and complex literature. I have focused on the most recent and relevant works, and have cited these in the notes. A full bibliography of all secondary works and further relevant tables are available online through the project website.

Manuscript Collections

Baring Archive, London
British Library, London
    Baring Papers, Microfilm, Public Archives of Canada
    John Bright Papers
    Richard Cobden Papers
    William Gladstone Papers
    George Henry Herbert Letters
    Austen Henry Layard Papers
    Florence Nightingale Letters
    Joseph Sturge Papers
    Henry John Temple, 3rd Viscount Palmerston Papers
Chicago Historical Society
    William Butler Letters
    Gunther Collection
    John Kirk Letterbooks
    Junius Mulvey Letter
    John Munn Collection
    Alexander Prentiss Letter
    William Savage Letter
    Robert Tarrant Datebook

Library of Congress, Washington, D.C.
  August Belmont Papers
  Cornelius Chase Papers
  Edward Frost Papers
  Garrett Family Papers
  Horace Porter Letters
Library of Virginia
  Board of Public Works, Blue Ridge Railroad Correspondence
  Executive Papers, Papers of Gov. John Floyd
  Executive Papers, Papers of Gov. John Letcher
  Executive Papers, Papers of Gov. Henry A. Wise
  Second Auditor, Internal Improvements Fund Records
National Archives and Records Administration (NARA), Washington, D.C.
  Record Group 21, Judiciary Records
    District of Columbia Supreme Court case files
    U.S. Supreme Court case files
  Record Group 92, Records of the Office of the Quartermaster General
  Record Group 92.6, Records of the Office of the Director and General Manager,
    Military Railroads United States
  Record Group 105, Bureau of Refugees, Freedmen, and Abandoned Lands,
    Headquarters, Washington, D.C.
  Record Group 107, Secretary of War Records
  Record Group 109, Confederate Records
National Maritime Museum Library, Greenwich
  William Schaw Lindsay Papers
Nebraska State Historical Society
  Sim Family Papers
  Union Pacific Railroad Records
Newberry Library
  Chicago, Burlington and Quincy Railroad Collection
  Ephraim C. Dawes Papers
  Grenville Dodge Papers
  James Taylor Graves Papers
  Illinois Central Railroad Collection
  Charles T. Kruse Papers
  Charles Elliott Norton Letter
  Johnson Paisley Papers
  Henry C. Parry Papers
  Union Pacific Railroad Company Records
Rothschild Archive, London
Smithsonian Institution, National Museum of American History
  Baltimore & Ohio Railroad Records
University of Chicago Library
  Ebenezer Lane Family Papers
  Illinois Central Railroad Company Papers
  Lincoln Collection, Lincoln Miscellaneous Manuscripts
  Sanford Truesdell Papers
University of Iowa Libraries Special Collections
  Levi O. Leonard Papers

University of Nebraska Libraries Special Collections
  Charles Kennedy Railroad Collection
  McConihe Papers
Woodruff Library, Special Collections, Emory University
  Richard Burch Jett Papers
  William Greene Raoul Papers
  Sue Richardson Diary
  Isaac Roseberry Diary

Online Primary Sources

American Periodicals Series
Ancestry.com
Confederate Railroads
Documenting the American South
Harpweek
Historical Census Browser, Geospatial and Statistical Data Center,
    University of Virginia
Library of Congress, American Memory
  A Century of U.S. Lawmaking for the Nation
  Civil War Maps
  Abraham Lincoln Papers
  Railroad Maps, 1828–1900
Making of America, Cornell University
Making of America, University of Michigan
Nineteenth-Century British Library Newspapers
Nineteenth-Century U.S. Newspapers
ProQuest Historical Newspapers
Territorial Kansas Online
Valley of the Shadow: Two Communities in the American Civil War,
    Virginia Center for Digital History, University of Virginia

Printed Primary Sources

Albert and Shirley Small Special Collections Library, University of Virginia
  *Fifteenth Annual Report of the Directors and Officers of the Nashville & Chattanooga
    Railroad Company.* Nashville, Tenn.: Roberts, Watterson and Purvis, 1867.
  Johnson, A. J. *New Illustrated (Steel Plate) Family Atlas: With Physical Geography and
    with Descriptions Geographical, Statistical, and Historical.* New York: Johnson and
    Ward, 1864.
  Memphis, El Paso and Pacific Railroad, Annual Report of the Officers. Clarksville, Tex.:
    Standard Print, 1857.
  Mississippi Central Railroad, Annual Report of the President and Directors. Holly
    Springs, Miss., 1855–1860.
  New Orleans, Opelousas and Great Western Railroad Company, *Annual Report of the
    President and Directors.* New Orleans: Clark and Brisbin Printers, 1850–1864.
  Political Speeches. 1826–1855.
  *Proceedings of the Stockholders of the Louisville, Cincinnati and Charleston Rail-Road
    Company.* Charleston, S.C.: A. E. Miller, 1841.

Speech of Wm. M. Burwell of Virginia, New Orleans, La., 1852.

"To the Members of the Permanent Committee on the New Orleans, Algiers, Attakapas, and Opelousas Railroad," 1851.

Creighton University

Cutler, Julia Perkins. *Life and Times of Ephraim Cutler: Prepared from His Journal and Correspondence*. With sketch of William P. Cutler by Ephraim C. Dawes. Cincinnati: Robert Clark and Co., 1890.

Dawes, Ephraim Cutler. "The Battle of Shiloh." In *Campaigns in Kentucky and Tennessee Including the Battle of Chickamauga, 1862–1864*. Papers of the Military Historical Society of Massachusetts, Vol. II. Boston, 1908, 101–172.

———. "The Confederate Strength in the Atlanta Campaign." In *Battles and Leaders of the Civil War*, Vol. 4 (1887): 281–283.

———. *In Memoriam, William Blackford Stephenson*. Cincinnati: Peter G. Thomson, 1879.

———. "Major Ephraim C. Dawes of the 53d Ohio Volunteers and the Battle of Dallas, Georgia, May 28, 1864." Compiled by Harriett D. Wilson. At head of text: The Accounting by Ephraim C. Dawes. Crum Letter Service. Elmhurst, Ill., 1967. Ohio Historical Society.

Duke, John K. *History of the 53rd Regiment Ohio Volunteers*. Portsmouth, Ohio: The Blade Printing Co., 1900.

Smith, William Prescott. *The Book of the Great Railway Celebrations of 1857; Embracing a Full Account of the Opening of the Ohio & Mississippi, the Marietta & Cincinnati Railroads, and the Northwestern Virginia Branch of the Baltimore and Ohio Railroad*. New York: D. Appleton and Co., 1858.

Stevenson, William G. *Thirteen Months in the Rebel Army, Being a Narrative of Personal Adventures by an Impressed New Yorker*. New York: A. S. Barnes and Co., 1862 and 1864.

Whitney, Asa. "A Project for a Railroad to the Pacific," 1849.

Library of Virginia

Baltimore and Ohio Railroad Company. *Annual Report of the President and Directors to the Stockholders, 1826–1827*. Baltimore, 1827.

Chesapeake and Ohio Railroad Company. *Annual Report of the President and Stockholders*. 1868.

Northwestern Virginia Railroad Company. *Annual Report of the President and Directors to the Stockholders*. 1851–1852.

Proceedings of the Annual Meeting, Richmond and Danville Railroad Company. Richmond: H. K. Ellyson, 1848–1857.

Raleigh & Gaston Rail Road Company. *Proceedings of the Fourteenth Annual Meeting of the Raleigh & Gaston Railroad Company*. 1864.

Richmond, Fredericksburg and Potomac. *Annual Report*. 1834/1835–1988.

Richmond, Fredericksburg and Potomac and Richmond and Petersburg Railroad Company. *Proceedings of a Called Meeting of the Stockholders, Held on Wednesday, June 26th, 1867*. Richmond: Examiner Job Office, 1867.

Richmond and Petersburg, Reports & Proceedings. Richmond, Va., 1836–1864.

Winchester and Potomac Railroad Company. *Annual Report, 1831–1832*. Winchester, Va.: Winchester Virginian.

Maryland Historical Society

Baltimore & Ohio Railroad Company, printed payroll lists, 1842, 1852, 1855, 1857.

Newberry Library

Fry, F. *Fry's Traveler's Guide*. Cincinnati: Applegate and Co., 1865.

Illinois Central, History of the Illinois Central Railroad and Representative
Employees, Chicago, 1900.

Seymour, Silas. *Incidents of a Trip Through the Great Platte Valley, to the Rocky
Mountains and Laramie Plains, in the Fall of 1866*. New York: D. Van Nostrand, 1867.

Texas A & M University

Colyer, Vincent. *Brief Report of the Services Rendered by the Freed People to the United
States Army in North Carolina in the Spring of 1862, After the Battle of New Bern*.
New York: Vincent Colyer, 1864.

Notes

Prologue

Epigraph: Diary of Asa Whitney, transcript, October 21, 1844, typescript page 116. (Asa Whitney Papers, University of Michigan Library, Special Collections).

1. Diary of Asa Whitney, transcript, September 3 to October 21, 1844 (Asa Whitney Papers, University of Michigan Library, Special Collections). I would like to thank Kathleen Dow, Head of Archival Cataloging, for her aid and expertise in tracking down these diary transcripts. On the speed of trains averaging 30 m.p.h., and the argument that railroads changed space, time, distance, and orientation, see Z. Pratt, "Railroads," *United States Democratic Review*, Vol. 21, No. 112 (October 1947): 338–344.

2. Diary of Asa Whitney, transcript, September 3 to October 21, 1844.

3. Ibid.

4. Quoted in Daniel Walker Howe, *What Hath God Wrought: The Transformation of America, 1815–1848* (Oxford: Oxford University Press, 2008), 697, and in William Weeks, *Building the Continental Empire: American Expansion from the Revolution to the Civil War* (Chicago: Ivan R. Dee, 1996), 85. 4. O'Sullivan's "manifest destiny" concepts also appeared in "The Great Nation of Futurity," in *United States Democratic Review*, Vol. 6, No. 23 (November 1839): 426–430; and in the *New York Morning News*, July 9, 1845. Also quoted in Thomas R. Hietala, *Manifest Design: American Exceptionalism & Empire*, revised ed. (Ithaca, N.Y.: Cornell University Press, 1985), 197. O'Sullivan also wrote other influential pieces emphasizing territorial expansion and technology; see "Annexation," *United States Democratic Review*, Vol. 17, No. 85 (July–August, 1845): 9, www.cornell.moa (accessed March 2011). For a useful analysis of the confidence in New England that railroads would lead to the breakdown of slavery, as well as of the blurring of partisan differences railroads caused, including creating a consensus among Democrats in favor of expansion and economic development, see Michael J. Connelly, "The Correction of Our Political Philosophy: New England Whigs and the 1851 Railroad Jubilee," *New England Quarterly*, Vol. 79, No. 2 (June 2006): 202–226.

5. Harriet Beecher Stowe, *Uncle Tom's Cabin* (New York: Library of America, 1982), 283; Henry Adams, *The Education of Henry Adams* (Houghton Mifflin Co., 1918), 240 and 330; Walt Whitman, "To a Locomotive in Winter," in *Leaves of Grass* (Doubleday, 1923), 253.

6. Herman Melville, *Moby-Dick; or, The Whale* (New York: Signet Classic, 1961), 118, 147. See especially Philip Armstrong, "'Leviathan Is a Skein of Networks': Translations of Nature and Culture in Moby-Dick," *ELH*, Vol. 71, No. 4 (Winter 2004): 1039–1063. Carolyn L. Karcher, *Shadow over the Promised Land: Slavery, Race, and Violence in Melville's America* (Baton Rouge: Louisiana State University Press, 1980), and Andrew Delbanco, *Melville, His World and Work* (New York: Knopf, 2005), 154. Stephen C. Ausband, "The Whale and the Machine: An Approach to Moby-Dick," *American Literature*, Vol. 47, No. 2 (May 1975): 197–211.

7. The classic works stressing space and time are Leo Marx, *The Machine in the Garden: Technology and the Pastoral Ideal in America* (Oxford: Oxford University Press, 1964), 194; and Wolfgang Schivelbusch, *The Railway Journey: Industrialization and Perception of Time and Space* (Sacramento: University of California Press, 1986). More recently, Richard White, "Information, Markets, and Corruption: Transcontinental Railroads in the Gilded Age," *Journal of American History*, Vol. 90 (2003): 19. "The Railroad Enterprise, Its Progress, Management and Utility," *New Englander* (1843–1885), Vol. 9, No. 35 (August 1851): APS Online, 321. For a detailed account of the rhetoric surrounding railroads, see Craig Miner, *A Most Magnificent Machine: America Adopts the Railroad, 1825–1862* (Lawrence: University Press of Kansas, 2010). The forthcoming work by Richard White addresses the way transcontinental railroads shaped Western space and time; Richard White, *Railroaded: The Transcontinentals and the Making of Modern America* (New York: W. W. Norton, 2011).

8. Henry David Thoreau, *Walden, Or Life in the Woods* (1854), 364, http://etext.virginia .edu/toc/modeng/public/ThoWald.html (accessed March 2011). Robert Sattelmeyer, ed., *The Writings of Henry D. Thoreau: Journal*, Vol. 2, 1842–1848 (Princeton, N.J.: Princeton University Press, 1984), 358–359.

9. The literature on modern slavery is large and growing. See Siddharth Kara, *Sex Trafficking: Inside the Business of Modern Slavery* (New York: Columbia University Press, 2008); Kevin Bales and Ron Soodalter, *The Slave Next Door: Human Trafficking and Slavery in America Today* (Berkeley: University of California Press, 2009); and David Batstone, *Not for Sale: The Return of the Global Slave Trade — And How We Can Fight It* (New York: Harper, 2007).

10. A recent narrative of this period has been exuberant about the role of technology in American society in these years. See Daniel Walker Howe, *What Hath God Wrought: The Transformation of America, 1815–1848* (Oxford: Oxford University Press, 2008).

11. The phrase "contending territorial empires" is C. A. Bayly's, in *The Birth of the Modern World, 1780–1914: Global Connections and Comparisons* (Malden, Mass.: Blackwell, 2004), 2. Bayly's seminal work emphasizes the broader nineteenth-century processes of state formation and processes of economic and political organization. The question of the South's modernity has been extensively debated. For a recent and thorough examination of the South's intellectual life, which argues the South "was not premodern but deeply implicated in modernity," see Michael O'Brien, *Conjectures of Order: Intellectual Life and the American South, 1810–1860*, vols. 1 and 2 (Chapel Hill: University of North Carolina Press, 2004), 17. For the leading argument emphasizing the South as premodern, see Eugene Genovese, *The Slaveholder's Dilemma: Freedom and Progress in Southern Conservative Thought, 1820–1860* (Columbia: University of South Carolina Press, 1992). On the question of similarities and differences between North and South, emphasizing the processes of modernity and economic organization, see William G. Thomas III and Edward L. Ayers, "The Differences Slavery Made: A Close Analysis of Two American Communities," *American Historical Review* (December 2003), http://www.vcdh.virginia.edu/ AHR, and Edward Pessen, "How Different from Each Other Were the Antebellum North and South?" *American Historical Review* 85 (1980): 1119–1149.

12. My concerns and approaches have been influenced throughout especially by "actor network theory," as well as by the literature on the social construction of space. Bruno Latour's views on the modern "constitution," with its separation of Nature and Society, on the importance of nonhuman objects (what he calls "hybrids") as actors, on the idea of a "sociology of associations," and on the mediation among actors in society have been especially important in my thinking about the role of the railroad and the war in southern and American society. Indeed, this book seeks to trace the ways the railroad served as a hybrid agent, mediating any number of social, political, and economic associations. My goal throughout is to follow the railroad's associations, map them, and place them in relation to one another. See Bruno Latour, *Reassembling the Social: An Introduction to Actor Network Theory* (Oxford: Oxford University Press, 2005) and

We Have Never Been Modern (Cambridge: Harvard University Press, 1993). The works on space and modernity have also influenced the overall emphasis in this book, including: J. Nicholas Entrikin, *The Betweenness of Place: Towards a Geography of Modernity* (Macmillan, 1991), esp. 27–59; Allan Pred, *Making Histories and Constructing Human Geographies: The Local Transformation of Practice, Power Relations, and Consciousness* (Boulder: Westview, 1990), esp. 126–170; and Anthony Giddens, *The Consequences of Modernity* (Cambridge: Polity, 1990). I have also been especially influenced by Peter Onuf and Nicolas Onuf, *Nations, Markets, and War: Modern History and the American Civil War* (Charlottesville: University of Virginia Press, 2006), for their understanding of the South as a nation and of the Civil War as a clash of modern nation-states.

13. For analysis on these lines, see Scott Reynolds Nelson, *Iron Confederacies: Southern Railways, Klan Violence, and Reconstruction* (Chapel Hill: University of North Carolina Press, 1999), 16–45. Allan Nevins, in his massive and important four-volume *Ordeal of the Union*, stressed that the South "lagged" in the development of trunk line (east-to-west) railroads, and asserted the "primary fact" of the age was "the completeness, closeness, and modernity of the great transportation web" of the Northeast and Northwest. Yet, this research shows the depth of the South's railroad penetration and its rapid growth. Certainly, the geography of the mountainous terrain made the South's engineering challenges formidable (Allan Nevins, *Ordeal of the Union*, Vol. 1 [New York: Scribner, 1947], 208 and 241). See also Max Boot, *War Made New: Technology, Warfare, and the Course of History* (New York: Gotham, 2006), 125, on the use of railroads to "overcome geography" in Germany and to link new places and identities. Also Sean McMeekin, *The Berlin-Baghdad Express: The Ottoman Empire and Germany's Bid for World Power* (Cambridge: Belknap Press of Harvard University Press, 2010), for an examination of German railroad building and its cultural and political influence.

14. On the importance of the increasingly sectional language of southern leaders, as well as northerners, see especially Elizabeth R. Varon, *Disunion! The Coming of the American Civil War, 1789–1859* (Chapel Hill: University of North Carolina Press, 2008), 292–293. New works on the Civil War appear regularly: David Goldfield, *America Aflame: How the Civil War Created a Nation* (New York: Bloomsbury, 2011), stresses the religious convictions of Americans and the war as avoidable; Adam Arenson, *The Great Heart of the Republic: St. Louis and the Cultural Civil War* (Cambridge, Mass.: Harvard University Press, 2011), argues the centrality of the West in the sectional struggle and the cultural clash over Manifest Destiny and slavery in the West. Also in press at this time are Gary Gallagher, *The Union War* (Cambridge, Mass.: Harvard University Press, 2011), and Adam Goodheart, *1861: The Civil War Awakening* (New York: Knopf, 2011). Tim Wu, *The Master Switch: The Rise and Fall of Information Empires* (New York: Knopf, 2011), offers an important new analysis that "industry structure" (311), more than hardware technology, governs how a communication revolution affects freedom.

15. The term "second nature" is drawn from William Cronon's *Nature's Metropolis: Chicago and the Great West* (New York: W. W. Norton, 1991), xix, 62–78, and in his edited volume, *Uncommon Ground: Rethinking the Human Place in Nature* (New York: W. W. Norton, 1995). Cronon, an environmental historian, is interested in the way rails, commodity markets, commercial lending, and other systems altered the natural landscape in the 1870s and 1880s, especially around the city of Chicago, but in the Civil War the distinction is equally significant. Cronon calls second nature "the artificial nature that people erect atop first nature" and recognizes the ambiguity in the terms and the "complex mingling of the two."

16. On the concept of "railroad generalship" see Christopher R. Gabel's excellent overview, "Railroad Generalship: Foundations of Civil War Strategy," in Command and General Staff College, Combined Arms Research Library, http://handle.dtic.mil/100.2/ADA445773 (accessed June 2008). See Boot, *War Made New: Technology, Warfare, and the Course of History*, 140, on the concentration and speed of forces made possible by railroads in the Austro-Prussian war in 1866, delivering 190,000 men and 55,000 horses in twenty-one days.

17. George P. Rawick, ed., *The American Slave: A Composite Autobiography*, Vol. 12, Georgia Narratives, Parts 1 and 2 (Westport: Greenwood): 274–275.

18. The importance of "soundscapes" and their competing cultural interpretations have been recently explored in Sarah Keyes, "'Like a Roaring Lion': The Overland Trail as a Sonic Conquest," *The Journal of American History*, Vol. 98, No. 1 (June 2009): 19–43. The locomotive whistle was an aural experience that signified for Euro-Americans the march of civilization, conquest, empire, and progress. Civilized places, Keyes points out, had particular "soundscapes" as well as economic activities.

19. Xavier Duran has recently argued that the transcontinental railroad proposals proceeded from a highly rational assessment of global capital markets, engineering considerations, global trade patterns, and risk. He has also asserted that American railroad entrepreneurs, North and South, in the 1850s operated in a context shaped by global trade and commercial opportunities (Xavier Duran, "Great Expectations: Trade Booms, Gold Rushes, and the Railroads to the Pacific," unpublished paper presented at the Western History Association, Lake Tahoe, Nevada, 2010). On this point see also T. J. Stiles, *The First Tycoon: The Epic Life of Cornelius Vanderbilt* (New York: Vintage, 2010), 170–177, 214–222.

20. Much of the modernization thesis comes from James M. McPherson's important work *Ordeal by Fire: The Civil War and Reconstruction* (New York: Knopf, 1982), in which he argued that "slavery and modernizing capitalism were irreconcilable" (p. 50). And more recently, in "Ante-bellum Southern Exceptionalism: A New Look at an Old Question," in *Drawn with the Sword: Reflections on the American Civil War* (Oxford: Oxford University Press, 1996), he has written, "The North—along with a few countries in northwestern Europe—hurtled forward eagerly toward a future of industrial-capitalism that many Southerners found distasteful if not frightening; the South remained proudly and even defiantly rooted in the past" (p. 22). The idea of the South as behind the times has continued. For a view of the South's claim to nationhood as backward-looking and afflicted with a "divided psyche," see Russell F. Weigley, *A Great Civil War: A Military and Political History, 1861–1865* (Bloomington: Indiana University Press, 2000), 10–12. For an analysis of the South as premodern and precapitalist, see Eugene D. Genovese and Elizabeth Fox-Genovese, *The Fruits of Merchant Capital: Slavery and Bourgeois Property in the Rise and Expansion of Capitalism* (New York: Oxford University Press, 1983). Historians continue to debate whether the South was an anachronistic premodern society or a variation of modern capitalism, but recent studies emphasize the latter. John Majewski's *Modernizing a Slave Economy: The Economic Vision of the Confederate Nation* (Chapel Hill: University of North Carolina Press, 2009), addresses the ways South Carolina and Virginia planters sought to improve their productivity and how these efforts helped give rise to ideas about an independent southern nation, secession, and eventually a strong Confederate central government. With its deep statistical analysis, Majewski's work explains the importance of the "modernizing secessionists" who created a Confederate nation (p. 152). A different debate over "total war" has also been important to Civil War historians. Some have seen the war as a more modern conflict in the sense that it became similar to World War I and twentieth-century wars. In explaining the Civil War as modern, I am not suggesting here that it was a total war nor that it bore any specific relationship to these later wars. The modern nature of the Civil War had little to do with whether it was or was not "total." For revisionist approaches to the total war thesis, see Wayne Wei-siang Hsieh, *West Pointers and the Civil War: The Old Army in War and Peace* (Chapel Hill: University of North Carolina Press, 2009), 10, and especially Mark Grimsley, *The Hard Hand of War: Union Military Policy Toward Southern Civilians, 1861–1865* (New York: Cambridge University Press, 1995).

21. For one of the best examples of modernist thought, see David Lowenthal, *George Perkins Marsh: Prophet of Conservation* (Seattle and London: University of Washington Press, 2000), 235–236 and 290. Marsh, one of the most influential writers about nature and society,

considered the Union cause in the Civil War, and antislavery more generally, linked inextricably to modernity and civilization. Marsh recognized that "the destructive agency of man" became "more energetic and unsparing as he advances in civilization" (George Perkins Marsh, *Man and Nature* [1864], 39–40). Lowenthal points out that even though Marsh wanted "to treat man and nature as a unity," his Calvinism and Enlightenment progressivism led him to "exalt" humanity (290). Despite his modernist views, what Lowenthal calls his allegiance to "environmental conquest," Marsh in fact questioned the confidence in "improvement"—the idea that all human action is better for nature—and he understood that human action was extensive and not always visible in the landscape (406). For one of the best overviews of the problem of modernity's emphasis on the supremacy of humans over nature, see Nick Lee and Paul Stenner, "Who Pays? Can We Pay Them Back?," in *Actor Network Theory and After*, ed. John Law and John Hassard (Oxford: Blackwell, 1999), 94–97 and 108–109.

22. The new interpretations of slavery as connected to the modern developments in the Atlantic world stand at the center of this argument, see Robin Blackburn, *The Making of New World Slavery* (London: Verso, 1997); Walter Johnson, *Soul by Soul: Life Inside the Antebellum Slave Market* (Cambridge, Mass.: Harvard University Press, 1999); Walter Johnson, ed., *The Chattel Principle: Internal Slave Trades in the Americas* (New Haven: Yale University Press, 2004); Edward L. Ayers, *In the Presence of Mine Enemies: War in the Heart of America, 1859–1863* (New York: W. W. Norton, 2003); Walter Johnson, "The Pedestal and the Veil: Rethinking the Capitalism/Slavery Question," *Journal of the Early Republic*, Vol. 24, No. 2 (Summer 2004): 299–308; Anthony E. Kaye, "The Second Slavery: Modernity in the Nineteenth-Century South and the Atlantic World," *Journal of Southern History*, Vol. 75, No. 3 (August 2009): 627–650; Thomas and Ayers, "The Differences Slavery Made"; Charles Taylor, *Modern Social Imaginaries* (Durham, N.C.: Duke University Press, 2004); and Sven Beckert, "Emancipation and Empire: Reconstructing the Worldwide Web of Cotton Production in the Age of the American Civil War," *American Historical Review*, Vol. 109, No. 5 (December 2004): 1405–1439, and "From Tuskegee to Togo: The Problem of Freedom in the Empire of Cotton," *Journal of American History*, Vol. 92, No. 2 (September 2005): 498–527. For a new collection of essays on the South promising to shed light on the South's modern development, see Frank Towers, Diane Barnes, and Brian Schoen, eds., *A New History of the Old South: Slavery, Sectionalism, and the Nineteenth-Century Modern World* (Oxford: Oxford University Press, 2011).

23. The literature on the concept of mobility and embodiment has been especially important in women's history. See Virginia Scharff, *Twenty Thousand Roads: Women, Movement, and the West* (Berkeley: University of California Press, 2003); Ginette Verstraete, "Railroading America: Towards a Material Study of the Nation," *Theory, Culture, and Society*, Vol. 19 (2002): 145–159; Alison Blunt and Gillian Rose, eds., *Writing Women and Space: Colonial and Post-Colonial Geographies* (New York: Guilford, 1994); and Doreen M. Massey, *Space, Place, and Gender* (Minneapolis: University of Minnesota Press, 1994). On the telegraph, racial identities, and the concept of "embodiment," see also Paul Gilmore, "The Telegraph in Black and White," *English Literary Review*, Vol. 69 No. 3 (2002): 805–833. Also, see George W. Pierson, "The M-Factor in American History," *American Quarterly*, Vol. 14, No. 2 (Summer 1962): 275–289.

24. The social effects of the railroad bear striking resemblance to those of the Internet, especially in the ways they transform culture and in their recursive politics and economics. I am especially interested in the ways these technologies are open-ended, enabling both freedom and oppression. The "iron way" could lead in either direction. I have been influenced in this approach by my experience as a digital historian and by much of the recent analysis of the digital revolution, such as Sherry Turkle, *Alone Together: Why We Expect More from Technology and Less from Each Other* (New York: Basic, 2011); Evgeny Morozov, *The Net Delusion: The Dark Side of Internet Freedom* (New York: Public Affairs, 2011); and Lee Siegel, *Against the Machine: Being Human in the Age of the Electronic Mob* (New York: Spiegel and Grau, 2008). Richard

White has also recently argued that railroads had both "software" and "hardware" systems; see http://spatialhistory.stanford.edu and Richard White, "Constructing Railroad Space," paper presented at the Social Science History Association, Chicago, Ill., November 2010. On the social construction of technologies, and for a recent account of the social meanings of technology and how people adapt technology to their use, see David Edgerton, *The Shock of the Old: Technology in Global History Since 1900* (New York: Oxford University Press, 2006). Edgerton emphasizes a history of "technology in use" rather than invention and the persistence of old technologies among the modern. He calls the tendency to overemphasize the impact of technology "futurism." Here, Edgerton's view is especially relevant because with railroads the question is how people adjusted to them, adapted, and came to terms with their use and meaning. This is predominately a cultural and social question. Other important works focused on this question include: Carolyn Marvin, *When Old Technologies Were New: Thinking About Electric Communication in the Nineteenth Century* (New York: Oxford University Press, 1988), esp. 193–209; and David Nye, *Technology Matters: Questions to Live With* (Cambridge: MIT Press, 2006), esp. 46–47. Nye emphasizes that technology is not deterministic and is "unpredictable," often with "no immediate impact."

25. For recent definitions and explorations of the methodology of digital history, see Daniel J. Cohen and Roy Rosenzweig, *Digital History: A Guide to Gathering, Preserving, and Presenting the Past on the Web* (Philadelphia: University of Pennsylvania Press, 2006); Orville Vernon Burton, ed., *Computing in the Social Sciences and Humanities* (Urbana and Chicago: University of Illinois Press, 2002); David J. Staley, *Computers, Visualization, and History: How New Technology Will Transform Our Understanding of the Past* (Armonk, N.Y.: M. E. Sharpe, 2003); Edward L. Ayers, "The Pasts and Futures of Digital History," Virginia Center for Digital History, 1999, http://www.vcdh.virginia.edu/PastsFutures.html; Orville Vernon Burton, "American Digital History," *Social Science Computer Review*, Vol. 23, No. 1 (2005): 206–220; Daniel J. Cohen, Michael Frisch, Patrick Gallagher, Steven Mintz, Kirsten Sword, Amy Murrell Taylor, William G. Thomas III, and William J. Turkel, "Interchange: The Promise of Digital History," *Journal of American History*, Vol. 95, No. 2 (2008), http://www.journalofamericanhistory.org/issues/952/interchange/index.html; and Douglas Seefeldt and William G. Thomas, "What Is Digital History: A Look at Some Exemplar Projects," *Perspectives on History* (May 2009). For critical analysis of spatial approaches, see also Richard White, "What Is Spatial History?" *Spatial History Project* (Stanford University), http://www.stanford.edu/group/spatialhistory/cgi-bin/site/pub.php?id=29; Timothy Mahoney, "Gilded Age Plains City," (Center for Digital Research in the Humanities, University of Nebraska), http://gildedage.unl.edu/; and David J. Bodenhamer, John Corrigan, and Trevor M. Harris, eds., *The Spatial Humanities: GIS and the Future of Humanities Scholarship* (Bloomington: Indiana University Press, 2010).

26. Digital history as a scholarly practice bears a close relationship to the wider field of Digital Humanities. Some of the key influences on my thinking about interfaces, texts, and narratives have been: Jerome McGann, *Radiant Textuality* (New York: Palgrave, 2001); Johanna Drucker, *Speclab: Digital Aesthetics and Projects in Speculative Computing* (Chicago and London: University of Chicago Press, 2009); Lev Manovich, *The Language of New Media* (Cambridge: MIT Press, 2001); Susan Schreibman, Ray Siemens, and John Unsworth, *A Companion to Digital Humanities* (Malden, Mass.: Blackwell, 2004); Anthony Grafton, *The Footnote: A Curious History* (Cambridge, Mass.: Harvard University Press, 1997); John Seely Brown and Paul Duquid, *The Social Life of Information* (Cambridge, Mass.: Harvard Business Press, 2000); Espen Aarseth, *Cybertext: Perspectives on Ergodic Literature* (Baltimore: Johns Hopkins Press, 1997); and Janet Murray, *Hamlet on the Holodeck: The Future of Narrative in Cyberspace* (New York: Free Press, 1997).

27. Melville, *Moby-Dick*, x.

Chapter 1. Slavery, the South, and "Every Bar of Railroad Iron"

1. Frederick Douglass, *Life and Times of Frederick Douglass: His Early Life as a Slave, His Escape from Bondage, and His Complete History to the Present Time* (Hartford: Park Publishing, 1881), 196–202, in *Documenting the American South Collection* (University of North Carolina at Chapel Hill), http://docsouth.unc.edu/neh/douglg2/menu.html (accessed March 2008).

2. Ibid., 200.

3. Ibid., 200.

4. Ibid., 201.

5. Frederick Douglass, "A Nation in the Midst of a Nation: An Address Delivered in New York, New York, on May 11, 1853," quoted in Lisa Brawley, "Fugitive Nation: Slavery, Travel, and Technologies of American Identity, 1830–1860" (Ph.D. diss., University of Chicago, 1995), 239.

6. Douglass, *Life and Times of Frederick Douglass*, 197.

7. Steven G. Collins, "Progress and Slavery on the South's Railroads," *Railroad History* (Autumn 1999): 6. See also Collins's dissertation, "Organizing the South: Railroads, Plantations, and War," Louisiana State University, Baton Rouge, 1999. The subject of slavery and the South's relative modernity is large; a few of the recent works relevant to this argument include: Gavin Wright, *Slavery and Economic Development* (Baton Rouge: Louisiana State University Press, 2006); Walter Johnson, *Soul by Soul: Life Inside the Antebellum Slave Market* (Cambridge, Mass.: Harvard University Press, 1999); Walter Johnson, ed., *The Chattel Principle: Internal Slave Trades in the Americas* (New Haven: Yale University Press, 2004); Edward L. Ayers, *In the Presence of Mine Enemies: War in the Heart of America, 1859–1863* (New York: W. W. Norton, 2003); James L. Huston, *Calculating the Value of the Union: Slavery, Property Rights, and the Economic Origins of the Civil War* (Chapel Hill: University of North Carolina Press, 2003); Tom Downey, *Planting a Capitalist South: Masters, Merchants, and Manufacturers in the Southern Interior, 1790–1860* (Baton Rouge, La.: Louisiana State University Press, 2006); L. Diane Barnes, *Artisan Workers in the Upper South: Petersburg, Virginia, 1820–1865* (Baton Rouge, La.: Louisiana State University Press, 2008); John Majewski, *A House Dividing: Economic Development in Pennsylvania and Virginia Before the Civil War* (Cambridge: Cambridge University Press, 2000); Robin Blackburn, *The Making of New World Slavery* (London: Verso, 1997); Robert Fogel, *The Slavery Debates: A Retrospective, 1952–1990* (Baton Rouge: Louisiana State University Press, 2003); Robert Fogel, *Without Consent or Contract: The Rise and Fall of American Slavery* (New York: W. W. Norton, 1989); and John Ashworth, *Slavery, Capitalism, and Politics in the Antebellum Republic, Volume I: Commerce and Compromise, 1820–1850* (Cambridge: Cambridge University Press, 1995), esp. 84–86. On the modern development of the South, see Susanna Delfino and Michelle Gillespie, *Global Perspectives on the Industrial Transformation of the American South* (Columbia: University of Missouri Press, 2006). For a recent examination of working class labor in the South, see Frank Towers, *The Urban South and the Coming of the Civil War* (Charlottesville: University of Virginia Press, 2004).

8. The most detailed analysis of slave labor on railroads is Theodore Kornweibel, Jr., "Railroads and Slavery," *Railroad History* (Fall–Winter 2003); see page 36 for the estimate of the workforce.

9. *The Emancipator*, October 11, 1838, from the Advocate of Freedom Recollections of Slavery by a Runaway Slave, http://docsouth.unc.edu/neh/runaway/runaway.html.

10. On railroads as the primary "exogenous" factor in the rise of slave prices, see Mark A. Yanochik, Mark Thornton, and Bradley T. Ewing, "Railroad Construction and Antebellum Slave Prices," *Social Science Quarterly*, Vol. 84, No. 3 (September 2003): 723–737. They conclude: "The economic connection between railroads and slave prices reconciles the views of

traditional economic historians who thought slavery was economically irrational and the views of the new economic historians who have concluded that slavery was highly profitable . . . it was public policy [of railroad construction subsidies] that provided the stimulant to slave prices, not the 'peculiar' culture of the antebellum South or the planter efficient management of slave labor."

11. The history of slavery's use on railroads has not been written. A few works have sketched the subject briefly: Allen Trelease, *The North Carolina Railroad, 1849–1871, and the Modernization of North Carolina* (Chapel Hill: University of North Carolina Press, 1991), 35, 63; *Proceedings of the Stockholders of the Louisville, Cincinnati and Charleston Rail-Road Company* (Charleston, S.C.: A. E. Miller, 1841), Special Collections, University of Virginia Library, Charlottesville, Va., 7–9; and Mississippi Central Railroad, *Annual Report of the President and Directors* (Holly Springs, Miss., 1855–1860), Special Collections, University of Virginia Library, Charlottesville, Va. See also Kornweibel, "Railroads and Slavery," 34–59; Steven G. Collins, "Progress and Slavery on the South's Railroads," *Railroad History* (Autumn 1999): 6–25; and the comprehensive and exquisitely compiled, Theodore Kornweibel, Jr., *Railroads and the African American Experience: A Photographic Journey* (Baltimore: Johns Hopkins University Press, 2010), 12–28.

12. Vicksburg and Mississippi Railroad Account Book, Illinois Central Railroad Records, Newberry Library, Chicago, Ill.

13. *Proceedings of the Stockholders of the Louisville, Cincinnati and Charleston Rail-Road Company.*

14. These figures come from a variety of sources. Exact numbers for railroad ownership of slaves are surprisingly difficult to pin down. The Virginia Central Railroad leased a dozen slaves in Staunton, Augusta County, Virginia (see *The Valley of the Shadow* project census database at http://valley.vcdh.virginia.edu/govdoc/slave_census.html). The online resource www.ancestry.com lists slaveholders but makes no distinction between railroads that hired slaves and those that purchased them, nor do the transcribed names make it possible to search for railroads (which were abbreviated often and cryptically). One of the best, but incomplete, sources online is Tom Blake's "Large Slaveholders of 1860" site, http://freepages.genealogy.rootsweb.ancestry.com/~ajac/, a detailed compilation of many southern county-level census records on slaveholders. The best records of slave ownership by railroads are the railroad company annual reports. Theodore Kornweibel, Jr., has compiled one of the most detailed accounts of slave numbers on railroads in "Railroads and Slavery," 34–59.

15. List of company officers and directors taken from Virginia Board of Public Works, *Annual Reports of Railroad Companies*, 1859, Box 105, Charles Kennedy Collection, Special Collections, University of Nebraska-Lincoln. Slaveholding for individuals compiled and checked against www.ancestry.com (accessed July 22, 2008). Company directors in South Carolina included 40 percent planters, 20 percent merchants, 20 percent lawyers, and 8 percent manufacturers and bankers. See Brian Schoen, *The Fragile Fabric of Union: Cotton, Federal Politics, and the Global Origins of the Civil War* (Baltimore: Johns Hopkins University Press, 2009), 205, and Thomas Downey, *Planting a Capitalist South: Masters, Merchants, and Manufacturers in the Southern Interior, 1790–1860* (Baton Rouge: Louisiana State University Press, 2006), 226.

16. *Railroad Advocate*, December 16, 1854; January 20, 1855; and January 27, 1855. Colburn's journal was based in the North and offers a different perspective on the industry's view of southern railroad development from the works of Frederick Law Olmsted. Olmsted's *A Journey in the Seaboard Slave States* (New York, 1856) depicted southern railroads as badly managed and as ultimately subversive of slavery because of their implicit modernity and culture. "They [railroads] cannot be prevented from disseminating intelligence and stirring thought," Olmsted wrote.

17. *Railroad Advocate*, December 16, 1854; January 20, 1855; and January 27, 1855.

18. The cost of railroad construction has been a subject of much debate among scholars rightly skeptical of the railroad accounting in this period. Colburn's *Railroad Advocate*, like many others at the time, used railroad annual reports and state commission data for his basis and admitted that these estimates were rough. The *1860 Census of the United States, Preliminary Report*, contained detailed construction costs and mileage for each state and railroad and reveals the major discrepancy between southern and northern railroad costs per mile. In addition, there are estimates in Dionysius Lardner's *Railway Economy* (London: Taylor, Walton and Maberly, 1850), 403–406. One of the best discussions of this problem is E. R. Wicker, "Railroad Investment Before the Civil War," *National Bureau of Economic Research: Trends in the American Economy in the Nineteenth Century*, Vol. 24 of *Studies in Income and Wealth* (Princeton, N.J.: Princeton University Press, 1960). Wicker states that as a rule New England costs were higher than those of the South (p. 512). For a full analysis of railroad construction costs, see Albert Fishlow, *American Railroads and the Transformation of the Ante-bellum Economy* (Cambridge: Harvard University Press, 1965), 342–347. Fishlow estimates U.S. construction costs at $35,000 per mile. Robert W. Fogel points out that engineers estimated the cost of the Union Pacific construction, for example, at $27,500 per mile, in Robert William Fogel, *The Union Pacific: A Case in Premature Enterprise* (Baltimore: Johns Hopkins Press, 1960), 57. On George Perkins Marsh, see David Lowenthal, *George Perkins Marsh: Prophet of Conservation* (Seattle and London: University of Washington Press, 2000), 192 and 195.

19. *Railroad Advocate*, December 16, 1854; January 20, 1855; and January 27, 1855.

20. "John C. Calhoun to David Hubbard," 1838, Gilder Lehrman Collection, Gilder Lehrman Institute of American History, New York, N.Y. See also, for similar correspondence, Clyde N. Wilson and Shirley B. Cook, eds., *The Papers of John C. Calhoun: Volume XXIV, December 7, 1846–December 5, 1847* (Columbia: University of South Carolina Press, 1998). See Vol. XXII, 1845–1846, 236, for Gadsden's letter. On Calhoun's plans for the West, see Charles M. Wiltse, *John C. Calhoun: Sectionalist, 1840–1850* (New York: Russell and Russell, 1951), 234–246. "General Brisbane's Compliments to the Conductors of the Press," *Charleston Mercury*, June 1, 1859, Issue 10,558, Col. D, in Gale Digital Collections, "Nineteenth Century U.S. Newspapers." See also Betty L. Plisco, *The Rocky Road to Nowhere: A History of the Blue Ridge Railroad in South Carolina, 1850–1861* (Salem, S.C.: Blue Granite, 2002), 69–73.

21. Means, "Empire, Progress, and the American Southwest," 67. See also Schoen, *The Fragile Fabric of Union*, 209–213.

22. A. H. Brisbane, "Detailed Report of General Brisbane, Dated June 30, 1849. Address to Richard Keily, Esq." in Richard Keily, *A Brief Description and Statistical Sketch of Georgia* (London: J. Carroll, 1849). See also Mark Wetherington, *Plain Folk's Fight: The Civil War and Reconstruction in Piney Woods Georgia* (Chapel Hill: University of North Carolina Press, 2005), 41. See also Bruce Eelman, "Progress and Community from Old South to New South: Spartanburg County, South Carolina, 1845–1880" (Ph.D. diss., University of Maryland College Park, 2000), 107, on the Spartanburg and Union Railroad as "the last in a system of works that is to bind up the country to the seaboard, in sympathy, interest, and daily association." Southern state railroad advocates spoke in terms of the "security" of their states against northern encroachment.

23. Mileage data based on Henry V. Poor's *Manual of the Railroads of the United States, 1868–69*, 20; *1860 Census of the United States, Preliminary Report*, 237; and E. R. Wicker, "Railroad Investment Before the Civil War," *National Bureau of Economic Research: Trends in the American Economy in the Nineteenth Century*, Vol. 24 of *Studies in Income and Wealth* (Princeton, N.J.: Princeton University Press, 1960).

24. See Majewski, *Modernizing a Slave Economy*, 118. The battles over railroad "state aid" schemes afflicted nearly every southern state in the 1850s and produced varying internecine political battles. J. Mills Thornton has compiled the most thorough examination of the

political transformations at work in a southern state in the 1850s, in *Politics and Power in a Slave Society: Alabama, 1800–1860* (Baton Rouge: Louisiana State University Press, 1978), 261. See especially Thornton's chapter 5, "Fear and Favor," 267–341, on the economic transformation of Alabama, largely from railroad development, that led to what Thornton calls a "society in vertigo." Thornton correctly points out that the South in this period was swept up in "the doctrines of the Victorian age" and that much of the South, even and especially the fire eaters, was Jeffersonian in outlook, for it "too strongly approved of the emerging urban and industrial world" (337).

25. See Kenneth Noe, *Southwest Virginia's Railroad: Modernization and the Sectional Crisis* (Urbana: University of Illinois Press, 1994), 43 and 70. On slave forced migration within southern states and counties, see Louis Kyriakoudes and Peter Colcanis, "The M-Factor in Southern History: Slave Forced Migration and the Slave Trade on the Internal Cotton Frontier, 1840–1860, A Labor Market Approach," unpublished paper presented at the Social Science History Association, Chicago, Ill., 2010. Kyriakoudes and Colcanis emphasize the variation in migration at the county level and intrastate patterns. Thirty percent of Virginia counties, for example, had significant in-migration of slaves in the 1840s and 1850s—these largely in the West, where railroads were under development. Adam Arenson, *The Great Heart of the Republic: St. Louis and the Cultural Civil War* (Cambridge, Mass.: Harvard University Press, 2011), 67. In 1850 Missouri's slave population was 87,422, and in 1860 it was 114,931; see Historical Census Browser, University of Virginia, Geospatial and Statistical Data Center (2004), http://mapserver.lib .virginia.edu (accessed March 2011). Historians have tended to excessively downplay the South's industrial development in these years. For an emphasis on southern industrial development as empty rhetoric, see John McCardell, *The Idea of a Southern Nation: Southern Nationalists and Southern Nationalism, 1830–1860* (New York: W. W. Norton, 1979), 126–127. The major work on the limitations of southern industry is Fred Bateman and Thomas Weiss, *A Deplorable Scarcity: The Failure of Industrialization in the Slave Economy* (Chapel Hill: University of North Carolina Press, 1981). See also Ronald L. Lewis, *Coal, Iron, and Slaves: Industrial Slavery in Maryland and Virginia, 1715–1865* (Westport: Greenwood, 1979). For a review of the economic arguments about southern industry, see John Ashworth, *Slavery, Capitalism, and Politics in the Antebellum Republic, Volume I: Commerce and Compromise, 1820–1850* (Cambridge: Cambridge University Press, 1995), esp. 90–100 and appendix, 499–509. Ashworth emphasizes the importance of slave resistance in shaping the context of southern industrial development.

26. Douglas J. Puffert, "The Standardization of Track Gauge on North American Railways, 1830–1890," *Journal of Economic History*, Vol. 60, No. 4 (December 2000): 933–960. Puffert points out that railroads had every incentive to use the same gauge as most proximate lines, not necessarily the majority gauge of the system as a whole; the gauge of the line the railroad will join mattered more than the gauge of the system or whole.

27. This research was made possible by the Center for Digital Research in the Humanities and data analysis by C. J. Warwas, GIS specialist and cartographer for the *Railroads and the Making of Modern America Project*, http://railroads.unl.edu. My concern is with passenger access and personal mobility, rather than with freight. The closest study of rail and canal and wagon road networks remains Robert W. Fogel, *Railroads and Economic Growth: Essays in Econometric History* (Baltimore: Johns Hopkins University Press, 1964). See especially pages 79–80 for Fogel's assessment of distance to rail and his use of a forty-mile buffer based on historical sources. We used a fifteen-mile buffer around railroad depots as a day's journey to an access point, because our focus was personal mobility rather than freight shipping. Railroads in the 1850s were significantly more oriented to passenger business than in the later period. The technique for measuring and estimating each county population's railroad access has been modeled on Ian Gregory, "Population Change and Transport in Rural England and Wales,

240 NOTES TO PAGES 26–28

1825–1911," paper presented at the Association of American Geographers, Boston, 2008 (in possession of the author). This graph includes data from National Historical GIS Data from the University of Minnesota, and railroad depot data compiled at the Center for Digital Research in the Humanities, University of Nebraska, based on original map sources in the Library of Congress American Memory, *Railroad Maps, 1828–1900*. Cartography by C. J. Warwas and Karin Callahan.

28. The term "second nature" is drawn from William Cronon's *Nature's Metropolis: Chicago and the Great West* (New York: W. W. Norton, 1991) and his edited volume *Uncommon Ground: Rethinking the Human Place in Nature* (New York: W. W. Norton, 1995).

29. Payrolls, Entry 91, January 1854, #216 Blue Ridge Railroad, Board of Public Works, Library of Virginia, Richmond, Va. For the most detailed account of slave hiring practices by railroads, see Aaron W. Marrs, "'This Is the Way to Build Railroads': Slavery and Railroads in Antebellum America," paper presented to the American Historical Association conference, New York, 2009. The R. F. & P. records at the Virginia Historical Society contain detailed "bonds" slaveholders signed with railroad companies to hire individual enslaved workers.

30. "Claudius Crozet to Board of Public Works," December 1, 1854, #216 Blue Ridge Railroad, Correspondence, 1854, Board of Public Works, Library of Virginia, Richmond, Va.

31. Ibid., November 5, 1854.

32. Ibid., January 4, 1854, and December 28, 1854. Marrs, "'This Is the Way to Build Railroads.'" Marrs found that of the 149 bonds for the year 1836 on the R. F. & P., 36 percent of them placed restrictions barring enslaved workers from working side by side with whites, likely for fear of escape.

33. In their annual reports nearly all southern railroads listed accidents in which slaves were killed. See, for example, the 1857 annual report, "181 slaves employed at depots, at shops, and at stations, on sections, and on trains"; the death of brakeman Ned Cole on August 8, 1857; and the payment of $994.30 to Dr. Strachan for "negro killed in Jan. 1856," all in Raleigh & Gaston Rail Road Company, *Proceedings of the Annual Meeting* (Richmond: H. K. Ellyson, 1848–1857), 41, Library of Virginia. On the military organization of the railroads, see an early essay by Leo Marx, "The Railroad-in-the-Landscape: An Iconological Reading of a Theme in American Art," in *The Railroad in American Art: Representations of Technological Change*, ed. Leo Marx and Susan Danly (Cambridge, Mass.: MIT Press, 1988), 183.

34. George Fitzhugh, *Cannibals All! Or, Slaves Without Masters* (A. Morris: Richmond, Va., 1857), viii. For a perceptive analysis of Fitzhugh's enthusiasm for technology and his "modern sense that the world was becoming too complex for understanding," see Michael O'Brien, *Conjectures of Order: Intellectual Life and the American South, 1810–1860*, Vol. 1 (Chapel Hill: University of North Carolina Press, 2004), 980–991.

35. Theodore Kornweibel, Jr., "Railroads and Slavery," *Railroad History* (Fall–Winter 2003): 34–59. "Ex-Slave Interview with Paul Smith," in *Born in Slavery: Slave Narratives from the Federal Writers' Project, 1936–1938*, Vol. IV, Part 3, Georgia Narratives, 336, Federal Writer's Project, USWPA, Manuscript Division, Library of Congress, American Memory Project, http://memory.loc.gov/ammem/snhtml/snhome.html.

36. "1853 Annual Report," in Opelousas and Great Western Railroad Company (New Orleans), *Annual Report of the President and Directors* (New Orleans: Clark and Brisbin Printers, 1850–1864), Special Collections, University of Virginia Library, Charlottesville, Va.

37. Memphis, El Paso and Pacific Railroad, *Annual Report of the Officers* (Clarksville, Tex.: Standard Print, 1857), Library of Virginia, Richmond, Va.

38. "Leslie Combs to Unknown, Friday," November 7, 1862, Series 1, General Correspondence, 1833–1916, Abraham Lincoln Papers, Library of Congress, Washington, D.C.

39. "Report of the President and Directors and of the Chief Engineer to the Annual

Meeting of the Stockholders of The Blue Ridge Railroad Company, in South Carolina, Held in Charleston, the 10th of November 1858," *Charleston Mercury,* November 13, 1858, Issue 10,388, Col. B.

40. "William F. Askew to Dickenson and Hill," February 13 and 19, 1856, Box 6, folder 6, Cornelius Chase Papers, Library of Congress, Washington, D.C.; "William D. Hix to Moore and Dawson," July 10, 1860, and numerous telegraphic messages, folder 10, in ibid.

41. "Winbush Young to E. H. Stokes," June 24, 1862, and numerous telegraphic messages, Box 6, folder 5 and folder 13, and Box 7, folder 1, Cornelius Chase Papers, Library of Congress, Washington, D.C.

42. James W. C. Pennington, "A Narrative of Events of the Life of J. H. Banks, an Escaped Slave, from the Cotton State, Alabama, in America," *Documenting the American South,* University of North Carolina, http://docsouth.unc.edu/neh/penning/penning.html.

43. Ibid.

44. *Semi-weekly Mississippian* (Jackson, Miss.), June 17, 1859, Issue 114, Col G.

45. "Anne Broome, Ex-Slave 87 Years Old," in *Born in Slavery: Slave Narratives from the Federal Writers' Project, 1936–1938,* Vol. XIV, Part 1, South Carolina Narratives, 104, Federal Writer's Project, USWPA, Manuscript Division, Library of Congress, American Memory Project, http://memory.loc.gov/ammem/snhtml/snhome.html.

46. Henry David Thoreau, *The Writings of Henry David Thoreau,* Vol. III, *Journal,* ed. Bradford Torrey (Boston and New York: Houghton Mifflin, 1906), 39.

47. See especially the outstanding work of Bonnie Maria Martin, "'To Have and to Hold' Human Collateral: Mortgaging Slaves to Build Virginia and South Carolina" (Ph.D. diss., Southern Methodist University, 2006), "Banks, Building Societies, and Speculators: Profiting from Human Collateral in Nineteenth-Century South Carolina," paper presented at the American Historical Association, New York, January 2009, and "Slavery's Invisible Engine: Mortgaging Human Property," *Journal of Southern History,* Vol. 76, No. 4 (November 2010): 865. Also Jennifer Oast, "'The Worst Kind of Slavery': Slave-owning Presbyterian Churches in Prince Edward County, Virginia," *Journal of Southern History,* Vol. 76, No. 4 (November 2010): 867–869, and J. Calvin Schermerhorn, "Against All Odds: Slavery and Enslaved Families in the Making of the Antebellum Chesapeake" (Ph.D. diss., University of Virginia, 2008), and his forthcoming *Money over Mastery, Family over Freedom: Slavery in the Antebellum Upper South* (Baltimore: Johns Hopkins University Press, 2011) and his forthcoming *Rambles of a Runaway from Southern Slavery.* For white proslavery ideas about the limits of black mobility, independence, and communication, see Stephanie McCurry, *Confederate Reckoning: Power and Politics in the Civil War South* (Cambridge, Mass.: Harvard University Press, 2010), 32.

48. For an example, see *Annual Report of the Philadelphia, Wilmington and Baltimore* (January 9, 1860) (Philadelphia: James A. Bryson), Charles Kennedy Collection, Special Collections, University of Nebraska-Lincoln. On the 1850s as a decisive break, see Lacy K. Ford, *The Origins of Southern Radicalism: The South Carolina Upcountry* (New York: Oxford University Press, 1988), 277, 359, 372; Bradley G. Bond, *Political Culture in the Nineteenth-Century South: Mississippi, 1830–1900* (Baton Rouge: Louisiana State University Press, 1995), 110–111. Bond notes that railroads helped unite white Southerners and convey a high degree of economic independence. Indeed, he argues the boom mirrored secession sentiments, as the railroad's success gave white Southerners unbounded confidence. For an important explanation of the South's understanding of its modernity, civilization, and nation, see especially Nicholas Onuf and Peter Onuf, *Nations, Markets, and War: Modern History and the American Civil War* (Charlottesville: University of Virginia Press, 2006), 166, 177, 185. Also Robert E. Bonner, "Americans Apart: Nationality in the Slaveholding South" (Ph.D. diss., Yale University, 1998), xv, 15, and 70, on the South's capacity to "perpetuate similarly profound contradictions" and the region as part of the American national empire in the 1850s.

Chapter 2. Railroads, the North, and "The Velocity of Progress"

1. Asa Whitney, "A Project for a Railroad to the Pacific," *Western Americana*, Reel 597, No. 6181, 41.

2. "Art. III.—The North and the South," *DeBow's Review and Industrial Resources, Statistics, etc. Devoted to Commerce* . . . (October 1854), Vol. XVII, No. 4, 361, American Periodicals Series Online, http://library.unl.edu/record=e1000040~S0 (accessed March 2008) (a paper read before the Franklin Society, Mobile, Alabama, by John Forsyth, 1854). On the rise of the Great Lakes economy and its importance in consolidating sectional orientations, see Marc Egnal, *Clash of Extremes: The Economic Origins of the Civil War* (New York: Hill and Wang, 2009), and "Rethinking the Secession of the Lower South: The Clash of Two Groups," *Civil War History*, Vol. 50, No. 3 (September 2004): 261–290.

3. George E. Baker, ed., *The Works of William H. Seward*, Vol. 1 (New York: Redfield, 1853), 70–93.

4. On the rival northern and southern land grants to internal improvement companies and their significance, see Jenny Bourne Wahl, "Stay East, Young Man? Market Repercussions of the Dred Scott Decision," *Chicago-Kent Law Review*, Vol. 82, No. 1 (2007): 368. On the congressional language in speeches for and against the Illinois Central, see Adele Josephine Cummings, "Governing the Economy: The Process and Politics of Government Involvement in the Railroads in Canada and the United States, 1850–1885" (Ph.D. diss., Duke University, 1995). Railroads were "nation builders," she argues, and brought unified state control over territories, creating and maintaining a sense of nationhood (16–17). On the importance of the West in shaping the sectional differences and conflicts, see Adam Arenson, *The Great Heart of the Republic: St. Louis and the Cultural Civil War* (Cambridge, Mass.: Harvard University Press, 2011), 82–107.

5. John Munn Collection, Journals, Vol. 21, 160–162, Chicago Historical Society, Chicago, Ill.

6. Ibid., 176.

7. Ibid., Vol. 22, 134–135, 139–140, and 170.

8. Railroads often complained that competing lines distorted maps. See September 28, 1858, letter to John W. Garrett, president of the Baltimore & Ohio from the Indiana Central Railroad officers complaining that "the studious enlargement of the lines leading from your city . . . on your maps" and the omission of the Terre Haute Railroad on the B & O maps were "well calculated to mislead." Garrett Family Papers, Box 68, Library of Congress, Washington, D.C.

9. "Benjamin F. Johnson to William Osborn," May 19, 1855, Series I J6.2, Box 92, folder 298, Illinois Central Railroad Records, Newberry Library, Chicago, Ill. (hereafter ICRR). Jeremy Atack and Robert A. Margo, "The Impact of Access to Rail Transportation on Agricultural Improvement: The American Midwest as a Test Case, 1850–1860," unpublished paper presented at the Organization of American History Conference, Houston, Texas, 2011, use Stanley Lebergott's estimate for land clearing and fencing—between $14 and $25 per acre in 1850. Even on the prairie, sod needed to be broken and fences put up.

10. Ibid.

11. Dorothy R. Adler, *British Investment in American Railways, 1834–1898* (Charlottesville: University Press of Virginia, 1970), 23 and 55–59.

12. "Benjamin F. Johnson to William Osborn," May 22, 1855, Series I J6.2, Box 92, folder 298, ICRR (emphasis in original).

13. *Guides to Illinois Land Sales, 1854–1860*, Series 7.22, Box 4, folder 72, ICRR.

14. Carlton J. Corliss, *Main Line of Mid-America: The Story of the Illinois Central* (New York: Creative Age, 1950), 82 and 87–88.

15. See Jay Sexton, *Debtor Diplomacy: Finance and American Foreign Relations in the Civil War Era, 1837–1873* (Oxford: Clarendon, 2005), 76.

16. Terre Haute and Richmond Railroad Annual Reports, Kennedy Collection, Box 182, University of Nebraska-Lincoln, Special Collections Library. Albert Fishlow, *American Railroads and the Transformation of the Ante-bellum Economy* (Cambridge: Harvard University Press, 1965), 202, contends that western railroads were high–passenger volume roads and earned their profits from this for several years after the rest of the nation's lines had switched to freight traffic as their main source of revenue. Instead, in the western states and territories in the 1850s passenger revenues remained higher longer, into 1857. By 1859, he argues, passenger revenues had fallen off and passenger traffic slowed. Passenger through-traffic on six major east–west trunk lines fell from 581,000 in 1857–1858 to 367,000 in 1859–1860, while the number of tons carried on these lines jumped from 797,000 to 1,026,000. "The difficulties of western railroads from 1857 on were thus a direct consequence of the break in the flow of migration westward, and not the result of a decline in freight shipments" (203) (see Appendix, Table 7).

17. Fishlow, *American Railroads and the Transformation of the Ante-bellum Economy,* 263 and 293. Economic historians have recently explained the important effects of the railroad on the Northwest economy in detail. On population growth, John J. Blinder, "The Transportation Revolution and Antebellum Sectional Disagreement," *Social Science History,* Vol. 35, No. 1 (Spring 2011): 43. Atack and Margo, "The Impact of Access to Rail Transportation on Agricultural Improvement," use a "difference in differences" analysis to find that railroads explain almost two-thirds of the increase in agricultural productivity, half of the urban growth, and "all of the increase in percent improved acreage over the decade."

18. Walter Licht, *Working for the Railroad: The Organization of Work in the Nineteenth Century* (Princeton, N.J.: Princeton University Press, 1983), 33. By 1880 approximately 10 percent of all industrial workers in the United States were employed by the railroads, but the number could be much greater, possibly as high as 18 percent. On the elaborate hierarchies in railroad work, see Paul M. Tallon, "Culture, Politics, and the Making of Railroad Brotherhoods, 1863–1916" (Ph.D. diss., University of Wisconsin-Madison, 1997), 47–50.

19. See William F. Deverell, "To Loosen the Safety Valve: Eastern Workers and Western Lands," *Western Historical Quarterly,* Vol. 19, No. 3 (August 1998): 269–285. The most influential and important account of free labor ideology remains Eric Foner, *Free Soil, Free Labor, Free Men: The Ideology of the Republican Party Before the Civil War* (New York: Oxford University Press, 1970), esp. 11–39. Foner argues that these ideas were connected to material development for Republicans and quotes William Henry Seward, for example—"Popular government follows in the track of the steam-engine and telegraph." Also David Montgomery, *Beyond Equality: Labor and the Radical Republicans 1862–1872* (Urbana: University of Illinois Press, 1981), 24–44.

20. Walter Licht has completed the most detailed account of first-generation railroad workers in the North. He tracked social mobility across the industry and emphasized the high levels of transience, upward mobility, and migration (Licht, "Working for the Railroad," 33, 73, 127, 153, and 158 ff.). Licht followed men from payroll to payroll—after two years 5–8 percent moved up; 40 percent did not change position; over 50 percent disappeared.

21. Licht, "Working for the Railroad," 220–224. In the South nearly all railroad employees were black except the engineers and conductors. This pattern persisted well after the Civil War. In 1880 the North Atlantic Population Project data shows that over 52 percent of railroad workers in Virginia were black, while in Maryland and Pennsylvania over 96 percent were white.

22. All 6,467 B & O workers were checked against the 1860 U.S. Census for possible matches and against the Baltimore City Directory for 1858. R. Edwards and W. H. Boyd, *The*

Baltimore City Directory, Vol. 1, 1858 (Polk, 1858). Three hundred and forty-seven employees were matched to the city directory, while 129 were matched to the U.S. Census for counties and cities in Maryland along the B & O line. Richard Healey, Katie Dooley, and William G. Thomas, "Migration, Economic Opportunity and the Railroads: Movement of Heavy Industrial Workers in the North-East USA 1850–1900," ESRC Grant No. RES-000-22-2420 (2009). Also Richard G. Healey, William G. Thomas, and Katie Dooley, "The Geography of Free Labor: The Baltimore and Ohio Railroad and Worker Mobility in Mid-Nineteenth Century American Society," unpublished manuscript, 2010.

23. Licht, "Working for the Railroad," 22.

24. *A List of the Officers and Employees of the Baltimore and Ohio Railroads with the Amount of Their Pay for 1857* (Baltimore: John Murphy and Co., 1868), Maryland Historical Society, Baltimore, Md.

25. Historical Railroad Employees Database, "Railroads and the Making of Modern American," Center for Digital Research in the Humanities, University of Nebraska-Lincoln, http://railroads.unl.edu. Baltimore & Ohio payrolls databases, with data for 1852, 1854, 1857, and 1858, were developed in collaboration with Richard Healey, University of Portsmouth, ESRC Grant No. RES-000-22-2420.

26. Robert William Fogel, *Without Consent or Contract: The Rise and Fall of American Slavery* (New York: W. W. Norton, 1989), 354–356. See Frank Towers, *The Urban South and the Coming of the Civil War* (Charlottesville: University of Virginia Press, 2005), 222–223. Towers's study of Baltimore's working men shows that between 1850 and 1860 native white workers' proportion of jobs in transportation fell from 50 percent to 39 percent, while immigrants gained.

27. Healey, Dooley, and Thomas, "Migration, Economic Opportunity and the Railroads."

28. "John R. Boyle to Samuel B. Reed," April 30, 1860, Reed Family Papers, Yale University Library, Manuscripts and Archives, New Haven, Conn.

29. "Samuel B. Reed to Jennie Reed," October 3, 1860, Reed Family Papers, Yale University Library, Manuscripts and Archives, New Haven, Conn.

30. Elizabeth Hoon Cawley, ed., *The American Diaries of Richard Cobden* (Princeton, N.J.: Princeton University Press, 1952), 41 ff. On Cobden, see Anthony Howe, ed. *The Letters of Richard Cobden, Vol. I, 1815–1847* (Oxford: Oxford University Press, 2007), xxxiii–lx. On Cobden's involvement in the Illinois Central Railroad and his role as an investor, see Carlton J. Corliss, *Main Line of Mid-America: The Story of the Illinois Central* (New York: Creative Age, 1950), 33, 65, 92, and 95–96.

31. Cawley, *The American Diaries of Richard Cobden*, 152.

32. "Richard Cobden to Parkes," December 4, 1861, MSS 43,660, and "Richard Cobden to Henry Ashworth," June 14, 1862, MSS 43,648, Richard Cobden Papers, British Library, London, U.K.

33. "Richard Cobden to Parkes," December 4, 1861, MSS 43,660, and "Cobden to John Bright," April 29, 1859, MSS 43,651, Vol. V, Richard Cobden Papers, British Library, London, U.K.

34. John J. Blinder, "The Transportation Revolution and Antebellum Sectional Disagreement," *Social Science History*, Vol. 35, No. 1 (Spring 2011): 41–42. On property rights, see Gavin Wright, *Slavery and American Economic Development* (Baton Rouge: Louisiana State University Press, 2006).

35. Cawley, *The American Diaries of Richard Cobden*, 176.

36. Gavin Wright, *Slavery and American Economic Development* (Baton Rouge: Louisiana State University Press, 2006), 48–49. See also William G. Thomas, III, and Edward L. Ayers, "The Differences Slavery Made: A Close Analysis of Two American Communities," *American Historical Review* (December 2003), http://www.vcdh.virginia.edu/AHR. For a different but

related explanation of southern planter confidence, see Stephanie McCurry, *Confederate Reckoning: Power and Politics in the Civil War South* (Cambridge, Mass.: Harvard University Press, 2010), 9.

Chapter 3. Secession and a Modern War

1. "Ephraim C. Dawes to Kate," October 27, 1856, and May 19, 1856, Series I, Box 1, folder 13, Ephraim C. Dawes Papers, Newberry Library, Chicago, Ill. (hereafter Dawes Papers).

2. "Ephraim C. Dawes to Henry Dawes," December 25, 1856, Series I, Box 1, folder 11, Dawes Papers.

3. For an analysis of the importance of the Great Lakes region in the developing sectional political crisis, and the influence of the "Yankee North," see Marc Egnal, "The Beards Were Right: Parties in the North, 1840–1860," *Civil War History*, Vol. 47, No. 1 (2001): 30–56.

4. I am grateful to Gregory R. Jones, who shared his seminar paper with me on this subject, "Connecting the 'Railway of Life': Southeastern Ohio in the 1850s," Kent State University, November 14, 2008.

5. "Ephraim C. Dawes to William Stephenson," October 28, 1861, Series I, Box 1, folder 44, Dawes Papers. Ephraim C. Dawes, *In Memoriam, William Blackford Stephenson* (Cincinnati: Peter G. Thomson, 1879), United States Army Military History Institute, Carlisle, Pennsylvania.

6. For a useful study of the language and enthusiasm surrounding railroad development, see Craig Miner, *A Most Magnificent Machine: America Adopts the Railroad, 1825–1862* (Lawrence: University Press of Kansas, 2010), xiv, 68–69, and 169.

7. Some guests regretted the invitation but applauded the B & O for opening "the facilities of social and commercial intercommunication incident to a small island, and thus unite us as one family, with one common interest"; and serving "to connect the different states of the union as one family and which by the facility of intercourse" reduce those "unreasonable and unnatural prejudices which mischievous demagogues are eternally laboring to prosecute"; "P. E. Thomas to W. P. Smith," May 20, 1857, and "John Minor Botts to W. P. Smith," May 23, 1857 (respectively), Garrett Family Papers, Box 64, Library of Congress, Washington, D.C.

8. Smith, *The Book of the Great Railway Celebrations of 1857* (New York: D. Appleton and Co., 1858), 96. The classic works stressing space and time include L. Marx, *The Machine in the Garden: Technology and the Pastoral Ideal in America* (New York: Oxford University Press, 1964), 194; W. Schivelbusch, *The Railway Journey: Industrialization and Perception of Time and Space* (Berkeley: University of California Press, 1986); and, more recently, R. White, "Information, Markets, and Corruption: Transcontinental Railroads in the Gilded Age," *Journal of American History*, Vol. 90 (2003): 19.

9. Smith, *The Book of the Great Railway Celebrations of 1857*, 96.

10. Ibid., 86–88.

11. On the rise of the Republican Party in Maryland from 300 voters in 1856, see "Maryland Affairs," *New York Times*, April 17, 1860. Smith, *The Book of the Great Railway Celebrations of 1857*, 86–88.

12. Frank Towers, *The Urban South and the Coming of the Civil War* (Charlottesville: University of Virginia Press, 2004), argues that the workers' political movements in the largest cities in the South—Baltimore, New Orleans, and Saint Louis—contributed to secession because planters feared the consequences and increasingly saw the large cities as "bridgeheads for a Republican Party invasion of the South" (14).

13. "Great Railroad Celebration," *DeBow's Review, Agricultural, Commercial, Industrial Progress and Resources*, Vol. XII (1857): 91–94.

14. "Military Defences of Virginia—No. 2," *DeBow's Review and Industrial Resources, Statistics, etc. Devoted to Commerce . . . Oct 1855,* American Periodicals Series Online, 445, from *Richmond Examiner,* August 10, 1855.

15. Lawrence A. Estaville, Jr., "A Strategic Railroad: The New Orleans, Jackson, and Great Northern in the Civil War," *Louisiana History,* Vol. 14 No. 2 (Spring 1973), 124. Also Miner, *A Most Magnificent Machine,* 158 and 165.

16. For an example, see *Annual Report of the Philadelphia, Wilmington and Baltimore* (Philadelphia: James A. Bryson, January 9, 1860), Charles Kennedy Collection, Special Collections, University of Nebraska-Lincoln. On the 1850s as a decisive break, see Lacy K. Ford, *The Origins of Southern Radicalism: The South Carolina Upcountry* (New York: Oxford University Press, 1988), 277, 359, 372; Bradley G. Bond, *Political Culture in the Nineteenth-Century South: Mississippi, 1830–1900* (Baton Rouge: Louisiana State University Press, 1995), 110–111. Nicholas Onuf and Peter Onuf, *Nations, Markets, and War: Modern History and the American Civil War* (Charlottesville: University of Virginia Press, 2006), 166, 177, 185. On the Confederate claim of self-determination and its significance in the way Confederates explained and understood their national ambitions in the world, see Drew Gilpin Faust, *The Creation of Confederate Nationalism: Ideology and Identity in the Civil War South* (Baton Rouge: Louisiana State University Press, 1992), and Anne Sarah Rubin, *A Shattered Nation: The Rise and Fall of the Confederacy, 1861–1868* (Chapel Hill: University of North Carolina Press, 2005).

17. William Freehling suggests that the timing of the completion of the Charleston & Savannah Railroad might have played a decisive role in the secession movement in South Carolina in December 1860. "A modern railroad might seem an ironic engine to further a reactionary revolution," Freehling writes, but the celebration brought Georgians and South Carolinians together at a crucial moment in the secession crisis. William W. Freehling, *The Road to Disunion: Secessionists Triumphant, 1854–1861* (New York: Oxford University Press, 2007), 406.

18. On the speed of disunion, see David M. Potter, *The Impending Crisis, 1848–1861* (New York: Harper, 1977). See also Allan Nevins, *Ordeal of the Union,* Vol. II (New York: Scribner, 1947), 320, on the rush of the delegates to Columbia as decisive in reversing the convention's decision to delay the vote and, therefore, in accelerating the momentum of secession by advancing its timetable.

19. James H. Moss, March 11, 1861, in *Journal and Proceedings of the Missouri State Convention* (Missouri, 1861), 70, 323. *Journal of the Public and Secret Proceedings of the Convention of the People of Georgia,* January 16, 1861 (Georgia, 1861), 395, 413, and 576. George H. Reese, ed., *Proceedings of the Virginia State Convention of 1861* (4 vols.), Vol. II (Richmond: Virginia State Library, 1965), 651. Charles B. Dew, *Apostles of Disunion: Southern Secession Commissioners and the Causes of the Civil War* (Charlottesville: University of Virginia Press, 2003).

20. Reese, *Proceedings of the Virginia State Convention of 1861,* Vol. II, 83 and 105.

21. Ibid., 75–108.

22. "John W. Davis to His Brother," March 3, 1861, MSS 1393; "J. W. Parrish to His Sister," March 27, 1861, MSS 1035; "Lawrence Pitman to O. P. Smith," March 11, 1861, Steele Family Papers, MSS 10616, in Albert and Shirley Small Special Collections Library, University of Virginia, Charlottesville, Va. "John H. Cochran to His Mother," March 19, 1861, Cochran Family Letters, MS 92–032, Civil War Collections, Special Collections, Virginia Tech, Blacksburg, Va. See also Peter Carmichael, *The Last Generation: Young Virginians in Peace, War, and Reunion* (Chapel Hill: University of North Carolina Press, 2005). On college campus reaction, Audra Hegney, "Virginia Students in the Civil War: The Heart of the Confederacy" (undergraduate senior thesis, University of Virginia, 2000).

23. Reese, *Proceedings of the Virginia State Convention of 1861,* Vol. IV, 58–59, for Jubal Early's decision not to support secession, and 80–82 for William G. Brown's concerns that his

western Virginia county near Pennsylvania would be "overrun" and that he would have to go to Philadelphia to get home.

24. Reese, *Proceedings of the Virginia State Convention of 1861*, Vol. II, 38 (emphasis in original). On Virginia secession, see William G. Shade, *Democratizing the Old Dominion: Virginia and the Second Party System, 1824–1861* (Charlottesville: University Press of Virginia, 1996); see also Kenneth Noe, *Southwest Virginia's Railroad: Modernization and the Sectional Crisis* (Urbana: University of Illinois Press, 1994), 7–8, 43, 70. The three railroad directors at the Virginia Constitutional Convention were Thomas Branch of Petersburg, William Ballard Preston of Montgomery, and Lewis E. Harvie of Amelia, although many of the delegates may have been stockholders and involved in railroad promotion.

25. See Reese, *Proceedings of the Virginia State Convention of 1861*, Vol. IV, 24. See also William H. Freehling, *The Reintegration of American History: Slavery and the Civil War* (New York: Oxford University Press, 1994), 8–9.

26. Reese, *Proceedings of the Virginia State Convention of 1861*, Vol. II, 345–351, 677–682.

27. Ibid., 673.

28. Ibid., 675. For a useful analysis of the Confederate moment of secession and national formation, see Robert E. Bonner, "Americans Apart: Nationality in the Slaveholding South" (Ph.D. diss., Yale University, 1998), 220–236.

29. Several monographs deal with railroads in the Civil War, and many historians have pointed to the poor management of its railroads as one reason for the Confederacy's defeat. For an analysis, see Collins, "Organizing the South: Railroads, Plantations, and War" (Ph.D. diss., Louisiana State University, 1999), chapter 3, and recently John E. Clarke, Jr., *Railroads in the Civil War: The Impact of Management on Victory and Defeat* (Baton Rouge: Louisiana State University Press, 2001), and Scott Reynolds Nelson, *Iron Confederacies: Southern Railways, Klan Violence, and Reconstruction* (Chapel Hill: University of North Carolina Press, 1999). Clark has shown how northern organization in 1863 allowed it to outrun southern interior lines. Robert G. Angevine, *The Railroad and the State: War, Politics, and Technology in Nineteenth-Century America* (Stanford, Calif.: Stanford University Press, 2004) examines the growth of the military and its relationship to big-business development. The classic works in the field are Thomas Weber, *The Northern Railroads in the Civil War* (New York: Crown, 1952; rpt. Bloomington: Indiana University Press, 1999), and Robert C. Black, *The Railroads of the Confederacy* (Chapel Hill: University of North Carolina Press, 1952; rpt. 1998). Another classic work, *Victory Rode the Rails: The Strategic Place of the Railroads in the Civil War*, by George Edgar Turner (Indianapolis, Ind.: Bobbs-Merrill, 1953; rpt. Lincoln: University of Nebraska Press, 1992), covers the strategic significance of railroads in the war. Turner's volume details nearly every major engagement in which railroads figured and is a thorough account of railroad strategy in the North and South. It remains important and useful, but it pays little attention to the broader currents of social change and the development of modernity. Similarly, Angus James Johnston II's *Virginia Railroads in the Civil War* (Chapel Hill: University of North Carolina Press, 1961), and Black's *The Railroads of the Confederacy* cover the detailed logistical failures of the Confederate war effort's use of railroads. For the best recent study of the development of gauges in the United States, see Douglas J. Puffert, "The Standardization of Track Gauge on North American Railways, 1830–1890," *Journal of Economic History*, Vol. 60, No. 4 (December 2000): 933–960.

30. See John Keegan, *The American Civil War: A Military History* (New York: Knopf, 2009), 70. The most recent treatment of strategy in the Civil War is Donald Stoker, *The Grand Design: Strategy and the U.S. Civil War* (Oxford: Oxford University Press, 2010), 24–26.

31. *Biennial Report of the Board of Public Works, Annual Reports of the Rail Road Companies of the State of Virginia Made to the Board of Public Works for the Year Ending September 30, 1861*, 36, Charles J. Kennedy, Railroad Collection, University of Nebraska, Lincoln, Neb.

32. Ibid., 71, 121, 142, and 159. Collins, "Organizing the South," 119, and Black, *The Railroads of the Confederacy*, 129–130. For an excellent collection of employee records, see Dave Bright, ed., *Confederate Railroads*, http://www.csa-railroads.com.

33. October 15, 1862 report, *Biennial Report of the Board of Public Works to the General Assembly of Virginia, 1861–62 and 1862–63*, 209, Norfolk and Petersburg, Charles Kennedy Collection, Box 102, Special Collections, University of Nebraska-Lincoln.

34. U.S. War Department, *The War of the Rebellion: A Compilation of the Official Records of the Union and Confederate Armies* (Lynchburg, Va., and Pasadena, Calif.: Broadfoot, 1985) (hereafter *OR*), Series III, Vol. 5, 976 and 979. Brian R Dirck, "Posterity's Blush: Civil Liberties, Property Rights, and Property Confiscation in the Confederacy," *Civil War History*, Vol. 48, No. 3 (September 2002): 250.

35. Charles Hildreth, "Railroads out of Pensacola, 1833–1883," *Florida Historical Quarterly*, Vol. 37, No. 3/4, 397–417. Collins, "Organizing the South," 113–121. Black, *The Railroads of the Confederacy*, 78–96.

36. Carlton J. Corliss, *Main Line of Mid-America: The Story of the Illinois Central* (New York: Creative Age Press, 1950), 137.

37. "Joseph G. Totten, Chief Engineer, to Secretary of War, April 3, 1861," *OR*, Series I, Vol. 1, 234.

38. John Disturnill, J. Goldsborough Bruff, E. Jones, G. W. Newman, and J. Probst, *A Correct Map of the Seat of War in Mexico*," 1847, David Rumsey Map Collection, www.davidrumsey.com/index.html.

39. "Joseph G. Totten, Chief Engineer, to Secretary of War," April 3, 1861, *OR*, Series I, Vol. 1, 234. Lloyd's American Railroad Map, New York, 1861, in *Lloyd's American Railroad Weekly*, Vol. 2, No. 8 (October 5, 1861), American Memory Collection, Library of Congress, Washington, D.C.

40. *Richmond Daily Dispatch*, May 4, 1861, in Dave Bright, ed., *Confederate Railroads*, http://www.csa-railroads.com.

41. "Simon Cameron to Giddeon Welles," May 29, 1861, *OR*, Series I, Vol. 1, 423.

42. Yael Sternhell, "Revolution in Motion: Human Mobility and the Transformation of the South, 1861–1865" (Ph.D. diss., Yale University, 2008), 39.

43. James I. Robertson, Jr., *Stonewall Jackson: The Man, The Soldier, The Legend* (New York: Macmillan, 1997), 217–218. *OR*, Series I, Vol. 1, 487.

44. *OR*, Series I, Vol. 1, 677–678, and "Jeff Thompson to Jefferson Davis," May 6, 1861, *OR*, Series I, Vol. 1, 690.

45. See especially James C. Scott, *Seeing Like a State: How Certain Schemes to Improve the Human Condition Have Failed* (New Haven: Yale University Press, 1998). On the South's capacity to organize itself for war, see Steven G. Collins, "System in the South: John W. Mallet, Josiah Gorgas, and Uniform Production at the Confederate Ordnance Department," *Technology and Culture*, Vol. 40, No. 3 (1999): 517–544.

46. One of the best accounts of Sherman's character and writing is Charles Royster, *The Destructive War: William Tecumseh Sherman, Stonewall Jackson and the Americans* (New York: Knopf, 1991), 358, 376–377, and 392.

47. "William T. Sherman to Edward Bates," Thursday, May 8, 1862, Series 1, General Correspondence, 1833–1916, Abraham Lincoln Papers, Library of Congress, Washington, D.C. See also "Sherman to John Sherman," September 11, 1862, "We ought to hold fast to the Mississippi River, as a great base of operations," in Brooks D. Simpson and Jean V. Berlin, ed. *Sherman's Civil War: Selected Correspondence of William T. Sherman, 1860–1865* (Chapel Hill: University of North Carolina Press, 1999), 301. See also William H. Goetzmann, *Army Exploration in the American West, 1803–1863* (New Haven: Yale University Press, 1959).

48. On Sherman's strategy, see Stoker, *The Grand Strategy*, 208–209 and 374–394.

49. *OR*, Vol. 5 (Part I), 757. "The Reclamation of the Trans-Allegheny," *Richmond Daily Dispatch*, February 10, 1862, Vol. XXI, No. 35.

50. *OR*, Vol. 5 (Part I), 7.

51. See Stephen Sears, *George B. McClellan: The Young Napoleon* (New York: Ticknor and Fields, 1988), 48–49. "George B. McClellan to J. Newton Perkins," August 28, 1857 and August 31, 1857, Illinois Central Railroad Company Records, IC 1 M2.1, Box 94, Newberry Library, Chicago, Ill. On the development of McClellan's plans and strategy, see Stoker, *The Grand Design*, 81–92. "George B. McClellan to Mary Ellen McClellan," November 14, 1861, in Stephen W. Sears, ed., *The Civil War Papers of George B. McClellan: Selected Correspondence, 1860–1865* (New York: Ticknor and Fields, 1989), 132. See also Kevin Dougherty and J. Michael Moore, *The Peninsula Campaign of 1862: A Military Analysis* (Jackson: University Press of Mississippi, 2005), 66–67.

52. On the concept of "railroad generalship," see Christopher R. Gabel, "Railroad Generalship: Foundations of Civil War Strategy," U.S. Army Command and General Staff College, Combat Studies Institute, http://handle.dtic.mil/100.2/ADA445773 (accessed June 2008). For an excellent study of West Point and its officer class, see Wayne Wei-siang Hsieh, *West Pointers and the Civil War: The Old Army in War and Peace* (Chapel Hill: University of North Carolina Press, 2009), 131–151. Hsieh argues that both North and South depended on the old army for its officers, who followed ad hoc doctrine, that few of them had any training in railroad warfare, and that throughout the war both sides experienced an "equilibrium of competence."

Chapter 4. Fighting the Confederate Landscapes

1. "Ephraim C. Dawes to William Stephenson," October 28, 1861, Series I, Box 1, folder 44, Ephraim C. Dawes Papers, Newberry Library, Chicago, Ill. (hereafter Dawes Papers).

2. The railroads kept detailed records of the troop transportation and reported to the Quartermaster's Department. See "Transportation of Troops, 1861," Record Group 92 1475, National Archives and Records Administration, College Park, Md. The forthcoming work of Timothy Mahoney on the middle West and the small town worlds the soldiers came from and returned to promises to shed new light on the importance of how men traveled into, and out from, the war. Mahoney is following the "spatial narratives" of individuals and regiments in the Civil War. For an example of spatial narrative, see Timothy Mahoney, "Gilded Age Plains City," Center for Digital Research in the Humanities, University of Nebraska, http://gildedage.unl.edu.

3. John K. Duke, *History of the 53rd Regiment Ohio Volunteer Infantry During the War of the Rebellion, 1861 to 1865 Together with More Than Thirty Personal Sketches of Officers and Men* (Portsmouth, Ohio: Blade Print, 1900). Even in the far west, other units too traveled largely by train and steamboat. The First Nebraska split as one part took steamboats from Omaha to Saint Louis, while the other boarded trains from Saint Joseph to Hannibal, Missouri, then took steamboats down the Mississippi to Saint Louis. The First Nebraska then took trains to Pilot Knob, a depot on the Saint Louis and Iron Mountain Railroad. The First eventually traveled by steamboat to Cairo, then up the Tennessee River to Fort Henry and back down to Pittsburgh Landing, where it arrived to fight in the Battle of Shiloh. The unit had marched only twelve miles in the first year of the war—from Fort Henry to Fort Donelson. See James E. Potter, "Standing Firmly by the Flag: Nebraska Territory, the Civil War, and the Coming of Statehood, 1861–1867," manuscript in possession of the author.

4. "Ephraim C. Dawes to Kate," November 10, 1863, Series I, Box 1, folder 18, Dawes Papers. On marching and the logistics of moving armies, see John E. Clark, Jr., *Railroads in the Civil War: The Impact of Management on Victory and Defeat* (Baton Rouge: Louisiana State Uni-

versity Press, 2001). Some armies in the western theater marched over thirty-five miles a day. For an excellent examination of Union soldiers' experiences on the long marches, as well as of their understanding of the landscape in the far west, I am grateful to Kaci Nash for sharing her seminar paper "'Steadily and Joyfully to Our Doom': On the March in the Union Army" (May 2010).

5. Ephraim C. Dawes, *In Memoriam, William Blackford Stephenson* (Cincinnati: Peter G. Thomson, 1879), United States Army Military History Institute, Carlisle, Pa. Ephraim C. Dawes, Pension File # 55520 Invalid, National Archives and Records Administration, College Park, Md. "Ephraim C. Dawes to Kate," November 10, 1863, December 18, 1863, and March 31, 1864, Box 1, folders 18 and 19, Dawes Papers, Newberry Library.

6. "Charles T. Kruse to Parents," August 24, 1862, Charles T. Kruse Papers, Newberry Library.

7. Ibid., January 15, 1863.

8. For one of the most useful accounts of soldiers' travels in 1861 from the home front into the cities and to army camps, see Yael Sternhell, "Revolution in Motion: Human Mobility and the Transformation of the South, 1861–1865" (Ph.D. diss., Yale University, 2008), 40, 44–48. Sternhell argues that, for Confederates, journeying "embodied" the new nation. Also Robert Hallock, "Soldier's Impressions of the Richmond Landscape, 1861–1865" (undergraduate thesis, University of Virginia, 2000). James A. Mumper, ed., *I Wrote You the Word: The Poignant Letters of Private Holt* (Lynchburg: H. E. Howard, 1993), 8.

9. On the importance of the environment and landscape in war, see Charles E. Closeman, ed., *War and the Environment: Military Destruction in the Modern Age* (College Station: Texas A. and M. University Press, 2009). On the ways scholars have portrayed war and natural landscapes as separate and unrelated, and why they instead should be interconnected, see Edmund Russell, *War and Nature: Fighting Humans and Insects with Chemicals from World War I to Silent Spring* (Cambridge and New York: Cambridge University Press, 2001).

10. On the peculiar features of the military landscape and its importance, see "Landscape as Seen by the Military," in John B. Jackson, *Discovering the Vernacular Landscape* (New Haven: Yale University Press, 1984), 131–137. Some very promising new histories of the environment in the Civil War will shed light on this important topic: see Lisa Brady, "The Wilderness of War: Nature and Strategy in the American Civil War," *Environmental History*, Vol. 10, No. 3 (July 2005); Mark Fiege, "Gettysburg and the Organic Nature of the American Civil War," in *Natural Enemy, Natural Ally: Toward an Environmental History of War*, ed. Richard P. Tucker and Edmund Russell (Corvallis: Oregon State University Press, 2004), 93–109. Jack Temple Kirby has also written an essay on the environmental effects of the war, "The American Civil War: An Environmental View," National Humanities Center, http://www.nhc.rtp.nc.us:8080/tserve/nattrans/ntuseland/essays/amcwar.htm (accessed May 2005). Also on "reading" a landscape, see Francis Pryor, *The Making of the British Landscape: How We Have Transformed the Land from Prehistory to Today* (London: Allen Lane, 2010).

11. See, especially, Jeffrey Alan Melton, *Mark Twain, Travel Books, and Tourism: The Tide of a Great Popular Movement* (Tuscaloosa: University of Alabama Press, 2002), 16 and 49–55, on the ways nineteenth-century travelers encountered "the other" and on their colonialist perspective in reading a landscape; also Jennifer Speake, *Literature of Travel and Exploration: An Encyclopedia, Vol. I: A to F* (New York: Taylor and Francis Books, 2003). Also Jerry Musich, "Mapping a Transcontinental Nation: Nineteenth- and Early Twentieth-Century American Rail Travel Cartography," in *Cartographies of Travel and Navigation* ed. James R. Ackerman (Chicago: University of Chicago Press, 2006), 120–121. Also Catherine Delano-Smith's "Milieus of Mobility: Itineraries, Route Maps and Road Maps" in the same volume for an excellent overview of mobility and the history of print- and mapmaking in the early modern era.

12. For data on access to railroads, see the graph on page 7 and Appendix Table 3.

13. "George F. Cram to Mother," October 15, 1862, in Jennifer Cain Bohrnstedt, *Soldiering with Sherman: Civil War Letters of George F. Cram* (DeKalb: University of Northern Illinois Press, 2000), 6–7.

14. "George F. Cram to Mother," November 20, 1862, in Bohrnstedt, *Soldiering with Sherman*, 15.

15. "George F. Cram to Mother," November 9, 1862, in Bohrnstedt, *Soldiering with Sherman*, 9–10. Union soldiers' diaries contain numerous references to what they perceived as either a desolate or an aristocratic landscape and, respectively, either an ignorant or arrogant people. Their language of observation was strikingly similar across regions. Alcander Morse wrote of his travels through Arkansas, "The people here are very ignorant and destitute . . . the ladies are very saucy." See Nash, "'Steadily and Joyfully to Our Doom,'" 17.

16. "Ephraim C. Dawes to Kate Dawes," May 30, 1862, Series 1, Box 1, folder 14, Dawes Papers.

17. "Ephraim C. Dawes to Kate," March 16, 1862, Series 1, Box 1, folder 14, Dawes Papers.

18. "George F. Cram to Mother," October 15, 1862, in Bohrnstedt, *Soldiering with Sherman*, 9–10. "Ephraim C. Dawes to Kate Dawes," 1862, Series 1, Box 1, folder 15, Dawes Papers. See Frederick Law Olmsted, *A Journey in the Seaboard Slave States: With Remarks on Their Economy* (New York: Dix and Edwards, Sampson Low, Son and Co., 1856).

19. "Ephraim C. Dawes to Kate Dawes," 1862, Series 1, Box 1, folder 15, Dawes Papers.

20. "Ephraim C. Dawes to Kate Dawes," August 3, 1862, Series 1, Box 1, folder 14, Dawes Papers.

21. "Ephraim C. Dawes to Kate Dawes," June 23, 1862, and August 3, 1862, Series 1, Box 1, folder 15, Dawes Papers.

22. "Ephraim C. Dawes to Kate Dawes," August 24, 1862, Series 1, Box 1, folder 15, Dawes Papers.

23. "Ephraim C. Dawes to Kate Dawes," September 16, 1862, and "Ephraim C. Dawes to Lucy," July 31, 1862, Series 1, Box 1, folder 15, Dawes Papers.

24. "Bob Taggart to Captain John Taggart," October 11, 1861, in Edward L. Ayers, William G. Thomas, III, Anne S. Rubin, and Andrew Torget, eds., *Valley of the Shadow: Two Communities in the American Civil War*, http://valley.lib.virginia.edu/papers/F0045.

25. John Keegan, *The American Civil War: A Military History* (New York: Knopf, 2009), 93 and 87. See also page 70 for Keegan's description of the South's rail system as disjointed, and page 11 on the region as not unified, both points with which I disagree. Keegan's argument about railroad gauges ignores the North's equally chaotic gauges. On McClellan's plans and correspondence with Lincoln, see Stephen W. Sears, *The Civil War Papers of George B. McClellan. Selected Correspondence, 1860–1865* (New York: Ticknor and Fields, 1989), 162–170.

26. For a detailed analysis of McClellan and the strategic considerations in the Peninsular Campaign, see Edward Hagerman, *The American Civil War and the Origins of Modern Warfare: Ideas, Organization and Field Command* (Bloomington: Indiana University Press, 1988), 65–68. And Keegan, *American Civil War*, 114–123, deems McClellan's strategy "a bad plan . . . too diffuse, insufficiently ruthless."

27. "McClellan to Lincoln," in Sears, *The Civil War Papers of George B. McClellan: Selected Correspondence, 1860–1865*, 162–170.

28. Hagerman, *The American Civil War and the Origins of Modern Warfare: Ideas, Organization and Field Command*, 64–65. Hagerman notes, "McClellan, ironically, was dismissed for inactivity . . . while leading over 100,000 men in one of the most impressive strategic movements of the war." Hsieh, *West Pointers and the Civil War*, 155.

29. "McClellan to Ambrose E. Burnside," January 7, 1862, U.S. War Department, *The War of the Rebellion: A Compilation of the Official Records of the Union and Confederate Armies*, (Lynchburg, Va., and Pasadena, Calif.: Broadfoot, 1985) (hereafter *OR*), Series I, Vol. 5, 37. Also in Sears, *The Civil War Papers of George B. McClellan. Selected Correspondence, 1860–1865*, 149.

30. "Dispatch to George B. McClellan," February 3, 1862, and May 24, 1862, in Roy P. Basler and Christian O. Basler, eds., *The Collected Works of Abraham Lincoln* (New Brunswick, N.J.: Rutgers University Press, c.1990). The differences between Lincoln and McClellan have been recently treated in James M. McPherson, "My Enemies Are Crushed: McClellan and Lincoln," in *Wars Within a War: Controversy and Conflict over the American Civil War*, ed. Joan Waugh and Gary Gallagher (Chapel Hill: University of North Carolina Press, 2009), 52–67.

31. David Herbert Donald, *Lincoln* (New York: Simon and Schuster, 1995), 155. Donald downplays Lincoln's legal career, arguing that he had "no consistent legal philosophy" because he appeared to be both for and against railroads. For a different, more generous interpretation, see Howard Schweber, *The Creation of American Common Law, 1850–1880: Technology, Politics, and the Construction of Citizenship* (Cambridge: Cambridge University Press, 2004), 43–44. On Lincoln's exceptional strategic capabilities, see James M. McPherson, *Tried by War: Abraham Lincoln as Commander in Chief* (New York: Penguin Press, 2008), 70–71 and 191.

32. See Stoker, *The Grand Design*, 81–92, for Lincoln and McClellan's strategy, especially Lincoln's "Occoquan Plan," and 218 and 410 for Lee's army as the Confederate "center of gravity." Also John C. Waugh, *Lincoln and McClellan: The Troubled Partnership Between a President and His General* (New York: Palgrave Macmillan, 2010), 56, 66–77.

33. "McClellan to Edwin Staunton," June 26, 1862, 12 a.m., in Sears, *The Civil War Papers of George B. McClellan*, 312.

34. On McClellan's failure to move the Army of the Potomac out of the Chickahominy flood zone, see William J. Miller, "I Only Wait for the River: McClellan and His Engineers on the Chickahominy," in *The Richmond Campaign of 1862: The Peninsula and the Seven Days*, ed. Gary Gallagher (Chapel Hill: University of North Carolina Press, 2000), 31. "McClellan to Mary Ellen McClellan, May 10, 1862," in Sears, *The Civil War Papers of George B. McClellan: Selected Correspondence, 1860–1865*, 263. McClellan also experienced the difficulty of mapping eastern Virginia as he went, and despite military balloons and other innovations he was unable to "see" the landscape very effectively; see Hagerman, *The American Civil War and the Origins of Modern Warfare: Ideas, Organization and Field Command*, 46–47. On the structural command problems McClellan faced in the newly created office of general-in-chief, see Ethan S. Rafuse, "McClellan and Halleck at War: The Struggle for Control of the Union War Effort in the West, November 1861–March 1862," *Civil War History*, Vol. 49, No. 1 (March 2003): 32–51. The Union commanders' keyword frequencies were compiled using the digitized volumes of *OR*, from Cornell's Making of Modern America digital library. These volumes, while exceedingly useful, have numerous scanning errors, so all analysis remains subject to some variation. In addition, the corpus analyzed unavoidably included the salutation and location from the headings in the correspondence. This distorts the prominence of some geographical features, such as Yorktown, where McClellan was headquartered for a time. Some keywords, moreover, could apply to both railroads and other systems, such as "bridge" and even "road." Still, the patterns we found were significant.

35. "George B. McClellan to Salmon P. Chase," May 14, 1862, in Sears, *The Civil War Papers of George B. McClellan: Selected Correspondence, 1860–1865*, 264.

36. "George B. McClellan to Edwin B. Stanton and Edwin M. Stanton to George B. McClellan," May 30, 1862, *OR*, Series I, Vol. 11 (Part III), 196 and 201,

37. "Abraham Lincoln to George B. McClellan," May 28, 1862, in Basler and Basler, *The Collected Works of Abraham Lincoln*, Vol. 5, 244. I am indebted to Kenneth Winkle for helping me find the relevant Lincoln dispatches and documents related to railroads. Stoker, *The Grand Design*, 146–149.

38. "Irvin McDowell to George B. McClellan," May 22, 1862, *OR*, Series I, Vol. 11 (Part III), 186.

39. "General Orders No. 128," May 25, 1862, *OR*, Series I, Vol. 11 (Part III), 191.

40. See Michael B. Chesson, *Richmond After the War, 1865–1890* (Richmond: Virginia State Library, 1981), 8, 12, 23; Midori Takagi, *Rearing Wolves to Our Own Destruction: Slavery in Richmond, Virginia, 1782–1865* (Charlottesville: University Press of Virginia, 1999), 1, 72, 126–128. Historian Gary Gallagher has noted that the Confederates chose Richmond in part because they were "overwhelmingly devoted to the idea of carrying the war to the enemy, holding on to or recapturing Confederate territory, and otherwise taking an offensive approach" (Gary Gallagher, *The Confederate War: How Popular Will, Nationalism, and Military Strategy Could Not Stave Off Defeat* [Cambridge: Harvard University Press, 1997]). But Richmond was the leading city in the South in terms of modern development and advanced forms of slavery and industry.

41. "Bob Taggart to Sam Taggart," June 24, 1862, in Ayers, Thomas, Rubin, and Torget, *Valley of the Shadow: Two Communities in the American Civil War*, http://valley.lib.virginia.edu/papers/F0048; John S. Robson, *How a One-Legged Rebel Lives* (Durham, NC: Educator Co. Printer, 1898), 70.

42. "Bob Taggart to Sam Taggart," June 24, 1862, in Ayers, Thomas, Rubin, and Torget, *Valley of the Shadow: Two Communities in the American Civil War*, http://valley.lib.virginia.edu/papers/F0048. Paul H. Hass, "A Volunteer Nurse in the Civil War: The Letters of Harriet Douglas Whetten," *Wisconsin Magazine of History*, Vol. 48, No. 2 (Winter, 1964–1965), 151 (July 13, 1862). I am indebted to Kaci Nash for bringing this source to my attention. Kaci Nash, "'In the Usual Southern Style': Northern Women and the Southern Landscape During the Civil War," unpublished manuscript, in possession of the author.

43. "Bob Taggart to Sam Taggart," June 24, 1862.

44. For the best overview of Jackson's campaign, see James I. Robertson, Jr., *Stonewall Jackson: The Man, the Soldier, the Legend* (New York: Macmillan, 1997), 369, for the movement from Brown's Gap back into the Valley on the Virginia Central Railroad.

45. "Abraham Lincoln to George B. McClellan," May 31, 1862, *OR*, Series I, Vol. 11 (Part III), 202.

46. On the importance of this campaign to the Confederacy's national aspirations, see Aaron Sheehan-Dean, *Why Confederates Fought: Family and Nation in Civil War Virginia* (Chapel Hill: University of North Carolina Press, 2007), 71–79.

47. Robertson, *Stonewall Jackson*, 459.

48. "McClellan to Hill Carter," July 11, 1862, "McClellan to Mary Ellen McClellan," July 22, 1862, and "McClellan to Henry Halleck," August 1, 1862, in Sears, *The Civil War Papers of George B. McClellan*, 352, 368–369, and 380–381.

49. "General Orders No. 5, 7, 11, and 19," *OR*, Series I, Vol. 12 (Part III). Harry S. Stout, *Upon the Altar of the Nation: A Moral History of the Civil War* (New York: Viking, 2006), 140–142 and 188. Stout argues provocatively that emancipation helped inaugurate a turn to "total war" in which civilians were targeted, and that Lincoln sanctioned an escalation when he approved General John Pope's General Orders No. 5. Stoker, *The Grand Strategy*, 228–230, also emphasizes the Emancipation Proclamation in the escalation of the war. Both suggest a "slippery slope" (Stout) or a gradual change in military destruction.

50. "Sanford Truesdell to His Sister," November 7, 1862, Box 10, folder 55, Lincoln Collection, Lincoln Miscellaneous Manuscripts, University of Chicago Archives, Chicago, Ill. (hereafter Lincoln Collection).

51. Ibid.

52. "Sanford Truesdell to Sister," October 5, 1863, Box 10, folder 55, Lincoln Collection.

53. "Sanford Truesdell to Sister," April 19, 1864, Box 10, folder 55, Lincoln Collection.

54. "Erastus H. Reed to Samuel Reed," January 25, 1863, Reed Family Papers, Box 2, folder 29, Yale University Library, Manuscripts and Archives, New Haven, Conn.

55. On Civil War photography, see the excellent analysis of Gardner's style and significance in Anthony Lee and Elizabeth Young, *On Alexander Gardner's Photographic Sketch Book of the Civil War* (Defining Moments in American Photography I) (Berkeley: University of California Press, 2008); Alan Trachtenberg, *Reading American Photographs: Images as History, Mathew Brady to Walker Evans* (New York: Hill and Wang, 1989), and "Albums of War: On Reading Civil War Photographs," *Representations* 9 (Winter 1985): 1–32, esp. 24–25 on George N. Barnard's images; William C. Davis, ed., *The Image of War, 1861–1865* (New York: Doubleday, 1984); Frances Fralin, *The Indelible Image: Photographs of War—1846 to the Present* (New York: Harry N. Abrams, 1985); and Francis Trevelyan Miller, *The Photographic History of the Civil War* (New York: T. Yoseloff, 1910).

56. Esther Hill Hawks, *A Woman Doctor's Civil War: Esther Hill Hawks' Diary*, ed. Gerald Schwartz (Columbia: University of South Carolina Press, 1984), 33–34 (October 16, 1862). Kaci Nash, "'In the Usual Southern Style': Northern Women and the Southern Landscape During the Civil War," unpublished manuscript, in possession of the author. On the broader themes and conventions of travel writing, see Melton, *Mark Twain, Travel Books, and Tourism: The Tide of a Great Popular Movement*, 55.

57. Robertson, *Stonewall Jackson*, 515.

58. "Jedediah Hotchkiss to Sara A. Hotchkiss," March 15, 1863, in Ayers, Thomas, Rubin, and Torget, *Valley of the Shadow: Two Communities in the American Civil War*, http://valley.lib .virginia.edu/papers/A4027.

59. "Abraham Lincoln to George B. McClellan," October 13, 1862, in Basler and Basler, *The Collected Works of Abraham Lincoln*, Vol. 5, 461. See also analysis of Lincoln's strategy of "concentration in time," McPherson, *Tried by War*, 70–71.

60. Robertson, *Stonewall Jackson*, 513. For a useful analysis of the military failures of the Confederate railroads, see Christopher R. Gabel, *Rails to Oblivion: The Decline of Confederate Railroads in the Civil War* (Fort Leavenworth, Kans.: U.S. Army Command and General Staff College Press, 2002), 9–10.

Chapter 5. The Railroad War Zones

1. Stephen Ash, *When the Yankees Came: Conflict and Chaos in the Occupied South, 1861–1865* (Chapel Hill: University of North Carolina Press, 1995), provides the best study of how the occupied South rearranged perceptions of the war and Confederate views of the struggle in the midst of occupation and war. Aaron Sheehan-Dean has similarly charted the violence in the Civil War, in "Two Wars in One: Violence in the U.S. Civil War," unpublished manuscript, in possession of the author. My views on the guerrilla violence in the Civil War have been influenced especially by Randall Collins, *Violence: A Micro-Sociological Theory* (Princeton, N.J.: Princeton University Press, 2008), as well as Stathis N. Kalyvas, *The Logic of Violence in Civil War* (Cambridge: Cambridge University Press, 2006). Collins emphasizes the situational, local context of violence, shaped by "a set of pathways around confrontational tension and fear" and a series of turning points (8). Rather than explaining violence as individual or culturally determined, Collins stresses situational dynamics. I argue that the railroads gave a situational structure not only to the large-scale or macrowar but also to the microprocess of violence in the guerrilla conflict. The broader history of American violence has been treated in Richard

Maxwell Brown, *Strain of Violence: Historical Studies of American Violence and Vigilantism* (New York: Oxford University Press, 1975). See also Charles Tilly, "Collective Violence in European Perspective," in *Violence in America: Historical and Comparative Perspectives*, ed. Hugh Davis Graham and Ted Robert Gurr, 2d ed. (Beverly Hills, Calif.: Sage, 1979), 83–118. Stuart Carroll, ed., *Cultures of Violence: Interpersonal Violence in Historical Perspective* (Hampshire, U.K.: Palgrave Macmillan, 2007). John Keane, *Violence and Democracy* (Cambridge: Cambridge University Press, 2004).

2. Paul F. Paskoff, "Measures of War: A Quantitative Examination of the Civil War's Destructiveness in the Confederacy," *Civil War History*, Vol. 54, No. 1 (March 2008). "Civil War Diary of Eva Honey Allen," June 14 and 15, 1864, folder 4, Gilmer Speed Adam Collection, Special Collections, Alderman Library, University of Virginia, Charlottesville, Va. For another account emphasizing the lack of destructiveness in the war, see Mark E. Neely, Jr., *The Civil War and the Limits of Destruction* (Cambridge: Harvard University Press, 2007).

3. See Russell F. Weigley, *A Great Civil War: A Military and Political History, 1981–1865* (Bloomington: Indiana University Press, 2000), 322, for an especially useful summary of the railroad's strategic consequences in the war. See also the classic on rail strategy, George Edgar Turner, *Victory Rode the Rails: The Strategic Place of the Railroads in the Civil War* (Lincoln: University of Nebraska Press, 1953).

4. On Lee's orders to move into Pennsylvania in 1863 and his objectives, see James M. McPherson, "To Conquer a Peace? Lee's Goals in the Gettysburg Campaign," in *This Mighty Scourge: Perspectives on the Civil War* (New York: Oxford University Press, 2007), 77–86. McPherson points out that Lee's strategic goals were predicated on a set of fundamental beliefs that the North's greater resources would wear down the South in a war of attrition and that therefore the only way to win Confederate independence was to achieve "battlefield victories while the South had the strength to do so, victories that would cripple the enemy's main army and demoralize the Northern people." McPherson correctly calls attention to the political dimension of Lee's strategic invasions and their goals. My point here is that the removal of the northern armies from the railroad network changed the dynamic of the war in the East in fundamental ways that allowed the Confederacy to maintain its idea of independence and functioning statehood, having repercussions all the way down to North Carolina and relieving pressure from Federal incursions throughout the region. On Vicksburg as a "distraction," see Donald Stoker, *The Grand Design: Strategy and the U.S. Civil War* (Oxford: Oxford University Press, 2010), 229.

5. On Buell, Rosecrans, Grant, and the strategy in the West, see Stoker, *The Grand Design*, 179, 238–244, and 223, noting the hallmark of Grant and Sherman's campaign—repairing the railroads as they advanced. For calculation of "railroad corridors," see Appendix, Table 9.

6. Several recent studies place Confederate guerrillas at the center of the war rather than at the periphery. See, especially, Daniel E. Sutherland, *A Savage Conflict: The Decisive Role of Guerrillas in the American Civil War* (Chapel Hill: University of North Carolina Press, 2009), and Clay Mountcastle, *Punitive War: Confederate Guerrillas and Union Reprisals* (Lawrence: University Press of Kansas, 2009). Scott Nelson and Carol Sheriff, *A People at War: Civilians and Soldiers in America's Civil War, 1854–1877* (New York and Oxford: Oxford University Press, 2008), 96–101. One of the pathbreaking studies in guerrilla conflict remains Michael Fellman, *Inside War: The Guerrilla Conflict in Missouri During the American Civil War* (New York: Oxford University Press, 1989). Regional studies include Daniel L. Schafer, *Thunder on the River: The Civil War in Northeast Florida* (Gainesville: University Press of Florida, 2010); Noel C. Fisher, *War at Every Door: Partisan Politics and Guerrilla Violence in East Tennessee, 1860–1869* (Chapel Hill: University of North Carolina Press, 1997); W. Todd Groce, *Mountain Rebels: East Tennessee Confederates and the Civil War* (Knoxville: University of Tennessee Press, 1999); and Jonathan Dean Sarris, *A Separate Civil War: Communities in Conflict in the Mountain South* (Charlottes-

ville: University of Virginia Press, 2006), emphasizing how the guerrilla conflict carried into Reconstruction.

7. On the concept of dying a good death in nineteenth-century America, see Drew Gilpin Faust, *This Republic of Suffering: Death and the American Civil War* (New York: Vintage, 2009).

8. *Charleston Courier, Tri-Weekly* (Charleston, S.C.), Saturday, March 22, 1862, col. C; *Daily Morning News* (Savannah, Ga.), Friday, May 2, 1862, Issue 100, col. D; *Scioto Gazette* (Chillicothe, Ohio), Tuesday, December 10, 1861, Issue [42], col. A, all in Gale Cengage Learning, *Nineteenth Century U.S. Newspapers*. For an excellent account of the Peninsular War and its guerrilla war in context, see David A. Bell, *The First Total War: Napoleon's Europe and the Birth of Warfare as We Know It* (Boston: Houghton Mifflin, 2007), 279–285.

9. *Daily Evening Bulletin* (San Francisco, Calif.), Wednesday, September 3, 1862, Issue 127, col. A; and *Milwaukee Daily Sentinel* (Milwaukee, Wis.), Tuesday, August 19, 1862, Issue 197, col. C, in *Nineteenth Century U.S. Newspapers*.

10. *Daily Evening Bulletin* (San Francisco, Calif.), Tuesday, October 28, 1862, Issue 18, col. D, in *Nineteenth Century U.S. Newspapers*. William G. Stevenson, *Thirteen Months in the Rebel Army, Being a Narrative of Personal Adventures by an Impressed New Yorker* (New York: A. S. Barnes and Co., 1862 and 1864), 8 and 108–110.

11. Mark W. Geiger, *Financial Fraud and Guerrilla Violence in Missouri's Civil War, 1861–1865* (New Haven: Yale University Press, 2010), 4, 100, and 156.

12. Geiger, *Financial Fraud and Guerrilla Violence in Missouri's Civil War, 1861–1865*, 156. Geiger points out that pro-Confederate Missourians were deeply connected to the national market, and "had been in the forefront of the railroad agitation in the 1850s." On Imboden's interest in a car coupling patent, see *Staunton Vindicator*, June 29, 1860. Forrest was closely connected to Samuel Tate, president of the Memphis and Charleston Railroad. On Mosby and the officer leadership in these partisan units, see Robert R. Mackey, *The Uncivil War: Irregular Warfare in the Upper South, 1861–1865* (Norman: University of Oklahoma Press, 2004), 123.

13. Mackey, *The Uncivil War: Irregular Warfare in the Upper South, 1861–1865*, 123. See also Simeon Miller Bright, "The McNeil Rangers: A Study in Confederate Guerrilla Warfare," *West Virginia History*, Vol. 12, No. 4 (July 1951): 338–387. Freddie Lee Johnson, III, "The Tracks of War: Confederate Strategic Rail Policy and the Struggle for the Baltimore and Ohio" (Ph.D. diss., Kent State University, 1999), 151 and 183.

14. Mackey, *The Uncivil War: Irregular Warfare in the Upper South, 1861–1865*, 136.

15. *Milwaukee Daily Sentinel* (Milwaukee, Wis.), Tuesday, August 19, 1862, Issue 197, col. C, in *Nineteenth Century U.S. Newspapers*.

16. *Daily Evening Bulletin* (San Francisco, Calif.), Thursday, November 13, 1862, Issue 32, col. B, in *Nineteenth Century U.S. Newspapers*. Mackey, *Uncivil War*, 139, on Don Carlos Buell's commission hearings and the characterization of Forrest and Morgan as "guerrillas." Buell explained that the term did not apply to these commanders.

17. Mark Grimsley, *The Hard Hand of War: Union Military Policy Toward Southern Civilians, 1861–1865* (New York: Cambridge University Press, 1995), 114–117. Also Sutherland, *A Savage Conflict*, 59–60 and 145–146.

18. For an example of the earliest guerrilla actions in Missouri during the summer of 1861, as well as Grant's and Sherman's comments about these incidents, see T. J. Stiles, *Jesse James: Last Rebel of the Civil War* (New York: Vintage Books, 2003), 73–74.

19. "War in the West—Approaching End," *New York Times*, June 16, 1862, in *ProQuest Historical Newspapers The New York Times* (1851–2004), 4.

20. Ibid.

21. "Ephraim C. Dawes to Kate Dawes," August 10, 1862, Series 1, Box 1, folder 14; "Ephraim C. Dawes to Lucy Dawes," September 15, 1862, Series 1, Box 1, folder 20; Ephraim C.

Dawes Papers, Newberry Library, Chicago, Ill. (hereafter Dawes Papers). "Jennie Reed to Samuel B. Reed," August 12, 1862, Samuel Reed Family Papers, Yale University Library, Manuscripts and Archives, New Haven, Conn.

22. "Ephraim C. Dawes to Kate Dawes," April 6, 1863, and April 13, 1863, Box 1, folder 16, Dawes Papers.

23. "Ephraim C. Dawes to Kate Dawes," March 23, 1863, Box 1, folder 16, Dawes Papers.

24. "George F. Cram to Mother," January 1, 1863, in Jennifer Cain Bohrnstedt, *Soldiering with Sherman: Civil War Letters of George F. Cram* (DeKalb: University of Northern Illinois Press, 2000), 34.

25. "George F. Cram to Mother," February 15, 1863, in Bohrnstedt, *Soldiering with Sherman,* 40.

26. "Charles T. Kruse to Parents," February 2, 1863, Papers of Charles T. Kruse, Newberry Library, Chicago, Ill.

27. "Charles T. Kruse to Brother and Sister," April 21, 1863, U.S. War Department, *The War of the Rebellion: A Compilation of the Official Records of the Union and Confederate Armies* (Lynchburg, Va., and Pasadena, Calif.: Broadfoot, 1985) (hereafter *OR*), Series I, Vol. 23 (Part I), 217, also Series 1, Vol. 24 (Part I), 485.

28. Julia Perkins Cutler, *Life and Times of Ephraim Cutler: Prepared from His Journal and Correspondence* (With sketch of William P. Cutler by Ephraim C. Dawes) (Cincinnati: Robert Clark and Co., 1890), 305. *Daily Evening Bulletin* (San Francisco, Calif.), Thursday, February 18, 1864, Issue 111, col. C, in *Nineteenth Century U.S. Newspapers.*

29. Correspondence of the Chicago *Times,* in *New York Times,* December 26, 1862.

30. No firm number of Confederate guerrillas has been determined. Albert Castel estimated around 26,000, but Daniel Sutherland has suggested as many as 35,000 could have operated. See Sutherland, *A Savage Conflict,* xii.

31. "J. H. Devereux to Hermann Haupt," August 2, 1863, *OR,* Series I, Vol. 27 (Part III), 831. *OR,* Series III, Vol. 5, 388.

32. "The Guerrilla Raid near Winchester," *New York Times,* August 26, 1862. Also *New York Times,* March 29, 1863, described a guerrilla attack on a train in which a "corpulent" gentleman could not take cover as the other passengers did because he could not fit between the seats to hide on the floor, while the other passengers "dropped from their seats on the floor with the expertness of practiced gymnasts." One woman, "perfectly cool and collected," sat in her seat "laughing heartily at the confusion of her less valorous passengers."

33. "Jacob Kent Langhorne to Mother," May 4, 1863, in Edward L. Ayers, William G. Thomas, III, Anne S. Rubin, and Andrew Torget, eds., *Valley of the Shadow: Two Communities in the American Civil War,* http://valley.lib.virginia.edu/papers/A0758. See also Stephen Ash, *When the Yankees Came: Conflict and Chaos in the Occupied South, 1861–1865* (Chapel Hill: University of North Carolina Press, 1995).

34. "The Amite Valley Expedition: Cleaning Out Guerrillas Cutting Off Supplies for Port Hudson Seizure of Rebel Stores—Details of a Week's Operations in Secessia," *New York Times,* June 7, 1863.

35. *New York Times,* November 20, 1862.

36. "Charles T. Kruse to Parents," July 29, 1863, *OR,* Series I, Vol. 24 (Part III), 129.

37. "W. W. Wright's Report," April 24, 1866, and "J. H. Devereux's Report," September 7, 1863, Record Group 9 1528, Box 1, Reports, National Archives and Records Administration, College Park, Md. (hereafter NARA).

38. "Arrival of Ninety-Seven Contrabands at Philadelphia," *Chicago Tribune,* April 3, 1862. On conditions of the freed people in Tennessee and the Union impressment of black labor by the Union army, see *Report of Thomas Hood and S. W. Bostwick,* 38th Cong., 2nd Sess., S. Exec. Doc. 28 (December 28, 1864). "Runaways," *Richmond Daily Dispatch,* August 7, 1862,

http://americanpast.richmond.edu/dispatch/articles/view/67146 (accessed January 2011). On John Henry, see Scott Reynolds Nelson, *Steel Drivin' Man: John Henry, The Untold Story of an American Legend* (Oxford: Oxford University Press, 2006). See also Richard D. Sears, "A Long Way from Freedom: Camp Nelson Refugees," in *Sister States, Enemy States: The Civil War in Kentucky and Tennessee,* ed. Kent T. Dollar, Larry Whiteaker, and W. Calvin Dickinson (Lexington: University Press of Kentucky, 2009), 233.

39. General Order No. 10, May 10, 1862, *OR,* Series I, Vol. 12 (Part I), 53.

40. Ibid., 280.

41. "W. W. Wright to Herman Haupt," September 17, 1862, *OR,* Series I, Vol. 12 (Part III), 814–816. Vincent Colyer, *Brief Report of the Services Rendered by the Freed People to the United States Army in North Carolina in the Spring of 1862, After the Battle of New Bern* (New York: Vincent Colyer, 1864), 9. "Runaways," *Richmond Daily Dispatch.*

42. "E. L. Wentz to D. C. McCallum, Norfolk," Oct. 13, 1862, Record Group 92, "Consolidated Correspondence File 'Railroad,'" Entry 225, Box 871, NARA. See also "September 12, 1862 Letter from Lt. G. T. Robinson Desiring 14–15 'Contrabands' to Work as Laborers on Repairs of Chain Bridge north of Alexandria, Virginia."

43. "W. W. Wright Report March 15, 1863 on R. F. and P. R.R.," in ibid.

44. "Testimony of Major Wentz, Superintendent of Norfolk and Petersburg R. R. [n.d. — probably May 1863]," in ibid. Thanks to Amy Murrell Taylor for directing this important document to me. Her forthcoming work on contraband camps will explore the families, labor, and lives of African Americans in the immediate wake of their self-emancipation.

45. Ibid.

46. "Report on Operations on U.S. Military Rail Roads by H. Haupt, for Year Ending June 30, 1863," Record Group 92, "Consolidated Correspondence File 'Railroad,'" Box 871, NARA.

47. "George Bruce to A. Anderson," October 16, 1864, Record Group 92, "Letters Received by A. Anderson, Sup.," Box 1, NARA.

48. "Captain George Rosser to Jonathan C. Crane," September 16, 1864, Record Group 92, "Letters Received by A. Anderson, Sup.," Box 2, NARA.

49. Construction Corps, Department of the Mississippi Payroll, and U.S. Military Railroads Payrolls, Record Group 92, Subgroup 1738, NARA.

50. "Ephraim C. Dawes to Kate Dawes," May 14, 1863, Series I, Box 1, folder 16, Dawes Papers; "Diary of Ephraim C. Dawes," May 14, 1863, Box 2, folder 75, Midwest Manuscripts, Ephraim C. Dawes, Newberry Library, Chicago, Ill.

51. *OR,* Series I, Vol. VI, 149, December 1, 1861.

52. *OR,* Series I, Vol. XIV, 176, October 23, 1862. For other examples of black guides for Union troops, see also *OR,* Series I, Vol. LII, 2 and 80.

53. For an excellent account of freedom and mobility, see Yael Sternhell, "Revolution in Motion: Human Mobility and the Transformation of the South, 1861–1865," (Ph.D. diss., Yale University, 2008), 170–171. See also Stephanie McCurry, *Confederate Reckoning: Power and Politics in the Civil War South* (Cambridge, Mass.: Harvard University Press, 2010), 218–248, on war zones and actions by the enslaved in these places. And Leslie A. Schwalm, *Emancipation's Diaspora: Race and Reconstruction in the Upper Midwest* (Chapel Hill: University of North Carolina Press, 2009), 43–80. And Schwalm, "'Overrun with Free Negroes': Emancipation and Wartime Migration in the Upper Midwest," *Civil War History,* Vol. 50, No. 2 (June 2004): 156 and 165. See also Jacque Voegli, "A Rejected Alternative: Union Policy and the Relocation of Southern 'Contrabands' at the Dawn of Emancipation," *Journal of Southern History,* Vol. 69, No. 4 (November 2003): 765–90. And Michael Johnson, "Out of Egypt: The Migration of Former Slaves to the Midwest During the 1860s in Comparative Perspective," in *Crossing Boundaries: Comparative History of Black People in Diaspora,* ed. Darlene Clark Hine and Jacqueline Mc-

Loud (Bloomington: Indiana University Press, 1999), 223–245. See also the escape of Louis Hughes from slavery by following the Mississippi and Tennessee Railroad, in Stephen Ash, *A Year in the South: 1865 — The True Story of Four Ordinary People Who Lived Through the Most Tumultuous Twelve Months in American History* (New York: Harper Collins, 2004), 128–129.

54. *OR*, Series III, Vol. 5, 121. African Americans, "induced by high wages," military officials noted, took employment on the transports and as "wood-choppers" around Louisville. "Report of D. H. Rucker," September 28, 1865, *OR*, Series III, Vol. 5, 388 and 394.

Chapter 6. The Confederate Nation "Cut Off from the World"

1. "Richard Cobden to John Slagg," February 4, 1861, Cobden Papers, Vol. 43676, British Library, London, U.K. "August Belmont Correspondence to N. M. Rothschild and Sons," January/February 1861, XI/62/10A, Rothschild Archive, London, U.K (hereafter RA). For example, January 4, 1861: "We may yet save the ship before she goes to pieces, but the chances are against us. Mad passion seems to direct the movements of the people in South Carolina. The indications are that the other Cotton States are rushing blindly towards the same infatuation."

2. "N. M. Rothschild to August Belmont," March 8, 1861, T6/346, II/10/28, RA.

3. Recently, historians have found evidence that Nathan M. Rothschild, the founder of the bank, may have profited from accepting slaves as collateral on loans to southern slaveholders who did business with Rothschilds. Rothschild, though, was not the only bank or business to do so, and often these loans were just a small part of the bank's overall portfolio. "Rothschild and Freshfields founders linked to slavery," Carola Hoyos, *Financial Times*, June 26, 2009. Also see "Legacies of British Slave-Ownership" database, University College London, http://www.ucl.ac.uk/lbs. Also see Niall Ferguson, "Rothschilds Gained Less from Slavery Than from Financing Its Abolition," *Financial Times*, June 30, 2009. Ferguson makes the important point that slavery in the Atlantic economy was "pervasive." In *The World's Banker: The History of the House of Rothschild* (London: Weidenfeld and Nicholson, 1998), Ferguson argues that the Rothschilds' attitudes toward slavery and the Civil War have been misunderstood and that the firm was neutral, not supportive of the South. Ferguson's balanced judgment is fair, yet Lionel de Rothschild was not "passive." And in the American letter books at the Rothschild Archive (Ferguson seems to have cited only the General Correspondence in the Rothschild Archive), Lionel appears more active as a promoter of mediation and intervention in the American conflict. Ferguson is correct that Rothschild's interest was not at all in preserving slavery or enabling a slave based Confederate nation, but instead in ending a bloody war. Humanitarian reasons and the recognition of national claims by various states were at the front of Lionel's arguments in his correspondence with Belmont.

4. "N. M. Rothschild to August Belmont," March 8, 1861, II/10/28, RA.

5. Matthew Guterl, *American Mediterranean: Southern Slaveholders in the Age of Emancipation* (Cambridge, Mass.: Harvard University Press, 2008), 6–9. See also David Armitage, *The Declaration of Independence: A Global History* (Cambridge, Mass.: Harvard University Press, 2008). On the importance of the London bankers, see Jay Sexton, *Debtor Diplomacy: Finance and American Foreign Relations in the Civil War Era, 1837–1873* (Oxford: Clarendon Press, 2005), 6 and 14, and 73–74 on Belmont's role in Caribbean expansion, and the various splits in the banking circles of London on the South and slavery. On the ways elites deliberately constructed modern national identities, see Rogers M. Smith, *Stories of Peoplehood: The Politics and Morals of Political Membership* (Cambridge: Cambridge University Press, 2003); Thomas Bender, *A Nation Among Nations: America's Place in World History* (New York: Hill and Wang, 2006); Dorothy Ross, "Lincoln and the Ethics of Emancipation: Universalism, Nationalism, Exceptionalism," *Journal of American History*, Vol. 96, No. 2 (September 2009): 379–399.

6. H. C. Allen, *Great Britain and the United States: A History of Anglo-American Relations (1783–1952)* (New York: St. Martin's, 1955), 91. Jay Sexton, "Transatlantic Financiers and the Civil War," *American Nineteenth Century History*, Vol. 2, No. 3 (Autumn 2001): 29–46. Sexton, *Debtor Diplomacy*, 11. Sexton estimates that the 1853 breakdown included: $111 million in state debt, $27 million in federal debt, $62.8 million in private debt (railroads, canals, banks), and $21.5 million in municipal debt. Also Mira Wilkins, *The History of Foreign Investments in the United States to 1914* (Cambridge, Mass.: Harvard University Press, 1989), 49–51, 66, 76, and 79.

7. Wilkins, *The History of Foreign Investments in the United States to 1914*, 80–81 and 100–101. See also Cleona Lewis, *America's Stake in International Investments* (Washington, D.C.: Brookings Institution, 1938), 29–30.

8. Duncan Andrew Campbell, *English Public Opinion and the American Civil War* (Woodbridge, Suffolk, U.K.: Royal Historical Society/Rochester, N.Y.: Boydell Press, 2003) 98–101. Bender, *A Nation Among Nations: America's Place in World History*, 131–132. Bender points out that the United States and its Civil War were unexceptional and that "the United States shared with many other societies the violent process of nation-making." Victor Hugo was one contemporary observer who characterized Italy's unification with approval as an example of "the forces of progress . . . necessary to civilization" while at the same time lamenting the breakup of the United States (Paul Meurice, ed., *The Letters of Victor Hugo from Exile, and After the Fall of the Empire* [Boston and New York, Houghton, Mifflin and Company, 1898] 161–163).

9. Stanley Lebergott, "Through the Blockade: The Profitability and Extent of Cotton Smuggling, 1861–1865," *Journal of Economic History*, Vol. 41 No. 4 (1981): 867–886, and Lebergott, "Why the South Lost: Commercial Purposes in the Confederacy, 1861–1865," *Journal of American History*, Vol. 70, No. 1 (1983): 58–74. Lebergott also estimated that 2.3 million man-years were allocated to raising cotton by slave labor from August 1861 to August 1864, which "far exceeded the average size of the Confederate armies." Stephen Wise, *Lifeline of the Confederacy: Blockade Running During the Civil War* (Columbia: University of South Carolina Press, 1991), 226, estimated that the Confederacy imported 400,000 rifles and 3 million pounds of lead through the blockade. He concluded that 1,000 voyages out of 1,300 were successful in breaching the blockade. See also Robert B. Ekelund and Mark Thornton, "The Union Blockade and Demoralization of the South: Relative Prices in the Confederacy," *Social Science Quarterly*, Vol. 73, No. 4: 890–902; Mark E. Neely, Jr., "The Perils of Running the Blockade: The Influence of International Law in an Era of Total War," *Civil War History*, Vol. 32, No. 2: 101–18; Marcus W. Price, "Ships That Tested the Blockade of the Carolina Ports, 1861–1865," *American Neptune*, Vol. 11: 279–90. Earlier narratives include Hamilton Cochran, *Blockade Runners of the Confederacy* (Tuscaloosa: University of Alabama Press, 1958). Kevin J. Weddle, "The Blockade Board of 1861 and Union Naval Strategy," *Civil War History*, Vol. 48, No. 2 (June 2002): 136. Also see Robert E. Bonner, "Americans Apart: Nationality in the Slaveholding South" (Ph.D. diss., Yale University, 1998), 276, on the critical importance of the blockade in shaping Confederate nationhood and purpose.

10. The South's receptivity to European ideas was substantial, but conversely many of its leading intellectuals, such as Thomas Dew, William Harper, George Fitzhugh, and John Calhoun, had no European reception. See Michael O'Brien, *Conjectures of Order: Intellectual Life and the American South, 1810–1860*, Vol. 1 (Chapel Hill: University of North Carolina Press, 2004), 587.

11. Catherine Cooper Hopley, *Life in the South: From the Commencement of the War by a Blockaded British Subject*, Vol. 1 (London: Chapman and Hall, 1863), 275. Hopley used the pseudonym Sarah L. Jones.

12. Ibid.

13. See "Report of the Confederate Postmaster General," in Francis B. C. Bradlee, *Block-*

ade *Running During the Civil War, and the Effect of Land and Water Transportation on the Confederacy* (Salem: Essex Institute, 1925).

14. "Chieves & Osborn, Petersburg, Virginia to N. M. Rothschild & Son," May 6, 1861, T6/346, II/10/28, RA.

15. "Chieves and Osborne to N. M. Rothschild," May 16, 1861, July 19, 1861, March 19, 1862, June 15, 1862, Box X1/115/11A, and October 20, 1863, Box X1/15/11B, RA. "N. M. Rothschild to Chieves and Osborne," July 25, 1862, 16, American Letter Books, Vol. 30, RA.

16. As early as 1848, Rothschild's house was buying hundreds of tons of tobacco and cotton bales; "Alphonse de Rothschild to Paris House," October 12, 1848, T49/47 XI/109/69B/1/103, and May 4, 1849, to cousins in London, T49/55, RA. Niall Ferguson has downplayed the Rothschild investment in the South before the war and overemphasized the bank's decision not to handle Confederate bonds in *The World's Banker: The History of the House of Rothschild* (London: Weidenfeld and Nicholson, 1998), 628–632, and *The Ascent of Money: A Financial History of the World* (New York: Penguin, 2008), 93–98. For a critical review of Ferguson's analysis of the debt markets in this period, see Jeremy Wormell, review of *The World's Banker: The History of the House of Rothschild,* in *Reviews in History,* No. 213.

17. "August Belmont to N. M. Rothschild & Sons," May 14, 1861, XI/62/10A, RA.

18. Campbell, *English Public Opinion and the American Civil War,* 98–101.

19. "August Belmont to N. M. Rothschild," June 7, 1861, X1/62/10A, RA.

20. "August Belmont to N. M. Rothschild," May 3, 1861, X1/62/10A, RA.

21. "August Belmont to N. M. Rothschild," June 7, 1861, XI/62/10A, RA.

22. "Baring Brothers Liverpool to Baring Bros. London," March 9, 1860, HC 3.35 Part 22, and 1862 Correspondence Letter Book, 210, "E. J. Forstall to Baring Brothers," September 19, 1862, Baring Brothers Archive, ING, 60 London Wall, London (hereafter BBA). Also Jay Sexton, "Transatlantic Financiers and the Civil War," *American Nineteenth Century History,* Vol. 2, No. 3 (Autumn 2001): 29–46.

23. "Baring Brothers Liverpool to Ward and Campbell, New York," July 13, 1861, and "Baring Brothers Liverpool to Edmond J. Forstall, New Orleans," June 1, 1861, Baring Papers, Microfilm Reel 67, Library and Archives Canada, Ottawa, Ontario, Canada.

24. On arms shipments, "Baring Brothers Liverpool to Baring Bros. London," March 30, 1863, HC 3.35 Part 22; and Account Books Ledger Series, 100795, Client Ledgers American, 1864–1865, BBA. Baring Brothers shipped 48,000 stands of rifles to New York, Boston, and Harford for its clients in 1861–1862 on Inman steamer lines. The shipments were labeled "hardware" or "merchandise" to avoid detection as contraband of war. Baring Brothers' partners refused to ship arms for Governor Pickens of South Carolina upon his request in 1861.

25. On the importance of Antietam for British opinion, see Campbell, *English Public Opinion and the American Civil War,* 103. See also Allen, *Great Britain and the United States,* 479. The most accurate figures for Antietam casualties are the National Park Service's estimates, http://www.nps.gov/anti/historyculture/casualties.htm.

26. "N. M. Rothschild to August Belmont," October 7, 1862, II/10/30, 48, American Letter Books, 1834–1918, RA. Belmont, a Democrat, predicted that the proclamation would make the South "more desperate than ever" and totally alienate whatever remaining Unionists there were in the border states. "August Belmont to N. M. Rothschild," July 22, 1862, T56/45, and September 23, 1862, T56/69, RA. Rothschild in particular (and British banks in general) have been unfairly criticized as pro-Confederate. Rothschild did seek to mediate the conflict for humanitarian reasons but avoided supporting the Confederacy. For a careful examination of this issue, see Sexton, *Debtor Diplomacy,* 151–157.

27. "N. M. Rothschild to August Belmont," March 24, 1863, II/10/30, 134, American Letter Books, RA. On the Erlanger loan, see R. J. M. Blackett, *Divided Hearts: Britain and the American Civil War* (Baton Rouge: Louisiana State University Press, 2001). Richard

Lester, *Confederate Finance and Purchasing in Great Britain* (Charlottesville: University Press of Virginia, 1975), lists the Erlanger bondholders—suggesting Gladstone and other prominent British leaders supported the Confederacy—but cites only John Bigelow, *Lest We Forget: Gladstone, Morley and the Confederate Cotton Loan of 1863* (New York: De Vinne Press, 1905). Bigelow's list has been proved a fraud; see Sexton, *Debtor Diplomacy*, 171–173.

28. "N. M. Rothschild to August Belmont," May 26, 1863, II/10/30, 170, and July 21, 1863, 200, American Letter Books, RA. See Niall Ferguson, "Wars, Revolutions and the International Bond Market from the Napoleonic Wars to the First World War," paper presented at the Yale International Center for Finance, 1999, in RA.

29. William Schaw Lindsay Papers, LND/7, National Maritime Museum, Greenwich, U.K.

30. "Rose O'Neal Greenhow to unknown," July 23, 1863, Duke University Libraries, http://scriptorium.lib.duke.edu/greenhow/1863-07-23/1863-07-23.html.

31. "Rose O'Neal Greenhow to Alexander Boteler," December 10, 1863, Duke University Libraries, http://scriptorium.lib.duke.edu/greenhow/1863-12-10/1863-12-10.html.

32. Robert Douthat Meade, *Judah P. Benjamin: Confederate Statesman* (Baton Rouge: Louisiana State University Press, 1943), 248–249.

33. "George Chambers to N. M. Rothschild," June 9 and 14, 1864, Sundry Correspondence, Box X1/15/11B, RA.

34. "N. M. Rothschild to Reuben Ragland," July 29, 1864, 201, American Letter Books, Vol. 31, RA.

35. All letters from Chieves and Osborne are in Sundry Correspondence, Box X1/15/11A and B, RA. Rothschild's replies are in American Letter Books, Vols. 29–32, RA.

36. "August Belmont to N. M. Rothschild," January 17, 1865, T56/185, RA. On the importance of the fall of Wilmington, see also James M. McPherson, *Tried by War: Abraham Lincoln as Commander in Chief* (New York: Penguin Press, 2008), 255.

37. Catherine Cooper Hopley, *Life in the South: From the Commencement of the War by a Blockaded British Subject*, Vol. II (London: Chapman and Hall, 1863), 91–94. Robert C. Black, *The Railroads of the Confederacy* (Chapel Hill: University of North Carolina Press, 1952, reprinted 1998), 196–200 and 214–224.

38. Mary A. Livermore, *My Story of the War: A Woman's Narrative of Four Years Personal Experience as Nurse in the Union Army, and in Relief Work at Home, in Hospitals, Camps, and at the Front, During the War of the Rebellion* (Hartford, Conn.: A. D. Worthington and Co., 1888), 145.

39. Ibid., 238.

40. J. Wilkinson, *The Narrative of a Blockade Runner* (New York: Sheldon & Company, 1877), 226. See Black, *The Railroads of the Confederacy*, 220–224.

41. Isabella D. Martin and Myrta Lockett Avary, eds., *A Diary from Dixie, as Written by Mary Boykin Chesnut* (London: William Heinemann, 1905), 374; see also 357 and 367 for the first sign of defeat in reduced train service. See, especially, Yael Sternhell, "Revolution in Motion: Human Mobility and the Transformation of the South, 1861–1865," (Ph.D. diss., Yale University, 2008), 173, on the slow process of disintegration in the southern nation visible on the roads. On the importance of women's travel on the railroads and the identification of spies, see Stephanie McCurry, *Confederate Reckoning: Power and Politics in the Civil War South* (Cambridge, Mass.: Harvard University Press, 2010), 102–103.

42. Martin and Avary, *A Diary from Dixie*, 400.

43. Jason K. Phillips, "The Grape Vine Telegraph: Rumors and Confederate Persistence," *Journal of Southern History*, Vol. 62, No. 4 (November 2006): 753–788, and *Diehard Rebels: The Confederate Culture of Invincibility* (Athens: University of Georgia Press, 2007). See also William G. Thomas, "'Nothing Ought to Astonish Us': Confederate Civilians in the 1864 Shenandoah Valley Campaign," in *The Shenandoah Valley Campaign of 1864*, ed. Gary Gallager

(Chapel Hill: University of North Carolina Press, 2006), 230, on the rumors whites heard from blacks about black Union troops.

44. "Diary of Joseph Waddell," July 26, 1864, *Valley of the Shadow: Two Communities in the American Civil War,* http://valley.lib.virginia.edu/papers/AD1500.

45. "Diary of Joseph Waddell," July 7, 1864, July 29, 1864, October 10, 1864, and November 19, 24, and 29, 1864, *Valley of the Shadow: Two Communities in the American Civil War,* http://valley.lib.virginia.edu/papers/AD1500 (accessed March 2011).

46. Sexton, *Debtor Diplomacy,* 178 and 244.

47. There is a large literature on the Union financing of the war, but on the deep crisis in the summer of 1864, the resignation of Salmon P. Chase as secretary of the treasury, and the botched congressional attempt to control the trading and speculation in gold, see Heather Cox Richardson, *The Death of Reconstruction: Race, Labor, and Politics in the Post-Civil War North, 1865–1901* (Cambridge, Mass.: Harvard University Press, 2001), 58–62 and 96–99. Also Sexton, *Debtor Diplomacy,* 82 and 128.

Chapter 7. The Railroad Strategy

1. "William T. Sherman to Ellen Ewing Sherman," June 2, 1863, May 25, 1863, and June 27, 1863, in Brooks D. Simpson and Jean V. Berlin, ed., *Sherman's Civil War: Selected Correspondence of William T. Sherman, 1860–1865* (Chapel Hill: University of North Carolina Press, 1999), 472, 477, 492.

2. "William T. Sherman to John Sherman," September 11, 1862, and "William T. Sherman to U. S. Grant," July 4, 1863, in Simpson and Berlin, *Sherman's Civil War,* 301 and 497.

3. "William T. Sherman to Ellen Ewing Sherman," June 11, 1863; "William T. Sherman to John Sherman," May 29, 1863; and "William T. Sherman to John T. Swayne," June 11, 1863, in Simpson and Berlin, *Sherman's Civil War,* 478, 473 and 480.

4. "Sherman to Grant," February 27, 1864, and March 7, 1864, U.S. War Department, *The War of the Rebellion: A Compilation of the Official Records of the Union and Confederate Armies* (Lynchburg, Va., and Pasadena, Calif.: Broadfoot, 1985) (hereafter *OR*), Series I, Vol. 32 (Part I), 173 and 176. See also Buck T. Foster, *Sherman's Mississippi Campaign* (Tuscaloosa: University of Alabama Press, 2006).

5. "William C. Wipple to Samuel Ross," July 2, 1864, *OR*, Series I, Vol. 58 (Part V), 27.

6. *OR*, Series I, Vol. 58 (Part V), 141. Sherman ordered the burning of Randolph, Tennessee, in September 1862 for harboring guerrillas; see Mark Grimsley, *Hard Hand of War: Union Military Policy Toward Southern Civilians, 1861–1865* (Cambridge: Cambridge University Press, 1995), 113–116. Grimsley argues that the "surgical" and selective destruction of burning in this incident demonstrated the very clear limits for Union soldiers and officers.

7. On Johnston's failure to understand or even prepare for the events after Dalton, especially the geography of the region between there and Atlanta, see Richard M. McMurry, *Atlanta 1864: Last Chance for the Confederacy* (Lincoln: University of Nebraska Press, 2000), 43, 72, 77, and 199–200. For detailed histories of the Atlanta Campaign, see Russell S. Bonds, *War Like the Thunder Bolt: The Battle and Burning of Atlanta* (New York: Westholme, 2009), and Albert Castel, *Decision in the West: The Atlanta Campaign of 1864* (Lawrence: University Press of Kansas, 1992).

8. "Ephraim C. Dawes to Kate and Lucy Dawes," May 21, 1864, Box 1, folder 20, Ephraim C. Dawes Papers, Newberry Library, Chicago, Ill.

9. "William T. Sherman to Governors of Indiana, Illinois, Iowa, and Wisconsin," May 23, 1864, *OR*, Series I, Vol. 38 (Part IV), 294.

10. M. A. DeWolfe Howe, *Marching with Sherman: Passages from the Letters and Campaign*

Diaries of Henry Hitchcock, Major and Assistant Adjutant General of Volunteers, November 1864–May 1865, (Lincoln: University of Nebraska Press, 1995), 56.

11. "George F. Cram to Mother," October 30, 1864, in Jennifer Cain Bohrnstedt, *Soldiering with Sherman: Civil War Letters of George F. Cram* (DeKalb: University of Northern Illinois Press, 2000), 146–147.

12. *OR*, Series I, Vol. 38 (Part I), 38 and 86.

13. "William T. Sherman to Philemon B. Ewing," January 29, 1865, in Simpson and Berlin, *Sherman's Civil War*, 810. The best account of the March is Joseph T. Glatthaar, *The March to the Sea and Beyond: Sherman's Troops in the Savannah and Carolinas Campaign* (Baton Rouge: Louisiana State University Press, 1995); also Grimsley, *The Hard Hand of War*.

14. "George F. Cram to Mother," December 18, 1864, in Bohrnstedt, *Soldiering with Sherman*, 151.

15. Edward Hagerman, *The American Civil War and the Origins of Modern Warfare: Ideas, Organization and Field Command* (Bloomington: Indiana University Press, 1988), 283–286.

16. "William T. Sherman to Ulysses S. Grant," December 24, 1864, in Simpson and Berlin, *Sherman's Civil War*, 774.

17. "William T. Sherman to Henry Halleck," December 24, 1864 and "William T. Sherman to Ulysses S. Grant," December 16, 1864, in ibid., 775 and 764.

18. "William T. Sherman to Ulysses S. Grant," December 3, 1864, and January 29, 1865, in ibid., 784 and 816.

19. "William T. Sherman to Philemon B. Ewing," January 29, 1865, in ibid., 810.

20. Ibid.

21. The debate over whether either the Civil War or Sherman's campaigns were "total" has occupied historians for some time. My argument does not seek to revisit this debate, but to place Sherman's railroad strategy within the framework of the war's modern character. On "total war" see Mark E. Neely, Jr., "Was the Civil War a Total War?," *Civil War History*, Vol. 37 (March 1991): 5–28; Lance Janda, "Shutting the Gates of Mercy: The American Origins of Total War, 1860–1880," *Journal of Military History*, Vol. 59 (January 1995): 7–26; James M. McPherson, "From Limited to Total War, 1861–1865," in *Drawn with the Sword: Reflections on the American Civil War* (Oxford: Oxford University Press, 1996), 66–86; Mark E. Neely, Jr., *Civil War and the Limits of Destruction* (Cambridge, Mass.: Harvard University Press, 2007); Stig Forster and Jorg Nagler, eds., *On the Road to Total War: The American Civil War and the German Wars of Unification, 1861–1871* (Cambridge and New York: Cambridge University Press, 1997), 155–157. For a useful explanation of the rise of total war and its definition, see David A. Bell, *The First Total War: Napoleon's Europe and the Birth of Warfare as We Know It* (Boston: Houghton Mifflin, 2007), 184, on the "dynamic of radicalization" and the idea that the "totality" of war did not derive from battlefield clashes of organized armies but from the erasure of the line between combatants and noncombatants.

22. "General U. S. Grant to Henry Halleck," July 15, 1864, *OR*, Series I, Vol. 43 (Part V), 144.

23. "General Ulysses S. Grant to Henry Halleck," September 21, 1864, 4 p.m., *OR*, Series I, Vol. 43 (Part I), 130, and September 22, 1864, 10 p.m. Grant congratulated Sheridan on his victory at Winchester: "It will open again to the Government and the public the very important line of road from Baltimore to the Ohio . . . and wipes out much of the stain" on the Army in the Valley. "General U. S. Grant to Henry Halleck," July 15, 1864, *OR*, Series I, Vol. 43 (Part V) 144.

24. "James R. McCutchan to Rachel Ann McCutchan," March 17, 1862, in Edward L. Ayers, William G. Thomas, III, Anne S. Rubin, and Andrew Torget, eds., *Valley of the Shadow: Two Communities in the American Civil War*, http://valley.lib.virginia.edu/papers/A0310.

25. "Stephen Dodson Ramseur to Ellen Richmond Ramseur," September 11, 1864, in Henry Steele Commager, ed., *The Blue and the Gray: The Story of the Civil War as Told by Participants* (New York: Fairfax Press, 1982).

26. For an eyewitness account of the violence, see "Sue Richardson Diary," August 18, 1864, 66 and 74, Department of Special Collections, Robert W. Woodruff Library, Emory University, Atlanta, Ga. Richardson's home at Rose Hill was the scene of Union general George A. Custer's retaliatory execution of seven of Mosby's men. See also "Report," September 11, 1864, in *OR*, Series I, Vol. 43 (Part I), 634. *Richmond Dispatch*, October 31, 1864. "Richardson Diary," September 23, 1864, 76. Three of the seven men Mosby captured were actually executed, two escaped, and two were shot and left for dead, but survived. See William E. Boyle, "Under the Black Flag: Execution and Retaliation in Mosby's Confederacy," *Military Law Review*, Vol. 144 (Spring 1994): 148–163.

27. "Richardson Diary," 79–80.

28. Robert R. Mackey, *The Uncivil War: Irregular Warfare in the Upper South, 1861–1865* (Norman: University of Oklahoma Press, 2004), 123. Virgil Carrington Jones, *Ranger Mosby* (Chapel Hill: University of North Carolina Press, 1944), 215.

29. "Report," September 11, 1864, in *OR*, Series I, Vol. 43 (Part I), 634. *Richmond Dispatch*, October 31, 1864. See also Jones, *Ranger Mosby*, 223. "John S. Mosby to F. W. Powell, S. A. Chancellor, I. G. Grey, W. D. Noland et al.," February 4, 1862, Papers of John S. Mosby, Library of Congress, Washington, D.C.

30. Gary W. Gallagher, ed., *The Shenandoah Valley Campaign of 1864* (Chapel Hill: University of North Carolina Press, 2006), 238–239.

31. *OR*, Series I, Vol. 40 (Part III), 223; *OR*, Series I, Vol. 37 (Part II), 202. See also Gallagher, *The Shenandoah Valley Campaign of 1864*.

32. "Philip D. Sheridan to Henry Halleck," November 24, 1864, in *OR*, Series I, Vol. 43 (Part I), 37.

33. "General Philip H. Sheridan to General Ulysses S. Grant," October 7, 1864, 9 p.m., in *OR*, Series I, Vol. 43 (Part I), 30.

34. "Stephen Dodson Ramseur to Ellen Richmond Ramseur," October 10, 1864, in Commager, *The Blue and the Gray*.

35. Indeed, historians ever since have focused most of their attention on the scale of "the burning" in the Valley and the destruction of civilian barns, crops, and livestock undertaken by Sheridan's forces. But almost no attention has been paid to Sheridan's failure to capture the railroad lines at Staunton and Lynchburg. William G. Thomas, "'Nothing Ought to Astonish Us:' Confederate Civilians in the 1864 Shenandoah Valley Campaign," in Gallagher, *The Shenandoah Valley Campaign of 1864*, 240–241. For an interpretation stressing the relatively limited nature of the destruction in the Valley, see Neely, *Civil War and the Limits of Destruction*, 126.

36. *OR*, Series I, Vol. 43 (Part I), 54. Sheridan filed this and his subsequent report on the February and March "Expedition" to Petersburg on July 16, 1865, from New Orleans.

37. *OR*, Series I, Vol. 46 (Part I), 48.

38. Ibid., 481–483.

39. Philip H. Sheridan, *Personal Memoirs of P. H. Sheridan*, Vol. II (New York: Jenkins and McGowan, 1886), 119.

40. Andre M. Fleche, "Uncivilized War: The Shenandoah Valley Campaign, the Northern Democratic Press, and the Election of 1864," in Gallagher, *The Shenandoah Valley Campaign of 1864*, 211.

41. "William T. Sherman to Philip H. Sheridan," November 6, 1864, in Simpson and Berlin, *Sherman's Civil War*, 752. "William T. Sherman to Philemon B. Ewing," November 10, 1864, in Simpson and Berlin, *Sherman's Civil War*, 755. One of the best and most significant

treatments of Sherman's war making, especially its relationship to nationalism, remains Charles Royster, *The Destructive War: William Tecumseh Sherman, Stonewall Jackson and the Americans* (New York: Knopf, 1991).

42. "Ephraim C. Dawes Diary," Midwest MS, Dawes Papers, Box 2, folder 75 and 76, Newberry Library, Chicago, Ill. For a similar account of a horrific facial wound, see Stephen Ash, *A Year in the South: 1865—The True Story of Four Ordinary People Who Lived Through the Most Tumultuous Twelve Months in American History* (New York: Harper Collins, 2004), 100–102, on the wounding of Edward McDonald at the Appomattox High Bridge.

43. Ibid.

44. Samuel D. Gross, *The Autobiography of Samuel D. Gross, M.D.*, Vol. II (Philadelphia: George Barrie, 1887), 360. *Report of the Proceedings of the Society of the Army of the Tennessee,* Vol. 27 (Cincinnati, 1895), 243, for Dawes's obituary. Rufus Robinson Dawes, *Service with the Sixth Wisconsin Volunteers* (Marietta, Ohio: E. R. Alderman and Sons, 1890), 312. Rufus Dawes includes a full letter from Julia P. Cutler to Jane (sister of Ephraim and Rufus), September 24, 1864, describing the operation and Dawes's recovery. *The Medical and Surgical History of the War of the Rebellion,* part I, Vol. 2, (Washington, D.C.: Government Printing Office, 1870–1888), 369. Thanks to my colleague Susan Lawrence for her help in locating the relevant medical history for Dawes and prosthetics.

45. Ephraim C. Dawes, "Sketch of the Life of William P. Cutler," in Julia Perkins Cutler, *Life and Times of Ephraim Cutler: Prepared from His Journal and Correspondence* (With sketch of William P. Cutler by Ephraim C. Dawes) (Cincinnati: Robert Clark and Co., 1890).

46. Papers of Lewis B. Parsons, Record Group 92, Subgroup 1379, National Archives and Records Administration, College Park, Md.

Chapter 8. After Emancipation

1. Dilly Yelladay, *Born in Slavery: Slave Narratives from the Federal Writers' Project, 1936–1938,* Vol. IX, Part 2, North Carolina Narratives, 426, Federal Writer's Project, USWPA, Manuscript Division, Library of Congress, American Memory Project, http://memory.loc .gov/ammem/snhtml/snhome.html.

2. Tom Randall, *Born in Slavery,* Maryland Narratives, Vol. VIII, 57.

3. Charity Austin, *Born in Slavery,* North Carolina Narratives, Vol. XI, Part I, 60.

4. Mississippi Central Railroad, *Annual Report of the President and Directors* (Holly Springs, Miss., 1855–1860), Special Collections, University of Virginia Library, Charlottesville, Va. *Fifteenth Annual Report of the Directors and Officers of the Nashville & Chattanooga Railroad Company* (Nashville: Roberts, Watterson, & Purvis, 1867), Special Collections, University of Virginia Library, Charlottesville, Va.

5. "The Atlanta and West Point Road Report of Its President, Hon. John P. King," *New York Times* (1857–Current file), August 20, 1865, 3, ProQuest Historical Newspapers (*New York Times* [1851–2006]), www.proquest.com (hereafter ProQuest).

6. See Matthew Guterl, *American Mediterranean: Southern Slaveholders in the Age of Emancipation* (Cambridge, Mass.: Harvard University Press, 2008), 122, on the "freedom of movement" as "the most powerful and dangerous freedom of all." In places where the U.S. Military Railroads employed large numbers of blacks, including Alexandria, Virginia, and Nashville, Tennessee, meetings took place to claim civil rights; see "Liberty and Equality Before the Law," in *Proceedings of the Convention of the Colored People of Virginia* (Alexandria, Va.: Cowing and Gillis, 1865).

7. Guterl, *American Mediterranean,* 187. For a useful overview of new work on Reconstruction, see Thomas Brown, ed., *Reconstructions: New Perspectives on the Postbellum United States* (Oxford: Oxford University Press, 2006).

8. "The South as It Is. From Our Own Correspondent," *New York Times* (1857–Current file), August 22, 1865, 2, ProQuest. For a white former Confederate's railroad trip in 1865, and his view of these movements and black mobility, see Stephen Ash, *A Year in the South: 1865— The True Story of Four Ordinary People Who Lived Through the Most Tumultuous Twelve Months in American History* (New York: Harper Collins, 2004), 190–191. Also William Cohen, *At Freedom's Edge: Black Mobility and the Southern White Quest for Racial Control, 1861–1915* (Baton Rouge: Louisiana State University Press, 1991).

9. "From Florida. From Our Own Correspondent," *New York Times* (1857–Current file), August 1, 1865, 5, ProQuest.

10. "North Carolina. From Our Own Correspondent," *New York Times* (1857–Current file), June 4, 1865, 2, ProQuest.

11. See the report of John B. Howard, in U.S. War Department, *The War of the Rebellion: A Compilation of the Official Records of the Union and Confederate Armies* (Lynchburg, Va., and Pasadena, Calif.: Broadfoot, 1985) (hereafter *OR,*) Series III, Vol. 5, 458–459, on how the U.S. Army quartermaster hired over 1,000 freedmen in Richmond in April 1865 to cut wood, repair wharves, and clear wreckage. *OR* reports of railroad operations described "crowds of negroes" going north and south at the railroad stations, as well as thousands of laborers working for the quartermaster in these occupied regions; see *OR,* Series III, Vol. 5, 72–76.

12. Tim Dennee, ed., *Miscellaneous Personal Data on Alexandria African Americans, 1862–1868,* Friends of the Freedmen's Cemetery, Alexandria, Virginia, http://www.freed menscemetery.org/resources/resources.shtml (accessed October 6, 2009). See Richard Ransom and Roger Sutch, *One Kind of Freedom: The Economic Consequences of Emancipation* (Cambridge: Cambridge University Press, 1977), for the classic argument on the withdrawal of black women from labor in the immediate post-emancipation South; also Eric Foner, *Reconstruction: The Unfinished Revolution, 1863–1877* (New York: Harper and Row, 1988), 85–87; Stephen Hahn, *A Nation Under Our Feet: Black Political Struggles in the Rural South from Slavery to the Great Migration* (Cambridge, Mass.: Belknap Press of Harvard University Press, 2005), and Heather Cox Richardson, *Death of Reconstruction: Race, Labor, and Politics in the Post-Civil War North, 1865–1901* (Cambridge, Mass.: Harvard University Press, 2004). Jacqueline Jones, *Labor of Love, Labor of Sorrow: Black Women, Work, and the Family from Slavery to the Present* (New York: Vintage, 1986). Recent scholars have shown that black women continued to work; see Julie Saville, *The Work of Reconstruction: From Slave to Wage Labor in South Carolina, 1860–1870* (Cambridge: Cambridge University Press, 1994), and Leslie Schwalm, *A Hard Fight for We: Women's Transition from Slavery to Freedom in South Carolina* (Urbana: University of Illinois Press, 1997). For an analysis in Virginia's tobacco region, explaining black women's roles and household structure, see Laura Edwards, *Gendered Strife and Confusion: The Political Culture of Reconstruction* (Urbana: University of Illinois Press, 1997).

13. "Atlanta," *New York Times* (1857–Current file), June 4, 1865, 3, ProQuest.

14. "The Aquia Creek Riot," *Chicago Tribune* (1860–1872), August 17, 1865, 4, ProQuest. "The News," *Chicago Tribune* (1860–1872), August 7, 1865, 1, ProQuest; for the movement of African Americans across the South, see "The South," *New York Times* (1857–Current file), January 16, 1867, 2, ProQuest. See also Scott Reynolds Nelson, *Steel Drivin' Man: John Henry, the Untold Story of an American Legend* (Oxford: Oxford University Press, 2006), 51, on the strikes and conflicts at City Point, Virginia. And Stephen Ash, *A Year in the South: Four Lives in 1865* (New York: Palgrave Macmillan, 2002), 146–151.

15. "The Aquia Creek Riot," *Chicago Tribune* (1860–1872), August 17, 1865, 4, ProQuest; "The News," *Chicago Tribune* (1860–1872), August 7, 1865, 1, ProQuest; "Riot at Aquia Creek," *New York Times* (1857–Current file), August 5, 1865, 1, ProQuest.

16. For a "negro fund" see Raleigh & Gaston Rail Road Company, *Proceedings of the Fourteenth Annual Meeting of the Raleigh & Gaston Railroad Company* (1864), Library of Virginia.

17. The restoration of the South's railroads received some analysis in the following: William J. Cooper, Jr., and Thomas E. Terrill, *The American South: A History* (New York: McGraw Hill, 2008), 464; Margaret E. Wagner, Gary W. Gallagher, and Paul Finkleman, eds., *The Library of Congress Civil War Desk Reference* (New York: Simon and Schuster, 2009), 350; Robert C. Black, *The Railroads of the Confederacy* (Chapel Hill: University of North Carolina Press, 1952; rpt. 1998), 282; John F. Stover, *American Railroads* (Chicago: University of Chicago Press, 1997), 58–60. Paul F. Paskoff, "Measures of War: A Quantitative Examination of the Civil War's Destructiveness in the Confederacy," *Civil War History*, Vol. 54, No. 1 (March 2008): 52 and esp. n 21.

18. "Railroads Seized, Captured, and Operated or Destroyed by the U.S. During the War Not Including New Road," Record Group 92, Box 870, and "Report of Col. W. W. Wright," April 24, 1866, Record Group 92, Subgroup 1528, Box 1, National Archives and Records Administration, College Park, Md. (hereafter NARA).

19. Ibid.

20. Ibid.

21. "Railroads Seized, Captured, and Operated."

22. "Railroads Seized, Captured, and Operated." See also "Report of L. C. Easton," July 22, 1865, *OR*, Series I, Vol. 53, 44–49.

23. "Railroads Seized, Captured, and Operated" and "Report of Col. W. W. Wright."

24. "Report of J. J. Moore," *OR*, Series III, Vol. 5, 72–84.

25. "Report of Captain J. D. Stubbs," January 1866, Consolidated Correspondence File, "Railroad," Box 871, NARA. Also "D. C. McCallum to Gen. Montgomery Meigs," April 20, 1863, Box 869, NARA.

26. Thomas Weber, *The Northern Railroads in the Civil War, 1861–1865* (Westport, Conn.: Greenwood, 1952), 214–219. See also correspondence in Record Group 105, "Washington Headquarters, Bureau of Refugees, Freedmen, and Abandoned Lands, Chief Quartermaster's Correspondence," Vol. 2, E.167, Letters Sent, "Henry Whittelsey to James R. Ogden," 210–211, requesting credit for East Tennessee and Virginia Railroad's transportation of freedmen using Bureau vouchers to be accounted against its "indebtedness" for the purchase of U.S. military railroad equipment; and "Whittelsey to Gen. D. H. Ricker" (91), regarding list of railroad companies "indebted to the United States for purchases of military railroad property," both in NARA. See General Order No. 34, April 16, 1867, for list.

27. U.S. military officials reported that the repaired lines, bridges, and water tanks were turned over in "first rate order"; report of W. J. Stevens, *OR*, Series III, Vol. 5, 90–91.

28. Lawrence A. Estaville, Jr., "A Strategic Railroad: The New Orleans, Jackson, and Great Northern in the Civil War," *Louisiana History*, Vol. 14, No. 2 (Spring 1973): 135. *Glasgow Herald*, June 11, 1866, in *Nineteenth-Century British Library Newspapers*, British Library, London, U.K.

29. "The South as It Is. From Our Own Correspondent," *New York Times* (1857–Current file), August 22, 1865, 2, ProQuest.

30. Mark W. Summers, *The Era of Good Stealings* (New York: Oxford University Press, 1993), 154. Nelson, *Steel Drivin' Man*, 69–70.

31. Allen W. Moger, "Railroad Practices and Policies in Virginia After the Civil War," *Virginia Magazine of History and Biography*, Vol. 59, No. 4 (October 1951): 423–457.

32. *Annual Reports of the Officers, Boards, and Institutions of the Commonwealth of Virginia, for the Year Ending September 30, 1872* (Richmond: R. F. Walker, Superintendent of Public Printing, 1872), 13. See also the best study of these practices in Nelson, *Steel Drivin' Man*, 83–86. Nelson has found that black railroad workers and miners went on strike at the C & O tunneling operations because the steam drills they were using produced so much dust, or "bad air," that they objected to further work unless conditions changed. Huntington's solution was

to use convicts in the dangerous work; Nelson speculates that nearly all of the convicts working on the Lewis Tunnel (100 or more) likely died from inhaling the fine dust made from the steam drills on sandstone.

33. Scott Reynolds Nelson, *Iron Confederacies: Southern Railways, Klan Violence, and Reconstruction* (Chapel Hill: University of North Carolina Press, 1999), 104–105 and 134. Mark W. Summers, *Railroads, Reconstruction, and the Gospel of Prosperity: Aid Under the Radical Republicans, 1865–1877* (Princeton, N.J.: Princeton University Press, 1984), 84–86. In West Virginia the KKK was strongest in places such as Kanahwa County, where the C & O brought large numbers of black laborers between 1868 and 1870. Stephen B. Engle, "Mountaineer Reconstruction: Blacks in the Political Reconstruction of West Virginia," *Journal of Negro History*, Vol. 78, No. 3 (Summer 1993): 137–165. And Edward John Harcourt, "The Whipping of Richard Moore: Reading Emotion in Reconstruction America," *Journal of Social History*, Vol. 36, No. 2 (Winter 2002): 270, on the white fear of black labor recalcitrance in Reconstruction and the idea of "hot cognition" motivating the violent reaction of whites.

34. Frederick Douglass, *My Bondage and My Freedom* (New York: Miller, Orton, and Mulligan, 1855), chapter 25. Harriet Jacobs, *Incidents in the Life of a Slave Girl* (Boston, 1861), 135. On Massachusetts law, see Leon Litwack, *North of Slavery: The Negro in the Free States, 1790–1860* (Chicago: University of Chicago Press, 1961), 106–110.

35. Elizabeth Hoon Cawley, ed., *The American Diaries of Richard Cobden* (Princeton, N.J.: Princeton University Press, 1952), 91, 176, and 208. The best account of the origins and legalities of segregation is Barbara Young Welke, *Recasting American Liberty: Gender, Race, Law and the Railroad Revolution, 1865–1920* (Cambridge: Cambridge University Press, 2001), 326–338.

36. See, for example, *Cong. Globe* (Washington, D.C.), March 17, 1864, and *Railroad Company v. Brown*, 84 U.S. 17 Wall. 445 (1873). Roger A. Fischer, "A Pioneer Protest: The New Orleans Street-Car Controversy of 1867," *Journal of Negro History*, Vol. 53, No. 3 (July 1968): 219–233. The "star" cars were taken over by whites, and blacks in 1865 protested that they were being entirely squeezed out. Also William C. Hine, "The 1867 Charleston Streetcar Sit-ins: A Case of Successful Black Protest," *South Carolina Historical Magazine*, Vol. 77, No. 2 (April 1976): 110–114. Bernard E. Powers, Jr., "Community Evolution and Race Relations in Reconstruction Charleston, South Carolina," *South Carolina Historical Magazine*, Vol. 101, No. 3 (July 2000): 214–233.

37. For an excellent overview of Brown and her case, especially the experience of federal employees, see Kate Masur, "Personal and Political in Kate Brown's Washington," C-SPAN, August 17, 2005, http://www.c-spanvideo.org/program/189371-1. See also Kate Masur, *An Example for All the Land: Emancipation and the Struggle over Equality in Washington, D.C.* (Chapel Hill: University of North Carolina Press, 2010), chapter 3. I am grateful to Kate Masur for sharing this chapter in page proofs with me as I made my final revisions. Masur is one of the first scholars to look deeply into Brown's case, and her forthcoming book on this subject will be especially useful. Our respective accounts rely on much of the same evidence in the congressional report and case files.

38. *Senate Reports*, 40th Cong., 2d Sess., Rep. Com. No. 131 (June 17, 1868), 12–14. *Journal of the Senate of the United States of America*, Vol. 61 (1868), February 10: 175; February 12: 182; February 17: 194; and June 20: 519. Also *Cong. Globe*, 40th Cong., 2d Sess. (1868), 1071, 1121–1125, 1204, and 3314.

39. *Senate Reports*, 40th Cong., 2d Sess., Rep. Com. No. 131 (June 17, 1868), 11. *Journal of the Senate of the United States of America*, Vol. 61 (1868), February 10: 175; February 12: 182; February 17: 194; and June 20: 519. Also *Cong. Globe*, 40th Cong., 2d Sess., (1868), 1071, 1121–1125, 1204, and 3314.

40. 1860 and 1870 United States Federal Census, Ancestry.com, Provo, Utah (accessed October 6, 2009) (original data: 1860 and 1870 U.S. census, population schedule, NARA micro-

film publication M653, 1,438 rolls [1860], NARA microfilm publication M593, 1,761 rolls [1870]. Washington, D.C.: National Archives and Records Administration, n.d.). American Society of Civil Engineers, *Proceedings of the American Society of Civil Engineers*, Vol. 23 (New York, 1897), 170–171.

41. For a detailed account, see Earl M. Maltz, "'Separate but Equal' and the Law of Common Carriers in the Era of the Fourteenth Amendment," *Rutgers Law Journal*, Vol. 17 (1985–1986): 558–68. Augusta's case drew attention to the problem and Senators Charles Sumner and Waitman Willey initiated an investigation by the Committee on the District of Columbia; see *Cong. Globe*, 38th Cong., 1st Sess. 553 (1864). Alexander Augusta, *Christian Recorder*, May 30, 1863, quoted in Christian Samito, *Becoming American Under Fire: Irish Americans, African Americans and the Politics of Citizenship During the Civil War Era* (Ithaca, N.Y.: Cornell University Press, 2009), 45.

42. *Senate Reports*, 40th Cong., 2d Sess., Rep. Com. No. 131 (June 17, 1868), 22.

43. Attorney William A. Cook handled Brown's appeal to the U.S. Supreme Court. Born in Pennsylvania, Cook was corporation council before becoming city attorney for Washington, D.C., until 1874 when Edwin L. Stanton, son of Lincoln's secretary of war, succeeded him. In 1871 Cook represented the disgraced Orville E. Babcock, Grant's personal secretary, as he faced criminal prosecution during the Whiskey Ring scandal. A Republican, Cook later directed some of the District's first black lawyers at Howard Law School, several of whom read law under him in the 1890s. For biographical information on Cook, Burgess, and Bond, see John Y. Simon, ed., *Papers of U.S. Grant*, Vol. 27 (Southern Illinois University Press, 2005), 45 and 316; *Dartmouth*, Vol. 1 (January 1867): 238; Wilhelms Bogart Bryan, *Various Forms of Local Government in the District of Columbia* (Columbia Historical Society, 1898), 33; and 1870 United States Federal Census, Ancestry.com.

44. On black efforts to gain jury service in the District, see the petition in *Proceedings of the National Convention of the Colored Men of America*, Washington, D.C., January 13–16, 1869 (Washington, D.C., 1869), 19 and 20. See *Statutes at Large*, 41st Cong., 1st Sess., Vol. 16 (March 18, 1869), 3. See also *Statutes at Large*, 43d Cong., 1st Sess., Vol. 18, Part 2 (1873–74, District of Columbia), 100–102, on the qualifications for juror selection in D.C. with no mention of race: U.S. citizen, twenty-one to sixty-five years or age, and "of good character." Washington, D.C., experienced a strike by black railroad workers in June 1871; see Richardson, *The Death of Reconstruction*, 100.

45. *Railroad Company v. Brown*, 84 U.S. 445 (1873), transcript in *The Making of Modern Law: U.S. Supreme Court Records and Briefs*, http://railroads.unl.edu/documents/view_docu ment.php?id=rail.gen.0059 (accessed October 6, 2009). Census Bureau data was consulted to obtain information about all the jurors; race could not be determined for three of the men (1870 United States Federal Census, Ancestry.com, accessed October 7, 2009).

46. Record Group 21, Case No. 4582, NARA. All witnesses checked in 1870 United States Federal Census, Ancestry.com (accessed May 2010). Other connections between Brown and the Treasury Department include Samuel Bond, Brown's lawyer, who rented a room in his house to Mary Chase, a twenty-year-old clerk at the Treasury Department.

47. *Railroad Company v. Brown*.

48. Ibid. A similar debate took place in Congress when Sumner introduced the language to require nondiscrimination. For the best account of this conflict within the Republicans, see Martz, "'Separate but Equal' and the Law of Common Carriers."

49. Ibid.

50. "Washington. Discrimination on Account of Color on Railroads," *New York Times* (1857-Current file), November 18, 1873, 1, ProQuest. "Legal Intelligence. Special Dispatch to The Chicago Tribune," *Chicago Daily Tribune*, November 18, 1873, 5, ProQuest

51 "The Negro Problem," *De Bow's Review, Agricultural, Commercial, Industrial Progress*

and Resources, Vol. 5 (New Orleans: J. D. B. De Bow), March 3, 1868, 248–264. George Fitz-hugh, "The Negro Imbroglio," *De Bow's Review,* June 1867, 518–522, and "Virginia—Her Past, Present, and Future," *De Bow's Review,* Vol. 1, No. 2, February 1866.

52. See Nelson, *Iron Confederacies,* 75–84, and 201 n. 46. Also William Bender Wilson, *History of the Pennsylvania Railroad Company,* Vol. I (Philadelphia: Henry T. Coates, 1899), 352.

53. See Foner, *Reconstruction: America's Unfinished Revolution,* 370–374.

54. The history of the origins of segregation is extremely large—what follows are limited sources relevant to this issue: Edward L. Ayers, *The Promise of the New South: Life After Reconstruction* (Oxford: Oxford University Press, 1992), 149; Catherine A. Barnes, *Journey from Jim Crow: The Desegregation of Southern Transit* (New York: Columbia University Press, 1983), 12; Patricia Hagley Minter, "The Codification of Jim Crow," (Ph.D. diss., University of Virginia, 1994); Joseph R. Palmore, "The Not-So Strange Career of Interstate Jim Crow: Race, Transportation, and the Dormant Commerce Clause, 1878–1946," *Virginia Law Review,* Vol. 83 (November 1997): 1773–1817; and Welke, *Recasting American Liberty.* C. Vann Woodward, *The Strange Career of Jim Crow* (New York: Oxford University Press, 1955), 117, pointed out the incongruence of technology and racial separation: "The arrival of the age of air transportation appears to have put a string upon the ingenuity of the Jim Crow lawmakers. Even to the orthodox there was doubtless something slightly incongruous about requiring a Jim Crow compartment on a transcontinental plane, or one that did not touch the ground between New York and Miami. No Jim Crow law has been found that applies to passengers while they are in the air. So long as they were upon the ground, however, they were still subject to Jim Crow jurisdiction." Railroad cars in the 1880s were run over increasingly interstate systems under company rules (not required by law) and may have been mixed in some parts of the South. In this way they were similar to air travel several generations later—forms of physical transportation technology that did not conform to state legislative boundaries. It should not seem surprising that southern states, driven largely by white supremacy and progressive reformism, attempted to create effectively an "interstate" set of legislative acts to bring coherence to this technological change.

55. For the best account of postwar southern railroad machinations and their significance in Reconstruction, see Nelson, *Iron Confederacies,* 80–81. Also, the best account of Reconstruction remains Foner, *Reconstruction: America's Unfinished Revolution,* 379 and 395.

56. Kate Brown's case, 84 U.S. 445 (1873), was not cited in the *Brown v. Board of Education* opinion in 1954, but her case was cited by the National Association for the Advancement of Colored people (NAACP) attorneys in their appellate briefs for *Sweatt v. Painter, Brown v. Topeka Board of Education,* and *Bolling v. Sharpe.* The literature on the *Brown v. Board of Education* case is especially large and complex; I have relied on Risa L. Goluboff, *The Lost Promise of Civil Rights* (Cambridge, Mass.: Harvard University Press, 2007), and Michael J. Klarman, *From Jim Crow to Civil Rights: The Supreme Court and the Struggle for Racial Equality* (Oxford: Oxford University Press, 2004).

Epilogue

1. See *New York Times,* April 1, 1869; "Oliver Ames to Thomas C. Durant," January 4 and 16, 1869, and December 23 and 24, 1868, Levi Leonard Papers, University of Iowa Libraries Special Collections, Iowa City, Iowa. One of the best accounts of the Credit Mobilier remains Arthur M. Johnson and Barry E. Supple, *Boston Capitalists and Western Railroads: A Study in 19th Century Railroad Investment Process* (Cambridge, Mass.: Harvard University Press, 1967), 195–221; also Mark W. Summers, *The Era of Good Stealings* (New York: Oxford University Press, 1993), 226–242.

2. The history of the early Credit Mobilier is drawn from the excellent account of

Fletcher M. Green, "Origins of the Credit Mobilier of America," *Mississippi Valley Historical Review*, Vol. 46, No. 2 (September 1959): 238–251.

3. Ibid., 245.

4. Ibid., 247.

5. See James A. Ward, "Power and Accountability on the Pennsylvania Railroad, 1846–1878," *Business History Review*, Vol. 49, No. 1 (Spring 1975): 37–59. The literature on the effects of the Civil War on economic growth is huge, especially on railroads. For relevant aspects of railroad change, see George Rogers Taylor, "The National Economy Before and After the Civil War," in *Economic Change in the Civil War Era*, ed. David T. Gilchrist and W. David Lewis (Greenville, Del.: Eleutherian Mills-Hagley Foundation, 1965); Thomas C. Cochran, "Did the Civil War Retard Industrialization?" *Mississippi Valley Historical Review*, Vol. 48, No. 2 (September 1961): 197–210, esp. 209; Albert Fishlow, "Productivity Change and Technological Change in the Railroad Sector, 1840–1910," in National Bureau of Economic Research, *Output, Employment, and Productivity in the United States after 1800*, Studies in Income and Wealth, Vol. 30 (New York: Columbia University Press, 1966), 583–646; Thomas Weber, *The Northern Railroads in the Civil War, 1861–1865* (Bloomington: Indiana University Press, 1952); Alfred D. Chandler, Jr., "The Railroads: Pioneers in Modern Corporate Management," *Business History Review*, Vol. 39, No. 1 (Spring 1965), 16–40; Alexander J. Field, "US Economic Growth in the Gilded Age," Social Science Research Network, January 2007, http://ssrn.com/abstract=1095897. On New Philadelphia's bypass in 1869 by the Hannibal and Naples Railroad Company, and its subsequent demise, see Christopher C. Fennell, "Damaging Detours: Routes, Racism, and New Philadelphia," *Historical Archaeology*, Vol. 44, No. 1 (2010): 138–154.

6. Adele Cummings, "Governing the Economy: The Process and Politics of Government Involvement in the Railroads in Canada and the United States, 1850–1885" (Ph.D. diss., Duke University, 1995), 16. Cummings has usefully compared U.S. and Canadian projects, as well as broken down all arguments in support and opposition into analytical categories. See 161–162 for the pro and con tabulations on goals in 1862 and 167–169 on the overall comparison of data.

7. "Report of the Commissioner of Indian Affairs, November 22, 1856," in *Annual Report of the Secretary of the Interior, 1856* (Washington: A. O. P. Nicholson Printers, 1857), 22–23.

8. "Report of the Commissioner of Indian Affairs," in *Annual Report of the Secretary of the Interior, 1860* (Washington: A. O. P. Nicholson Printers, 1860), 103. "Report of Thomas B. Sykes, Delaware Agency, Fort Leavenworth, Kansas Territory, September 16, 1860," in *Annual Report of the Secretary of the Interior, 1860*. For copies of the original treaties, see Ayer collection, Volume 3. oE 95 .U69 1825, Newberry Library, Chicago, Ill. Thomas Ewing considered the railroad fraud in Kansas reason enough to worry that corruption might overtake the republic; see Summers, *The Era of Good Stealings*, 9. Clinton Alfred Wesieger, *The Delaware Indians: A History* (New Brunswick, N.J.: Rutgers University Press, 1972), 414. A balanced account of the treaties and the possible advantages of the railroads for Indian groups is in H. Craig Miner and William E. Unrau, *The End of Indian Kansas: A Study of Cultural Revolution, 1854–1871* (Lawrence: Regents Press of Kansas, 1978), chapter 2. Also, for a critical account, see Paul Wallace Gates, *Fifty Million Acres: Conflicts over Kansas Land Policy, 1854–1890* (Ithaca, N.Y.: Cornell University Press, 1954). And Francis Paul Prucha, *American Indian Treaties: The History of a Political Anomaly* (Berkeley: University of California Press, 1994), 235–287. For the most recent biography of Ewing, see Ronald D. Smith, *Thomas Ewing Jr.: Frontier Lawyer and Civil War General* (Columbia: University of Missouri Press, 2008).

9. Louis S. Warren, *Buffalo Bill's America: William Cody and the Wild West Show* (New York: Knopf, 2005), 42, 58. Also Don Russell, *The Lives and Legends of Buffalo Bill* (Norman: University of Oklahoma Press, 1960), 84–89. See Andrew Isenberg, *The Destruction of the Bison:*

An Environmental History, 1750–1920 (New York: Cambridge University Press, 2000); Elliott West, *The Contested Plains: Indians, Gold Seekers, and the Rush to Colorado* (Lawrence: University of Kansas Press, 1998).

10. For an excellent overview of the excursion, see David Howard Bain, *Empire Express: Building the First Transcontinental Railroad* (New York: Viking, 1999), 290–295. Also, for photography and Pullman contracts, see Levi Leonard Collection, University of Iowa Libraries, Iowa City, Iowa.

11. *Cincinnati Gazette,* June 5, 1867, Box 32, Papers of Levi O. Leonard, University of Iowa Libraries, Special Collections, Iowa City, Iowa.

12. For an excellent analysis of Cody and the show's "amnesia about the nation's most recent wounds," including the lack of visual or literary references to the Civil War, see Louis S. Warren, *Buffalo Bill's America: William Cody and the Wild West Show* (New York: Vintage, 2005), 264.

13. Henry Adams, *The Education of Henry Adams* (Boston: Houghton Mifflin Co., 1918), 240 and 330.

14. Ibid., chapter 25, "The Dynamo and the Virgin, 1900." Adams remarked that he had had his "historical neck broken by the sudden irruption of forces totally new." In the display of machines at the Paris Exposition in 1900, history, Adams thought, was a "sequence of force." See also Adams's brother, Charles Francis Adams, Jr., *Chapters of Erie and Other Essays* (New York: 1886), 98. He described the grasping, scheming railroad corporations as "a new power, for which our language contains no name."

15. "East and West," *New York Times,* May 11, 1869, 1, ProQuest Historical Newspapers, *New York Times* (1851–2003). For a different emphasis on this well-documented event, see David Nye, *American Technological Sublime* (Cambridge, Mass.: MIT Press, 1994).

16. *Harper's Weekly,* May 29, 1869.

17. Thanks to Ann W. Gaffney for her help in locating information about Vinton, especially his tenure as rector of Grace Church, Brooklyn. Vinton quoted in "East and West," *New York Times,* May 11, 1869, ProQuest Historical Newspapers (accessed March 2011).

18. Ibid.

19. "Speech of Mr. Colfax," *Chicago Tribune,* May 11, 1869, 4, ProQuest Historical Newspapers, *Chicago Tribune* (1849–1985).

Index